A SECRET WORLD

Sexuality and the Search for Celibacy _____

A.W. RICHARD SIPE

Foreword by Robert Coles, M.D.

BRUNNER/MAZEL, PUBLISHERS • NEW YORK

Library of Congress Cataloging-in-Publication Data
Sipe, A. W. Richard
    A secret world : sexuality and the search for celibacy / by A. W.
Richard Sipe.
        p.   cm.
    Includes bibliographical references.
    ISBN 0–87630–585–0
    1. Celibacy—Catholic Church.   2. Catholic Church—Clergy—Sexual
behavior.   I. Title.
BX1912.9.S57   1990
253'.2—dc20   90–32435
                                                                    CIP

Published by
BRUNNER/MAZEL, INC.
19 Union Square West
New York, New York 10003

Manufactured in the United States of America

10 9 8 7 6 5 4 3 2 1

To the memory of
the Very Reverend Ulric Conrad Beste,
whose celibate example inspired
the beginning of this study
and
to James Willard Sipe, M.D.,
whose courage assured
its completion

FOREWORD

As I read this book I remembered a patient of mine, whom I saw when I worked in the Alcoholism Clinic of the Massachusetts General Hospital in the late 1950s. I was completing my training in psychiatry, and I had the privilege, so doing, of being supervised by a wonderfully astute and knowing psychoanalyst, Alfred O. Ludwig ("Dutch," we all called him), who ran the clinic. The patient was a priest of about 40 who had serious drinking problems, and had decided to come see us, rather than to join a program run by the Catholic Church for its hard-drinking clergy. Dr. Ludwig kept telling me that there was probably "another reason" that prompted this priest's turn toward us secular doctors—and soon enough, I learned of it: a struggle with his sexuality. This priest had a habit, when drunk, of carousing with women who also drank a lot, and the result was not only a sexual life, but intense anxiety and guilt during his time of sobriety—and depression, serious bouts of it. I still remember some of our exchanges, and I especially remember a remark he once made to me as we tried to figure out what he ought do with his increasingly troubled life: "There's so much going on, below the surface." I thought, at first, he was talking personally, psychologically—the struggles within his mind as instincts confronted conscience, not to mention that well-known staple of our time, the reality principle. But he had a more sociological line of thought to share with me: "The world thinks of us [priests] as good, very good—and we are sinners, like everyone else." I was not inclined to disagree with him—and noticing my lack of surprise, he escalated his remarks, and started telling me particular stories meant, I slowly realized, to "give scandal," a phrase he had used several times in the course of our conversations. When *I* now used that phrase with him—asked him whether (and if so, why) he was trying "to give scandal" to his priestly vocation, he answered with a "yes" of some defiance. Needless to say, we had much, in that regard, to discuss, to try to understand.

If this book, the result of many years of work—hundreds of interviews done with priests and others—had been available then, I rather suspect both my priest-patient and I, as his doctor, might have had an easier time in the course of our effort to find a way out of what seemed to be a particular life's grave impasse. The historical information alone, in the first section of the book, is of great importance—a reminder that sexuality has indeed figured strongly in a church that has espoused the ideal of celibacy with such determination. For that matter, celibacy is itself an aspect of sexuality, in the broad definition of that latter word—a mode of coming to terms with one's sexual energies. In a sense, then, Freud's view of the workings of the human mind turns out to be helpful and enlightening to some of us who have great respect and affection for the Catholic Church, and for its nuns and priests, and who with the help of psychoanalytic studies, as well as this one by Richard Sipe, can understand how complex and demanding and challenging a priestly life is, how serious the possible jeopardy, even as the moral and spiritual achievements can, of course, be substantial. "His life is, on the whole, exemplary," I recall Dr. Ludwig saying about my priest-patient during our staff "work-up"—and then this further interesting comment: "I can understand how he feels demeaned by his drinking and his sexual activity; but if I were treating him, I would try to address his troubles as an aspect of his God-given humanity, rather than as evidence of some singular sinfulness—and it's our job to do that, to try to help him understand himself, not lacerate himself even more, as if he's not done plenty of that already." Yes, I thought then, and still do as I recall the meetings I had with that priest, and as I read of the other priests whose lives and struggles and stories appear in the pages that follow—pilgrims, all, with the special but quite human difficulties that a particular vocation can evoke.

ROBERT COLES, M. D.
Professor of Psychiatry and Medical Humanities
Harvard University, Cambridge, Mass.

Faculty, Department of Psychiatry,
Cambridge Hospital

CONTENTS _____

LIST OF FIGURES

ACKNOWLEDGMENTS   ————————

I would like to express my thanks to all who helped bring this work to its completion—first and foremost to the priests who shared their stories. Many gave their time during seminars, in workshop settings, and at scores of consultations. The priests who shared their observations in clinical settings deserve special note because the depth of their perception and their struggle to achieve celibacy added greatly to our understanding.

There are those few priests who have remained involved with the study since it started some 25 years ago and others for up to 15 years—and their fidelity and insights have been invaluable. Likewise, those priests who have reviewed and criticized our observations as they developed, and offered their thoughts from their considerable experience with celibate living, have been encouraging and equally indispensable to our final estimates and valuations. These men remain nameless only to avoid useless speculation and to ensure anonymity where it is desired.

The non-clerical informants—both male and female—who shared their stories either within or outside the clinical setting added a dimension that shattered the wall of secrecy and strongly corroborates our other data, making the difficulty of celibacy apparent but the achievement more possible in the long run.

I owe a debt to each of the following colleagues and friends who have offered advice, consultation, encouragement, information, or revision somewhere along the line between 1960 and 1985: Leo H. Bartemeier, M.D.; Donald Bartley, M.D.; Marianne Benkert, M.D.; Richard Benson, M.S.W.; Teresa Boria, M.D.; Francis J. Braceland, M.D.; John Brickner, M.D.; Sara Charles, M.D.; Louis F. Cleary, M.D.; Michael Cowen, Ph.D.; Dana L. Farnsworth, M.D.; Robert H. Felix, M.D.; Gregory B. Fernandopulle, M.D.; Jamie Garcia-Saavedra, M.D.; Francis Gearty, M.D.; Alan Greenwald, Ph.D.; Marjorie Harley, Ph.D.; Donald W. Hastings, M.D.; Elizabeth R. Hatcher, Ph.D., M.D.; John W. Higgins, M.D.; J. Cotter Hirschberg, M.D.; Walter O. Jahrreiss, M.D.; Ivan D. Junk, M.D.; William King, M.D.; J. Alfred LeBlanc, M.D.; David LeGrand, M.D.; Thomas Lynch, M.D.; Noel Mailloux, Ph.D.; Robert J. McAllister, M.D.,

Ph.D.; Francis McLaughlin, M.D.; John P. McNamara, M.D.; Desmond P. McNelis, M.D.; Paul W. Pruyser, Ph.D.; Joseph J. Reidy, M.D.; Marie-Claud Rigaud, M.D.; Clarence J. Rowe, M.D.; Nathan Schnaper, M.D.; Toni Sussman; and Henry Tom, Ph.D.

The Seton Psychiatric Institute of Baltimore, Maryland, provided the work setting for five years of this study (1965–1970). Thanks are owed to the Daughters of Charity and to a dozen secretaries and nurses who made learning and healing possible. Concurrently, the St. John's University Institute for Mental Health at Collegeville, Minnesota, garnered treasured insights from priests from all parts of the United States.

Although this study was begun and would have been completed without the following people, it would never have been published without their input. First, Bernie Mazel, who has made an accurate assessment of every one of my publishing ventures since 1970. Indispensable were the love, encouragement, and help of my wife Marianne and our son Walter, who spent valuable hours in libraries meriting the rewards of a research assistant. Andrew Jezic did likewise. Dr. Herbert Hauptman, Ph.D., director of the Medical Foundation of Buffalo, inspired the tetrahedron model for the celibate process. Kathy Wieman from the research departments of Johns Hopkins medical schools deserves credit for all diagrams. Dr. J. Alfred LeBlanc, secretary of the Washington Psychoanalytic Institute, read the manuscript and made valuable corrections and comments.

In addition, my family and I enjoy the friendship of dozens of priests who have not participated in this study. Most of them have been understanding and indulgent about my project. One of this group has to be named: Father Joseph Gallagher, established essayist, spiritual writer, and poet of note, labored over the manuscript. There is hardly a page that was not improved by his unerring clarifications. We treasure his judgment as a literary *imprimatur.* Joan Chittister O. S. B. gave me the crucial push that suppressed my natural timidity in favor of speaking out.

Finally, words are insufficient to express the debt this publication owes to Marjorie Nelson. She came forward and offered her help at a time when the topography of celibacy was clear but the cartography was a menacing challenge. Her superb editorial skills transformed the journey of 25 years into a readable road map over some forbidding and heretofore uncharted terrain.

In spite of the help of all of the above, I reserve for myself credit for any limitations and errors.

U.I.O.G.D.
July 31, 1989

Part I
THE BACKGROUND AND THE CONTEXT _____

Chapter 1

WHY THIS SUBJECT?
Apologia Pro Studiis Suis ___

His great subject was the relation of corruptible action to absolute principle; of worldly means to transcendent ends; of historical commitment to personal desire.

—Irving Howe
Introduction to Bread and Wine (Silone)

The potential value of this study lies in the questions that it addresses: What is celibacy? How is it really practiced by those who profess it? What is the process of celibacy? What is the structure of celibate achievement?

In short, this is a search for a structural and dynamic model of an ancient practice that crosses cultural and religious boundaries. Although this study is limited to Catholic priests in the United States, the questions are meaningful to the understanding of celibate practice universally, including the Buddhist and Hindu traditions. The most commonly assumed definition of "celibate" is simply an unmarried or single person, and celibacy is perceived as synonymous with sexual abstinence or restraint. Those assumptions, although incomplete for the purpose of our study, will be sufficient to sustain the reader for the first three chapters. In Chapter 4, a more precise definition will be delineated both to amplify and to challenge incomplete notions.

In spite of the fact that celibacy has not been a constant tradition even in the Roman Catholic Church, there is a common psychic presumption of a "virginal" clergy which even extends to the Jewish rabbinate. More than one psychologically sophisticated rabbi has told me that they are aware of this phenomenon among members of their congregations. Especially in the celebration of any sacred service or in the recitation of sacred texts, clerical acts and words need to be separated in the minds of the faithful from the sexuality of the minister, much as children must separate their parents from any sexual "contamination."

3

Questions about celibacy are not commonly asked, nor do they very often stir common interest. Some justification—apologia in the traditional sense—may help the reader understand why anyone would pursue such questions systematically for 25 years and, more important, why the subject of celibacy should merit a reader's time and interest.

SEX/CELIBACY: BREAKING THE TABOO

The time period spanned by this search is the quarter-century that has marked the "sexual revolution." We have learned a great deal about/from sexual expression and sexual indulgence in these 25 years. However, there is also much to be learned about sexuality from sexual restraint and abstinence. C. S. Lewis noted that you learn more about an army by resisting it than by surrendering to it.

What better examples of sexual control are there than those who publicly profess a life full of meaning yet devoid of sex—Roman Catholic priests? Yet information that would seem so easily accessible from every priest by the simple question—*What is your sexual/celibate adjustment?*—is often shrouded in secrecy, denial, and mystery, even to the priest himself.

"Before the 60s, celibates were presumed to have no sexuality. Any priest who showed signs of sexuality was considered at least strange," said a priest participant in a dialogue on the sexual maturing of celibates (Tetlow, 1985). Asking a priest about his celibacy is like asking a banker about his honesty—if one questions the closely guarded and highly defended assumptions, insult, confusion, and even rage result.

Carl Eifert, a lay spokesman for the National Conference of Catholic Bishops, asserted in an interview with Gustav Niebuhr that statements by U.S. bishops on the issue of celibacy are "based on the assumption that priests are consistent in their adherence to their vows" (Niebuhr, 1989). A priest spokesman for the same agency was typically defensive about the suggestion made in prepublication material from this work that a substantial proportion of professed celibates do indeed have a sexual life. Said he, "Priests are humans and have feelings; but the great, great majority of priests that I know are faithful to their vows. I know hundreds and hundreds of priests—it's certainly not true." (Niebuhr, 1989).

This study looks for fact beyond all the assumptions—both positive and negative—about celibacy, for there are equally unfair contrary suppositions surrounding celibacy, and not only among secular nonbelievers. One middle-aged priest, a poetic cynic, said, "Celibacy is like the unicorn—a perfect and absolutely noble animal. . . . I have read eloquent descriptions of it and have seen it glorified in art. I have wanted desperately to believe in its existence, but alas, I have never been able to find it on the hoof" (personal communication).

In short, even priests who know "hundreds and hundreds of priests" often do not know the sexual/celibate adjustment of even their closest friends, as we found time and time again in our search. This adjustment is mostly a secret one. A priest's sexual/celibate life becomes visible primarily through a scandal in which a pregnancy, a lawsuit, or an arrest comes to public attention.

Some priests will share the secret of their celibate achievement or compromise in the confessional or, as it is called now, the sacrament of reconciliation. However, many priest informants in our study revealed that they do not consistently confess what might at least technically be termed a transgression of the vow or the practice of celibacy, e.g., masturbation.

Whereas confession can be accomplished in the dark and anonymously, spiritual direction and psychotherapy are two areas in which a priest can reveal his intimate life-style and deal openly and yet in a privileged manner with issues of sexuality. During the period of our study, priests increasingly talked more openly to friends or in small groups about their sexual struggles. In Chapter 2, I expand on the shifting sociosexual context that made this study of celibacy possible. Individual revelations and collections of data can make the penetration of the veil of secrecy possible and useful both to those who wish to understand sexuality better and to those who wish to live celibacy effectively.

The factors outlined in Chapter 2 are among many that provided a window into the hitherto secret world of the celibate. The ideal of celibacy has been gloriously extolled throughout history, just as it has been ingloriously ridiculed. However, it has never been examined in a way that could open it to scientific research. This study is an attempt to make such research more plausible.

There is no unseemliness in attempting to examine the secrets of celibate practice and achievement. In fact, Pope John Paul II, in speaking to journalists on January 27, 1984, said, "The Church endeavors and will always endeavor more to be a house of glass, where all can see what happens and how it fulfills a mission" (*Baltimore Sun*, Jan. 28, 1984). He was speaking in a general sense, and certainly not specifically about celibacy, but how could he exclude an element so vitally entwined with the priesthood? Personal celibacy is a public stance. Religious leaders and their own personal standards contribute significantly to the understanding of sexuality and sexual morality among their flocks. Certainly, the public witness and teaching of the clergy cannot be separated from their personal attitudes toward sexuality and the observance of their vow.

HISTORY: THE BROADER CONTEXT

Henry C. Lea wrote a classic nineteenth-century study of sacerdotal celibacy. He hoped that his study would be of interest to the general reader,

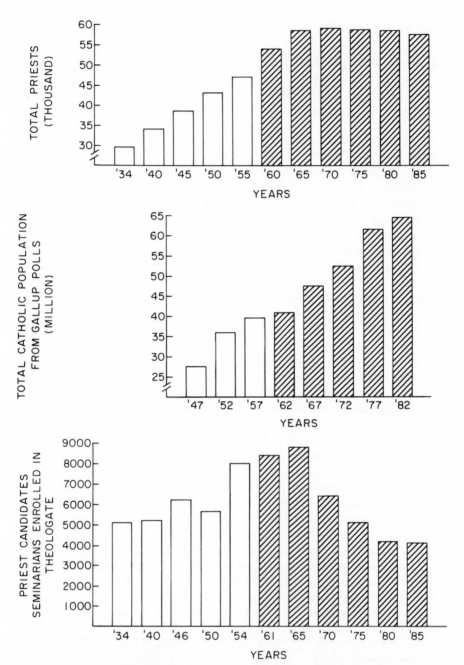

FIGURE 1:1. *Top*, growth in the U.S. priest population from 1934 through 1985. *Center*, growth in the general U.S. Catholic population during the same time period. *Bottom*, number of priest candidates enrolled in the seminaries in the United States during this period.

"not only on account of the influence which ecclesiastical celibacy has exerted, directly and indirectly, on the progress of civilization, but also from the occasional glimpse into the interior life of past ages afforded in reviewing the effect upon society of the policy of the church as respects the relations of the sexes" (Lea, 1884). Lea wrote that for the preface to the 1867 edition of his study.

However, where Lea focused on the interior life of past ages, I focus on the current picture and hold the same hope that he did. I have invoked the broader context of celibacy and historical connections wherever I thought they would help the reader understand the aspects of celibate practice being discussed or wherever they might be of interest. Unlike Lea, I do believe that celibacy has its genuine origin in the apostolic community, but I am well aware that it was not then nor in the first Christian millennium a universal requirement for the priesthood. I think that it is necessary to put celibacy into its historical reality (cf. Chapter 3) for two reasons: (1) for an understanding of its relationship to ministry, and (2) to delineate clearly the problems of charism (or spiritual grace) versus discipline (church law).

I believe that the careful reader will find this study free of some of the bias attributed to Lea.

One final comment on the historical context is in order. In 1960, there were 53,796 Catholic priests in the United States and about 8,000 men in the final four years of their preparation for ordination. In 1985, 57,317 priests were recorded as active, with 4,063 men studying (Hoge, 1987, p. 229). If one looks at the priest population since 1934 (see Figure 1.1, top), one cannot help but be struck by the steady progress in numbers between 1935 and 1965 in glaring contrast to the plateau and decrease in total numbers between 1965 and 1985. The leveling of the total priest population is another factor that made this study possible during these years. This leveling does not reflect the growth in the total Catholic population in the United States (see Figure 1.1, center) during this same time period. The concomitant decrease in candidates for the priesthood (Figure 1.1, bottom) is at least in part due to a decline in the understanding and appeal of celibacy (Hoge, 1987).

FORMAT AND SCOPE OF THE STUDY:
WHAT IT IS AND WHAT IT IS NOT

There is currently a hot debate in clerical circles about a married clergy versus a celibate priesthood. This study is not a defense of either position. The facts and analysis that follow can be used to support either view, just as they challenge partisans of both to a deeper understanding and clarification of their arguments.

This work is based upon interviews with and reports from approximately 1500 people who have firsthand knowledge of the sexual/celibate adjustment of priests. One-third of the informants were priests who were in some form of psychotherapy either during inpatient or outpatient treatment. The clinical setting provides a tremendous advantage in gathering personal information because of the depth and duration of the observation. It is not merely the sexual behavior or the celibate ideal that is revealed or recorded, but the person—the history, development, and context of a life that can be observed and analyzed. Brief evaluations and longer treatment modalities have both contributed to the insights garnered for this study. Several reports from psychoanalysis were available to us; the longest involved 1700 sessions.

A word of caution is necessary for those who are unaware of psychotherapy or who have a bias against persons who enter it. To see those who use psychotherapy as "sick" and thereby dismiss them and their observations is like denigrating anyone who uses the sacrament of reconciliation as merely a "sinner" who has nothing to teach us about values and virtue. Also, one who is sexually active, even if vowed to celibacy, may indeed be beset by a conflict of values but may be "healthy" sexually.

Another third of the informants were clergy who were not patients but who shared information during meetings, interviews, and consultations, both individually and in small groups. The secular cultural upheaval of recent decades as well as that resulting from the Second Vatican Council (1962–1965) made priests more self-aware, as well as open and searching, especially during retreats and workshops, as well as in training programs. Each man knew not only his own sexual/celibate history but also had some observation, experience, or knowledge of the sexual/celibate experience of the group with whom he lived or worked. As a confessor, religious superior, or confidant of others, he brought a perspective to the subject that no outsider could expect to master alone or through a mere attitudinal survey. A number of men from this group have kept contact with this study from five to 10 years, and a handful endured most of the 25 years.

The remaining third of the informants were especially valuable in validating and corroborating the priests' observations and conclusions because they had a perspective on priests who themselves would never have reported on their sexual/celibate adjustment. This group had firsthand information on the priests' behavior because they were their lovers, sexual partners, victims, or otherwise direct observers of it. This group included both men and women, married and single, nuns, seminarians, and men who had left the priesthood. The first data were recorded from this group in 1960 but increased as the study progressed, especially in the years 1975–1985.

There are undoubtedly readers who will cry "foul" at the fact that estimates of celibate practice and achievement are made on the basis of the life experience of 1500 men. "They are the sick ones," or "They are the exceptions," may be the first lines of defense against the simple facts. All of us involved in making generalizations and estimates from the facts available to us were so cautious and had so much time and opportunity to revise our calculations that I am confident that if we have erred at all, it is on the side of conservative percentages.

We consistently asked informants to estimate the sexual/celibate practice among their group or in their area. We took into account the relative viewpoint of each man reporting. If there was a vested interest in a response, that interest was taken into account. For instance, a bishop or religious superior would sometimes present a case or series of cases for consultation while stating defensively that these were the "only" such instances, whereas active homosexual priests who knew of one or more other active homosexual priests tended to make relatively high estimates. Persons with a relatively long association with the study or who had broad past experience within clerical circles offered estimates remarkably close to ours. Older participants tended to have higher rather than lower estimates; however, there were startling exceptions to that rule also.

Priests have at their disposal an important tool enabling them to be in touch with the "sexual truth"—confession. Michel Foucault (1978), in *The History of Sexuality*, points out the broadest implications of this vehicle of knowledge and power:

> Since the Middle Ages at least, Western societies have established the confession as one of the main rituals we rely on for the production of truth: the codification of the sacrament of penance by the Lateran Council in 1215, with the resulting development of confessional techniques, the declining importance of accusatory procedures in criminal justice, the abandonment of tests of guilt (sworn statements, duels, judgments of God), and the development of methods of interrogation and inquest, the increased participation of the royal administration in the prosecution of infractions at the expense of proceedings leading to private settlements, the setting up of tribunals of Inquisition: all this helped to give the confession a central role in the order of civil and religious powers. (p. 58)

A confessor will have an approach different from a therapist. A priest is trained to "forgive sins" as an agent of God. The slate is wiped clean upon the acknowledgment of an act, its repentance, and a firm resolve not to repeat it in the future. The observer of human behavior cannot be quite so segmented in evaluating the sexual/celibate behavior of a person. For instance, a priest may be sexually involved with another person only four times a year for a period of a few years. According to the former calculation, this man can be judged to be celibate with some periodic lapses due to human frailty. The student of celibacy who cannot relegate the behavior merely to the category of sin will not necessarily see the sexual behavior as unrelated sexual acts or as behavior divorced from the man's sexual/celibate orientation or adjustment. As one lay informant said of these four annual "lapses," "That's as much sexual activity as some married folks have."

In some instances we have included the ages of informants, but the geographic areas or dates of the interviews or reports are consistently omitted. That is mainly in the interests of anonymity. Also, we have not made any distinction between men who hold positions of authority in the church and the foot soldiers. There is a natural selection process that tends to eliminate grosser manifestations of noncelibate behavior, but there is no evidence that positions of authority or responsibility alone ensure celibate practice or achievement. The same laws of nature and the same demands affect the process and achievement of both superior and subject.

Most of the histories used as examples have been recounted by informants who have given their permission for inclusion. In some instances, the histories are of people now deceased. Other examples are so common that the example cited is an accurate representation of a whole subgroup. In all cases, the identity of informants is carefully guarded. The reader should be aware that there is no likelihood that he or she will guess the informants' identities. There is, however, a very good chance that the informed student will recognize someone "like" that. In fact, if this study has really tapped the essences of the practice, process, and achievement of celibacy, *every* priest will find himself included, and *no* person will find himself exposed.

This work is not a survey. It did not carefully select a representative sample of priests and ask each of them the same standardized questions during a structured interview. I doubt that the informants in this study could have been gathered by any scientific survey. One such survey of priests so scrupulously devised reports that 96.1 percent of 4600 priests responding said they "never had" mental illness, and 93.3 percent "never had" a problem with alcohol. These numbers are remarkable and questionably higher than national figures for the population generally (Bishops' Committee on Priestly Life and Ministry, 1985).

This work also is not a sociological study in spite of the fact that there is always a societal context to sexuality, and sexuality is important in every known culture (Marshall & Suggs, 1971). No culture is indifferent to sexuality because physical pleasure and self-disclosure are the building blocks of all human relationships. Over the past 25 years, Ira Reiss (1986) has worked extensively to develop a comprehensive sociological theory of human sexuality. His perspective has profound implications for the understanding of celibacy, which, like sexuality, has deep societal implications—certainly in terms of ecclesiastical societies.

Celibacy has to be learned and maintained within the church structure. Since the priesthood exists in many cultures, the cross-cultural comprehension that Reiss advocates is open to those who would study celibacy in its broader context. The current development of the Catholic church in Africa—a culture with such distinct sexual traditions as compared with those of Europe—will challenge the coming decades (Otene, 1982). It was during the 1960s that we frequently heard in the closed circles of the church that blacks were not well suited for the priesthood because they were not constitutionally capable of celibacy. This view was not voiced as often in the 1970s and 80s, but the social implications of it certainly add to the challenge of interracial understanding and respect.

I am aware that celibacy has economic implications and special links to the authoritarian structure and power of the church and religion. These are important considerations, although I do not deal with them within the scope of this study.

Gender roles and biological determinants of celibacy are introduced in Chapters 6 (homosexualities) and 10 (the sexual drive). Both areas need more study.

SEARCH AND RESEARCH

The reader may well ask, "How did this study come about?", "Who is responsible for it?", and "What motivated it?" These are not unfair questions, but are the reasonable challenge to any serious exploration. I will stand by what I have written earlier:

> The limitations of any scientific study are practical, theoretical, and ethical. Among the practical limitations is the notorious human proclivity toward bias. Even if causes could be linked to effects with certainty, the scientists would still have to reckon with the fact that, while experiments may be objectively carried out, they are never objectively set up. Michel Foucault, in *The Archaeology of Knowledge* [1972, pp. 50–53], argued that any description should include what behavior is observed, where such behavior emerges (meaning, in the case of human behavior, the workplace, the family, the church, etc.), who made the observation (for instance, doctor, employer, or priest), the vantage point of the observer, and which "grids of spec-

ification" pinpoint these observations. By considering these questions, Foucault asserted, scientific description can be corrected for bias. (Sipe, 1987, p. 88)

A search is related to, but distinct from, research. The value of a search is in its ability to disregard assumptions and to proceed asking questions and collecting data without a set hypothesis. It is not bound by the constraints of research and suffers from the limitations of its informal design. This does not mean that its conclusions cannot be verified and duplicated. Search can often get at facts that need to precede more formal studies. The facts, estimates, conclusions, and analysis presented here invite challenge and verification.

As a search, this work was directed as much by providence as by design. That is its strength. This information could not have been amassed if it had been sought for its own sake and not genuinely in the service of clinical understanding and intervention. Similarly, its limitations, marked by the lack of design and primary structure, in the end are the means by which we are able to extrapolate its many rich implications. Yet the simplicity of its pastoral intent remains intact. This work has always been geared to those who would like to understand more about the mystery of celibacy, its nature, and its practice, and how to achieve it.

I began studies for the priesthood during high school and entered a monastery when I was 20 years old. I was inspired by the idealism manifested by the men around me and had no reason to question anyone's celibate struggle but my own during the years of training. Celibate behavior was taken for granted by everyone around me as far as I could tell.

The writings of a monk/psychiatrist, Dr. Thomas Verner Moore, (1924, 1938, 1939, 1943a, 1943b, 1944, 1948, 1956) intrigued me even during my first year in the novitiate, and although I never met him, I was later greatly influenced by two of his students and friends, Dr. Leo H. Bartemeier and Dr. Walter O. Jahrreiss.

However, the man who first inspired me to search more deeply for the dynamic of celibacy was the Very Reverend Ulric C. Beste. I was a student in Rome at the time that he was a professor of canon law and on the staff in the Vatican's Holy Office. I had chosen him as my confessor and made my weekly confession to him. He was 75 years old. A foot injury incapacitated him during the summer of 1956, and I served his Mass each morning and delivered his supper tray to him each evening.

After supper, we would sit on the upper courtyard, and he would speak about his work in the curia during the war years; he had been in Rome since 1939 under Pope Pius XII and was privy to the workings of the Vatican. He spoke of his life in the monastery and of his early development in a small farming community. He also spoke of his own sexual development and his celibacy as easily as he had spoken about all the rest. "He has truly achieved celibacy," I thought to myself. Of course, that revelation also brought about my awareness that not everyone else had.

Father Ulric had a quirk that also proved decisive for me: He kept numerical count of all of the confessions he had ever heard and of the Masses he had said. He had done this since his ordination. After I was ordained, it was that quirk that inspired me to begin keeping data I thought would be useful in understanding and helping others.

In 1960, I began to focus my interest because of two groups of priests. The first group was 120 newly ordained priests who gathered that summer from all over the United States for a six-week workshop at Conception Abbey in Missouri. It was the first time I had heard my contemporaries share their sexual/celibate struggles and experiences. In conversation with some of these men, I began to form my first thoughts about the process of celibacy. A few of the men maintained contact with me for many years.

The second group who fostered my resolve in those early years met regularly in a town adjacent to where I taught high school. I attended their meetings only occasionally, but their frank discussions about the priesthood and their spirit of open questioning were what I needed at that time to maintain my search. One member of the group eventually led the National Conference of Catholic Bishops in Washington, D.C., and himself became a bishop. The senior member of the group, a pastor, subsequently spent 25 years as a missionary in Central America; another became rector of a seminary; and one, who at that time was a member of the John Birch Society, is currently pastor of a parish where only Latin Masses are celebrated. Three members resigned from the active priesthood after 10–12 years.

My contact with the St. John's University Institute for Mental Health (Collegeville, Minnesota) and my pastoral training at the Menninger Foundation in the mid-1960s increased my interest in the problems of the priesthood. When I spoke to Dr. Bartemeier about my observations in 1964, he invited me to come to the Seton Institute in Baltimore, where he was Medical Director, to study with him the counseling of priests and religious. Dr. Bartemeier was actively involved in my work from that time on.

The data collected from all these sources would have remained merely anecdotal were it not for the opportunity provided by him and the institute to establish contacts from every section of the United States, focus the material without the benefit of a standard set of interview questions, and build a consultation system that could measure estimates of sexual/celibate practice and achievement within a few typical groups of priests.

When Dr. Bartemeier retired from Seton, I engaged his services and we met for one or two hours each week until 1979. My teaching in major seminaries from 1967 through 1983 kept me in close contact with the clerical atmosphere. The core of my motivation in pursuing the understanding of celibacy has remained constant.

The clinician/consultant is often granted the privileged position of the "stranger." He is given the inside story quickly by the seeker in the hope of an objective assessment and subsequent relief. Dr. Bartemeier, who had been President of the American Psychiatric Association (1951–1952), the American Psychoanalytic Association (1944–1945), and the International Psychoanalytic Association (1949–1951) was a Catholic, had treated numerous priests, and had maintained a lifelong interest in the problems of religious and psychiatry (Bartemeier, 1972). He was consulted by a wide variety of bishops and religious superiors over an extended period of time. This study is as deeply indebted to his lifetime of knowledge and observations as a Catholic layman and psychiatrist as it is to my 18 years of religious life and 15 years of celibate practice.

In my mid-thirties, I experienced a depression I could not shake or explain. I consulted a Baltimore psychoanalyst, Francis McLaughlin, for evaluation. At the end of it, he said simply, "If in the course of treatment you discover that your vocation is the cause of your depression, will you be able to leave the priesthood?" I spontaneously and surprisingly said, "Yes." To the casual observer, that exchange may seem trivial, but to one whose identity, aspirations, and energies had been focused on one goal since childhood, it was monumental.

Marjorie Harley was the analyst with whom I chose to work out my personal concerns. She was consistently supportive of clerical goals, but was neutral to my decisions. Two years into analysis, I became convinced that celibacy was no longer a goal I wished to pursue. My religious superior was understanding of the struggle and helpful in directing me toward an ecclesiastical dispensation from the vow of celibacy.

Soon after I made my internal resolve about my own celibate goal, I met a missionary nun psychiatrist. I consciously pursued the relationship. Three years later, after she too was dispensed from her vows, we were married in a Roman Catholic ceremony.

Beginning in 1967, I lectured part-time in two Catholic theological seminaries. With the exception of the school year 1970–1971, I resumed teaching theological students in another major seminary from then until 1983. A good personal relationship and active professional exchange have continued with my initial religious community. Certainly this is a tribute to their strength, clarity of vision, and tolerance.

My own psychoanalysis and marriage have added dimensions of richness and a perspective to the project which could not have been achieved without them, but they have not altered the goal.

There will be those who are eager to speculate about the motives for such a prolonged and lonely search. A kinsman of mine, seeing the manuscript, speculated that my interest in the sexual/celibate lives of priests—a secret realm—was motivated by the public propriety of our father versus his secret life. Others will project less kind or more noble motives. Motivation is both simpler and more complex than can be speculated about. It is part of a life search inspired and maintained by the nobility of service and self-sacrifice which I have witnessed and from which I have benefited. It has also been conditioned by empathy for good people struggling, in Paul Ricoeur's (1964) words, "In a dynamic equilibrium of intersubjectivity where [Agape] is achieving the integration and spiritualization of Eros" (p. 162). Certainly it is inspired by a need to set the record straight and to do one's part to seek the Truth that sets us free. The reader is free to judge as to the success of the inspiration.

I have tried to avoid psychiatric classifications and moral judgments wherever possible in favor of a simple recounting of a life history. Some brief conversations with Margaret Mead in 1966 had a decisive impact on the direction of my study. To some of my assumptions about behavior and its origin, she issued challenges that took me a good 10 years to absorb and apply to my thinking about celibacy. Her influence was critical in making this study ethnographic. Celibacy, from the celibate's point of view, is hardly separable from the religious tradition, community, and beliefs that give it form and sustain it. My own interest in religion and psychiatry were compatible with a broadly anthropological approach. As Iago Galdston explained, "Anthropology is the study of the extended history of mankind; psychiatry, that of the short-range behavioral history of man. The former is the matrix of the latter and affects it profoundly" (1971, p. ix).

Celibacy truly is a culture apart from the average person's understanding, but, as with sexuality, there really is so little known about it that it is difficult to formulate the right research questions. The participant observer and the interested outsider could team up as so many anthropologists and psychiatrists had done since the 1930s to understand culture and personality. Leo Bartemeier, again, was essential to this evolution. He helped me grasp the melding of anthropology and psychiatry in the words of Edward Sapir, "The true locus of culture is in the interactions of specific individuals and on the subjective side, in the world of meanings which each one of these individuals may unconsciously abstract for himself from his participation in these interactions" (Wittkower & Dubreuil, 1971, p. 6).

To study human nature is to be confronted constantly with ambiguity and deviance as well as with purposefulness and ideals. This book's simple recounting of celibate histories and its analysis of the process will hopefully open up the subject of celibacy—a variant of one's sexual capacity—to further scientific examination.

Chapter 2

CELIBACY AND THE
SEXUAL REVOLUTION _

"Grow up, boy! . . . We're talking about life, death and the hereafter. No one gets an absolution from reality."

—*Morris West*
The Clowns of God

Priests striving for celibacy live, move, and have their being in a distinctly sexually aware and sexually active world. This was never more true than in the quarter-century under consideration.

Seven elements have critically structured the framework of celibate practice during the last 25 years: the shifting image of the clergy, sexual awareness, sexual explicitness, oral contraceptives, women's rights, the gay movement, and androgyny. Although I acknowledge that the Second Vatican Council (1962–1965) is an event with major implications for religion and ministry, I leave it to other, firsthand observers to recount its effect on clergy and celibate practice. One competent treatment that places ministry in its appropriate theological and historical context was written by the Dutch theologian, Edward Schillebeeckx (1988).

The decline in numbers of priests with respect to the growth of the general population, which we pointed out in the preceding chapter, has been matched by a blurring of the popular image of the priest and a concomitant lowering of priestly morale.

SHIFTING IMAGE

"Image" is a relatively amorphous concept, at least as popularly used, but usually it is regarded as a straightforward reflection of a person or a

17

reality. It is more like a house of mirrors that greatly depends on angle, lighting, and momentary glimpses of the medium and the person transmitting the image. Many people who see a photograph or portrait of themselves have a hard time accepting the "reality" on paper or canvas. On the other hand, every image is more or less a distortion of the truth even as it reflects *some* truth about that reality.

Catholic priests ordained prior to 1960 were generally viewed as public icons of strength, virility, honesty, and dedicated service. To follow that conception from the height of its Hollywood portrayal, during the 1940s especially, into the 1980s is to witness it mutate into precisely its opposite. The priest of today emerges more generally as a weak man of questionable masculinity or outright wimpishness. He is seen as at least less than honest or at worst hypocritical and is surrounded by an aura of monumental irrelevance. This trend is not an industry anticlerical campaign; on the contrary, the American cinema, dedicated as it is to commercial success, has been primarily a reflection of the times and only secondarily a forger of attitudes.

I have chosen examples from Hollywood films to demonstrate my point about the changing image of the priest in the hope that they will be more available in the memory of the general reader than theological or sociological considerations. The advantage of movies is that they are experiences shared by the most diverse segments of the population, validated by the numbers who see and react to them.

In their treatise *Hollywood and the Catholic Church*, Les and Barbara Keyser (1984) sketch the line of reasoning I want to follow. They say, "Church and cinema co-exist, co-mingle and frequently compete in modern life. Each offers a vision of reality so complete that it threatens to preempt the other's existence" (p. xii). I am indebted to their research and analysis to help make my point.

Consider, first, the priest movies from 1938 to 1948—years that were formative for priests ordained by 1960. Spencer Tracy portrayed Father Edward Flanagan of *Boys Town* (1938). This was an image anyone could be proud of; it made his work an American institution and immortalized in popular culture two phrases: "There's no such thing as a bad boy" and "He ain't heavy, he's my brother" (Keyser & Keyser, 1984, p. 68). Pat O'Brien as a priest in both *Angels with Dirty Faces* in 1938 and *The Fighting 69th* in 1940 consolidated the image of the priest as strong and fearless. There are echos of this same image as late as 1961 in the portrait of *The Hoodlum Priest* that is "a semidocumentary account of Father Charles Dismas Charles's work with juvenile offenders" (Keyser & Keyser, 1984, p. 72).

One of the most moving, popular films about priests was the 1944 Academy Award–winning *Going My Way*. Barry Fitzgerald as Father Fitzgibbon and Bing Crosby as Father O'Malley displayed a spectrum of priestly styles from dogmatic-dignified-rigid to practical-casual-accessible. All the human elements, even the vain and stubborn aspects of the older priest and the vivacious worldliness of the younger are a suggestion of humanity informed by sanctity (Keyser & Keyser, 1984, p. 102). Naturally, the younger priest plays golf.

In 1945, Father Chuck O'Malley appears again, this time with Ingrid Bergman as the authoritarian nun Sister Benedict, in *The Bells of St. Mary's*—a film that hints of sexual awareness beneath the clerical surfaces. The Keysers report that the film critic James Agee "was not alone in recognizing the sexual tension in a film about two young, healthy, vibrant personalities, both pledged to vows of chastity" (p. 111). The sexual humanity of priests becomes increasingly apparent from that point on in popular awareness. *The Cardinal* in 1963 was an attempt, in the words of director Otto Preminger, to portray "a hero moving from immaturity to maturity" and "a mature man who knows how to combine his own feelings with the laws of the Church, and to live within the Church without giving up his own personality or hurting his conscience" (Keyser & Keyser, 1984, p. 134).

Contrast that intent, if not the movie, with a 1982 release, *Monsignor*. Calling it "sleazy and tasteless," one reviewer synopsized the protagonist as "a totally worldly adventurer interested in arousing and sampling all the pleasures of the flesh. In no way does he seem like a man of God" (Keyser & Keyser, 1984, p. 128). However, reviewer Vincent Canby, speaking of the same film, says "Junk movies tell us a lot more—more effectively—about the secret fantasy lives of Americans." The Keysers point out that the sexual episodes in this movie "do have an importance far beyond this one sleazy film. The Catholic clergy's renunciation of carnal pleasures and of marriage has long made priests and nuns objects of curiosity and sexual fantasy" (p. 129).

What the authors fail to note is that the sexual behavior of some priests (however few) *is* sleazy, opportunistic, and cheap. The trouble with this negative image is that, like the child of failure, it is an orphan no one wishes to claim. This negative image is very unlike the earlier images that *everyone* claimed—the strong priestly figures of the 1930s and 40s (Spencer Tracy, Pat O'Brien) who were untouched by sexual emotions and who could be every future priest's equivalent of a sports hero, which was what he wanted to be when he grew up. It is also unlike the human and somewhat sexually vulnerable priests of the later 1940s (Bing Crosby) to the

1960s, like Father O'Banion (William Holden) in Satan Never Sleeps in 1962, who fights off the sexual invitations of a beautiful young woman as vigorously as he fights communism. These figures are certainly representative of some priests, but however many they may represent, they are not every priest.

1970 launched the image of the priest as sweet and nice, authentically religious, and incredibly inconsequential. As the chaplain in M*A*S*H, Dago Red emerges as harmless and irrelevant, participating in a mock last supper without ever realizing the sexual parody that is being played out (Keyser & Keyser, 1984, pp. 187–192). In that same decade, The Exorcist in 1973 presented the struggling but flawed priest, and The Omen in 1976 showed us priests who were frankly evil and satanic, along with others who were orthodox and fanatic.

The late 1970s and early 80s presented clerical images worse even than piously irrelevant or clearly evil—those of the laughable and ridiculous. Although there were vignettes of priest buffoons in many movies of the time (most less attractive and amiable than the canny Father Guido Sarducci of "Saturday Night Live"), the Keysers (1984) select Burt Reynolds' 1978 movie The End as a mean-spirited parody of Catholicism. The image of the immature Father Benson is devastatingly and graphically portrayed in his confessional behavior and his response especially to the sexual exploits of the film's macho hero. "Having dismissed the Church as a serious sanctuary for modern man and besmirched its clergy with images of immaturity and imbelicity, Reynolds dismisses them as childish masturbators not worth another thought" (p. 141).

In real life, one mature priest has said, "It brings me to my knees when, after living my life, there are no young men who want to follow my example." Perhaps the reason is that the living representations known to adolescents are not always positive. A movie that was designed to evoke memories of the Catholic high school experience was Heaven Help Us in 1985. With the focus on the adolescent coming of age sexually, this film gives us a good guy, the young humane brother, counterparted by a bad guy, the frankly sadistic disciplinarian, balanced by the older, more authoritarian principal. Against this background the students struggle. The priest/chaplain, Father Abruzzi, is a sniveling, lisping character, drawling his way through a warning about the dangers of lust as he blesses the students before a dance. "There is a beast within each of you," he says. "That beast is lust!" he screams as he describes the brutal tortures of hell as punishment for a "brief look at someone's buttocks."

This is the same priest who is shown as overeager and overintrusive with the boys in confession as they fumble to confide to him their sexual transgressions. Clearly, this movie reflects the priest and religion through the adolescent mirrors of the fun house. However, it is also clear that many people—Catholics and non-Catholics alike—retain this adolescent portrayal in matters religious, while receiving ever-maturing images of most other professions.

The general regression of the film priest from hero to clown has its exceptions. *The Trial of the Catonsville Nine* in 1973 was a biographical account of a 1968 war protest by several priests, among them Father Daniel Berrigan. This film was a straightforward and unglamorized testament to the convictions of a number of priests regarding war and peace. It may not have had the appeal of some of the other biographical presentations, but it did more or less accurately depict priests being themselves. We should not forget that Father Flanagan of *Boys Town*, Father Duffy of *The Fighting 69th*, Father Michael Logan of *I Confess* (1963), Father Barry (Father John Carridan) of *On the Waterfront* (1954), and Father Clark, the hoodlum priest, were all based on the lives of real priests.

The less flattering, if less individualized, are no less biographical; they are not merely figments of imaginative minds that have "no similarity to anyone living or dead." Together, the chimera constructed by movies is unjustly afflicted on the majority of priests, but it is also an image that some priest or other has made possible and believable. Not every priest working with children is a Father Flanagan, not every chaplain is a Father Duffy, and not every political or social activist is a Father Carridan or Berrigan. However, neither is every chaplain an irrelevant Dago Red or every adolescent counselor a lascivious Father Abruzzi or every assistant an underdeveloped Father Benson.

Since celibacy has to do partly with the public image and perception of priests, it is important to deal with the questions and doubts about priests and address them not in whispers and innuendos or in the groans of a beleaguered minority but in the open forum. Taken in its totality, American cinema has probably covered the spectrum of priestly celibate adjustment from the unquestionably observant to the frankly deviant and has included the admirable, amazing, and pathetic characters in between.

The fact is that sex puts the average Catholic at variance with the Church's teaching, especially since 1968 and the anticontraceptive papal encyclical statement *Humanae Vitae*. The discrepancy between law (doctrine) and practice has heightened an interest in the priest and his sexual example. The lay image of the clergy not only affects a priest's self-esteem, it also influences the source of clerical vocations—the laity. The lay joke is "the trouble with the priesthood is that they have only clerics and no lay people," and the clerical response is "the trouble with the clergy is that they have only lay people to draw from." In reality, clergy and lay both contribute to and suffer from the popular image of the celibate priest. Although fleeting and fickle, images are nonetheless powerful forces in determining as well as reflecting behavior.

SEXUAL AWARENESS: 1960–1985

There is another amorphous phrase—"the sexual revolution"—that is not easily defined but still impinges on behavior and awareness. The change in the sexual climate during the past quarter-century has challenged sexual meaning and practice and has made a formerly mute population articulate in describing their own sexual practice and questioning the sexual assumptions of others, including priests and clerical celibacy in general. Two areas that have come into focus during this period are contraception and the place of women in the Church and in society.

Several events prior to 1960 set the stage for a revolution of sexual behavior and being. Perhaps the earliest of these events was the 1944 discovery of penicillin, the first drug found to treat syphilis effectively. This discovery ushered in for one brief Camelot-like era a pause in the human medical record when every known sexually transmitted disease was curable. Syphilis and its concomitant fear that dread disease could accompany sexual pleasure were genuine threats that for some people reinforced abstinence or at least inspired caution. A Wasserman test was a standard requirement for entrance into many religious communities of men. A few priests in our study population reported having contracted and been treated for syphilis after their ordination. A few priests also reported parents or close relatives who had died of syphilis or were confined to mental hospitals as a consequence of this disease.

Tertiary syphilis is the killer that ravaged Europe after 1492. Both Christopher Columbus and Henry VIII died from it. In the early 1940s, more than half of all mental patients in the United States were hospitalized because of tertiary syphilis (cf. Langsley, 1980, p. 2860; Smillie & Kilbourne, 1962, p. 205; Seltzer & Frazier, 1978, p. 308).

Kinsey, Masters, and Playboy

In 1948, Alfred Kinsey, an entomologist from the University of Indiana, and colleagues published a study entitled *Sexual Behavior of the Human Male*. This record of questionnaires and interviews of 5300 subjects who detailed their sexual behavior won wide acceptance in both scientific and popular circles. It made sexual behavior a legitimate object of scientific study and wrested it from the exclusive domain of moral judgment. Its appearance was not marked by a grand outcry of indignation; generally, it was well received and gained additional grant money to continue its research.

Although Kinsey and colleagues' subsequent study of women (1953) anticipated a whole new area of awareness that I will deal with in a moment, I want to point out the contrast between the reactions to the two studies. One might have expected that *Sexual Behavior in the Human Female* would win the same open-minded response as its predecessor. Not so. The Rockefeller Foundation withdrew its financial support. Senator Joe McCarthy denounced Kinsey. Gould reports that Congressman Heller said: "The most disturbing thing is the absence of a spontaneous, ethical repulsion from the premises of the study." Presumably, talking to women about their sexuality should cause a moral aversion distinct from the same discussions with men. The dean of Union Theological Seminary in New York, Van Dusen, was even more condemnatory. "He [Kinsey] is hurling the insult of the century against our mothers, wives, daughters and sisters under the pretext of making a great contribution to scientific research." Women and celibates are presumed not to have a sexual life that can be talked about (cf. Gould, 1985, p. 155).

In 1966, William Masters—a gynecologist—and Virginia Johnson—a psychologist/researcher—published their landmark *Human Sexual Response*. While Kinsey's work was unsurpassed in its sociological significance, Masters and Johnson provided something different: physiological observation and analysis. For the first time in recorded history, sexual response was scientifically studied. In their preface, Masters and Johnson say:

> If problems in the complex field of human sexual behavior are to be attacked successfully, psychologic theory and sociologic concept must at times find support in physiologic fact. Without adequate support from basic sexual physiology, much of psychologic theory will remain theory and much of sociologic concept will remain concept. (p. vi)

In 1970, the same team recorded the results of 15 years of treating sexual dysfunction and problems in their book *Human Sexual Inadequacy*. Physiological observation was applied to clinical treatment and to the alleviation of suffering. Inevitably, their work opened up the floodgates of sexual observation in printed forms. What previously would have been considered pornographic or prurient was now openly written about and published by popular as well as by scientific publishing houses.

Homosexuality in Perspective followed in 1979 and used the same methods of observation and research of the earlier studies. In 1982, *Masters and Johnson on Sex and Human Loving* appeared. Coauthored by Robert Kolodny, it not only summarized research observations but organized them in the context of a manual for sexual education.

Already in 1955 *Playboy* magazine had published its first issue and became increasingly a symbol and voice of sexual freedom and expression. Propounded in what was termed the "playboy philosophy," it reached the pinnacle of its financial and popular success in the late 1970s. It also sponsored a number of "clubs" that flaunted the style of a sexually "liberated" clientele, although many poseurs and merely curious swelled the ranks of the true believers. The last club closed its doors in the mid-1980s, signaling a shift in attitudes as much as the opening of these clubs had. The Playboy Foundation sponsored surveys and studies that had sufficient scientific respectability to reflect, as accurately as surveys ever do, the changing awareness in sexual knowledge and behaviors. The magazine was so representative of the average American male during this period that at least one religious group of men ran advertisements in its pages for vocations to the priesthood.

Whether or not priests read Kinsey, Masters and Johnson, or *Playboy*, the thrust that these forces represented affected the entire climate of sexual sophistication at that time. The priest who had previously been the most educated expert on all subjects touching moral behavior now was challenged in his expertise about "res sexualis." Even in the 1950s, one of the most popular English language texts in moral theology (Davis, 1938, four volumes) presented in Latin the sections on the sixth and ninth commandments ("de sexto"). Increasing numbers of engaged couples who in earlier times could not be instructed about intimate marital sexual exchange prior to the very night before their wedding (lest they use the information to sin), now found any talk of sex superfluous or redundant. (Four out of five U.S. women married after 1975 had had intercourse prior to marriage, according to a 1983 report by the National Center for Health Statistics, while in 1960, 40 percent of women were virgins at marriage.)

SEXUAL EXPLICITNESS

Sexual explicitness bordering on exhibitionism invaded or exploded in every corner of the media. Radio, television, movies, and even the telephone service expanded understanding of what was legal, tasteful, moral, or at least commercially profitable.

Music, always a sensual medium, had long used poetic lyrics allowing for broad interpretation and offering great latitude for innuendo. Now songs became sexually blatant. *Sexual Healing, I Want to Love You All Over, I Want a Man with Slow Hands, I Want Your Sex,* and *Dirty Mind* are titles of songs or albums or lyric phrases that fill the airwaves. Sex sells in the music industry. It always has, but its modern explicitness and at times its alliance with violence make it startling. One album jacket shows a codpiece with an electric saw dripping blood under the title *Animal (F--- like a Beast)*. Names of music groups are more than merely sexually suggestive. "Sex Pistols" and "Circle Jerk" (a colloquial term signifying group masturbation) almost exhaust the limits of directness. Performers vie with each other for visual stimulation in costume and gesture. One performer in concert kneels on his speakers, strokes his guitar suggestively, and the instrument sprays the audience with water. The same performer has come onto the stage in bikini underwear, women's stockings, and an overcoat. One rock group flashes the slogan "Show us your tits" on the front of its tour bus.

Long gone are the movie ratings of the Legion of Decency. Sex that could be shown in an ordinary family movie from the mid-1970s to the 1980s would have merited an ecclesiastical condemnation in 1960. The double entendres lacing the Rock Hudson-Doris Day romances of the 60s look mildly off-kilter or contrived compared with *Last Tango in Paris, I Am Curious Yellow,* or hosts of others.

Radio and television talk shows have unveiled more sexual issues than did Dr. Reuben, author of *Everything You Wanted to Know about Sex but Were Afraid to Ask* (1969). True confession has become the name of the game, and the line between private and public life is frequently blurred for financial gain. Frankly sexual themes have increased steadily over the last quarter-century, and television has probably not yet reached the boundaries of its boldness nor has the public found its saturation point. The sexual audacity of some popular cable networks is causing the older networks to stretch their previous standards. The general population, in fact, seems willing to give television a great deal of freedom in exploring sexual themes, as fictional characters discuss intercourse, abortion, orgasm, ejaculation, condoms, diaphragms, making out, and getting laid—just like life.

In the 1980s, a research survey sponsored in part by the National Catholic Education Association and conducted among fifth through ninth graders found that Catholic students "worried" about sex more than youngsters from other religious groups, but also "report higher frequencies of thinking about sex" and "are more interested and active in the area of sexuality" (Foriliti, 1984).

Obviously, Catholic adolescents are not alone in their expression of sexual interest. In 1969, a review opened on Broadway that would run for more than two decades. It was called *Oh Calcutta!*—a sly play on the French phrase "Oh Quelle Cunt"—although one wag said it "gave pornography a bad name." The play was intended to be "something that was about sex, for intelligent people, with no holds barred, but without trying to shock people," in the words of the noted critic Kenneth Tynan. Nudity took over the stage of this production more than it did in the musical *Hair*, in which the chorus sang of masturbation, fellatio, and pederasty.

The 60s peace movement that extolled love above war gave way in the 80s to love and war inextricably intermingled. No hero is more exalted than the secret agent, James Bond, who is a law unto himself and whose lust, aggression, and violence are in the service of his nation's cause and the defeat of its enemies.

The celibate warrior dims before the glow of these glamorous modern crusaders. However, that is not the greatest challenge to the celibate ideal. Explicitness of sexuality, popularly accepted, challenges the denial of sexuality that many celibates must use to keep their practice somewhat in place. It also threatens, not entirely in a hostile way, the structure of celibacy: Explicitness can be an invitation to truth, nonsecrecy, and accountability—delicate areas, to be sure, for religious.

ORAL CONTRACEPTIVES

No single event has rocked the credibility of the Church's teaching on sexuality more than the discovery of oral contraception by a Catholic doctor, John Rock. Introduced to the market in 1960, oral contraceptives enabled women for the first time to control their own reproductive function, thereby giving them sexual equality with men. More than that, they offered to married couples a rational choice about family planning and childbirth. Rock wrote his own defense in 1963 (*The Time Has Come*).

Even at that time, many Catholic couples accepted the morality of contraception. Later, a vast majority of Catholics embraced contraception, some in neglect of papal teaching, and many in conscious rejection or defiance of *Humanae Vitae*, which formed a watershed of sexual authority for the celibate priesthood as well as for married couples. The majority of Catholic couples in the United States rejected the reasoning of the encyclical, and many thoughtful priests dissented. I was able to talk with a score of priests who, in 1968, signed statements of conscience in opposition to it, and I observed firsthand how two archbishops handled that opposition. In one jurisdiction, there was a simple order to recant or be suspended; in the other, each priest was asked individually if he could acknowledge the official Church teaching on birth control as official and recognize the authority of the magisterium of the Church. There was no demand to reject one's conscience. No one was suspended.

A number of synods of bishops (e.g., the West German bishops in the Koenigsteiner statement) presented the teaching of *Humanae Vitae* in a manner that left room for those who had grave reservations about its pastoral application. For at least one bishop, James P. Shannon of St. Paul, the pastoral challenge was insurmountable:

> He did not speak out publicly, but he stopped hearing confessions at [his parish] so that he would not tell parishioners something at odds with church doctrine.
>
> Then he was visited by the young woman, apparently not from his parish, who was worried about her relationship with her husband.
>
> They had tried to practice the rhythm method of birth control, she said. But they had had two children in two years, they were poor and they could not afford more.
>
> The night before she went to see Shannon she had prepared a special dinner for her husband's birthday, "wine, candles, the whole bit," Shannon said. It was an act of love. Her husband came home and saw what she had done, came up behind her in the kitchen and kissed her. But the fear of another pregnancy caught her. She fled to the bedroom, shut the door and cried herself to sleep.
>
> She went to Shannon because she wanted to use artificial birth control, to restore her relationship with her husband. Shannon remembers telling her, "Under the circumstances, you have a right to practice birth control."
>
> "Would the pope say the same thing?" she asked. "Any pastor would," he said, "and the pope is a pastor."
>
> "She hugged me, and the tears ran down her cheeks," Shannon said. "I've never seen her since."
>
> The woman left by the front door. Shannon left by the back door to tell his archbishop that, for the first time, he had overtly contravened the church's teaching on birth control. He wrote to the pope to express his concerns.
>
> Two months later, in November 1968, Shannon resigned from his Twin Cities duties, saying he realized that he had become a problem for his superiors. (Franklin, 1988)

The profound effect of *Humanae Vitae* was that it called into question the whole range of teaching on human sexuality. In the 1960s, the time had come, as Rock said, to face the question of contraception squarely. The World Council of Churches approved artificial means of birth control only in 1959, and there were still anti-birth control laws in more than a dozen states in 1964. Only the Anglican church had approved the use of birth control methods other than total abstinence at the Lambeth Conference in 1930.

The magisterium has chosen to formulate the essence of its moral judgment in the statement "Every conjugal act must be open to the transmission of life." Likewise, it holds that any sexual act outside marriage is mortally sinful. Once the question of the validity of these statements was raised in the context of contraception, not all responsible moral theologians were convinced by the papal arguments for a position that was not solemnly defined and was not infallibly declared. A principle of moral teaching asserts that a statement "is not true merely because authority says so; rather it can be asserted and taught authoritatively only to the extent that it can be proven true" (Haering, 1986, p. 336).

One of the most dramatic consequences of oral contraceptives for Catholic practice has been the diminution of the use of confession by both lay people and religious. In the early 1960s, a priest in an average city parish would spend several hours at a time in the confessional, and before Christmas and Easter a large proportion of the congregation would avail themselves of the Sacrament of Reconciliation. In the 1980s, 15 minutes to a half-hour on a Saturday afternoon or evening is as much as is practical in any parish. In the 60s, priests would go weekly or every two weeks to confession; in the 80s, they can go literally for years without it, even bypassing their annual retreat.

It is almost impossible to overstate the effect that the contraception controversy has had on the celibate clergy. It has attacked their self-confidence in three areas: (1) their credibility as a moral authority on sexual matters has been irreparably assailed; (2) the source of their assurance on those matters has been compromised; and (3) the validity of their own sexual sacrifice has been called into question.

WOMEN'S RIGHTS

Soon after Rock's apologia appeared, Betty Friedan published *The Feminine Mystique* (1967). Although the book is not standard reading for priests, there is not one who has not been confronted by the changing consciousness of women's rights. The equality of women is a cause that cannot be turned back; and yet no other shift in awareness has so threatened the celibate authority structure of the Church. In all of Christian tradition, only the original Society of Friends under George Fox fully embraced the equality of women in every respect (Nickalls, 1985).

Not until 1988 did the American bishops address at any length women's concerns, in a document entitled *Partners in the Mystery of Redemption*. They quote as a starting point a 1963 encyclical, *Pacem in Terris*, which said, "Since women are becoming ever more conscious of their human dignity, they will not tolerate being treated as mere material instruments, but demand rights befitting a human person both in domestic and public life" (p. 759).

The Second Vatican Council (1962–1965), concluded under Pope Paul VI, had some prescience for the ground swell of women's rights when it stated, "For in truth, it must still be regretted that fundamental personal rights are not yet being universally honored. Such is the case of a woman who is denied the right and freedom to choose a husband, to embrace a state of life or to acquire an education or cultural benefits equal to those recognized for men" (p. 759).

Actually, there is little support for women's equality in the celibate tradition.

Within the time frame of our study, these two popes (John XXIII and Paul VI) strongly endorsed the theory of women's equality, but the practical implications of such a theory still wait to be unfolded because of the peril they bode to a celibate male hierarchy. Nevertheless, like Joshua's marches around the walls of Jericho, the movement continues, and the trumpets are being heard, if not yet triumphant. St. John Chrysostom, in his famous treatise on the priesthood (written around A.D. 386), is witness to just how long the siege has been going on.

> Divine law has excluded women from the ministry . . . but they endeavor to force their way into it. Because they can do nothing of themselves, they seek to accomplish everything through others. They have gained such power that they can appoint to the priesthood and depose from it whomsoever they wish. . . . Everything is topsy-turvy, and the old saw is certainly true—'Servants lead their masters.' . . . And would that it were men who do this, rather than those who are not permitted to teach. . . . Did I say teach? The Blessed Paul did not permit them even to speak in the Church. . . . Yet I have heard someone say that women now assume such liberties as to rebuke the bishops of the Church more sharply than masters do their slaves. (Jurgens, 1955, p. 17)

The male virgin—described in scripture as the celibate—is one *not defiled by woman*. Sexual defilement and the threat to power are inextricably bound to a concept of woman as the weaker sex and as the spoiler.

Equality of the sexes can find a scriptural basis in none other than the champion of celibacy, St. Paul, who wrote, "In Christ there is neither slave nor free, Jew nor Greek, male nor female. We are all one" (Galatians 3:28).

This is a beautiful ideal—limited only by one factor: sex. Women cannot have *power*. Women are equal, necessary, one in Christ if they keep their *place*. The idea that the place of women is subordinate to men runs deep not only in the history and culture of the Church, but in the conscious fiber of many men and women who justify this bias as natural (sanctioned by grace).

Society as well as the Church has effectively conditioned women to avoid power. Dr. Jean Baker Miller (1982) put it trenchantly:

> For many a woman [the prospect of using her own life forces and power—individually motivated in a self-determined direction] is perceived as the equivalent of being destructive. On the one hand this sets up a life-destroying [controlling], psychological condition. On the other hand it makes sense if one sees that women have lived as subordinates, and as subordinates, have been led by the culture to believe that their own, self-determined action is wrong and evil. (p. 4)

Men who seek power are seen as resourceful and leaders; women who seek power are considered scheming and avaricious. Men who express anger are seen as forceful; women who express necessary and just anger are called bitches (Lerner, 1986).

The justification for male superiority and the introduction of evil into the cosmic system via sex both hinge on the Church's view of women.

According to Church tradition, the only good woman is silent, sexless, and subservient. My study of celibacy has left no doubt that this attitude is still alive and well in clerical circles.

There is an ancient book that few priests in our study have read. It was sanctioned by Pope Innocent VIII in 1486 and for two hundred years was a standard guide in all the major theological schools of Europe. No priest today would dare openly espouse the expression of Kramer and Sprenger's (1971) translation *Malleus Maleficarum* (Witches' Hammer). They don't need to. Many of the attitudes in this volume are ground into the unconscious of the celibate system. Much of the tone of the book can be recognized as a prepubertal defensiveness, that of priests who say, "Women can never be priests, they can't keep secrets," or "Women are so jealous, they could not be ordained," or more simply, "There is no head above the head of a serpent, and there is no wrath above the wrath of a woman." The last is quoted by Kramer and Sprenger from Ecclesiasticus 25.

What about John Chrysostom, mentioned above? Heard today just as convincingly as when cited by Kramer and Sprenger, this is the same man who spoke so eloquently about the priesthood. How does he justify nonmarriage? He comments freely on Matthew 19: "It is not good to marry!" Why? "What else is a woman but a foe to friendship, an inescapable punishment, a necessary evil, a natural temptation, a desirable calamity, a domestic danger, a delectable detriment, an evil of nature, painted with fair colours!" (Jurgens, 1955, p. 49).

Women are seen as essentially wicked. Kramer and Sprenger (1971) even appeal to Seneca: "When a woman thinks alone, she thinks evil."

"Women are naturally more impressionable . . . they are feebler both in mind and body." Of course it is assumed here that Man is the norm. Again, from the *Malleus,* "Women are intellectually like children" (p. 44). "Women also have weak memories; and it is a natural vice in them not to be disciplined, but to follow their own impulses without any sense of what is due" (p. 45). Inferiority is, the celibate authors erroneously claim, supported even linguistically, for they say "*Femina* comes from *Fe* and *Minus,* since she is ever weaker to hold and preserve the faith."

This attitude toward women is still a reality that is denied and skirted, smirked about, and rationalized every day in the operation of the Church.

Kramer and Sprenger warn about domination by women. Citing Cicero, Seneca, St. Jerome, and John Chrysostom, they conclude, "If we inquire, we find that nearly all the kingdoms of the world have been overthrown by women" (p. 46). Not just that, but "She is a liar by nature." And now we come to the core of the matter: "She is more carnal than a man, as is clear from her many carnal abominations" (p. 44). Carnal lust "in women is insatiable" even according to the Book of Proverbs 30. But Kramer and Sprenger are very graphic about it, expanding the image by saying, "the mouth of the womb" is never satisfied.

There is an oft-quoted image, undoubtedly the product of the male psyche—"A woman is a temple built over a sewer" (Alexander & Selesnick, 1966, p. 67).

There are those men of good will who would like to distance themselves from these attitudes and yet who cling to the theological bias that justifies all of them. "And blessed be the Highest Who has so far preserved the male sex from so great a crime [witchcraft]: for since He was willing to be born and suffer for us, therefore He has granted to men this privilege" (Kramer & Sprenger, 1971, p. 47).

These may seem like outlandish and archaic expressions of the rationale for limiting the role of the priesthood to celibate men. Yet one can hear them voiced sentiment for sentiment by priests and even bishops currently in private. Unfortunately, this negativity toward the person and place of women is unconsciously but effectively fostered as a support of celibacy. These attitudes are being increasingly exposed and assailed. The National Conference of Catholic Bishops has at least gone on record in their conference report (1988) as being aware of the danger of unconscious assimilation of a concept of masculinity marked by "domination and violence, sexual aggression and indulgence" and concluded that sexist attitudes are "negative indications for fitness for ordination." In the words of the report, "Women have suffered from profound as well as petty discrimination because of an attitude of male dominance which, in any form, is alien to the Christian understanding of the function of authority" (p. 781).

THE GAY MOVEMENT

Homosexuality, a word that was not accepted into English until this century (Lewes, 1988, pp. 69–70) was the focus of a great deal of attention in the quarter-century of our study. In their 1948 study, Kinsey and colleagues estimated that 4 percent of American males were exclusively homosexual throughout their lives and that 40 percent of adult males had at least one homosexual experience to orgasm some time in their lives. Gay advocacy groups often claim that 10 percent of American men are homosexual in orientation. A 1970 survey conducted by the National Opinion Research Center in Chicago, and validated in 1988, said that 3.3 percent of males have sexual contact to orgasm with another man occasionally or fairly often and about 20 percent of males have had at least one such contact (Thompson, 1989).

Whatever the numbers, people engaging in homosexual behavior have in the past formed a generally silent minority. Homosexuality was a topic that even in the 1960s still merited the scorn applied half a century earlier to heterosexual activity when the famous Doctor Howard Kelly of Johns Hopkins University told the 1899 meeting of the American Medical Association that the discussion of sex "is attended with more or less filth and we besmirch ourselves by discussing it in public" (Hollender, 1983, p. 228).

The 60s rebellion and the demand for rights for women, blacks, and war resisters was now extended to homosexuals. Probably the most symbolic event marking the emergence of a new social awareness to be reckoned with occurred on June 27, 1969, in Greenwich Village in New York, when a half-dozen policemen entered a homosexual bar, the Stonewall, and demanded to see identification cards. Four officers were injured when patrons formed a crowd outside the bar and fought the police with rocks and bottles.

Theoretically and pastorally, priests were challenged to serve the men and women in their care who acknowledged with a growing sense of acceptance, if not pride, their minority sexual orientation. The same flourishing honesty and openness about sexuality encouraged a number of clergy to question or acknowledge their own homosexual orientation and plunged the moral consideration of this topic into the center of the theological arena.

The acceptance of homosexuality as a topic of study and controversy made it fashionable to speculate about the possible sexual orientations of all people, especially the unmarried. Freud's daughter, Anna, remained single all her life, and her biographer defends the successful sublimation of her sexuality and insists that she was not homosexual (Young-Bruehl, 1988). In an earlier time, the need to defend meaningful singleness would not have required so energetic an effort.

The entire authority structure of an organization comes under analytic scrutiny when it insists not only that power is reserved to one sex, but that all participants in it be free of any sexual or affective attachment to the complementary sex. Years ago these questions would not have been interfaced with those of sexual orientation or with broader considerations of sexual analysis. Now having been raised, both the questions and the analysis have to be faced and completed. The answers are a task only begun.

AIDS

The acquired immune deficiency virus has almost accidentally been identified with homosexuality in the United States. In Africa, it is a disease that afflicts men, women, and children indiscriminately. However, because the virus was introduced into the United States via homosexual contact, and because up until this time the majority of reported cases involve homosexuals, AIDS has the reputation of being a "gay" disease. This belief is an illusion, since a virus is indifferent to sexual orientation. The first case of AIDS was diagnosed in the United States in 1981 and increasingly has impinged on the clerical and religious conscience. Already there are researchers who claim that clergy are overrepresented among AIDS patients. The broader implications of that possibility for the general population have captured the interest and concern of religious. Since sexual abstinence, self-control, and education are the best protections against contracting the disease, moral leaders dedicated to celibacy should be able to help stem the tide of infection.

ANDROGYNY

Clear sexual role definition is important to the sustenance of the celibate stance. The role of "Father," if defined in traditional authoritarian terms, can be understood and maintained with the rights, duties, and privileges that fit clerical structure. The "Pater Familias"—kind, firm, wise, and the ultimate local representation of moral and religious authority—supported male identification and gave the clergy a model that could match secular power roles.

When the deeper questions of sexual identification are raised by gender-blending customs in dress and social roles, they challenge the traditional power structure itself, not just the image. Increasingly in the 1960s and 70s, expressions of sexual role and identity diffusion grew and affected society generally. Some cross-dressing entertainers epitomized androgyny in style and song ("Girls will be boys and boys will be girls"). Unisex hairstyles and dress were only the surface manifestations of the real changes going on in role definition and sexual expectation. "Macho" and "sensitive" received new definition and value when applied to men. "Assertive" and "strong" were no longer pejorative terms for women. Helping professions like medicine and ministry were now revealed as having a large "feminine" core. The facades and stereotypes of masculinity and femininity were stripped from traditional frameworks and the bare substructures that looked oddly homologous and undefined were exposed. Clerical life and celibacy have not escaped the process.

By the mid-1980s, there was a clear polarization within culture and the Church on all the issues of sexuality that impinge on celibate practice. If the 1960s touted the age of sexual freedom and liberation, the 1980s were a harbinger of moderation. Alcohol consumption, tobacco smoking, and sexual promiscuity seem to be on a downward curve. Most likely, AIDS will continue to have an adjusting effect on sexual practice and exposure. Some revival of romantic love instead of casual recreational sex and of Victorian propriety instead of uninhibited individualism may gain in popularity and promote a revival of the "new celibacy" predicted by Gabrielle Brown (1981). But there has been too much laid bare, too much sexual knowledge registered, too many issues of sexual identity raised for the celibate structure of pre-1960 to be reestablished.

The sexual turbulence of the past quarter-century, with its discoveries and consciousness of equality, will have its lasting impact on celibate practice and achievement; but the generation of celibates who were part of the 25 years after 1960 have been in a unique position to expose and examine their celibacy and to contribute to the understanding of this mysterious "sign of contradiction" that can coexist with and participate in the history and service of civilization.

Chapter 3

THE ORIGINS OF CELIBACY _____

"No word and no gesture can be more persuasive than the life and, if necessary, the death of a man who strives to be free, loyal, just, sincere, disinterested. A man who shows what a man can be."
—Ignazio Silone
Bread and Wine

"Deeper than any changing idea of man, the world, and God (three correlative moments of a single attitude toward life), although inextricably bound to it, lies the unspoken religious experience that is God's inner word to man's heart: the intuition of faith which strives for expression." So says Dutch theologian Edward Schillebeeckx (1968, p. 13) in his study of the origins and motivations for the present practice of Roman clerical celibacy.

That intuition of faith historically was often expressed by the maintaining of what Schillebeeckx calls "cultic purity." The notion that sacrifice offerers must remain untainted by sexual encounters goes back to ancient civilizations. The yellow-capped Lamas of Tibet, the ascetic hermits of Egypt, the virgin priestesses of Thebes, the Astarte cult of Syria, the primitive Greek worshippers of Dodona, the Vestal Virgins of ancient Rome, and the temple priests of the Aztecs all lived in celibacy.

In the Roman Catholic Church of today, celibacy is understood to mean "an absolute chastity, even of thought and desire. . . . The purpose of celibacy is to attain complete freedom to devote oneself to the work of the kingdom of God. The meaning of the vow is virginity as a way of life" (Pfliegler, 1967, p. 13).

Present tradition rests mainly on two quotations from the New Testament. In Matthew 19:12, Jesus says ". . . and there are eunuchs who have made themselves eunuchs for the sake of the kingdom of heaven. He who is able to receive this, let him receive it." This thought is echoed by St. Paul in his first letter to the Corinthians (7:7) in which he says, "I wish that all were as I myself am. But each has his own special gift from God, one of one kind and one of another."

Neither quotation is a demand for celibacy; each is rather a granting of permission to practice it. As Schillebeeckx (1968) says, "In the synoptic gospels, 'celibacy' is not presented as an abstract ideal, nor as a requirement imposed from without, nor even as a desideratum. Jesus approvingly states a fact of religious psychology: in view of their joy on finding the 'hidden pearl' (Mark 4:11), some people cannot do other than live unmarried. This religious experience itself makes them unmarriageable, actually incapable of marriage; their heart is where their treasure is" (p. 25).

Christ was celibate. There is no serious tradition that contradicts that assumption. Christ was unique. He was the epitome of moral perfection, therefore the sexual drive and his other instincts were also subject to his perfection. Such perfection does not, in and of itself, obviate an active sexual life or marriage. Neither does it solve all the theological questions about Christ's humanity nor dismiss the heuristic challenges presented by the prospect of a "perfect" man without sex. These are theological conundrums that have to be faced eventually for the full understanding of the psychology of Christ as well as of human sexuality and celibacy.

Paul, celibate by choice, tells us something about his own decision and the life-style of the other apostles when he writes, "Have we not . . . the right to take a Christian woman [wife] around with us, like all the other apostles and the brothers of the Lord and Cephas [Peter]?" (I Cor. 9:5). It makes no sense to claim, as St. Jerome did, that all or even most of the other apostles were celibate. That figment does not enhance the stature of the celibate ideal, which, to have power, must be based on truth. The celibate ideal must be the genuine diversion of all sexual energy into an alternate pathway, resulting in proportionate productivity. In short, it must lead to the expansion of lovingness.

Paul—the popularizer of celibacy or, at any rate, its only articulate advocate in all of Scripture—is an example of sex transformed, and yet he, too, is a unique character. He wishes and counsels Christ's followers to be as he *is*, but not as he *was*. In the context of speaking to married couples about their sexual life, and recommending periodic abstinence for the sake of prayerfulness, he acknowledges the need for the couple to come together again, "in case Satan should take advantage of your weakness and tempt you" (I Cor. 7:5). This is not the voice of abstract speculation. This is not hearsay. Like Saul the Jew—a conformist in all things Jewish—Paul was proud of his heritage, his religious orthodoxy, his education and practice (Acts 21:39; Rom. 11:1; II Cor. 11:22; Gal. 1:14). Paul's education with Gamaliel (Acts 22:3) and the responsibility given to him as a member of the Sanhedrin (Acts 26:10) mean that he must have been more than 40 years old at the time of his conversion. "Paul was converted in middle age, and . . . was married. . . ." (Brown, Fitzmyer, & Murphy, 1968, 64:14, p. 217).

Paul certainly writes like a man who had experienced marriage. In midlife, having found his life's work after being widowed, he was free of family obligations to serve his Christ. This is quite a different picture from that of a young man without a married background. This picture also fits with the early Church Fathers' repeated discussion of remarriage after the death of a spouse, i.e., if the will of God has made the person single again, should he or she not accept that as an invitation to serve as Paul himself was now serving? (I Cor. 8:8–9). In Paul's case, clearly his present life as a Christian, with his goals, devotion and fulfillment, so far surpassed his former condition and happiness that he recommended it to "all who can take it."

Jesus was not so emphatic about recommending celibacy. He was younger by 10 or 15 years when he *finished* his ministry than Paul was when he *began* his. Psychologically and sexually, they had quite different points of departure when they began their ministries.

In the apostolic days of the early Church, married leaders coexisted with celibates. The Church was tightly woven into the context of the family, with followers meeting exclusively in each others' homes. As Schillebeeckx (1968) says, "There is no indication of any rejection of women or sexuality in connection with the priesthood. Church life and family life (in the broad sense of the word) are carried on in the same 'profane' environment: that of the Christian home with wide-open doors" (p. 21).

Along with men like St. Paul, whose ministry excluded by definition a wife and family, there were men like St. Peter. His "existential inability to do otherwise" took another more gradual turn. Peter—priest and first "pope"—was not celibate. He had a family. Schillebeeckx (1968) again describes that experience of giving up all for the kingdom of Christ as follows: "Actually, it is a growth of perhaps several years. After Christ's 'calling of the apostles,' as the synoptics tell it . . . we often see them still 'at home' and in the same circles where they were working before their calling. Although they were married before they had this experience, they did not go back to their family lives but on the contrary devoted themselves completely, and their wives also, to their ministerial work" (p. 141).

Family life did not cease. It was transformed and incorporated into the early Church. It existed side by side with those men and women who could not integrate the two. Neither way of life was perceived as superior to the other.

PAPAL PRONOUNCEMENTS AND EXAMPLE

Let us now take a close look at priestly celibacy and put it in its broadest historical context. To do this simply, I would like to consider the popes—all called to the priesthood, by definition. Although Gelasius I (492–496) was the first pope to be called the "Vicar of Christ" on earth, there is a tradition since the time of St. Peter himself that the Bishop of Rome held a special place among the other bishops (cf. Cullmann, 1962). This position of spiritual and political preeminence makes the pope an appropriate focus for studying celibacy. The history of papal celibacy is a microcosm of the practice, process, and achievement of celibacy, with its triumphs and defeats, spiritual exaltation of the first rank and deceptions of base rankness, marked with full humanity and all to which the human spirit can aspire.

Celibacy Not an Essential Element

If priesthood and papacy are essentially connected, celibacy and the papacy are not. This is the first important fact to keep in mind about celibacy—it is not intrinsically essential to any role, function, state, or ultimate goal (i.e., salvation) articulated by Christ. Its unquestionable gratuity makes it all the more intriguing as a puzzle, whether viewed as a charism (a special gift of grace) or as a discipline.

The list of popes who fathered future popes reads like an Old Testament lineage recitation: Anastasius I (399–401) begat Innocent I (401–417); Hormisdas (514–523) begat Silverius (536–537); Sergius III (904–911) begat John XI (931–935).

Other popes were the children of lesser clergy: Theodore I (642–649) was the son of a bishop; Damasus I (366–384), Boniface I (418–422), Felix III (483–492), Anastasius II (496–498), Agapitus (535–536), Marinus I (882–884), and John XV (985–986) were the sons of priests; and Deusdedit (later Adeodatus I, 615–618) was the son of a subdeacon.

Many future popes were not necessarily born into the office but were groomed for it as children, growing up in Rome's Lateran Palace. Benedict II (684–685) was enrolled with the clergy as a child, and studied in the choir-school. Leo III (795–816), son of middle-class, southern Italian parents, and Marinus I, son of a priest, served in the papal bureaucracy from boyhood.

Stephen III (752–757), Paul I (757–767), Hadrian I (772–795) and Stephen IV (816–817) were all the offspring of wealthy Roman nobility, orphaned in childhood and raised under the wing and tutelage of the Church, rising in her hierarchy, and attuned to her politics early. Political underpinnings may, in fact, have been responsible for the most notable act of Paul I's reign—his transferring of a number of bodies from the catacombs to the local parishes in Rome, including the body of Petronilla, regarded and revered by the Franks as the daughter of St. Peter.

Parenthetically, the children of popes were not always venerated. The daughter of Hadrian II (867–872) was raped and brutally murdered with her mother during Hadrian's reign as pope.

Several popes did not become priests until after the death of a spouse. Felix III (483–492) was a widower and father of two children, with whom he was buried in St. Paul's basilica. Clement IV (1265–1268) had been married, had two daughters, took his vows shortly after his wife died, and moved rapidly up the ecclesiastical ladder. Felix V (1439–1449) was so distraught following the death of his wife in 1422 and eldest son in 1431 that he founded an order of knight-hermits in 1434.

Clearly, a sense of the reality of sexuality as opposed to "angelism" pervaded the Church for centuries. Early attempts to separate sex from the Church began while celibacy was still trying to be worked out as a discipline. Little by little, the working-out finally became law in the 12th century. The law was based on both political and economic pressures and justified in the name of piety.

Ironically, the legislation against marriage and sexual activity for clerics produced two notable side effects in the Church: (1) an increase in the transgressions against chastity and the rearticulated rule of celibacy; and (2) a continuing degradation of women. The two issues are inextricably intertwined, and once again I would like to deal with them in their historical perspective.

In the pagan cultures, women other than virgins were the stirrers of sexual desire, which was considered somehow unclean. The ancient Babylonians bathed and burned incense offerings after intercourse to atone for its sinfulness. In some areas of Judaism, a man and his wife were ritually unclean until the evening of the day following their intercourse. In India, birth was bound with death. As Pfliegler (1967) says, "The goddess of lasciviousness is Bhavari, but she is also the goddess of Death and Destruction" (p. 2). He continues: "The very fact that the sexual instinct was so strong and overpowering made many races regard it as inspired by devils; under the influence of this force a man was in the power of evil spirits. It was ancient Indian tribal law that any man who had scalped an enemy must abstain from eating meat or from touching a woman for six months; otherwise he would be killed by the spirit of the dead man" (p. 2).

Because of their association with earthly desires and the power of demons, women were often excluded from pagan religious rituals, as their presence might interfere with the workings of the gods at sacrifices.

Only as virgins—i.e., nonsexual beings—were women exalted among the religions of ancient Thebes, Syria, Rome, and Mexico, for example. A slip from their virginal pedestals was punishable by impaling, flogging, dismembering, or walling up alive the formerly pure.

In Old Testament Judaism, marriage—often polygamy—and sex for the sake of producing sons were common practices among the prophets and kings. Gideon had 70 legitimate sons, as well as a collection of concubines; Jephte had 30 sons and 80 daughters; Abdon, 40 sons; Solomon, 700 wives and 300 concubines.

Within this mixed framework, Christianity had its beginnings. However, in his letter to the Galatians (3:28), Paul says, "So there is no difference between Jews and Gentiles, between slaves and free men, between men and women; you are all one in union with Christ Jesus."

The Roles of Women

Such equality did not last long. Soon women were again seen as distractors from worship. Within the first 100 years after the death of Christ, extreme asceticism was cropping up among some of the orthodox followers. In the year 170, Dionysius, bishop of Knossos, urged other bishops in his area to be less strict in matters pertaining to marriage and celibacy. As Fox (1987) says, "Women had so much to overcome. By Mary, said the second-century theologians, the Fall of Eve had at last been reversed: formerly, woman had been the 'gateway of the Devil,' though now she could be closed and restored, by maintaining her virginity" (p. 372). Virginity

> became a distinguishing feature of Christian life, where it created its own forms of organization, and has survived ever since wherever the faith takes root. It inspired its own poetic imagery, using the symbols of whiteness and transposed erotic desire: in a Church in the age of Augustine, we would have found the virgins seated apart, screened behind a balustrade of chill white marble. To become a Christian was to live with this constant evidence of the striving for perfection. . . . Striving, however, was not attainment, and the majority did not strive at all, [since virginity was exalted in a society that maintained public baths where men and women bathed naked together.] (p. 373)

By about A.D. 200, degrees of Christians had evolved, with extreme punishments for levels of sins, imposed during the preparation time for adult baptism. As a leveler of the classes of Christians, the higher of whom held themselves up as holier than the rest, Pope Callistus (217–222) ordained men who had been married two or three times, and refused to condemn the married clergy.

A double standard clearly existed, with many popes and followers urging and condoning marriage, while the ascetics demanded celibacy for all believers as well as for clergy.

Around A.D. 260, virgins began living in the households of priests and bishops as housekeepers, and in about 300, when the Church no longer supported virgins financially, women established celibate households of their own.

Anthony of the Desert (d. 356) was the model *par excellence* of man's inner struggle to authenticate and integrate his religious ideals by way of celibacy. He was a spiritual giant. He had power—the kind that allowed him to be unimpressed when he was summoned and consulted by Emperor Constantine. The mere story of his life "shocked Augustine out of his desire to marry and launched him on a trajectory that within a few years would lead to his ordination as Bishop of Hippo. . . ." (Veyne, 1987, p. 287).

While Augustine gathered a group around him for the support of his vows, it was John Cassian (c. 400) who articulated the spiritual power of community so celibates could be organized into self-sustaining units economically and politically. The papacy drew its candidates from men imbued with the ethos of each era and reflecting the development of the ideals of priesthood and celibacy. Increasing numbers of popes were chosen from the monastic ranks over the succeeding thousand years.

Political power and economic questions were intrinsically bound up with even the first decisions made about priestly celibacy at the national episcopal levels. In Spain, the Synod of Elvira (305) forbade those in holy orders to marry. If a priest was already married, he had to discontinue having intercourse. Any child born into a priest's household was grounds for permanent excommunication.

An attempt to make this ruling binding on priests outside Spain was defeated at the first Council of Nicaea in 325, though the ascetics gained some ground, as Schillebeeckx (1968) points out. "The rule that was clearly formulated for the first time by this general council—no marriage *after* the reception of an important office in the Church—has remained fundamental in both the eastern and western Churches" (p. 34).

Despite the Council of Nicaea, the exalting of virginity and efforts to legislate it into the Church continued. The Virgin Mary was held up as the model female—wife, mother, and virgin. As Fox speculates, "Were Christian tracts on virginity expressions of a deep antifeminism by which the male Church leadership desexed the women whom they did not understand and perhaps even feared?" (p. 372).

The double standard also continued. Fox (1987) reports an incident occurring in the 370s in which a Christian priest in Cappadocia "so far from excluding his Church's virgins . . . ran away with them and was later reported at a festival, a pagan one, it seems, at which he showed them off as chorus girls. The spectators admired their routine, and when their parents asked for the girls back again, the priest refused, insulting them" (p. 374).

In 390, John Chrysostom best summed up the situation in his address to the Church in Antioch:

> There ought to be a wall inside this Church to keep you apart from the women, but because you have refused one, our fathers thought it necessary to barricade you off in these wooden partitions. . . . I hear from other people that in the past, there was no need even for partitions. In Christ, there was "neither male nor female. . . ." But now it is quite the opposite. The women have learned the manners of the brothel, and the men are no better than maddened stallions. (Fox, 1987, p. 374)

Two years later, Pope Siricius excommunicated the monk Jovinian, who disagreed with clerical celibacy and said that the Blessed Virgin lost her virginity by giving birth to Jesus.

In 441, the Synod of Orange exacted a promise of perpetual virginity from clergy before their ordination, and in 445, Pope Leo I recommended a "Joseph's marriage"—continence for those priests already married. Both the promise and the recommendation were largely ignored until the 12th century.

Church Property and Political Power

During the next 50 years or so, the question of a priest's home and sexual life began to evolve into one of power and property.

Pope Gelasius I (492–496) outlined in a letter to Emperor Anastasius the reasons for the superiority of the Church over the State—namely that although God gave royal power to the emperor, He gave spiritual authority to the bishop, which extended beyond political boundaries. His letter would be used for centuries in the struggle between Church and State. The struggle for spiritual superiority, even over material and sexual matters, would surface immediately when the successor pope, Symmachus (498–514), a convert from paganism, was charged with misuse of Church property and unchastity.

Pope Agapitus (535–536) tightened the knot between celibate practice and control of material possessions by opposing what had been the common practice of popes picking their successors, and Pelagius I (556–561) made his episcopal candidates who already had a wife and children sign a document stating that the children could not inherit Church property.

"Gregory the Great," pope from 590 to 604, tried unsuccessfully to enforce clerical celibacy. It was during his reign that the Council of Seville (592) declared the sons of priests to be illegitimate. Church property would remain Church property, but ecclesiastical authority would expand its material care of its celibates. A few years later, Pope Adeodatus—the son of a subdeacon—was the first to leave a one-year stipend as a bequest to his bishops.

Not all popes were models of the purity being clamored for among the ascetics. Pope Leo III (795–816) was unpopular among the aristocratic Christians who attacked him, tried to cut out his eyes and tongue, and charged him with perjury and adultery. Pope Boniface VI—son of a bishop named Hadrian—had been defrocked for immorality during his subdeacon years by Pope John VII, had been rehabilitated, reinstated, and defrocked a second time before being elected pope by a rioting crowd in 896 as a political gesture. He lasted only 15 days in the office.

With Sergius III (904–911) came an alliance of Church and aristocracy, if not State. Sergius had the close support of Theophylact, a wealthy nobleman who served as his financial director, consul, and commander of the militia, and of Theophylact's wife, Theodora. He also had the close support of their 15-year-old daughter, Marozia, by whom he had an illegitimate son—the future Pope John XI.

Papal dependency on this wealthy family continued through the next three popes, including John X (914–928) who had been Theodora's lover when he was a deacon. John's own close relationship with Berengar I, king of Italy, and his political ambitions and successes prompted him to try to separate himself from the powerful Theophylact family. They proved more powerful than he, however, and after the death of Berengar, John was deposed and suffocated with a pillow.

Women may not have had power within the Church, but some of them in essence ran the papacy.

Marozia inherited the house of Theophylact, and was responsible for the election of Popes Leo VI, Stephen VII, and ultimately her own son, John XI, who presided at her wedding to the then king of Italy, Hugh of Provence.

Political families continued to dictate the occupancy of the papal throne through the reign of John XII (955–964), illegitimate son of Alberic II, a powerful prince of Rome. John became pope at age 18 and is described as having a "disinterest in spiritual things, addiction to boorish pleasures, and an uninhibitedly debauched life. Gossipy tongues accused him of turning the Lateran palace into a brothel" (Kelly, 1986, p. 126). He died in his mid-twenties, having suffered a stroke while he was in bed with a married woman.

Political reversals and a strong alliance with King Henry II of Bamberg allowed Pope Benedict VIII (1012–1024) to prohibit through the Synod of Pavia in 1022 the marriage and concubinage of all clergy, including subdeacons. Anticipating nonobedience, the Synod further decreed that children of these unions would become serfs. Under Henry, these canons became imperial code, and allayed Benedict's fear that Church property would dissipate among clerical offspring.

In the years that followed, celibacy legislation became more serious, and women became inconsistent baggage to the ministry. The Councils of Limoges and Bourges in 1031 declared that a man could not be ordained to the subdiaconate unless he left his wife or lived with her with a promise of continence. Under confusing circumstances and politically conflicting forces, Pope Benedict IX abdicated the papacy, some say to marry. In 1049 Pope Leo IX made priests' wives slaves of the Church. In the latter part of the 11th century, two priests led a movement to root out women living in priests' homes, married or not.

In 1059, under Pope Nicholas II, a Lateran Synod declared that people could not attend the masses of married priests or receive sacraments from them. For the first time, clergy of one church were required to share a common life. As a response to the Synod, bishops quietly urged their priests to be discreet in their marriages. Celibacy was still viewed by many as an absurdity, even as the laws enforcing it became stricter and more numerous.

Four years later, Pope Alexander II found it necessary to reinforce the decrees of Nicholas' Synod, and in 1074 Gregory VII reinforced them again and suspended from the priesthood the "concubine-keepers." In reply, the German clergy drew up counterpetitions, charging the pope with trying to make men live like angels and stating that by forbidding the way of nature he was actually forcing *incontinence.*

In 1081, the Synod of Melfi declared again that clergy women and wives were slaves, and children of these unions illegitimate. Another witch hunt for priests' women was the result.

In 1123, Pope Callistus II pronounced the marriages of higher clergy invalid, and in 1139 the historic Second Lateran Council under Innocent II declared all marriages of priests to be null and void, and further demanded that existing marriages be severed before a man could be ordained to the priesthood. It was the first time that continence and celibacy were identified as the same thing.

Clerical behavior did not immediately change, and in 1180 Alexander III confirmed the Lateran laws.

In 1266, as a reaction by the Germans to bishops who were giving dispensations to clergy to marry, the Synod of Bremen excommunicated bishops not upholding the Lateran decisions, excommunicated people whose daughters married priests, dismissed again the concubine-keepers, and reiterated that the children of priests could not inherit Church property. Despite many attempts by bishops in the 13th and 14th centuries to have the more liberal Eastern laws adopted in the Western Church, the clamping down continued. Separate Synods in Valladolid (1322), Valencia (1388), Cologne (1415), and Paris (1429) denied Christian burial to women who had affairs with priests.

With marriages forbidden, the 14th and 15th centuries saw a rise in concubinage. As Kelly (1986) says of Clement VI (1342–1352), though he was devout and a protector of the poor, "the charges brought by contemporaries against his sexual life cannot be explained away" (p. 221). The antipope John XXIII (1410–1415) was rumored to have seduced 200 women during his five-year reign.

Neither Pius II (1458–1464) nor Innocent VIII (1484–1492) married, but both left trails of illegitimate children fathered prior to their ordinations.

The bitter irony is that while the male half of these liaisons moved upward into power and esteem in the Church, the women who were involved were increasingly persecuted.

The Inquisition and Anti-Eroticism

The psychiatrists, Alexander and Selesnick (1966) pointed out:

Centuries of imposed celibacy had not inhibited the erotic drives of monks or nuns, and underground passageways were known to connect some monasteries and nunneries. Townspeople often had to send prostitutes to the monasteries in order to protect the maidens of the village. It became increasingly imperative to the Church to start an antierotic movement, which meant that women, the stimulus of men's licentiousness, were made suspect. Men's unsavory impulses could no longer be tolerated, so they were projected upon women. (p. 67)

I have already commented on the handbook of the antierotic movement, *The Malleus Maleficarum.* It was approved by Innocent VIII, who set in motion the subsequent Inquisition. He also used his own papacy and alliance with the powerful Medicis to marry his bastard children into wealthy families. In *Malleus*, witchcraft is essentially connected to woman by her inferior carnal nature:

She is more carnal than a man, as is clear from her many carnal abominations. . . . All witchcraft comes from carnal lust which is in women insatiable. . . . Three general vices appear to have special dominion over wicked women, namely, infidelity, ambition and lust. Therefore, they are more than others inclined towards witchcraft who more than others are given to these vices. . . . Women being insatiable it follows that those among ambitious women are more deeply infected who are more hot to satisfy their filthy lusts. (p. 47.)

While the Inquisition raged, Alexander VI (1492–1503) succeeded Innocent to the papal throne. Alexander had been born Rodrigo Borgia, nephew of the bishop of Valencia, who became Pope Callistus III and made Rodrigo a cardinal deacon. Rodrigo served as vice chancellor under the next four popes, fathering a number of children along the way. His favorites were the four by Vannozza Catanei, including the notorious Cesare and Lucrezia Borgia. It was said of Alexander "that his consuming passion, gold and women apart, was the aggrandizement of his relatives, especially Vannozza's children" (Kelly, 1986, p. 253). His son, Cesare, tried to establish a hereditary monarchy, became the subject of Machiavelli's *The Prince*, and murdered the second husband of his sister, Lucrezia. Alexander himself excommunicated and ordered the torture and eventual execution of the reformer Girolamo Savonarola, who, among other things, denounced papal corruption.

Julius II (1503–1513), patron of Michelangelo, Raphael, and Bramante, followed Alexander VI. Kelly (1986) says of him "As a man he was headstrong, irascible, sensual (as cardinal he fathered three daughters), and was nicknamed 'Il terribile'; as pope he had policies which were at least disinterested and intelligible, even if they aimed no higher than making the papal State the first power in Italy" (p. 256).

The Reformation

In Germany the Reformation was taking hold as Martin Luther nailed his 95 theses to the door of All Saints Church in Wittenberg in 1517, and was excommunicated by Leo X three years later. Luther had sought to correct the abuses within the Roman Church, not break from it. He married in 1525.

In the Roman Church, sexuality at the highest levels remained operative. Paul III, cardinal deacon under Alexander VI, was pope from 1534 to 1549. Nicknamed "Cardinal Petticoat" because his sister Giulia had been one of Alexander's mistresses, Paul himself had a mistress, three sons, and a daughter.

Divergencies between the letter and spirit of the law were not confined to the continent. As Sanderson (1986) says of David Beaton, Cardinal of Scotland from 1494–1546, "What was particularly denounced and pilloried in literary satire was a life of profligacy supported by a rich living and high ecclesiastical office. Professor Cowan remarks in his recent book *The Scottish Reformation*, 'If there had been any moral outrage it related to the bishops and commendators with their many mistresses rather than to the humble parish priest with his loyal housekeeper who also shared his bed and bore his children.' " (p. 36).

In 1545 the Council of Trent convened and tightened pro-celibacy legislation even further. "Every attempt to waver from the path of celibacy was anathematized" (Pfliegler, 1967, p. 40). Rules for clerical training, forming of seminaries for young boys, dress codes for priests, and edicts for how and where priests would live were handed down. Female housekeepers were still allowed; however, priests would continue to be excommunicated if they married.

Predictably, the more sexuality was outlawed, the more it flourished. Pope Julius III (1550–1555) had a homosexual involvement with a 15-year-old boy whom he named a cardinal. In 1552, Pope Pius IV reconvened the Council of Trent but deferred the issue of married priests. He himself was the father of three children.

Popes continued their political and military involvements, and resisted new ideas. Gregory XIII (1572–1585), a professor of law with a natural son, militarized the Counter-Reformation, endorsing plots to have Queen Elizabeth I of England assassinated. Urban VIII (1623–1644) insisted that bishops and cardinals live in their dioceses. This was partially an attempt to curtail the sexual immorality of the clergy. He also ordered the torture of Galileo and condemned the Copernican theory.

Innocent X (1644–1655), like other popes before him, enjoyed a special relationship, which was rumored to be immoral, with a powerful woman—in this case, his sister-in-law, Donna Olimpia Maidalchini—whom he consulted on all important decisions.

In an effort to desexualize the art of the time, Pope Clement XIII (1758–1769) ordered all nudity in Vatican statuary and paintings to be covered up.

Questions about celibate observance continue in our own century. In the early 1920s, Cardinal O'Connell's nephew, Monsignor O'Connell of Boston, secretly married. When Rome found out, the younger O'Connell fled with his wife and $75,000 of Church funds. The cardinal denied the marriage to Pope Benedict XV, who in turn produced the marriage license and remarked, "He who gives the red hat can take it away" (Cooney, 1984, pp. 26–27).

Pope Pius XII (1939–1958) was generally well regarded for his sanctity. However, there are two questions historians still have to sort out: his relationship to Nazism and his relationship with a German nun who loathed the Nazis. He has been criticized for his failure to speak out against the Nazi atrocities. A biography, itself not above serious question, claims that Pius had as his closest confidant Sister Josefine Pascalina, a German nun who eventually rose to unprecedented heights of power during his reign, was the only woman ever to have lived with a pope in the papal quarters, witnessed a papal election, and served in effect as Vatican Secretary of State (Murphy & Arlington, 1984).

Another painful and questionable sexual allegation was leveled at Pius' successor. Pope Paul VI (1963–1978) was accused in both the French and Italian press by an author, Roger Peyrefitte, of having a homosexual relationship early in his priesthood. The incident itself is unremarkable except that Vatican officials overreacted loudly by calling for a universal "Day of Consolation" for calumny against the Holy Father (April 4, 1976). The 78-year-old pope himself unnecessarily graced the charge when he addressed a crowd of 20,000 in St. Peter's Square with these words: "We know that our cardinal vicar and the Italian bishops conference have urged you to pray for our humble person, who has been made the target of scorn and horrible and slanderous insinuations by a certain press lacking dutiful regard for honesty and truth. We thank you all for these demonstrations of faithful piety and moral sensibility" (*National Catholic Reporter*, April 1976).

Modern historians will have to sort out silly and salacious speculation from serious psychohistorical exploration of the sexual/celibate adjustment of church leaders. Conscientious students of history and religion are increasingly aware of the importance of a psychodynamic element in assessing men, their actions, and their influence.

THE POWER AND PERSISTENCE OF CELIBACY

From where does a nonessential practice as difficult and unique as celibacy derive its power and persistence? In the Roman priesthood, there are three sources: spiritual, political, and economic. The Gospel, with its message of universal love, has intrinsic power to transform lives, inspire heroic acts, and confront overwhelming opposition from culturally dominant views of reality. Chastity, freedom, and equality are worthy ideals. However, when one translates them into practical action and daily reality, they challenge any established order.

Celibacy is the great validator of one's beliefs. A priest's statement that "I am so convinced of the Message and my mission that even my sexuality is unimportant in the face of this reality" is startling and strong proof of his convictions, if nothing else. And this strength of conviction is what makes revolutions. There is, after all, something revolutionary (and subversive of established order) about every genuine religious movement.

The early Christians did not greatly need celibacy to validate their revolution. At odds with the Roman world around them, they had ample occasion to prove their devotion and adherence to their beliefs.

It was the man of the desert, the monk (the man alone), who would consolidate celibacy within the Western discipline. This was not just Paul's recommended abstinence, however soundly motivated, but a quantum psychological leap into self-awareness, which I will discuss later under celibate achievement. The switch was from the idea of the devil on the outside tempting one to the idea of the inner workings of one's heart, mind, and body in the service of the Gospel ideal.

> The spiritual masters of the desert, most notably Evagrius and his Latin exponent, John Cassian, came to treat the fact of sexuality as a privileged sensor of the spiritual condition of the monk. Sexually based imaginations, the manifestation of sexual drives in dreams and through night emissions, were examined with a sensitivity unheard of in previous traditions of introspection, and in a manner entirely independent of any opportunities for contact with the other sex. To see sexuality in this manner was a revolutionary change of viewpoint. From being regarded as a source of passions, whose anomalous promptings might disrupt the harmony of the well-groomed person if triggered by objects of sexual desire, sexuality came to be treated as a symptom that betrayed other "passions". It became the privileged window through which the monk could peer into the most private reaches of his soul. . . . The slow remittance of the lingering, intensely private meanings associated with sexual dreams heralded the passing away from the soul of those far greater beasts, anger and pride, distant echoes of whose heavy tread appeared in the form of sexual fantasies. With this the monk had closed the last, razor-thin fissure in the single heart. (Veyne, 1987, pp. 299–300)

If political power and economic questions had been absent, I doubt that celibate practice would have been legislated beyond monastic walls. What makes celibacy a tempting broker of political and economic power is its simplicity. Marital, family, and sexual ties are complicated, engendering obligations, bonds, and alliances of marvelous intricacy. They form the kind of net that can entwine nations together and ensnare the mightiest.

According to Luke's account (23:29), Jesus acknowledged the luck of those who were not blessed or burdened with family. He acknowledged that following him would involve a rejection of family—at least by means of some internal freedom—and a reevaluation of priorities. Followers could not rely on a home or be bound even by the sacred family duty to bury a parent (Matt. 8:19–22).

Questions about Church property and religious power and authority were recurrent themes for centuries of popes. There is a natural awareness that unmarried men are less encumbered socially, freer, and economically more flexible than those who are married. If only married men could fight in wars, the latitude of most combat would be greatly restricted. The vow of celibacy institutionalized nonmarriage, and gave the practitioner (or the avowed) superior control over his political and economic destiny.

Celibacy became an even more treasured weapon in the political and spiritual armamentarium of the Church as the conflicts between Church and State evolved. The power of Christ that he refused to use in his own defense was now unleashed—or at any rate enlisted—in his name and in the service of his mission and property. No longer just a gift to some of the apostles (the repository of spiritual power), it became a requirement for all who would aspire to hold authority. Every pope (and priest) has had in some way to struggle with the idea of man and his sexual nature, the world and its power and property, and God and His eternal transcendent truths.

AT WHAT COST CELIBACY?

There is a price to pay for every shift of power. In the history of the popes' celibacy, we see that the shift sexually was from the essentially horizontal power base of the Gospel, where there was "no difference between Jews and Gentiles, between slaves and free men, between men and women," (Gal. 3:28) to one of male dominance over property and women. What Duby (1983) describes within the family in 1030 France was paradigmatic of the sexual shift in the whole Church:

> What had been an equal association between husband and wife gradually changed into a miniature monarchy in which the man ruled as king. This male predominance was reinforced by the tendency for family relations to be defined more and more in terms of vertical lineage. . . . The splitting up of family fortunes was undesirable; the number of claimants to them needed to be limited—and that number could be halved simply by excluding women from the succession. So, as we can see from these various indicators, women's power over hereditary property was gradually retracted. (p. 99)

As celibacy became codified, the power of women and the development of a Christian theology of sex were sacrificed. In some instances, sexuality and heresy became synonymous, especially in relationship to the homosexualities (Boswell, 1980). Women became increasingly associated with sin intrinsically and with witchcraft lustfully. It is hard to overestimate the importance of antifeminism in the formation of celibate consciousness and priestly development for over two centuries when the discipline of celibacy was being solidified (1486 and following).

The outlandish and archaic expressions of the rationale for limiting the role of the priesthood to celibate men can be matched sentiment for sentiment in current clinical examples.

The spiritual essence and integrity of celibacy do not need to support themselves by an incomplete theology of sex or a distorted concept of women. There is a power inherent in celibacy proven by those who have achieved it.

The Church has come to demand celibacy—the discipline—but does not educate for it or support it effectively. Many who care about religion as a moral force are vocal and direct both in demanding celibacy from those who claim the charism or who willingly embrace its discipline "on account of the kingdom" and in supporting its practice or achievement. Pretense is intolerable. Dissimulation serves neither authentic religion nor Christian values.

The questions about celibate development will never be solved by celibates alone. The development of a theology of sex will not be effectively addressed by celibates alone. Married persons and celibate priests need each other to proceed with the important practical challenges to effective Christian living. This is the authentic apostolic and Christian tradition.

Chapter 4

THE MEANINGS OF CELIBACY

"I hold that a life of perfect continence in thought, speech and action is necessary for reaching spiritual perfection. And a nation that does not possess such men is poorer for the want."

—*Gandhi*
All Men are Brothers

What is celibacy? One might think that definitions of celibacy are easy to come by—"ask any priest." This is not the case. In the mid-1980s, four bishops from different dioceses were essentially asked that question during a deposition each had to give regarding the sexual behavior of a priest in each of their jurisdictions. It was clear, as it is with the average priest in the United States, that there simply is no clear operational definition of celibacy.

In the last 20 years, there has been a growing consciousness of the need for celibate definition. The emphasis, however, has been primarily on the negatives—what to avoid—rather than on the positive—how you do it.

Donald Goergen, himself a vowed celibate, wrote *The Sexual Celibate* in 1974. He took as his starting point sexuality instead of abstinence, and treated celibacy from the vantage point of the psychology and theology of sexuality. The book is admirable, generally revolutionary in its directness, and includes concrete suggestions for living a chaste life. Father Andrew Greeley was insightful in his evaluation of Goergen's work, and was willing to endorse it on the book jacket: "For too long we were celibates because we had to be and no reflection was needed beyond the repetition of bromides and clichés. . . . Many of us sense that our commitment to celibacy was neither irrevelant nor adolescent, but the Church lacked the theory to propound the vision of the celibate life in terms that made sense to our contemporaries. Goergen has made a major step forward toward developing a new theory of celibacy." Goergen is bold in asking some questions about celibate living, and he moves beyond where many priests

52

are—what really is celibacy? Merely abstinence or periodic abstinence? Only an ideal like perfect beauty to which many aspire but few if any attain?

I became progressively more fascinated with this glaring lack of precise characterization as I taught successive classes of seminarians in their deacon year. They were the ones who articulated the question most succinctly: "What *is* celibacy?" Priests representing several generations have confirmed that, surprisingly, this was not a query easily or adequately handled in their education. One priest said, "The extent of my formal training about celibacy in the seminary was a statement by the rector: 'Celibacy means no sex, hetero, homo, auto, basta cosí!' "

I have received over the years varied responses from clergy when I have spoken about this deficit in celibate training. A priest in a position of authority defended the current system in a letter: "I can attest that such training takes place in many ways and in many contexts. It is simply not true that 'very little attention is paid to direct training for celibacy.' I would be troubled indeed if I thought that the whole matter were thought to be taken care of in 'a single semester course.' Celibacy is a whole way of life and is a fundamental component in priestly spirituality. It is not something which is learned in an exclusively academic setting."

However, another priest in a position of equal authority said, "Most seminaries have a workshop or lectures on the subject of celibacy. But it is true that they do not have full semester courses on the subject. Given its importance in the life of the priest and religious, one might expect a more extended treatment."

The majority of priests in our study felt that their education for celibacy and about sexuality was inadequate. When asked how their questions about sexual concerns were handled in the seminary, they said the most frequent replies were: "Pray about it"; "Don't think about it"; "Play sports"; "Just accept it, it's human nature."

The focus here is not on a "course" for the training of celibacy but rather on the need for an open and adequate arena wherein the full and honest discovery of the structure and practice of celibacy can be debated and considered. The ideal and the law of celibacy need critical and practical examination before mastery can be expected. We require no less of any other area of vital intellectual and practical interest.

Dr. Leo Bartemeier had a lifelong dream of speaking to the American bishops on the training of priests. He felt that training could be done much more effectively if emotional and sexual concerns were addressed in a direct way. He reiterated frequently his evaluation: "We take promising young men from thirteen to twenty years of age, feed them well, educate them diligently, and eight to twelve years later we ordain them, healthy, bright, emotional thirteen-year-olds" (Sipe, 1980, p. 43). The acceptance of older candidates for the priesthood will not necessarily alter that reality.

Those who claim that celibacy is adequately taught through the whole system of regulated hours, spiritual direction, confession, and so on are in the minority. Many priests will tell you that they do not feel well served by that system. It is rare that any young priest ever hears the direct witness of an older celibate such as, "I know what celibacy is; this is the process I have experienced, and this is how I have achieved it." Without living role models with whom to identify explicitly in the area of handling one's sexual drive, the priest is left to the secret arena and isolation of his own fantasy, where fear and guilt proliferate and sap his psychic energy.

What I. F. Stone said in a radio interview regarding the Iran-contra affair can be applied to celibate practice: "You cannot have secrecy and accountability at the same time." There is no other single element so destructive to sexual responsibility among clergy as the system of secrecy that has both shielded behavior and reinforced denial.

More and more during the 1970s, celibacy was touched upon in the context of moral theology. One- to three-day seminars were and are used, sometimes including outside consultants invited to address the issues. These seminars are well intentioned but insufficient to deal with the understanding and mastery required by the celibate goal. It is not at all obvious that canon law is really observed in regard to training for celibacy in any major seminary of the United States, where not so much as a semester course is offered in how to be celibate. Canon 247 states, "The students are to be prepared through suitable education to observe the state of celibacy, and they are also to learn to honor it as a special gift of God. . . . They are to be duly informed of the duties and burdens of sacred ministers of the Church; no difficulty of the priestly life is to be kept back from them."

One study of Catholic clergy reported that 68 percent agreed "that the traditional way of presenting the vow of chastity during their religious training often allowed for the development of impersonalism and false spirituality" (Greeley, 1972, p. 363).

A 1983 guide prepared by the Bishops' Committee on Priestly Life and Ministry of the National Conference of Catholic Bishops acknowledged the sexuality of human beings as intrinsic. The fact that the conference would even direct its attention to the importance of sexuality is a step forward. It said:

> To be a human person is to grow, develop and mature throughout the life span from cradle to grave. To be a human person is to be a sexual person—the marvelous mystery of human sexuality permeates every moment of human existence. . . . The human person is so profoundly affected by sexuality that it must be considered as one of

the factors which give to each individual's life the principal traits that distinguish it. (National Conference of Catholic Bishops, 1983, p. 7)

Two years earlier, the conference decreed but did not implement the following guidelines for the training of seminarians for celibacy:

This education should deal specifically with such topics as the nature of sexuality, growth toward sexual maturity, marital and celibate chastity, the single state, premarital and extramarital sexual relationships, and homosexuality. . . . It is clear that confidence in being able to live out the response of celibacy is based on God alone. Seminarians, with a sensitive appreciation of women and their natural attraction to them, will base their determination to lead a celibate life on their special love for Christ. (National Conference of Catholic Bishops, 1982, pp. 24–25)

ABSTINENCE

In *Sexual Dimensions of the Celibate Life* (1979), William Kraft says, "Celibacy, however, does not simply denote an unmarried status. In a more positive sense, celibacy (which etymologically means to be alone) can also be a distinct and meaningful life form" (p. 9).

The current system of training for celibacy is deficient. First and most importantly, celibacy is not simply sexual abstinence, any more than honesty is simply not stealing. A few years ago I was amused when I heard a rock star on a late night talk show expounding on the "new celibacy." He said that for the first time since he was a teenager he had been abstinent for a whole month. He waxed eloquent on the sense of freedom and relaxation he was experiencing.

Priests striving for celibacy, even if they lack a complete comprehension of the nature of the ideal, know instinctively that sexual abstinence alone is not celibacy. One middle-aged priest voiced the concern of many when he said, "I don't want to be celibate by default—just too tired and bored to have sex."

There are many people who are sexually abstinent for shorter or longer periods of time—for some healthy and loving reasons, others through neurotic fear or even psychotic disarray—but who would never view celibacy as desirable, much less as an ideal.

LAW AND IDEAL

There are two similarities between the law and the ideal of celibacy. The first is that each remains operative regardless of whether celibacy is practiced or not; and the second is that one must work to make them operative or applicable to one's own existence.

The few brief canons that deal with clerical celibacy and those concerning clerical spirituality are probably sufficient to sustain a celibate lifestyle for those who observe them with full understanding and commitment. I will address these issues more completely in the chapter on the achievement of celibacy.

It is enough to point out here that canon law decrees that priests are to be celibate. We saw in the preceding chapter that this has not always been the case, but for every priest in our study the law—specifically, canon 277—was binding:

> Clerics are obliged to observe perfect and perpetual continence for the sake of the kingdom of heaven and therefore are obliged to observe celibacy, which is a special gift of God, by which sacred ministers can adhere more easily to Christ with an undivided heart and can more freely dedicate themselves to the service of God and humankind. . . . Clerics are to conduct themselves with due prudence in associating with persons whose company could endanger their obligation to observe continence or could cause scandal for the faithful.

The question that is debated more and more in clerical circles is whether one can legislate a charism. The obvious response from an authoritarian point of view is that the charism must be presumed to be present prior to ordination, as demonstrated in canon 1037: "An unmarried candidate for the permanent diaconate and a candidate for the presbyterate is not to be admitted to the order of diaconate unless in a prescribed rite he has assumed publicly before God and the Church the obligation of celibacy or professed perpetual vows in a religious institute."

There are a number of ordained men who claim a vocation to the priesthood and yet who feel they neither possess the charism of celibacy nor are inclined to practice it. Those who resign the exercise of the priesthood are actually more easily dealt with administratively than those who abandon celibacy but retain clerical practice, as I will show in the following chapters. Suffice it to say that *the law* is clear: it requires perfect and perpetual abstinence in order to serve like Christ.

CHRIST THE IDEAL

The ideal, of course, is Christ. The priest is to serve others as Christ did. It is the personal relationship and identification that in the end give meaning and possibility to the total striving. Priests are the first to admit the impossibility of celibacy without a personal relationship with Christ. (Those who are not acquainted with this mode of spiritual thinking should focus on the essential psychological element—the capacity for and achievement of a personal relationship.)

We all know that distance and time do not destroy a mature relationship in spite of the great difficulty its maintenance demands. St. Paul, even though he never met Christ, knew him well. St. John the evangelist, who was a friend of Christ, remained vibrantly alive to that relationship years beyond the physical separation of the two men. "What we have seen and heard we announce to you also, so that you will join with us in the fellowship that we have with the Father and with his Son Jesus Christ. We write this in order that our joy may be complete" (I John 1:3–4).

As the history of the apostles and popes demonstrates, celibacy is not necessary for the maintenance of a meaningful relationship and identification with Christ. However, celibacy is not possible without the capacity for involvement with some reality beyond the self, and the involvement must be practically effective in the service of one's fellow humans. These elements were essential to Gandhi's celibacy in a different religious tradition.

St. John Chrysostom points to the priesthood as the greatest evidence of love for Christ and uses the triple questioning of Peter by Christ as an example: "If you love me, shepherd my sheep" (Jurgens, 1955, pp. 15–16). In the same treatise on the priesthood, Chrysostom explores the loftiness of the ideal and its demand for identification with Christ: "The soul of a priest ought to be purer than the very rays of the sun, so that the Holy Spirit will not abandon him, and so that he may be able to say 'It is no longer I that live, but Christ that liveth in me' " (Jurgens, 1955, p. 92). The ideal of the priesthood thus articulated in the fourth century is at the heart of the decision of many men to be priests—their sense that they wish to be *like* Christ. Naturally, this intention does not occur in pure culture. Their sense is mixed with whole spectra of emotions and ambitions, both holy and gross, that need to be refined by the process of seeking the ideal.

LOVE

In the early 1970s, Yves Raguin (1974) talked about the nature of celibate love: "So love is to say yes to another, to say yes not merely with the lips or even with the heart, but with one's whole being. The yes is uttered before the total giving, and yet it is the yes which guarantees the certainty of love" (p. 11). The images ring true, but the day-to-day directives are completely vague. What the ideal means as applied in a particular person-

ality and how it is achieved in the face of conflicting demands are nowhere spelled out.

The goal of Christian celibacy is, of course, the enhancement of love.
Irving Singer's philosophical exploration (1984) into the nature of love
demonstrates how easily one speaks about it but how complex the reality
of love is. He is correct when he says: "What in primitive religions had
served to idealize the natural functions of man now became a means of
transcending nature. Love turned into a *super*natural device, and in Christianity it became the very essence of God. In the ancient and the medieval
world philosophical idealizations were primarily transcendental" (p. 42).
The celibate, removed from sexual activity and involvement, is forced to
grapple with that transcendental nature of love, and it is that struggle that
has proven so pregnant for Western civilization and culture precisely because the transcendent reality of love has to be translated or activated into
projects or services that transform the man, making him a "man for others"—a man of service to humanity.

DEFINITION OF CELIBACY

These realities, then, are at the roots of any viable definition of celibacy.
In the course of my study, I have come to a definition of celibacy that
includes six essential interrelated elements:

> *Celibacy is a freely chosen dynamic state, usually vowed, that involves
> an honest and sustained attempt to live without direct sexual gratifi-
> cation in order to serve others productively for a spiritual motive.*

In order to apply the legalistic and idealized roots to my definition, I
will comment on each of the six elements.

1. A Freely Chosen Dynamic State

To be free in matters that are related to sexuality is in itself not easy.
There were many priests in our study who said after years in the priesthood that they had had no real idea of what celibacy was all about when
they were ordained. They had been happy as seminarians and had somehow assumed that the supportive environment would follow them into
their pastoral settings. The fact that one is not initially free or not fully
informed does not vitiate one's pursuit of celibacy. Freedom is itself a process. Gandhi (1960) records the struggle in a way to which other celibates
can relate when he says:

> The spirit in me pulls one way, the flesh in me pulls in the oppo-
> site direction. There is freedom from the action of these two forces,

but that freedom is attainable only by slow and painful stages. I cannot attain freedom by a mechanical refusal to act, but only by intelligent action in a detached manner. This struggle resolves itself into an incessant crucifixion of the flesh so that the spirit may become entirely free. (p. 71)

This kind of struggle is necessary to enter a "state," i.e., a lifelong situation that is free of sexual involvement. This process entails knowledge of one's embodiment, an acknowledgment that humans are sexed and sexual beings, and it demands sexual realism and self-determination—all areas that have been neglected in seminary training and which probably cannot be elucidated adequately by celibates alone. Marriage as well as celibacy are meant to lead Christians to the "freedom of the children of God," and probably nowhere else is there as acute a need for cooperation between marrieds and celibates as in the sexual training of those who are contemplating a celibate dedication.

The celibate should be free from sexual dependency—that is, his sexual orientation or internal adjustment should not interfere with his physical or mental health, his interpersonal relationships, or his effective and efficient functioning. This does not mean that he must be virginal; but one who has been subject to any compulsive sexual behavior such as pedophilia, committed homosexuality, or heterosexual activity without regard for the reality of relationships will have a hard time choosing the state of celibacy convincingly. Celibacy is not a running away from sex. It knowingly embraces reality with the subjective conviction that one existentially is not able to do otherwise. In short, it is the sense of vocation.

2. Usually Vowed

Although there may be exceptional instances where celibacy is pursued without a conscious or public declaration, I do not know of any. For Catholic priests, the vow precedes ordination as a requirement, and the Church places such emphasis on the vow that it remains even if one loses the clerical state. According to canon 291: "Loss of the clerical state does not entail a dispensation from the obligation of celibacy, which is granted by the Roman Pontiff alone" (*Code of Canon Law*, 1984, p. 103).

There is something about the public nature of the commitment and the declaration of one's intent that is necessary for the efficaciousness of the endeavor. Celibacy is not meant to be a harbor for the fearful or a refuge for the sexually incompetent, but a witness by those dedicated and concerned for humanity. A powerful impact is made, even on nonbelievers, when a believer is so convinced of his cause and so dedicated to his beliefs that he is willing to give up all sexual pleasures in their behalf. It is the kind of admiration one has for those who give up their lives for the country they believe in or for the person they love. The connection between martyrdom and celibacy is not accidental. There has to be an element of the heroic striving in both, and there has to be a relatedness to the community. It declares the most private—sex—as a most public promise. Groeschel (1985) describes an example of this:

> A few years ago a young religious sister shared the following experience. She was enrolled at a state university in a course entitled "Human Sexuality." She attended the class anonymously and was unrecognized as a sister. For reasons unknown (and probably unknowable), the students were required to share with the class the wildest sexual encounter they had experienced. Sister resolved to stand her ground and admit the awful truth—she had never had a sexual encounter.
>
> As this exhibitionists' round-robin made its way to her, she disclosed her dreadful secret. The students thought they had been prepared for everything, but not for this! Chastity was just too far out. Between their gasps of incomprehension and guffaws of unbelief, she managed to explain that she was a religious sister. The response of the group completely reversed. Her classmates were delighted, awestruck and deeply moved. They all agreed that she should stay right where she was and not have an encounter. Even the most jaded were impressed to know that someone, somewhere, had managed to preserve her humanity and yet be chaste for the Kingdom of God. (p. 11)

3. An Honest and Sustained Attempt

The fulfillment of the vow of celibacy is not accomplished by the public declaration. The constant daily living and implementation of leading a sexless life demand a quality of control and inner freedom which is devoid of self-deception and rationalization. In short, it takes a kind of integrity that has balance, self-knowledge, consistency, and commitment.

A key factor is the equilibrium of needs and demands. Many priests throw themselves into their work without regard for their other personal needs. All of their sexual energy is thus translated into their work effort. Breakdown and oftentimes rebound are inevitable. This unbalanced approach is matched at the other extreme by priests who feel that because they are deprived of sexual gratification they have a right to every other comfort. Celibacy requires that a person find a parity among internal versus external demands, individual versus communal forces, and immediate versus ultimate needs—not an easy task for anyone. However, if one is to renounce sexual gratification as a means of tension reduction, then the building of relationships and the transmission of spiritual life challenge that person to a level of creative living not commonly experienced.

Self-knowledge is absolutely indispensable for the celibate pursuer. Denial is the great betrayer of celibacy.

> Accepting and living with the reality that God made us bodily creatures does not mean that we must voluntarily indulge in sexual pleasure. It does mean recognizing that our sexuality will often be felt and experienced in many ways. Because sexual expression in its highest form is linked with tender emotions and the need for intimacy, the person seeking to be a chaste celibate must not suppress tenderness and emotion while seeking to avoid pregenital or genital behavior. As in most areas of human accomplishment, advance is along a knife-edge, avoiding on the one hand an unrealistic puritanism and on the other an indulgence of inappropriate behavior which is disguised as virtue. I have come to suspect both the angelic battle of the 1940s and the "third way" of the 1970s as being denials of sexual reality. (Groeschel, pp. 35–36)

The celibate must face honestly his physical and spiritual assets and liabilities. A deep search of one's personal history and a social awareness alone can keep the daily struggle in perspective. There is an intensely private and personal side to the sustained attempt to be celibate. Transgressions can be incorporated into the *attempt* to be celibate, but a sexual incident that can very quickly turn into a pattern obliterates celibacy as a reality. The priest, for instance, who regularly, even though infrequently, seeks out a sexual liaison is not a practicing celibate. There are scores of examples of priests who have had to abandon celibacy for a time in order to find out what it is and later practice it, but that abandonment must be honestly acknowledged lest the public image become a cover for hypocrisy. The masturbations pose a specific and special problem for the celibate. Although masturbatory activity is technically and legally forbidden in celibate practice, our study shows that it is not an uncommon activity even among those who in every other regard observe celibacy and strive honestly to attain it.

Each celibate develops adaptive patterns that are consistent with his characterological formation. Some personality structures are more readily compatible with the discipline required of a celibate. The required constancy will be assailed by the impulsive character or the narcissistic. Some people have to work harder for constancy than others.

Commitment to others as well as to oneself is measured by the allegiances and loyalties one has and above all by the quality of one's existing relationships and the capacity one has to develop new ones. Sustained celibate living is really not possible in a schizoid vacuum. Without the commitment to others, celibacy breaks down, if not in technique, at least in its goal.

4. To Live without Direct Sexual Gratification

The core of celibacy involves necessary sublimation. The sexual instinct of the celibate is defused and directed to the service of other pursuits. Not a few priests have said that celibacy means that they will not *marry*. They hold that *chastity*—that is, the virtue of purity—is reserved for those who, like nuns, take a specific vow of chastity. As celibates, therefore, they feel they can engage in sexual activity without breaking their vow or violating their state, in spite of the fact that they may sin. This is simple rationalization and has no merit.

At first glance celibacy seems an impossible and even outlandish course of life; for most people direct sexual pleasure is a necessary component of their personal growth and development and can be a means of loving and serving. Upon reflection, however, one realizes how many of the joys of life and truly meaningful interactions do not involve direct sexual gratification: the love between parents and children, brothers and sisters, and friends, as well as work and career accomplishments. In addition, there are those few persons who are so in touch with the transcendent that they achieve profound relatedness and universal love of other humans almost constitutionally.

5. In Order to Serve Others Productively

Sexual denial that is without a social or community goal is meaningless and probably not possible. I have said already that celibacy is not merely abstinence. By its essence it has to be *on account of something,* and that something has to be perceived as valuable and worth the sacrifice. Canon law again speaks to nuns and religious brothers and to priests when it says: "The evangelical counsel of chastity assumed for the sake of the kingdom of heaven, as a sign of the future world and a source of more abundant fruitfulness in an undivided heart, entails the obligation of perfect continence in celibacy" (*Code of Canon Law,* 1984, p. 227).

Celibacy reaches beyond oneself. It aims first at the familial model of early Christianity, where all men and women are brothers and sisters, genuinely loving, and serving because Christ is present in each. Genital behavior is excluded not because it is evil—that was a later development consolidated by St. Augustine (cf. Pagels, 1988)—but because of the relative superiority of building up the kingdom of God—that what Christ taught could become a reality so "that all may be one" (John 17:23). Celibacy is meant to be an eschatological witness to these values.

It is also meant to be a witness to the ability of grace to overcome nature and to the fact that courage can surmount biological imperatives, that hope is stronger than death, and that one can give even one's life (and energies) for others. Although not all priests today agree that celibacy frees them for unencumbered service of others (cf. Hoge, 1987), there is an essential link between being free *from* sexual demands and being free *for* service. By embracing celibacy, one eschews relationship bonds that impose an exclusive mutuality. There is a commitment to universality of accessibility inherent in celibacy as well as a valuation of all humanity independent of external merit or presentation. Rich and poor, healthy and sick, saints and sinners all have equal claim to the celibate. Transcendental love translated into universal relatedness: this is the core of celibacy's freedom for service.

There is also a singleness of purpose demanded by celibacy, a single-heartedness of one who has discovered the pearl of great price and is willing to sell all for it. Again, that kind of dedication has its parallel in the service of other goods—the athlete, the actor, the scholar. Persons of excellence in every field sacrifice deeply and focus all their available energy and efforts to the achievement of their goal. That dedication, sometimes bringing fame and fortune, is extolled and understood even if it cannot always be emulated.

The depth of the aloneness that must be embraced to support celibacy cannot be minimized. As Father Keith Clark (1982) says, "Celibate people have a special relationship to loneliness because they make a commitment to enter life's moments of loneliness more completely and more vulnerably than is possible for the married" (p. 55). There is no way that celibacy can be practiced and achieved other than by penetrating the aloneness, not merely sustaining it, for it taps the wellsprings of spirituality and leads to the sixth essential element of my definition.

6. For a Spiritual Motive

There should be no question about this: Celibacy is not proposed as a natural phenomenon. Several priests recalled that they were told in school that every boy is called to the priesthood but only a few respond. The priesthood may be an option for every Christian; celibacy is not. Celibacy is a highly specialized gift that presumes an awareness of existence and reality beyond the ordinary as well as a charism—that is, a special gift of grace and of spiritual witness. The priest will want to know, eventually, if his sexual struggle is with the development of his genuine charism, or if it is a conflict arising from a discipline he accepted as part of his ministerial role without the benefit of the special gift.

Priests believe in grace. A charism is a grace and not a product of nature, although it is usually supported by a special combination of genetic endowment, environmental luck, and deep subjective awareness that one "cannot do other." Surprisingly, there is not a great deal of direct literary witness to the experience. We have the scriptural witness of Christ's life of love. St. Paul, who was most likely over 40 years old and widowed at the time of his conversion, is most explicit in his decision to remain celibate rather than to remarry. I have always liked this explicit description of Gandhi's discovery of his celibate vocation:

> It was in South Africa that Gandhi learned to translate . . . tremendous ideals into effective action. . . . Night and day, carrying . . . stretchers across the vast deserted hill country of Natal, he plunged himself deep into prayer and self-examination in a fervent search for greater strength with which to serve.
> The intensity of his desire led him to the source of power itself. Deep in meditation Gandhi began to see how much of his vital energy was locked up in the sexual drive. In a flood of insight he realized that sex is not just a physical instinct, but an expression of the tremendous spiritual force behind all love and creativity which the Hindu scriptures call kundalini, the life-force of evolution. All his life it had been his master, buffeting him this way and that beyond his control. But in the silence of the Natal hills, with all his burning desire to serve focused by weeks of tending to the wounded and dying, Gandhi found the strength to tap this power at its source. Then and there he resolved to be its master, and never let it dictate to him again. It was a decision which resolved his deepest tensions, and released all the love within him into his conscious control. He had begun to transform the last of his passions into spiritual power. (Easwaran, 1972, pp. 37–38)

There is currently a sharp debate in theological circles about the legal requirement of celibacy for the priesthood. There are many priests who firmly believe they are called to the ministry of the priesthood and at the same time called to the married state.

I remember the psychoanalyst Dr. Gregory Zilboorg commenting in 1955 on a consultation he had conducted with a Jesuit scholastic he felt to be obviously schizophrenic. His conclusive proof was that the man wanted to be both a priest and married. Zilboorg's diagnosis might have been correct, but his criterion would be very unreliable in our consultation office today. I have always wondered, incidentally, whether that patient was truly psychotic or merely ahead of his time!

This distinction between celibacy as a discipline and as a charism has always existed. The reality that has brought it into painful practical focus for many priests now is the shift in support systems that used to surround clerical life. Privilege, prestige, educational advantage, social, political and spiritual power, exclusivity, and secrecy all conspired to form a protective barrier and source of sublimation for the priest dealing with his sexual drives. Within such a system it was not so essential to deal with the distinction between charism and discipline. The celibate charism will always remain, as it has in the Buddhist tradition; however, the discipline primarily—and even secondarily the charism—is greatly strained without significant external supports.

Seminary education has been gravely remiss—certainly from the psychological perspective—by not examining actively enough the distinction between charism and discipline. The Church also does itself a grave disservice as well as personal injustice by requiring the practice of celibacy without actually supporting it (cf. Sipe, 1988, pp. 45–47). Only a spiritual (i.e., transcendent) motivation can sustain celibate striving. Gandhi makes this clear in his pursuit. Only a love that can match or exceed what is possible with sexual love can sustain celibacy.

This briefly is the legal and ideal framework that situates celibacy. It is an ideal that defies easy understanding or easy practice. As with all ideals, some merely profess, some strive, and a few achieve. This chapter should give the reader sufficient theoretical background to proceed to the second question of our study. How, really, is celibacy practiced and not practiced by those who profess it?

Part II
THE PRACTICE VERSUS THE PROFESSION _____

Chapter 5

PATTERNS OF HETEROSEXUALITY ___

"Si non caste, tamen caute" ("*If not chastely, at least carefully*")
—*Albert, Archbishop of Hamburg, 1040*

THE HETEROSEXUAL PRESUMPTIONS

There are two presumptions about Roman Catholic priests: that a majority of men who pursue a life of celibacy are heterosexual in orientation; and that heterosexual impulses, distractions, or "temptations," if you will, pose the greatest threat to the practice of celibacy. Both assumptions are justified by our study, repeatedly and consistently. All groups sampled demonstrated at least a 2 to 1 ratio of heterosexual to homosexual behaviors (with the exception of estimates of two small groups noted in the chapter on the homosexualities).

The landmark studies on the Catholic priests in the United States—especially the *Sociological Investigations* chaired by Father Andrew Greeley (1972), and the *Psychological Investigations* under Father Eugene Kennedy (1972)—were quick to point out that "the priests in the United States are ordinary men" faced with extraordinary ideals and demands. Generally, the tendencies in studies on the priesthood reflect an attempt to be fair and are not eager to label people as sick, or deviant, or different. They also seek to find the solid humanness that sustains us all.

What has happened, however, in the subsequent research on the clergy has not matured on the solid and provocative foundation laid down by these early studies. Greeley's early work especially ferreted out opinions about celibacy and attitudes toward sexual morality (although not behavior). But today, in the popular press, Greeley (1983b) minimizes the differences between the married state and celibacy when he says:

> It is no more impossible, if we are happy in our work, than fidelity is for a normally heterosexual married man (or woman, for that

69

matter) who is reasonably satisfied in his (or her) marriage. Which is to say that there are times when it is only mildly difficult and other times when it is extremely difficult indeed. (p. 6)

Greeley also feels that there is every reason to believe that priests in the United States keep their celibacy; "While celibacy is not necessarily honored all the time, perhaps, it is nonetheless the normal behavior of most American priests," he says, (1983b). It is that *not necessarily all the time* that needs to be respected, understood, and researched.

Several myths about celibacy need to be dispelled. First, it simply is not true that marital infidelity and celibate infidelity are identical. Put positively, celibate fidelity and married fidelity are *not* similar or parallel, at least sexually. There is a vast gap on the one hand between "no sexual activity" (even on account of the kingdom) and sexual activity with another person, as the celibate may experience these states, and on the other hand, sexual activity with one partner (married fidelity) or with several different partners. Both infidelities may involve a betrayal of trust or promise; but the experience of celibacy and of marriage, genuinely embraced, are psychic horses of very different colors.

To be precise, they are not even both horses! Celibacy and active sexual involvement operate on two separate circuits of tension reduction. To blur this fact minimizes the significance of the reality and perniciously undermines the achievement of both. Celibates do not help themselves or each other when they deny the reality of this difference. The average healthy and stable avowed celibate will have to use inordinate amounts of unconscious mental defenses to move from the celibate mode to an active sexual mode: denial, rationalization, reaction formation, and splitting are the most common. A married person, even to be unfaithful, does not have to go through a shift in psychic mode. Direct sexual activity—already chosen—is free from the need to defend it excessively. The married man may have conflicts over his choice of partner; he may have guilt; but he does not move from one psychic mode to another.

Celibacy cannot be kept in place without sublimation. If sexual activity is chosen by the celibate, some other mental mechanism must be employed to keep him psychically in place while he compromises the incompatibles—direct sexual activity and no sexual activity. Without such a mechanism, celibacy is a sham and a pretense, and does not really involve the attempt to channel sexual energy into nonsexual outlets. Periodic sexual abstinence is not celibacy.

Second, it is not usual or ordinary to be celibate. One is *different* if one chooses to live one's life—even for the highest of motives—without direct sexual gratification. St. Paul and all of spiritual tradition agree that the celibate is a man set apart, with a special grace of spiritual charism. To argue that celibates are ordinary men is simply to avoid the questions of *what is different* about the person who chooses to live without sex, and what nature the grace of celibacy transforms.

Research published in 1984 under the auspices of the National Conference of Catholic Bishops points to traits that are stronger among seminarians studying for the priesthood than among the general population:

1. Dependency—a tendency to depend on others rather than on oneself.
2. Low sexual interest in the complementary sex.
3. Heightened aesthetic interest as opposed to athletic or mechanical pursuits.
4. Mother dominance, or a prevalence of a dominant unconscious mother image (an idealized view of women). (Hoge, Potvin, & Ferry, 1984, pp. 23–23)

Whether these tendencies are generally connected with the role of minister, regardless of which religion, is debated; noncelibate seminarians tend to show the same characteristics on testing—characteristics normally associated with the complementary sex. Greenwald says this profile remained constant in 1954 and 1968 (Hoge, Potvin, & Ferry, 1984).

The question that seems to frighten everyone is whether or not these characteristics invalidate the heterosexual presumption of the ministry. In other words, is this finding a reflection of a larger homosexual component among the celibate clergy than in the general population? The answer is yes. (See Chapter 6 on the homosexualities.) The estimate is about double that of the general population. But these psychological dispositions, interests, and attitudes have to be reconciled with celibacy. It is one thing to be open to marriage; quite another—regardless of one's testing profile—to put oneself in a structure and organization that allow no place for women or for direct sexual gratification.

Father Greeley makes it all sound so simple when he tells large audiences:

> Is celibacy difficult? For some priests. I don't think so. Like some married men, some celibate priests don't find women all that attractive sexually. They can do without them rather easily. Others are so caught up in the game of ecclesiastical power that they transfer the urge for pleasure to that all-consuming game. There have always been a few priests whose sexual orientation is in the other direction, and most of those also keep their vows. (Greeley, 1983b)

The attitudes toward women, power, and the homosexualities are not, I have found, that easily dismissed by priests who are talking directly about their sexual-celibate lives and struggles.

The third myth is that the hierarchical structure and clerical organization by which the celibate is absorbed and to which he is committed are heterosexually dominant—where, therefore, both sexes are regarded equally. This simply is not so—neither at the highest echelons of the Vatican nor at the smallest diocesan and parish levels. The idealization of the mother image—that reaches its psychological perfection in devotion to the Blessed Virgin Mary—is often purchased at the price of devaluing all other women. Aesthetic drives do not need the presence of women for their fulfillment. Michelangelo and Palestrina, for example, filled the Vatican with enduring beauty without the inspiration, companionship, or participation of women.

Lack of interest in the complementary sex can translate institutionally into disregard for and even hostility toward women. Seminaries, especially since the Council of Trent, were bastions against the intrusion of women. At one time there were strict penalties if a woman by her presence defiled a male cloister—it had to be reconsecrated! Protection-against fosters negative defenses. Woman becomes the evil one and the source of sin and temptation.

In houses of learning, this attitude then is justified by theological speculation. Woman is eliminated as a social equal, and a homosocial support system is established. Women enter only to be served pastorally, or to play a subservient role as cook, housekeeper, or secretary. A priest's chance for advancing politically is dependent upon his committing himself to a structure not only socially insulated from women, but positively and universally exclusive of one sex. Hierarchically, there is no place for any women.

Those who say the military ranks and the halls of government share in this pattern are correct. However, the possibilities for sexual alliance and influence in some spheres of operation make the military and political arenas vastly different from the Church.

Organizational and structural dependency for the clergy is on Mother Church, and for many this bond is an affiliation of glorious loyalty as well as an umbilical cord of monumental proportion. Forged from a close alliance with (or in some cases against) mother, often reinforced by deep devotion to the Blessed Virgin Mary, Mother Church is an idealized source of strength and nourishment, spiritually and economically. Unadorned, that ideal, of course, strips each woman of any adult sexual identification. They are all mothers—sexually unavailable in fantasy. Women celibates can be the brides of Christ and they can find and serve Christ in their ministries. Therefore, a heterosexual ideational structure is available to them within the context of their celibacy. Male celibates are in a more difficult stance heterosexually.

In practice, the brokers of all the power are male: God-father; Jesus-son; Spiritus-male spirit of love; Pope and Bishop. This is not very different from the Roman *Pater Familias,* who held power over the life and death of his household, free and slave alike (Veyne, 1987). The desire to participate in this male strength and dominance has preserved the presumption of the heterosexuality of the celibate priesthood.

My point is that the traditional definitions of heterosexual—especially as polarized against homosexual—are inadequate when we enter into a deeper exploration of what celibacy is and how it is protected.

In their study of 271 Catholic priests, Kennedy and Heckler (1972) provide some clues to the level of psychosexual development of each of them, even though this research did not specifically focus on the celibate-sexual behaviors of the respondents. Celibacy was approached as "hardly separable from the context of the priest's overall understanding of himself, his faith commitment, and his attitude toward his vocation" (p. 32). Inherent in that statement are precisely the elements we pointed out above: the homosocial organization of at least the seminary training program, the homosexual power structure of the Church, and the identification with Christ. What is important to remember is that a priest's sexual behavior is out of this context, and that it is not necessarily victimless. The maintenance of the system socially and hierarchically is often at the expense of women or the sacrifice of self-maturity.

THE ELEMENTS OF SPLITTING AND SECRECY

Two similarities running through the patterns of priests' sexual relationships are the elements of splitting and secrecy. The sexual behavior is psychically separated from the priest's professional life, and this splitting allows him to carry on his daily work with a degree of efficiency and comfort. The relationship is usually kept secret from every other person. Often it is shielded from the scrutiny of a best friend or even a confessor; when it is shared, there still can remain something public and something secret. The secrecy element protects the splitting, reinforcing the denial of the conflict in a double mode of operation—celibate on duty, noncelibate off.

Rationalization can also flourish under the cover of secrecy: "Sex is good"; "I am now a better priest"; "No one is being harmed"; "It helps me understand and love others better."

Three priests who had a close social association over a period of 20 years—seeing each other for recreation at least once a week and sharing annual vacations and family gatherings—felt they knew everything about each other. Two of them were then genuinely shocked when they read in the newspaper that the third was being sued—named in a paternity suit filed by an irate husband.

When the sexual activity is more socially unacceptable, involving pedophilia, child pornography, or the homosexualities, there may be an added incentive to preserve secrecy. The lack of guilt—the depth of the splitting—and the power of the denial and rationalization are reinforced by the official structure of support for the priest. "The avoidance of scandal" is the primary goal when the sexual activity of a priest comes to the attention of authority, and standard solutions usually involve sending the priest away—on retreat, to another district, or even to a mental hospital.

HETEROSEXUAL RELATIONSHIPS

About 20 percent of priests vowed to celibacy (estimate from all sources) are at any one time involved either in a more or less stable sexual relationship with a woman or, alternatively, with sequential women in an identifiable pattern of behavior. An additional 8 to 10 percent of priests are at a stage of heterosexual exploration that often involves incidental sexual contacts. The latter is like dating and predating behavior, where no relationship exists, nor any particular pattern of sexual involvement. This behavior can be the limit of the priest's experimentation, or can evolve into a pattern of sexual activity or a relationship. The reverse is also recorded: A failed relationship can result in the priest's avoiding a subsequent relationship, but not necessarily sexual activity.

It would be incorrect to think that priests who have long-term relationships with women are unsuccessful as priests. The following is an accurate description of a priest who had a 40-year mutually satisfying love relationship with one woman.

Father was a lover of life, a vital and enthusiastic man, an excellent and fascinating speaker, an intellectual, a teacher and writer, an athlete, a motivator, a generous friend.

He was a very committed priest. He was opinionated and strongwilled; he never said "no" when people needed him. People always wanted to be around Father. He also served as a chaplain in World War II and as a Judge on the Matrimonial Court, and was active in many other religious and educational functions.

He loved golf and magic tricks and electronic toys, and had a very special place in his heart for children.

No one can capture the essence of this wonderful human being in such a short space, but perhaps this might give you some flavor of his dynamic personality.

He was very proud of his 50 years as a priest—50 years of service to God and his Church.

He had many wonderful women friends and a very clear picture of the value of women as mothers and religious persons. But I question whether his training and/or the vision of the Church gave him a full and mature view of all that women can be and have to offer the Church. I feel that his lack of full appreciation of the appropriate role of women was a part of what made him sexually vulnerable.

Housekeepers

This group of hardworking and dedicated women has been maligned and often unjustly accused of being the sexual partners of the priests they serve. Most are not—which, of course, does not mean that the practice is unknown. The problem of the living arrangements for priests and bishops is an old one. Legislation by the early Church councils regulated the clerical household and in some instances limited the women living there to close relatives. Obviously, there had been abuses, especially with the growing custom of dedicated virgin women serving in the houses (Fox, 1987, p. 369). The protection of the virgins rather than celibacy seemed to be the primary concern of these early legislators.

Writing in 397, St. John Chrysostom addressed the problem of men and women ascetics living under one roof:

Adversus eos qui apud se habent virgines subintroductas, . . . is addressed to the clerics and condemns the custom followed by some priests of having consecrated virgins in their homes to keep house for them, pretending to live with them as sisters in devotion. (Quasten, 1960, p. 464)

The concern of Church authorities to protect the virtue of women was not always evident in the reports of our study. On the contrary, we have dozens of informants who were told by a bishop or pastor that if they had a problem with celibacy, they should take a woman as a housekeeper, or as a mistress. Any arrangement that was private and did not give scandal was seen as a preferable alternative to resignation from the priesthood. Time after time, superiors ignored the deeper personal relationship of the sexual involvement, and the emotional implications of the priest's behavior. "Make a retreat!" is common advice; "Look at all you stand to lose"; or even "What would your mother think?" are misguided attempts to help where real understanding of the struggle fails.

A 37-year-old priest informant had spent the first 10 years of his priesthood on the staff of a diocesan high school. He was popular and successful, and had received several indications from his bishop that there were greater things in store for him in the future. The bishop, subsequently infuriated when this man signed a statement of disagreement with the papal encyclical *Humanae Vitae,* transferred the priest from his high school post to a small parish of 30 families. The priest said he thought he "would go crazy" there. Accustomed to the high-pitched demands of adolescents, classes, sports activities, and the congenial community of other teachers, he could not adjust to the new unstructured and, for him, unchallenging environment. Although he was developing his celibate commitment adequately with some regular, if brief, prayer and confession, he knew he did not have the spiritual reserves to withstand the change.

In his first parish assignment, there had been a girl in one of his classes who had joined the convent. He and she had maintained an appropriate and warm but casual contact over the years. After eight years in the convent, and prior to her solemn vows, the girl, who was now a young woman of 27, decided to leave religious life. In the meantime, in the loneliness of his new position, the priest became aware that this woman friend was the only relationship he had developed over the years. There was a specialness to it that he had not previously focused on. With his growing insight and infatuation with the woman as they explored their friendship, the priest consulted his confessor before he and the woman initiated any sexual activity. He was quite surprised at the advice: "Take her as your housekeeper. If anything happens, God will understand. It's better than leaving the priesthood."

Most housekeeping arrangements that end up as sexual relationships do not start out that way by design. Loneliness, unexpected compatibility, and simply growth in appreciation from proximity seem to draw some men into a satisfying sexual liaison that is compatible with their work. Many of these relationships last into old age. Morris L. West portrayed this phenomenon with sensitivity and accuracy in his novel *Devil's Advocate* (1959). Informants in our study told stories strikingly similar in affect and development.

Married Women

For priests without sexual experience prior to their ordination, married women are the most frequent sources of their first sexual relationship. Next in frequency are alliances with younger women who themselves have had limited sexual experience.

The naturalness of a priest as a family friend is oftentimes the context in which the relationship grows. This seemingly safe arrangement is extolled in the popular press even by serious priests like Fr. Andrew Greeley, who says:

If a young married woman has a confidant relationship with a priest, her own marital satisfaction is, on the average, higher than is the satisfaction of a woman who does not have such a relationship. Moreover, the husband of the woman who has a priest-confidant is more likely to report a high level of sexual fulfillment than is a husband whose wife is not in such a relationship.

Both the husband and the wife profit from the wife's relationship with a celibate priest. (Greeley, 1983b)

Our informants confirm both the frequency and the viability of these celibate relationships, but they also report that the relationship does not always remain nonsexual. A woman's marriage is frequently the setting for a long-term love relationship with a priest, although at other times it is only a brief excursion into sexuality and part of a priest's experimentation and education.

One relationship that ended with the death of the priest and divorce for the woman may itself be extreme, but the dynamic is not. The priest was in his early forties, and was befriended by a couple and their five children. The priest was a welcome companion to the husband on the golf course on Wednesday afternoons and Saturday mornings. He related well to the children—the younger ones were fascinated by the stories he would tell, and the teenagers could argue freely with him. He was a family delight. It was one of those situations that Greeley glorifies, in which the wife becomes the priest's confidant, even as he had become hers. Everyone in this particular family felt better and functioned more efficiently because Father was a part of them. It was accidental that he and the wife became lovers, or at least neither had consciously planned it.

A series of business trips had left the already busy husband distressed and pressured. The wife, in turn, was left feeling neglected, and the priest's own work stress was weighing heavily on him. It was natural in the context of the family setting for the wife and the priest to share drinks at this time, as they had always done, and then to begin to express their feelings for each other—something that had not occurred until this point, one and a half years into their acquaintanceship.

The sexual liaison between them continued for four years after that time, upset finally when the priest suffered a fatal heart attack. He had been serving as the financial officer of his religious community, and had shared with the wife internal matters of his community—financial and otherwise. He had also purchased a home in his own name and had promised to give it to her. At the priest's death, the wife insisted that the religious community honor that promise or she would publicize all that she knew of their workings. The religious superiors acquiesced to her threats, and her husband divorced her.

Another situation involving a 12-year relationship between a priest and a married woman had a different outcome. This woman had moved into the priest's parish. She had several young children—the reason she gave for not leaving her abusive husband. She felt she was a woman of parts— "part daughter, part beaten wife, part broken mommy, and part a woman and compassionate person," as she said. She felt held together and proudest of "the part that was a lover of a special man." She suffered great pain when the priest was transferred to a new parish, quite some distance from her home. She lamented:

> *The 12 years prior to this one were beyond a doubt the best years of my life. I grew and had a reason to live. Church and priest. Or the other way around. I was wanted and needed and loved by both. I guess priest and Church all ran together; I couldn't imagine a life without either one.*
>
> *I would give almost anything to have them again. But that is impossible. I'll never have them again. Now I don't know what to look for to fill the space that they left. There is a big part of my life that doesn't exist any more. I guess a woman who suddenly becomes a widow goes through pretty much the same thing. I guess I'm a very insecure person not to be able to pick up and get on with living. I should be finished with my grief by now; it's been almost a year. I can't seem to be able to take the first step, and I'm terribly afraid. I said I just wanted to be left alone. It's lonely by yourself. You can't live just for yourself. There's nobody to do anything for. Nobody to make something for. Father has visited and stayed all night with me, but it's not at all the same. I resent that he lives in a place I'm not a part of. That he does things I'm not involved in.*

She also added that she knew Father would find a new friend in his new parish.

> *I was not the first, and I know I won't be the last. I always knew that. But I also know his needs. He can't get along without a woman. I wouldn't expect him to.*

That sentiment is relatively common among married women involved with priests. Some are quite nonpossessive. One woman told of the joy she experienced in her long relationship with a priest and ended her account with these words:

> *Well, why not find another church? Easier said than done. It all comes back to Father. See what happens when you fall in love with a*

*priest? He made me happy. He was my best friend. He gave me
things to do to keep me busy. He cooked me dinners. Told me stories. Introduced me to interesting people. Listened to me ramble on
about things. Asked my opinion. Gave me a wink when he thought
no one was looking.*

I miss him very much.

It seems surprising that few of the husbands appear to be conscious of
the sexual dimension of their wives' friendships with the priests. When
the couple is "caught," often the husband becomes angry, and the wife's
relationship with the priest ends. The priest's involvement with the whole
family is essential to this dynamic. If the whole family is included socially
while the relationship continues, everyone—including the husband—feels
better off. This balance is also possible with a divorced woman or one
who is widowed, with her extended family taking the place of the husband. However, when the family bond is ruptured by strain, competition,
by the wife or husband requesting a divorce, or if the priest's equilibrium
is shaken by vocational dissatisfaction, the pattern fails.

An example of this disruption occurred when a suspicious husband became increasingly distressed because he sensed a growing competition
between himself and his parish priest. His wife seemed to be too defensive
of the priest. The couple were in their late 20s and the priest was approaching 50. One day the husband came home from work at noon—not
at all his habit—to find the priest and his wife in bed. The priest, making
his exit as hastily as possible, said, "My son, come to my office and we
can talk about this calmly." The young man was not pacified.

Religious and Coworkers

Those who work together, share the same values, and have similar
training and goals can come to admire and understand each other more
profoundly than can those outside their shared vocations. From these satisfying working relationships between priests and religious women there
will occasionally develop a special closeness overreaching the bounds
of celibacy.

Contrary to some popular opinion, most nuns do not have sexual relationships with priests. One reason it does not occur more frequently is
that the aura of secrecy is difficult to maintain within a community that
is interdependent. Over the 25-year period of our study, however, many
more Church jobs—besides teaching in grade school or high school—
have opened up for nuns. Rectory assistanceships, team ministries, and
diocesan offices of supervision, as well as secular positions, have put
many nuns outside community life for extended periods of the workday

or even for months at a time—and outside the protective atmosphere and more easily maintained community system of spiritual and physical restraints.

History is not devoid of examples of sexual relationships between priests and coworkers. Early Christian literature is rife with concern for virgins. They were the bishops' responsibility. By the year 250, abuses against virginity were common. Fox (1987) quotes St. Cyprian, who wrote about that time: "Frequently the Church mourns over her virgins as a result, she groans at their scandalous and hateful stories" (p. 373).

Nature being what it is, there had to be transgressions involving those who were meant to shield. More is said in the early literature about virgins than about celibate males, reflecting an attitude toward sexuality and women. Certainly, after St. Augustine, the idea of women and sex as the sources of evil was solidified in the Western theological mind (cf. Pagels, 1988, Chapter 5). But early literature reinforces the idea of separate quarters. Chrysostom again is as good a source as any. His treatise, *Quod regulares feminae viris cohabitare non debeant,*

> . . . insists that canonical women . . . must not have men residing permanently with them under the same roof. Chrysostom admits that there has been no great amount of actual wrongdoing, but points out that scandal must inevitably arise. Though the two treatises breathe an apostolic zeal for a reform of the clergy, their language is often harsh and biting, comparing such houses even with brothels. Palladius mentions that "this caused great indignation to those among the clergy who were without the love of God, and blazing with passion." (Quasten, 1960, p. 464)

In our own time, one priest who was the pastor of a parish had a sexual relationship of several years' duration with the principal of his grade school. Each kept a very rigorous daily schedule of predictable and regulated associations, but set aside time every week for each other. Their sexual interaction was regulated like clockwork, just as was the rest of their lives.

When ordinary work brings two people into a satisfying shared opportunity for at least limited open social contact appropriate to each person's state, the sexual component can be incorporated and maintained with a minimum of effort as long as the shared work goal remains reasonably predominant. If that focus shifts, then marriage is an alternative—which, of course, ordinarily, but not necessarily, disrupts their ecclesiastical vocations (cf. covert marriage, below).

Nuns are not the only female coworkers of priests who share their religious ideals and values. Other women—either married or single—can participate in a sexual relationship whose dynamic differs from that of the married women previously mentioned in that the latter have a focus of family rather than the shared work goals.

Priests traditionally have had more social latitude than nuns. Association with lay women, especially those who are professionals or Church-related, is usually accepted without question if the work relatedness is in order and no other "danger" signals are emitted. Travel with priests, even for extended periods, is not uncommon among this group.

Many women in this coworker group are energetic, loving, and conscientious in their occupations. However, also included among them are those who have burned out in their work and have found a sexual relationship as one way of going on.

To the Served

Pastoral work is a source of great satisfaction. Teaching, preaching, counseling, crisis intervention, comforting, and facilitating the growth of people is what many a priest says, "I was ordained for." In 1972, a sociological study of priests showed that about 80 percent felt that their ministry was aided by celibacy—that because of celibacy they had an enhanced measure of availability of both time and energy. The denial of sexual gratification should in theory promote their development toward the goal of universal love for all mankind.

> ... the overwhelming majority of the priests agree that celibacy provides a priest with more time to be available to the people, but slightly less than half think that celibacy is essential to fulfill the potential of the priesthood, and only one-third think that the nature of the priest's relationship with God excludes companionship with another in marriage. On the other hand, approximately half think that celibacy may be harmful to some priests and half also think that many men are kept from the priesthood by the requirement of celibacy. (Greeley, 1972)

Denied physical and emotional satisfaction in other areas of life, a priest can be driven to overinvest emotionally in those he serves. This, coupled with a basic ambivalence reflected in Greeley's study, can lead to a special kind of relationship—an unexpected treasure, not sought out, but found while conscientiously tilling the field.

A 46-year-old priest, who had a remarkable life history of active and energetic work as a pastor and chaplain, had a host of devoted and appropriately loving and grateful followers whom he had rescued from various precarious life crises. With insight and humor, he said of himself, "I walk down the street and all the stray dogs and cats follow me. There must be something in my personality—that's been my priesthood too, only with people. And I love it." He became sexually involved with a woman half his age while counseling her. She had been unwillingly impregnated by an abusive and abandoning boyfriend. The priest was captivated by her predicament. He also reported having had a similar affair earlier in his priesthood, but this time he described himself as "head over heels" in love for the first time in his life.

He had entered the priesthood after making a promise to his mother on her deathbed when he was 15 that he would become a priest and "save" people. However, he had grown to feel a genuine aptitude for the work and the life of a priest, and knew he could not duplicate the opportunity for work satisfaction in any other setting.

He and his young friend continued their relationship for several years. It was mutually gratifying and retained the quality of the helper and the helped, while incorporating sexual satisfaction for them both.

Another priest had contact with the study for 10 years prior to his death at age 65. He had had a 30-year relationship that had begun when the woman was only 16 years old. At the time they met, the girl—a member of his parish—had made a serious suicidal attempt. Her whole family credited the priest with having saved her life, and she became a devoted and active parishioner. The priest presided at her marriage, baptized all her children, attended to all of their first communions, and was the honored guest at their weddings.

This picture is what everyone but the priest and the girl saw. In truth, she was for him the first and only source of all his sexual satisfaction. She ministered to him and his needs as she grew in sexual experience and maturity in her marriage. There was a genuine friendship between the two, and they enjoyed and shared the ballet, theater, and gourmet restaurants—things that did not interest her husband, and that at times the family could not afford.

At its base, the relationship began and remained on a level of a good priest serving his parishioner. He felt that this unique personal relationship helped him to carry on his ministry. He denied ever thinking of leaving the ministry to marry. He could not have had an affectionate and sexual relationship with anyone who did not understand the importance to him of the priesthood and its work. His companion did not want to marry him. She wanted to be the perfect parishioner and, in addition, wanted to "minister" to him in some way.

This situation is not an isolated one. The dynamic is represented with frequency in our study population. Two points are salient to it. First, the relationship usually begins with an initially profound pastoral experience of genuine spiritual significance for both parties. Convert instruction;

spiritual awareness from counseling; a confessional exchange that leads to value reorganization; comforting from death, loss, or illness of a loved one—all can become a unique experience for the priest who has served the same function with perhaps hundreds of others. However, there is something "special" about the serving of *"this"* woman. And, of course, there is mutuality in the specialness.

Second, this specialness of the spiritual experience is shared by two people who are basically content, each with his or her state. He does not want to be anything but a priest. She, at least for more or less long periods, does not want to be other than a special parishioner. The genuineness of the bond and the compatibility of mutual needs make this kind of relationship remarkably durable.

The Alien

Priests who assiduously avoid any sexual contact with women with whom they work, serve, or share their ordinary social circle at times find a relationship in a surprising quarter. Some priests find excitement in the uniqueness of a sexual relationship with a woman from a religious background, value system, or social circumstance entirely different from their own. They are attracted by not being treated in the manner to which they are accustomed. Some of these men find a freedom of self-expression for the first time in their lives—sometimes after years of ministry and celibate practice. These women are either unacquainted with or not overwhelmed by the social reverence and reserve that surround the priest. To them, he is "just another man," and it is this lack of constraint that seems to be so refreshing and attractive to some priests.

A 50-year-old priest entered into a sexual relationship with a woman— an avowed atheist—whom he met at a convention. She was "not like any other woman" he had ever encountered. She related to him as an intelligent and interesting man, not as a priest, and was singularly unimpressed by the trappings and ready answers others seemed to relish. For the priest, she was a first—enabling him to make challenging and stimulating exchanges with a woman. He was delighted with her intelligence and by her view of life, so unlike his own. "I'm in love for the first time," he confided, "and it's the most wonderful experience!" Although he had some trouble adjusting the relationship to the demands of his ministry, it endured for three years.

Women who share religious values but different religious traditions also bring the quality of taboo breaking to the relationship. Women of the priest's usual acquaintance, although attractive to him, may not be as free to defy or at least question openly his life assumptions, including his celibate practice.

A priest ordained for 12 years met a woman—a hostess at a restaurant—while he was on vacation in a large city several hundred miles from his own diocese. He was not wearing his clerical garb at the time, nor did he present himself as a priest. He was simply a man on vacation. Several pleasant days of socializing provided the foundation for a growing friendship between the two. Raised in a large fundamentalist family in the mountain country, she was a young widow with four children. He was the product of an urban Catholic ghetto. They met on territory that was far removed from both of their roots and embarked on an 18-year relationship that involved regular telephone contact and a monthly visit of three or four days. The priest became a surrogate father to all her children, who called him "Uncle" as they grew to adulthood.

The alien background and geography allowed the relationship to coexist with his continuing priestly commitment and a minimum of guilt.

The Asexual Marriage

What we are doing with the reported sexual relationships of priests is—without resorting to either unnecessary psychiatric or moral judgment—extrapolating the features that allow these relationships to continue for extended periods of time in the face of avowed celibacy.

Power and prestige rather than lust or adult sexual strivings seem to be at the core of some relationships priests have with women. Since our report records only the *known* sexual behavior of priests, I tentatively include in this category the involvement of Pope Pius XII with a Holy Cross sister named Pascalina and only as an example of a durable man-woman relationship that may or may not have included direct sexual exchange. I do not even imply that sex was involved in the case of Pius XII; in itself it makes little difference as far as the psychic structure of the relationship is concerned. Their acquaintanceship lasted from 1917 when she was 23 years old until the Pope's death in 1958. They lived together both in Munich and in the Vatican (Murphy, 1985). These long-term affective relationships are not infrequent among the ranks of ordinary priests, but they can be remarkable among men of authority.

I have often heard it said, "Power is the lust of the clergy." The core of the dynamic of the asexual marriage is that, to one degree or another, power replaces adult sexual strivings. As Fenichel (1945) commented:

The exaggerated striving for power and prestige has, in such persons, a history that leads back again into infantile sexuality. Power and prestige are needed as defenses against an anxiety that has become connected with infantile sexual strivings. (p. 244)

Perhaps the most perceptive and articulate exponent of the dynamic between power and sex is Eugene Kennedy—writer, psychologist, and resigned priest, whom I mentioned earlier with regard to his study of the psychosexual development of 271 Catholic priests. In an article (1986) in the *National Catholic Reporter,* he continues this theme:

> Asexuality connotes a lack of personal development, an immaturity characterized by a failure to achieve adequate differentiation of sexual identity. It is observed in many persons who use power to dominate others. The gratification experienced from this asexual model of functioning is in some sense a substitute for mature sexual gratification.

Kennedy weaves a sensitive portrayal of his viewpoint in the novel *Father's Day* (1981). There the choice the priest must make is not between a sexual relationship and a celibate existence, but between power and a woman. The essence of the relationship described is bound up with authority—some personal, but essentially institutional and bureaucratic—through which the priest realizes his existence as a man.

This phenomenon cannot coexist with sexual equality. To maintain such a relationship, both parties need to acknowledge that the authority or power system is supreme, and both must derive their primary meaning and satisfaction from their alliance with the power structure. In an article entitled "The Problem with No Name," Kennedy (1988) comments:

> As ecclesiastical leaders move uneasily around the issue of women's equality in the Church, they reveal not only something about themselves, but something about the deepest historical authoritarian instincts of the bureaucratic Church. (p. 423–424)

In our study, both priests and women who revealed this kind of power-based relationship reported that for them sexual intercourse was always secondary to authority and could be absent entirely for long periods of time. In general, deep, affective and often romantic bonds are reinforced by regular contact and sharing, and since physical affection is limited, the relationships can flourish at a great distance and sustain prolonged separations. The telephone is the great gift to these people, as were Héloise's letters to Abelard. Every emotion and secret is shared, and the parties have no doubts that each is the other's best friend. In most emotional ways, the relationship is like a marriage—long term, but based on a shared alliance with and devotion to the authority structure of the Church. Also in practice there is what amounts to a tacit agreement that neither party will elevate adult sexuality above a minimal level.

Covert Marriage

There are some priests who enter into civil marriages and continue their ministries within the ordinary Church structure. Awareness of these secret marriages is surprisingly easy to come by. They have increased appreciably over the period of our study—especially among chaplains in the military, where celibacy has little cultural meaning, and where personal freedom and security are enhanced or at least protected in their isolation from routine ecclesiastical supervisors. In his biography of Francis Cardinal Spellman, John Cooney (1984) ran across two married priests—both monsignors—one of whom, as I mentioned earlier, was the nephew of Boston's Cardinal O'Connell (pp. 26 and 324).

Frequent among our informants reporting legal marriage was their desire to be "honest," or to provide for the security of the women they loved and the legitimacy of their children. They strove—several successfully and for many years—to continue their assigned ministries. Some hoped they could live their "honest" double-lives until their retirement. In every instance, the priests were aware of the ecclesiastical penalty for "a cleric who attempted marriage even if only civilly" (Canon Law No. 194, 1:3). They knew they could be removed from office—but, as one said, "only if I get caught."

Marriage in spite of the law is also not a new phenomenon. Among the many historical accounts, one from around the year 1206 reads as follows:

> Although Lambert was a priest, he made no secret of being married, and he had at least two sons, both of whom became priests like himself. This was a century after the Gregorian offensive against concubinage among the clergy, and demonstrates the distance between ecclesiastical theory and practice in the matter of morals. (Duby, 1983, p. 253)

HETEROSEXUAL BEHAVIORS

Not all heterosexual activity of priests takes place within the context of a durable relationship. Some of their sexual activity forms behavior patterns limited in their very essence by the constraints of the priests' emotional immaturity, compulsion, impulsivity, or psychopathology. In each instance, the primary focus is on the act—the relationship is at the service of the sexual behavior rather than the other way around.

Some priests say that they went through a sexual "practice phase" prior to the formation of a continuing involvement with a woman; some used their practice experiences to form a deeper realization of the meaning of celibacy for their lives and priestly vocations. Other priests and their sexual behavior remain immature, transient, exploitative, or essentially narcissistic, from which they learn little about either their own life or the lives of others.

Transitional Behavior (The Prove-Myself Experience)

There is a kind of sexual involvement that can last for a few months or even a few years with the same person, yet remains a transitional sexual encounter for its entire duration. The object is never really the mutuality of partners. The relationship's reason for being is either in the service of the priest's growing up or the rededication of himself to his vocation—a sadder if wiser priest. The woman is essentially a tool of his growth or salvation. She is used.

The priest may likewise be a victim of a woman's immaturity or exploitation. Both are fairly common occurrences, and Father Andrew Greeley portrays them frequently in his earlier novels (cf. *Cardinal Sins*, 1981; *Thy Brother's Wife*, 1982; *Ascent into Hell*, 1983a). Greeley must be taken seriously, not only because of his monumental research into Church life, but also because of his broad human contacts. His own celibacy is not diminished by his writing. A priest and art historian said that he firmly believed that Greeley had "never had intercourse with a woman. His writings betray his innocence." That particular priest had had intercourse himself in the midst of his own transitional phase of psychosexual development, and stated, "I knew all the works of Picasso, but I never really saw them—understood them—until I had experienced sex with a woman. What a difference!"

In the early 1980s, seminarians were perceptive when they coined the phrase "The Greeley Syndrome." When I asked them what they meant by this, they said, "I have to have sex with a woman, be conflicted, and then reject her so I can get back to celibacy and be a bishop." That "syndrome" pretty well sums up the quality of much of the initial sexual activity of priests. The activity appears sexually relational in comparison to anything else the priest has experienced previously. But one cannot ignore that he has ensconced himself in a protective position where marriage or a permanent sexual union is theoretically impossible. One priest who had his first sexual experience at age 54 said, "Thank God I have the security of my priesthood while I go through all this turmoil!"

Another priest, who had been ordained three years, was aiding a young couple grieving the loss of their youngest child, and became sexually involved with the woman. On her side, she needed special reassurance and support in her crisis—which her equally grief-stricken husband could not provide. As for the priest, he needed to grow up sexually. Although the involvement lasted for a year and was meaningful for both the woman and the priest, the priest was aware that there was no permanency asked or promised, nor equality of emotion exchanged.

The core of their sexual activity was transitional because the *act* was central—substituting for a genuine pastoral involvement on the one hand, and on the other, for the woman, providing a stand-in for her husband. Later, the priest was able to identify the nature of his experience. He believed he had "proved" something about himself and felt more secure in that he was now "like other men" and would be more sympathetic to his parishioners' marital distresses and sexual tensions.

This kind of transitional sexual involvement is almost taken for granted in a certain phase of clerical development. One young woman informant who was working at a parish was distressed by the sexual advances of the curate. There were many things about him that attracted her, but she did not want to become seriously involved, nor did she want to lose her job. When we asked why she did not talk to the pastor about her situation, she replied, "I can't do that; he's involved with my mother."

Another young woman informant related that she had had this type of involvement with three priests, each encounter lasting about a year. She actually took some pride in the educational service she had provided to each, but had become distressed when she found herself more deeply attached to one of the priests than she had intended to be. He was unwilling to commit himself emotionally to a more involving relationship—a situation she had been able to accept previously because of her devotion to the Church and the priesthood. In this instance, however, she was experiencing the deprivation side of the inequality, and found it not to her liking.

Another example of the casualness with which these encounters are sometimes viewed was that of a deacon who had been referred for psychiatric evaluation by the rector of his seminary. The deacon had become involved with a married woman who worked around the facility. He had been seen necking with her in a car not far from the campus. When he was interviewed, the deacon insisted that he wanted to continue in the program to ordination in spite of the sexual liaison. He was embarrassed by the exposure and frightened by the woman's husband, who had heard rumors of the young man's activity.

When postponement of ordination was recommended on several grounds, including the student's ambivalence as demonstrated by his sexual encounter, the rector disagreed and replied, "He has been a good student and wants to proceed. A thing like this is not sufficient to keep a man from ordination. It can be a good growth experience. I think he's learned his lesson." The student was ordained and remained in contact with our study for three years thereafter. During that time, he became aware that the rector himself had periodic sexual friendships, which in the older man's words, "kept him human."

Salient in all of these examples is the unevenness of involvement, expectation, gratification, and dedication to the priesthood. Sometimes it is the woman who recognizes the importance of the priesthood to her partner and is, therefore, unwilling to make the relationship permanent or equal. She "saves the priest" for his vocation by treating the sexual encounter as a phase of his learning.

There is a lovely account in the *World of the Desert Fathers* (1986) that demonstrates this phenomenon:

> A brother was sent on an errand by his abbot, and arriving at a place which had water, he found a woman there washing clothes. Overcome, he asked her if he might sleep with her. She said to him, "Listening to you is easy, but I could be the cause of great suffering for you." He said to her, "How?" She answered, "After committing the deed, your conscience will strike you, and either you will give up on yourself, or it will require great effort for you to reach the state which is yours now: therefore, before you experience that hurt, go on your way in peace." When he heard this he was struck with contrition and thanked both God and her wisdom. He went to his abbot, informed him of the event, and he too marvelled. And the brother urged the rest not to go out of the monastery, and so he himself remained in the monastery, not going out, until death. (p. 14)

This story dates from around the year 300 and leads us to a consideration of another type of sexual behavior.

The Curious and Immature Dynamic

This is a behavior that is even further removed from a relationship than the transitional dynamic. It is conduct pursued by the immature and is driven essentially by curiosity. As we mentioned earlier, priests most typically keep to themselves the development of a relationship with a woman, or at most share it only with a close friend. Curious and immature priests, on the other hand, are likely to have a band of priest friends to whom they can confide their distress. These are the priests who are encouraged by their buddies, for example, "Go and get it out of your system. You'll find it's not so great."

There is some precedent in ancient wisdom for this advice. An old Talmudic saying counsels the following:

> Many suggestions, courses of action, and admonitions are offered by the talmudists to combat this powerful and controlling basic urge. Nonetheless, in their wisdom, they were cognizant of the force of compulsion and the "irresistible impulse." For the person who struggled sincerely but unsuccessfully with his impulse, they offered advice. . . . He was to dress in black (as a sign of mourning) and go

to a strange place where no one would know him and discharge his desire. Although it was acknowledged that God was aware, even when one sinned in secret, a man was admonished to sin in a place where he was not known, lest he set an example and encourage others to sin. . . . (Schnaper, 1970, p. 192)

It is very clear here that an *act* rather than a person is central to those afflicted.

A woman lost her father when she was 16 years old, after which she became unruly and promiscuous for about three years. Upon entering college, she determined to change her life, and became very devout, attending daily Mass and participating enthusiastically in religious activities. She chose a young priest from the ministry staff as her confessor, and during the annual retreat, made a general confession to him of all her past sins. Subsequently, the priest became more attentive to her and by the end of the year had unburdened himself to her, confiding to her his sexual inexperience. He asked her to teach him to French kiss, since he had never done it.

Dependent personalities are prominent here. Priests in this category need to be agreeable and approved of, and have great fear of rejection. They don't like to be alone and are more willing to take advice from others than to make decisions for themselves. They can conform very well through seminary training and in the clerical system. Their need for approval and fear of criticism make them conformists and generally good organizational men. They do not want a relationship that disrupts the system, but their sexual curiosity can be piqued beyond endurance once they become exposed to the lives and problems of the lay people they serve. In addition, if they feel at all disappointed in or disapproved of by the clerical system or by those they count on within it, they can be drawn to other avenues for acceptance.

The loner is also prone to sexual behavior that involves no relationship but satisfies his curiosity or psychic immaturity. Prostitutes are sometimes employed to gratify this urge. Loners are men who find a refuge in the clerical system rather than companionship or shared goals and values. They are often considered a bit odd, and are certainly different from the average priest. They do not have close friends and tend to be naturally suspicious—both factors that can be misread by others as signs of spirituality. Because they generally conform to the system and do their job, their discomfort with people and their eccentricities are tolerated and in some cases even extolled as "holy." Their sexual life will be episodic, secret, and completely devoid of any personal feeling.

A priest displaying these characteristics went periodically to massage parlors where he was fellated at the culmination of each encounter. The satisfaction of his sexual curiosity was limited to this experience. Even when the women would offer him intercourse, he would decline, as his psychic immaturity was locked into a level of impersonal exchange.

The hardworking, devoted priest who is willing to sacrifice everything for the perfect accomplishment of his tasks is also vulnerable to immature, curiosity-satisfying sexual encounters. These men are overconscientious and even scrupulous in the execution of their duties. Oftentimes they exhibit a rigidity in their lives and their relationships and prefer hard work even to the exclusion of recreation and friendship. They are men of the letter and are, accordingly, valuable lieutenants in the clerical army because of their devotion to detail, rules, and order. Their inflexibility can be interpreted as conviction, and their restricted ability to express affection as discipline and objectivity. These are men who agonize over their sexual transgressions, which they see painfully as sinful. They do not have the time for the development of a sexual relationship and are not prone to deny or split off sexual activity from their consciousness. A sexual encounter sends them to conscientious repentance and a renewed dedication to their work and to their usually well-ordered lives.

One priest informant of this type was not only active in ordinary priestly activities, but in addition dedicated himself to a spiritual group of laymen and priests, which demanded further sacrifices of his time, energy, and resources. Each month he would fit into his already crowded schedule a day of spiritual renewal with this group. Then, on the way home, he would stop sometimes at several bars where women would be available for sexual activity. He was fascinated by the atmosphere and clientele of these bars, so different from the ambience of his own life. Most of the time he would simply have a drink, talk with the women, and then refuse sex—almost as if he were testing his power to resist temptation. Once in a while, however, he would have sex, return guiltily to his residence, wake a fellow priest, and make a confession.

Anxiety, Depression, Mania, and Stress

There are certain emotional symptoms that at times are so intimately bound up with the sexual activity of priests that it is difficult to know which is the cause and which the effect. For the avowed celibate, sexual activity is a forbidden outlet for tension reduction. If his ordinary channels of tension reduction fail, or if stress becomes periodically overwhelming, the priest becomes more vulnerable to his sexual desires.

The priesthood is a vocation of concern—if not worry—over the condition of the human race and its salvation. Worry and anxiety can seem natural to the conscientious priest, and at what point he crosses the emotional line between justifiable concern and pathological anxiety is not always easy to detect. Those who have had a long involvement in the medical care of priests say that these men will suffer hosts of physical symptoms—shortness of breath, heart palpitations, dizziness, difficulty concentrating or sleeping, as well as irritability and exhaustion. These symptoms indicate anxiety, but will often be treated first as manifestations of physical disease.

When the priest is threatened with loss of his internal control, his anxiety symptoms can increase and lead him to justify or rationalize some sexual activity intended to reduce them. Such outlets ironically can lead to even more sexual frustration and anxiety. As a result, the priest's fear of sexual contact or release can be so inhibiting that it can develop into a true panic.

A priest in his early 30s became so concerned about his sexual thoughts and so fearful of sexual contamination that he grew unable to distribute Holy Communion lest he touch a woman's lips or hand in the process. Eventually he had to be reassigned to a position that obviated duties that would rouse his distress.

There are a certain number of priests who are literally agoraphobic, but who can function adequately within the confines of their clerical assignment—usually in a community setting. They experience genuine panic attacks any place outside their "home." It is the combination of their sexual aversion, their dependence on their priestly state, and their fear of separation from it that holds them in place. Their sexual activity is infrequent and almost always impersonal.

Although depression often diminishes the sexual drive in the average person and can have the same effect in the depressed priest, it is noteworthy that for some priests a depressed mood is the trigger for *increased* sexual activity. Because of its self-destructive nature, I speculate that this behavior is directly connected with their sexual control and uncompensated or unsublimated instinct.

One monsignor who was well known in his locale became depressed and began frequenting a part of town harboring bars and brothels, where he and his car were easily recognized. His activity came to the attention of Church authorities, who recommended that he seek professional help. In treatment, his depression was diagnosed and a subsequent course of medication and psychotherapy restored him to his former level of celibate functioning.

A priest in his 40s who had considerable ecclesiastical responsibility became depressed, exhibiting the classic signs of weight loss, early morning awakening, fatigue, and persistent thoughts of death. In spite of encouragement by his subordinates, he resisted any medical treatment.

Instead, he became sexually involved with a divorced woman, whom he experienced as compassionate and understanding. Several times a day his telephone conversations with her seemed to buoy him up, temporarily relieving his mood and aiding his ability to work.

In retrospect, after his eventual treatment, he acknowledged that this relationship had been not only detrimental to his career, but very punishing to him personally—confirming his sense of unworthiness and increasing his already overwhelming sense of guilt.

Another priest was encouraged by his brother—who was also a priest—to experience sex with a woman. He was reluctant to do so and resisted his brother's suggestions. Eventually, however, he acquiesced, and became involved with a woman who was eager to initiate him into the rites of sex. Afterwards, the priest became severely depressed and required hospitalization. During the course of his stay, he came to terms with his celibate decision, and realized that, unlike his brother, he was unable to combine his priesthood with sexual activity. Subsequent to his release, his celibate resolve remained, and his depression lifted.

Hypomania and frankly manic episodes involving increased sexual activity are also recorded in some priests.

One naturally busy and productive priest entered into a period of unusually fierce professional activity. Since he was successful and extraordinarily resourceful in his ministry, it was not initially noticed that his expansiveness had become out of line. He initiated several ambitious projects that he had been thinking and talking about previously, and then decreased his sleep time and stepped up his work schedule to meet the new demands created by them. Other priests grew concerned about him when he began telephoning them at midnight and later, sometimes talking about the same matters again and again. During this frenetic time, he also became sexually involved with a woman. Eventual treatment with lithium carbonate and psychotherapy allowed him to reduce his activity and simplify his schedule to their former levels. He continued thereafter to be a very successful priest.

Sometimes a change in a priest's sexual activity can have a hormonal root. One priest who became involved with a women was subsequently diagnosed as having Graves' disease (hyperthyroidism). Treatment with surgery and regulation with synthetic thyroid enabled him to resume his ordinary functioning.

Both within and outside of the celibate discipline, the relationship, balance, and interaction between mind and body are delicate and are still quite mysterious. We have yet a great deal to learn about how biochemistry and mood affect sexual functioning, and also how they in turn are influenced by sexual deprivation.

Idealization, Impulsiveness, and "I"-Centered Behavior

There are priests who go largely undiagnosed, but who could most appropriately be put in the category of borderline personality—and indeed are so classified if they come to psychiatric attention. They are often at the center of conflict or controversy within a group; or, to be more precise, they are effective in splitting a group into factions. This kind of priest overidealizes those to whom he wishes to become close, only to denigrate and devalue them later on. He has a profound capacity for the psychic mechanism of denial, and in this way keeps his sexual activity—which is mostly impulsive in character—out of his conscious integration. He is a man who literally does not know who he is. His identity is not solidified, and he is as likely to be involved in homosexual behavior as with heterosexual. This kind of priest finds it difficult to be by himself, yet at the same time his friendships and associations are marked by intensity and instability.

I have no reason to believe that more of this personality type is represented in the priesthood than in the general population—but I also do not believe it is less represented either. Two factors making the priesthood compatible with it are the priesthood's tolerance for lack of self-definition and of sexual differentiation. In addition, the sense of emptiness and boredom these men experience seeks relief and amelioration in the ideals of selfless service. The Church offers ample opportunity for idealization and devaluation. One's rage and anger can be directed with impunity against sin and sinners. Invariably, however, it is the impulsiveness of these men rather than any of their other disagreeable traits that is least absorbable by the clerical system. This is what trips them most frequently in the end.

A young priest informant had a history of assignments, each of which usually began with great promise, but ended in acrimony and strife. Throughout his career, he maintained a coterie of staunch supporters who were delighted with his quick wit and agile mind. Always more promising than productive, and most impressive on a first or brief contact, the priest managed to come through a series of community skirmishes barely scathed. His first conflict was in the novitiate of his order, where he was the focus of a split between the director and his assistant. In the end, the assistant was relieved of his duties.

This priest's pattern in his ministry was one that raised questions in successive parishes. He would surprise the congregation and colleagues with his fits of rage—sometimes in private, but most disturbingly from the pulpit—that caused controversy among the other priests or consternation in and alienation from a segment of the congregation. His sexual contacts were impulsive. They would always demand attention and his eventual reassignment to another house, where he would repeat the same behavior. He had little insight and presented a formidable administrative and therapeutic challenge.

A number of these men never come to treatment. They remain minor malcontents, accumulating florid histories and much administrative attention over the period of their lives.

Other priests in this self-aggrandizing category are those who have a remarkable overestimation of themselves, their work, and their value. They feel they are special and unique. Their vocations as "other Christs" and recipients of the highest calling only serve to validate their conviction of self-importance. They take advantage of others because they feel they are entitled to do so. Thus, the clerical role of these priests lends itself to their personal ends when many people are willing and eager to serve the Church by "doing for the priests" as part of that service.

One priest who, among other accoutrements, enjoyed lavish furnishings in his private apartment, expensive Oriental rugs, and a complete Waterford crystal bar set, said, "They're not for me personally. They're because of Christ."

The attention these people need is accessible to them by virtue of their role and not because of merit. They have rich fantasy lives involving idealized power, love, and success—themes that their sermons tend to reveal. When they "fall in love," it is with deep appreciation for their own needs and experience, with markedly little for those of their partners.

They tend to be most critical and demanding of others, yet are sensitive themselves to any slight, criticism, or correction from someone else. As priests they can do adequate work for the Church. In instances where they identify closely with their projects, they can accomplish remarkable things. Dr. Richard Gilmartin, a psychiatrist who has treated many priests, refers to this phenomenon as "altruism in the service of narcissism."

These men are not noted for their celibate achievement. They really do not believe that the rules which apply to others—or even about which they preach—apply to them. At the same time, their demandingness does not lend itself to a mutuality that fosters relationships. That is why I have categorized this group with "behaviors" instead of with "relationships." This pattern and its variants are so familiar to the average thoughtful reader that no examples need to be supplied here.

The Gantry Syndrome

In his 1927 novel *Elmer Gantry,* Sinclair Lewis fully painted the charming, dynamic, shallow yet convincing cleric who is opportunistic and promiscuous. A small number of priests fit this description well. They have charisma and oftentimes tremendous dramatic ability. They really do put on a good show, and can demand respect and popularity in both clerical and lay circles. But what they say and preach is so irrevocably split from what they do that "hypocrite" becomes simply an adjective rather than a judgmental term when applied to them. Their behavior is invariably heterosexual. Psychoanalysts question the internal dynamic of this behavior, and say that there tends to be a latent homosexual component at its core. Based on the reports I have reviewed, I would tend to agree, but since I have chosen to avoid both moral and psychiatric categories wherever possible and simply record the behaviors, I have included the Gantry Syndrome among the heterosexualities.

In our study, one priest who was interviewed for a period of several months had had sexual relations with 22 women. A follow-up record several years later revealed that although his sexual activity had diminished, his basic behavior pattern was essentially unchanged.

Other priests who report sexual relations with six to 10 women do not consider themselves promiscuous. Indeed, there are priests representing other categories of behavior who over the period of their lives are sequentially involved with a number of women. What distinguishes them from men in the Gantry category is the quality of the relationship and/or presence of a conscience. Priests who are promiscuous in the Gantry sense experience no regrets and exhibit little perturbation at the prospect of being caught.

The characterological deficit behind this behavior is not very amenable to known forms of treatment, although rare "conversions" have been reported. An environment with clear and stable limits is needed to maintain this type of person in any celibate resolve.

PATTERNS OF ASSOCIATION

There are priests who have respectful, healthy, and satisfying friendships with women, all within the structures of celibate dedication. The history of religion records major examples. The New Testament places Mary and Martha and Mary Magdalene in close association with Christ; St. Paul refers with affection and regard to Phoebe (Romans 16), whom he calls his sister. Virgins and widows were important elements in the early Christian communities from the middle of the second century. By the third century, celibate priests and Christian virgins lived under the same roof and in mixed communities. Remarkable spiritual friendships between celibate men and women are noted in the biographies of the founders and foundresses of religious orders—St. Francis of Assisi and St. Clare, or St. Francis de Sales and St. Jane de Chantal, for example.

These relationships are so thoroughly directed to spiritual goals, and the sublimation of sexual instinct so clearly manifest in the productivity and integrity of dedicated service, that they literally are above question. We will deal with this phenomenon in the section on the achievement of celibacy.

My concern here is with a type of association that is more ambiguous. Although such an association has elements of clearly shared spiritual strivings or elements of sexual sublimation, the social and sexual aims are still so viable that they can quite easily overshadow the celibate elements. Some associations are clearly dating patterns or thinly veiled excursions into social experimentation that skirt the edges of sexual involvement. These patterns can easily lead to the sexual relationships and behaviors mentioned earlier.

To some extent, the patterns of association between priests and women will be influenced by the fashion of the day—what is considered appropriate in one era will not be countenanced in another. For example, King Henry II failed in his attempt to discredit Thomas à Becket—the Archbishop of Canterbury in the late 12th century—by trying to compromise Becket's chastity through one of the king's mistresses. Although Becket's youthful behavior had been indistinguishable in its lusty zeal from the behavior of the other youths of his time, as an adult he proved "capable and versatile; he was a favorite with all. Several of his biographers underline both his lavish generosity and his extreme desire for popularity. They are unanimous, citing their witnesses, that he never lost his chastity, but three of them remark that he followed the fashions of his companions *in the use of emotional language and affectionate caresses*" [italics mine] (Knowles, 1970, p. 9). What talk and caresses precisely were in fashion in 1170? The implication is that, whatever they were, they would not be fashionable or appropriate at every time.

Fashions do change. What can be humorous on one occasion becomes gross or even repugnant at another time or in a different context. Certainly the association of priests with women shifted considerably between 1960 and 1985.

One group of five priests was typical of the early 1960s. The priests were all in their mid to late 30s, and each held a responsible position in the diocese. They worked hard and took their social cues from the schedule of parish and diocesan activities—confirmations, weddings, parish missions, bazaars, fund-raising dinners, communion breakfasts, priests' retreats, and so on. Their general demeanor with women was formal; if friendly, it was not familiar, and allowed only a warm handshake rather than an embrace except from family members, and often not kisses even from them.

Twice a year they would vacation in groups of three to five. Sometimes their focus was golf, skiing, or some other sport. During this time they would shed their clerical collars, don mufti—lay clothes—and socialize in bars and spas as though they were not priests. Protected by the group, they could venture into conversations and brief encounters with women they met. The unspoken rules of the game allowed for some intimate sexual exchange—necking and petting, but not intercourse, as though somehow intercourse but not the rest would be a violation of the celibate trust. The limits of celibacy could be tested, but the group rules had to prevail. If one of the group became too troubled by sexual desire, he was advised by the rest to go find a woman somewhere and get it out of his system, but the group setting was simply for "play" within the safety of priestly association.

Such groups were common in the 60s. More than one priest in our study recounted an incident similar to the following.

Having finished a round of golf, a group of priests were sitting in the clubhouse lounge waiting to be served. A waitress passed by their table, and said, "I'll be with you in a minute, Fathers." The priests were flabbergasted, not knowing how they had blown their cover. When the waitress returned, they asked her how she had recognized them as priests. She responded: "Priests are always impatient for service, and besides, none of you has a wedding ring."

In fact, in the early 1960s, except for military chaplains, priests in mufti were oftentimes easy to pick out of a crowd: their lay clothes were ill fitting, ill matched, out of fashion, and invariably included black dress shoes, regardless of the setting.

The late 1960s and early 1970s saw a metamorphosis from the dating-like behavior within groups of priests to the frank pairing of priests and women—often nuns—in a clear pattern called "the third way." Neither marriage nor traditional celibate practice, the third way allowed for and even extolled close personal relationships between priests and women that included all the behavior open to any other dating couple—dinner, dancing, shared leisure time, and socializing. The relationship was not intended to lead to sexual intercourse, and marriage was never its goal.

In the pseudo-psychological mid-1960s, a "deep, meaningful relationship" with a woman became *de rigueur* for the bright, young, restless cleric. It was a kind of adolescent rebellion within the bounds of the law. Affectionate language and caresses were legitimate; intercourse was not. Eugene C. Kennedy, then an active priest himself, told the press, "Through these relationships you might say that the Roman Catholic Church is allowing its latent heterosexuality to come out" (*Newsweek*, December 3, 1973). The third-way pairing—without group protection and with little life experience preceding it, and with no integration possible between a celibate spirituality and sexual immaturity—was a treacherous ideal to maintain. Frequently it evolved into one of the sexual relationships or behaviors mentioned earlier, or would lead to the priest's giving up his vocation.

The third way and its dangers were not unique to this period. Cyprian—Bishop of Carthage in the eary 200s—was alarmed by a parallel practice:

> In bishoprics near Carthage, young virgins were cohabiting with Christian men, with clerics, even, and deacons, with whom they were said to be sleeping chastely in the same bed. The risks were obvious, and Cyprian was quick to deplore them. (Fox, 1987, p. 169)

Obviously, Cyprian is referring to "language and caresses" that were fashionable but of which he disapproved.

Certainly, in some instances an episode of third way experimentation led to a priest's reevaluation of his vocation and subsequent rededication to celibate living. One priest in his early 50s commented on his experience during that era: "I kissed everyone, and hugged everyone. I just thought it was the mature thing to do. I'm more conservative now; it's hard to keep all hugs and kisses nonsexual."

Many men who left the priesthood credit their experience in the third way as the catalyst for their departure. They entered into an honest relationship, thinking it could be reconciled with their celibate ideal. They welcomed the semi-openness and the psychological and social support given the practice by priest psychologists and moralists, but then found themselves incapable of leading a comfortable double life and sustaining the irreconcilable confict with their vocations as priests.

In this period, the simultaneous freedom accorded nuns—their opportunity to attend summer school on university campuses far from the familiar schedule and ambience of the convent, the discarding of traditional religious habits—created an atmosphere and setting where like-minded, similarly valued, and mutually concerned priests and nuns could meet and associate. The *zeitgeist* was one that did away with the externals and nonessentials of spiritual life and celibacy, hopefully in favor of greater maturity and self-reliance.

However, some people discovered how intricately intertwined their internal observance of celibacy was with the external structure they had unconsciously come to depend on. When structure was removed, inherent immaturity was revealed for reevaluation and redefinition—which did not always lead back to a more mature celibate commitment. At times the restructuring became a springboard into a more or less secret sexual relationship as described previously. In other cases, it became a failed attempt at a relationship that in turn initiated a pattern of sexual behavior within the priesthood.

In a significant number of instances, the formation of a real relationship led observant priests to choose marriage over the priesthood. Many of these priests entered the third way in good—if naive—conscience, but they were men who could not easily tolerate a secret or dual existence. They had been happy and effective in the priesthood and refused to compromise either themselves or, more significantly, the women they genuinely loved. Of course, some priests also chose marriage or a relationship as a way out of an unhappy existence and a misguided vocation.

Regardless of whatever the unconscious factors are that motivate two people who share a conscious ideal of celibacy to initiate a close "meaningful" relationship that has neither sex nor marriage as its goal, the result is inevitable psychic conflict when they find themselves in a mutually inclusive affectionate bond. Choices must be made. The political, economic, and social structures surrounding celibacy and providing some of its external support fluctuate from era to era and place to place in the Church. In spite of their heterosexual strivings, some priests have found that the economic and sociopolitical advantages of their vocation simply outweigh the risks of existence outside the clerical structure. Again, it was Eugene Kennedy who called priests of the 1970s "the last of the vested gentry."

Frank Bonnike, who founded CORPUS (Corps of Reserve Priests United for Service) left the priesthood himself in 1973 and was identified in the national media as "the former president of the National Federation of Priests' Councils . . . among those third-way priests who are unwilling to live a public lie. 'I was happy as a celibate,' Bonnike wrote recently to friends in a letter announcing his plans to marry Janet Proteau, a former nun. 'I do not wish to be an unhappy or a compromising one. . . . Once I discovered myself closer to God because of Janet, I knew I could not just be open with Him about our relationship, but that I had to be open about it before people, too' " (*Newsweek*, December 3, 1973, p. 110B).

Perhaps the best statement of the purpose of CORPUS was reflected in the goals of their 1988 conference held in Washington, D.C.:

> To gather men and women whose experience and status speak to the issue; to assess the loss which the Church suffers through mandatory celibacy; to facilitate the reconciliation of celibate and married priests; to publicize findings and recommendations of the Conference; to formulate methods to effect the needed changes within the Church. Moreover, through our networking and conferencing, we hope to foster optional celibacy within the Latin Rite

Catholic priesthood; to study the 'mysterious' model of marriage as applied to Christ and the Church; to involve resigned priests more and more in the work of the Church; to evidence the compatibility of marriage and the priesthood; and to affirm the authentic charism of celibacy as an option in ministry. (CORPUS, 1988)

A good number of priests who are now married desire to continue in the active priesthood as married men. Some of them were among the most observant of their celibacy for the major part of their ministries.

It should be noted that not all former celibates achieve good marriages. Marriage for some ends in regret and pain for both parties; divorce is sometimes the result. I was told by a member of the Roman Curia that one of the reasons Rome has become more resistant and obstructionistic toward priests' requests for dispensations from their vows in order to marry is the large number of requests for reinstatement to the priesthood and celibacy from priests who had been previously dispensed. From 1965 through 1970, under the influence of the Second Vatican Council, Rome had been quite willing to dispense—a policy that was reversed in 1971. Nevertheless, priests continue to leave the priesthood in substantial numbers—most of them to marry.

Although the number of priests who are involved in heterosexual relationships and behaviors has remained relatively stable at 20 percent throughout the period of our observation, the number of priests involved in patterns of association where the conscious intent is nonsexual has fluctuated between 6 and 12 percent, in our estimation.

The only consistent exceptions to these figures are those of the strictly cloistered men we interviewed. A different dynamic operates among them. The isolation, silence, and interiority demanded by their lives increase their fantasies to an exquisite pitch. Even among the cloistered, the association with women can transcend fantasy. Thomas Merton developed an intense affective relationship with a young nurse he met in 1966 while he was a surgical patient. The relationship is important for an understanding of the dynamic of celibacy, because it flowered after Merton pursued a celibate life for more than 25 years. Also, the sexual struggles of one who has left a rich legacy of literary and spiritual significance add a dimension of understanding not duplicable in other life accounts. Merton knew this, and explicitly stated in his trust that his relationship with this woman should not be permanently suppressed, only delayed in its disclosure. Whether their love was sexual in nature is not known now. However, as Merton's biographer quoted him regarding this love:

It needs to be known too, for it is part of me. My need for love, my loneliness, my inner division, the struggle in which solitude is at once a problem and a "solution." And perhaps not a perfect solution either. (Mott, 1984, p. 458)

In the 1980s, the patterns of dating association are less blatant, more subdued, and yet not quite secret. Many nuns report the frank invitations by priests to enter into a "buddy" relationship. In a sexually conscious and explicit age, these relationships, plus the group dating patterns described earlier, persist as a protection against sexual naivete and the homosocial structure.

We have many examples of groups of young priests in the 1980s who recreate in bars and spas just as small groups did in the early 1960s. One group chided one of their number when he confided to a girl he met on one of the group outings that he was a priest. That dynamic of the pattern has remained constant—the alliance to the group and anonymity. Of course, the *use* of the woman for one's growth, experience, or recreation is clear. This element is not acceptable to many young priests.

Likewise, the third-way theme is still humming along. A 60-year-old pastor approached a young nun who worked on his parish staff and carefully explained to her that he would like to have a nonsexual friendship with her—that he wanted a companion for dinner, for visiting museums, and for attending athletic events. Although the nun had no doubt as to the sincerity of the pastor's conscious intentions, she was too attuned to the unconscious human agendas to be comfortable with the invitation. And therein lies the crux of the heterosexual patterns of association between priests and women—not in the conscious intent to embrace both the celibate ideal and a mature friendship with a woman, but in the unconscious sexual striving and immature attitudes toward women and the unsublimated elements of the priest's life and spirituality.

It is easy and reasonable from the perspective of Church authority for women to be viewed as the greatest danger to the priesthood and celibacy. Of course, the real danger is not in women, but lies within the priestly striving for this ideal in a Church structure whose authority is sexually underdeveloped.

Chapter 6

THE HOMOSEXUALITIES __

"Homosexuals have the same emotional and sexual needs as straights, only more dangerously and frustratingly."
—*Fr. Joseph Gallagher*
The Business of Circumference

There is no area of sexuality more misunderstood, distorted, maligned, and actually feared than the homosexualities. The use of the plural is not accidental. Since we do not have a sophisticated moral and behavioral vocabulary with regard to homosexual development, orientation, and behavior—as we do with heterosexuality—the use of the plural is necessary to avoid glibness and to pursue accurate definition and delineation.

For instance, the man who loves his wife and is devoted to his daughters prides himself that he is "heterosexual" in orientation and behavior. But he hardly would put himself in the same category as the man who stands by the schoolyard eager to engage little girls in sexual activity, or as the man who lurks in dark corners looking to overpower some woman with his sexual passion. He would insist that one be identified as a pedophile and the other as a rapist. He would not be satisfied that all be described as heterosexual in orientation and behavior, but would demand more accurate definition and more precise categories. Heterosexual orientation or behavior is not necessarily a *good* in and of itself.

Generally speaking, the only distinction made about "homosexuality" is between orientation and behavior. Both are assumed to be, and often labeled, "bad" or "defective"—although orientation can be tolerated by some moralists more readily than behavior. There is little understanding of the place of the homosexualities in the developmental process, in spite of Freud's pioneering explorations in his *Three Essays on Sexuality* (1905). He distinguished three types of people having "contrary sexual feelings": "absolute" (obligatory), "amphigenic" (bisexual), and "contingent" (situational). He also dealt with the questions of innate predisposition versus acquired character of the sexual instinct, and degeneracy.

103

Three shifts in awareness are needed to understand the homosexual facets of reality:

First, one must abandon the simplistic assumption that the distinction between homosexual orientation and behavior is sufficient to define accurately the reality, any more than merely distinguishing between heterosexual orientation and behavior tells the whole story.

Second, one must develop an equal neutrality about the concepts *homosexual* and *heterosexual*. *Homosexual* is no more "bad" than *heterosexual* is "good," just as the idea of *food* in and of itself tells us nothing about its being good or bad, since it can be applied to pheasant under glass in the most expensive restaurant as well as to a carcass in the middle of the jungle.

Third, *homosexual* and *heterosexual* are not oppositional concepts, at least developmentally, as if being heterosexual or behaving heterosexually obviated or protected one against homosexual feelings or behaving homosexually. Leo Bartemeier, along with all the early psychoanalysts, assumed early psychic bisexuality. He used to put it in a homespun way: "We all have a father and a mother. It would be foolish to think that we inherited qualities only from the parent of our same sex. Boys are like their mothers and girls are like their fathers, just as much as being like the parent of the same sex" (personal communication).

Kinsey's work also made me aware of the need to expand my own understanding of the homosexualities. A passage that jarred me at first was from his *Sexual Behavior in the Human Female* (Kinsey et al., 1953): "Heterosexual coitus is extolled in most cultures, but forbidden to Buddhist and Catholic priests. Homosexual activity is condemned in some cultures, tacitly accepted in others, honored as a religious rite in others, and allowed to Buddhist priests" (p. 320).

When I consulted Buddhists about Kinsey's statement, I quickly became aware that their frame of reference regarding the homosexual-heterosexual spectrum was distinct from the Western Judeo-Christian tradition of discontinuity and opposition. The Eastern view, as I understand it, sees sex as one, and homosexuality is part of a developmental phase or variation. One Buddhist monk said he was sure that homosexual activity was common, but it would be seen as a failure of growth and detachment, and would be "smiled upon" much the same way one indulges a child involved in some naughtiness that must pass if he is to be promoted or grow up.

A visitor to a Tibetan monastery received a different response to his inquiry: "Celibacy is an important element in Tibetan Buddhist monasticism. It is taught as a value from the earliest years and is one of the four musts in terms of monastic vows. The four initial vows are: not to steal, not to kill, not to have sexual relations, not to lie. The breaking of any one of these four is cause for immediate expulsion. As far as celibacy is concerned, any violation with another is a serious matter. I asked Kalsang about homosexuality. He said it is not a problem with Tibetans. If any incident between males did happen, it would mean the end of one's monastic life" (Kelly, 1986, p. 37).

These are not far removed from the attitudes held by seminary officials in the mid-1960s. Both expulsion and tolerance were recorded. Limited homosexual experience in a candidate's background could be better tolerated than an experience of heterosexual intercourse; the logic was that if one had experienced coitus, one was not likely to complete the course of studies. As one seminary professor put it: "Once they get a taste of that, it is very tough to keep the discipline"—meaning, of course, celibacy. The shame and guilt of an isolated homosexual encounter, plus the structure of the seminary schedule, were presumed to be positively motivational rather than a deterrent to celibacy.

Here again we see the split between the official teaching (homosexuality is bad) and the practical application (homosexual experience can be tolerated, at least in one's past). Also, the system of secrecy is foreshadowed here. This attitude of pastoral tolerance is in contrast to certain fundamentalist Christian ministries (i.e., the Assembly of God, and the Baptists) where homosexual behavior is an automatic and irreversible disqualification for ministry.

Data from a total of 20,000 men and women led Kinsey and colleagues (1953) to say:

> The data indicate that the factors leading to homosexual behavior are (1) the basic physiologic capacity of every mammal to respond to any sufficient stimulus; (2) the accident which leads an individual into his or her first sexual experience with a person of the same sex; (3) the conditioning effects of such experience; and (4) the indirect but powerful conditioning which the opinions of other persons and the social codes may have on an individual's decision to accept or reject this type of sexual contact. . . . In actuality, sexual contacts between individuals of the same sex are known to occur in practically every species of mammal which has been extensively studied. (pp. 447–448)

HOMOSEXUALITIES AND THE CLERGY

"People who mediate between different levels—between mankind and the gods in the case of priests, or between youth and adulthood in the case of initiates—are often made sexually ambiguous and, therefore, sacred. Indeed, part of their sacred quality results from this sexual ambiguity" (Hoffman, 1985, p. 32).

The problems of understanding the homosexualities are complex and not limited solely to questions of behavior or even orientation. Developmental, situational, and stress factors influence both ideation and behavior—sometimes in the service of growth as well as of regression. The Roman Catholic clergy is an exclusive one-sex institution; that fact alone makes it a productive well of information about sexual functioning and orientation.

A January 30, 1976, article appearing in the *Baltimore Sun* read as follows:

> The Vatican daily, *Osservatore Romano,* expanded yesterday on a papal document dealing with homosexuality, saying such behavior occasionally may not be 'sinful' because of gays' psychological and physical factors.
>
> It urged churchmen to adapt general rules to individuals.
>
> A Vatican document released two weeks ago (*Declaration on Certain Questions Concerning Sexual Ethics* from the Sacred Congregation for the Doctrine of the Faith—S.C.D.F.) reasserted that homosexuality and sexual behavior outside marriage were "sinful" in principle. In a 4,000-word article *Osservatore* urged prudence and understanding in dealing with individuals.
>
> *Osservatore* said homosexuals were suffering from "discrimination which is unjust except for some reservations—unjust because homosexuals often have a richer personality than those who discriminate against them."

One of the authors of the *Declaration,* Father Jan Visser (1976), was quoted in the *London Clergy Review:*

> When one is dealing with people who are so predominantly homosexual that they will be in serious personal and perhaps social trouble unless they attain a steady partnership within their homosexual lives, one can recommend them to seek such a partnership and one accepts this relationship as the best they can do in their present situation.

This relatively liberal and tolerant pastoral attitude is in stark contrast to the October, 1986, *Letter to the Bishops of the Catholic Church on the Pastoral Care of Homosexual Persons* (1986), also from the S.C.D.F. Here, there is little pastoral encouragement for latitude or understanding of circumstances or individual conscience. All homosexual acts are described as "intrinsically disordered," and under no circumstance are to be approved of. Although homosexual orientation in itself is not called sinful, a strong condemnatory stance is taken in these words: "It is a more or less strong tendency ordered toward an intrinsic moral evil; and thus the inclination itself must be seen as an objective disorder." Father Visser's earlier compassion is rejected: "Therefore special concern and pastoral attention should be directed toward those who have this condition, lest they be led to believe that living out this orientation in homosexual activity is a morally acceptable notion. It is not."

This shift in pastoral regulation coincides with an increase in the homosexualities among the clergy reported in our study. Generally, 18 to 22 percent of clergy (estimates established from all sources) are either involved in homosexual relationships, have a conflict about periodic sexual activity, feel compelled toward homosexual involvements, identify themselves as homosexual, or at least have serious questions about their sexual orientation or differentiation. Not all of these men act out any sexual behavior with others. This baseline was validated in groups in the 1960s, 1970s, and 1980s.

Between 1978 and 1985, the reporting of homosexual behaviors increased significantly and the reliable estimates almost doubled to between 38 and 42 percent. Sexually active homosexual clergy tended to give higher estimates of homosexually oriented or active clergy in their areas. This phenomenon may be partly due to projection, but also in part to their greater awareness of and sensitivity to the cues to the secret life-style and to multiple shared sexual contacts—both verbal and physical. The highest estimates given were 75 percent in two dioceses. These figures could not be corroborated or validated by interview material in those areas.

Between 1982 and 1985, several informants—none homosexual in orientation or sexually active—estimated the homosexualities in their districts approached 50 percent. In the same time period, we had enough information from two small separate subgroups to know that 50 percent fit into the category of the homosexualities.

In keeping with the policy of our study, when there was any question, I have always chosen the lower estimate rather than the higher. But the discrepancies in the reporting in the time periods 1960–1977 and 1978–1985 have to be acknowledged. There are undoubtedly aspects of the differences that are real, but some are merely apparent:

1. It is far more acceptable today to speak directly and openly about sexual matters—even the homosexualities—than it was in 1960. Men talk to each other—not merely in the privacy of the confessional or the consulting office—about their sexual fantasies, problems, and behaviors. This makes certain questions seem more prevalent, when they merely were not voiced previously.

2. Proportionately more men left the clerical state to marry than to avail themselves of a homosexual partner. This gives an appearance of an increase of numbers of homosexually oriented active priests, when in fact it is not. It is merely an adjustment in the proportion of sexual orientations and behavior.

3. The feminist movement and the gay liberation movement have made people conscious of the homosocial organization of clerical life (seminary, parish, religious house)—that is, men are central and necessary to the organization, whereas women are adjunctive and dispensable. Also, the hierarchical structuring of the Church is monosexual—that is, power is reserved to one sex. These are realities that have existed for centuries, but we have only recently gained an awareness of them and an ability to name them. This is an important shift, but only makes the reality more apparent.

4. The gay liberation movement between 1970 and the early 1980s encouraged open expression of sexual affection. This movement has gained acceptance among a certain proportion of the clergy. Overt sexual activity has increased in a segment of the clergy, in spite of their profession of celibacy.

5. The open expression of the homosexualities in the clergy community, the greater tolerance of individual behaviors, the freedom of movement that makes various life-styles possible, and the increasing need to recruit more priests which has altered admission standards to seminaries and religious houses have all increased the appeal of the priesthood to some who openly identify themselves as gay.

These last two factors do represent a *real*, not merely an *apparent*, shift, which, if not redirected, will result in a shift in the total clergy population to a point at which the majority could be involved in the homosexualities over the next two decades.

PSYCHOLOGICAL DENIAL OF THE HOMOSOCIAL STRUCTURE

Although the Vatican has spoken more voluminously about heterosexual behavior than about the homosexualities, it is in this latter area that celibates have a great deal to teach about sexual development and homosexual reality. There is, however, an aura of psychological denial that surrounds questions of homosexualities and the clergy. Although the official pronouncements from Rome are consistent in condemning homosexual behavior (cf. S.C.D.F. statements from 1976 and 1986), the pastoral practice has become more tolerant with regard to lay persons. Both directives are addressed essentially to the pastoral care of the laity by bishops and priests. However, since *any* sexual activity for celibates is a violation of the "perfect chastity" ordained by canon law, the shift to stricter pastoral application of Vatican teaching has only theoretically to do with lay persons.

There is no acknowledgment in the papal documents that there is a clerical problem with homosexuality. This is partially attributable to the fact that all sexual activity among celibates tends to exist in the secret forum—the predominant pattern of sexual practice, whether it is heterosexual or homosexual. An average cleric can proceed through seminary training, even 12 years of it, without observing "the slightest sexual impropriety." He may be aware of his own sexual struggles (especially masturbation), and may confide to a priest in the secrecy of confession one or the other of his own transgressions or preoccupations that he may think are unique to him.

In the early 1960s, the pattern of seminary life scheduling was such that every segment of the day was regulated and most activities monitored. Thus, little chance was left for the serious and observant student to get into sexual trouble. The summers and vacation periods when many diocesan seminarians returned to their homes were periods when both heterosexual and homosexual experimentation or at least temptation presented themselves. Some wealthier dioceses had summer villas or camps where attendance reduced the time spent out of a supervised daily regimen.

In 1966, a psychiatric team was invited to consult about a problem with the rector and faculty of a large diocesan seminary. The record of the consultations notes the physical surroundings: "All of the seminarians were dressed in cassocks, several still wearing surplices and carrying birettas. Those we assumed to be subdeacons and deacons proudly carried their breviaries. It was noon and this large group moved in an orderly and quiet fashion down the long arch-lined corridor from the chapel to the refectory."

This regimented and homogeneous procession was noteworthy in its contrast to other college-age groups. The cause of the upset within the halls of this institution in retrospect seems even more amazing now than then. The reason the consultants were called in was the serious request by the students that a Coke machine be available to them in one of the corridors. The rector's response had been, "If we allow them a Coke machine now, soon there will be women in their rooms!"

The logic of the rector's comments made sense and demonstrated his knowledge of the structure of his institution, each part of which was intricately interwoven with and interdependent on the rest. The time schedule for rising and retiring, for meals, prayers, and classes, the regulated recreation and periods of silence were intended to make each boy into a disciplined man, and each man into a celibate. The regulation did in some small way acknowledge the danger of homosexual behavior or attraction, however, as evidenced by the periodic warnings to the students to avoid "particular friendships." The theory was that if one kept the *horarium* (the regular hours of activities) and did not become a friend of just one other man, one would naturally be celibate. This theory was built on the presumption that the world outside the seminary walls—that is, women—constituted the major temptation against celibacy.

As it turns out, even though the introduction of the Coke machine— and the breakdown of the finely tuned seminary schedule—did not generally result in "women in the rooms" of the seminarians, 20 years later that breakdown in the structure did result in a realignment as the rector had predicted—that is, relationships with sexual objects. In 1985, in taking a deposition from a local insider, a lawyer was told: "Everybody in the gay community knows that you can pick up a trick there [the seminary] any time of day or night."

The shift in the social atmosphere of this seminary can be recorded as the history of the Coke machine that evolved into an in-house cocktail lounge. Both lay and clerical observers reported the open flaunting of behavior reminiscent of and consonant with that of a gay bar. It was common for the students to call each other by pet names and girls' names, and both faculty and students reported a knowledge of individual seminarians and groups of them who frequented gay bars in a neighboring city as part of their personal recreational program.

The question becomes whether the homosexual behavior over the two decades among the faculty and students increased, or whether the inner reality just became apparent. The answer is that both occurred. There is no doubt that the reporting of homosexual behavior doubled between 1978 and 1985. However, it must be remembered that the clergy population itself did not remain stable in those years. More significantly, the homosocial organization of the seminary that was designed to keep women at bay and thereby secure celibacy revealed part of its essence as homosexual only under the pressure of the dissolution of its protective facade.

These men who are set aside and given the prestige of being special— whose very existence will in some way bless their families—who have a spiritual perspective, are assured an honored place in society and financial security—who enjoy the economic and productive advantages of not being responsible for child care—who will bless the community by their ceremonial significance, moral instructions, and visionary leadership—are more similar to the American Indian *berdaches* than to students in other professional schools. A look at Williams' *The Spirit and the Flesh* (1986) clarifies the role of the *berdache* in the Indian culture:

They are set apart as a kind of order of priests or teachers . . . [who] devote themselves to the instruction of the young by the narration of legends and moral tales . . . spending the whole time in rehearsing the tribal history in a sing-song monotone to all who choose to listen. (p. 55)

THE MALE MATRIX

In spite of increased sexual behavior, the seminary is not homosexual in the same sense as a gay subculture. However, it *is* homosexual in the real sense that it lacks masculine and feminine definition that can come only from a system wherein men and women are tied together in an interdependent system of reciprocity.

Especially since the Council of Trent, the seminary is really an extension of the hierarchical system of the Church. It participates in its structure and its essence: only male figures have power; the ultimate justification for this power structure is that God is sexed. The Ideal for whom one gives one's life is Jesus Christ, masculine and divine. As minister, one is to see Christ in every person. A virginal mother is provided as an inspiring and loving support. All other women are disregarded as love objects, valued only in subservient roles. Spiritual functions are not complementary (male and female), but infused by one saving Spirit of God, also masculine.

Have seminaries attracted men who are inclined to the homosexualities or does the homosocial organization of the clerical world foster and develop consciousness of and involvement in the homosexualities? About the first question, I have only impressions, since I do not have enough consistent data to make judgments. Fewer than 10 percent of young men who began the minor seminary in high school completed the training to ordination. Recent reports show that a majority of men can tolerate a homo*social* environment without becoming active sexually with each other.

I have scores of reports from priests about affectionate or sexual approaches or responses from teachers or elders during their training. One informant related a situation that occurred while he was in the philosophy phase of his training—equivalent to the last two years of college. There had been a series of student departures in the middle of the term— disruptive enough for the authorities to call in a consultant to ascertain the cause. Some of the students who departed were disgruntled and had muttered and mumbled about a bunch of what they called "queers and fairies" around. It was the repercussion from these mumblings and nonspecific accusations that impelled the investigation. The consultants were told nothing except that an unusually large number of the most promising candidates had left the program precipitously.

After interviewing a number of students and teachers, the consultants saw clearly that the concern of those who left was "sexual," but an aura of denial surrounded any causal explanation within the organization itself. Secrecy prevailed even in the face of consultants whose aid had been solicited and paid for. The authorities were looking for a culprit among the student body who was driving their students away! The informant reported that one of the most popular professors, whom many seminarians sought out as a confessor, had a practice of embracing and even kissing certain penitents, especially after a particularly difficult spiritual unburdening. The confessor's conscious intent was to "show God's love, mercy, and acceptance." The isolation of the confessional itself, the intimacy of the confessional sharing, and the unconscious affective strivings of the men were more than some of the students could tolerate. One single clear picture does not emerge either of those who were threatened by the experience or of those who could deny the sexual implications of it.

The underlying assumptions that reinforce denial of the homosexualities in the priesthood are deeply ingrained in the clerical organization structure. After all, celibacy is taken up in the service of religion—"on account of the kingdom"—and it has to have religious and theological justification for its existence and continuance. Appreciation of the male matrix is central to the theological justification of celibacy (and all the sexual teaching of the Catholic Church). The traditions of male exclusiveness and superiority are deep and central to the Old Testament even if personal celibacy was not.

THE SYSTEM OF SECRECY

The line between affectionate and frankly sexual interaction from priest to seminarian is not always clear. Reports of hugs and kisses in the public and open forum seem to be in the same category as the exuberant embraces after an athletic contest. They are generally easily absorbed psychically and pose no threat to celibate practice if other elements in the man's life are balanced or not sensitized by some particular developmental stage or internal crisis. Hidden, exclusive exchanges that threaten to break the defensive denial have to be preserved and shielded by the system of secrecy, are defended as "acts" rather than "relationships," and form the core of problematic homosexualities in priestly training.

Over 100 priests reported incidents of problematic sexual approaches while each was in the seminary. Some of these proved to be merely a part of the priest's "growing up," while a few had the force of real sexual abuse where the betrayal of the generational barrier was severely traumatic to the subsequent development of the individual.

Each of three elements is essential to the preservation of the problematic system.

First, denial is employed. This literally keeps any sexual problem out of consciousness. "It doesn't exist," or "It is not important." This defensive manner keeps at bay the reality implications of sexual incidents on the development of men who are challenged to work out their sexual identity not only in a homosocial setting, but in one that presumes sexless men.

Second, a system of secrecy is employed to encapsulate any breakthrough either into conscious awareness or behavioral expression. Certainly the system of secrecy is partially in the service of confidentiality, necessary for the individual's growth, but it is also in the service of "not giving scandal," thus sealing institutionally the system into a mode of operation that perpetuates the very problems it is designed to eradicate. Secrecy obliterates accountability. There is no other single element so destructive to sexual responsibility among clergy as the system of secrecy that has both shielded behavior and reinforced denial.

The third element is the definition of any sexual problem as an "act" isolated from its developmental and relationship implications. This element is reinforced by equating incidents with sin. The sin is submitted to the system of secrecy (the sacrament of confession may or may not be involved). It then is "forgiven" or "forgotten," with minimal awareness of the relationship of the behavior to the person and his responsibility. Some priests can continue the same sexual behavior for years, several times each year. If they confess at all at other times, they will do so to their regular confessor, but these special acts are confided to an anonymous priest. The reality of the sexual behavior simply does not break into consciousness because when one system of secrecy threatens self-exposure, a subsystem is added.

A 50-year-old priest was productive and well adapted to his celibate life-style every part of the year, with the exception of two or three periods he spent with a long-time priest friend. They would golf together, share their intellectual and social concerns, have a few good meals, attend some cultural event, and sleep together. Before parting for their respective assignments, they would pray together and return home refreshed. Neither ever confided this sexual activity to anyone else. Nor did either have sex with anyone else. When one of the partners died, the other sank into a deep depression. During the course of his psychotherapy for the depression, the priest for the first time asked himself about the sexual implications of his relationship with his friend. He had had no guilt while his friend lived and neither man had ever identified himself as a homosexual.

Another example of how resistant the system of denial and secrecy is to reality was revealed by the psychiatric treatment of a 45-year-old man whose responsibility was for the initial training period of candidates for his religious order. After his daily lecture, he would gather the men in their recreation room, where they were instructed to form a circle, each man facing the back of the man in front of him, and then to form an "elephant line" around the circle, each man holding onto the penis of the person behind him. This had been explained carefully to the group as an exercise to "desensitize" them and prepare them for their future ministry.

What struck the psychiatrist when the man was referred for treatment was not the psychotic process of the priest himself, who had finally succumbed under prolonged, severe personal pressure, but the fact that the situation had existed for several sessions before any of the candidates reported the behavior to his superiors. Because the priest was a genuinely good and conscientious man with a reputation for liveliness and wisdom within the community, even such a frankly bizarre psychotic episode could be for a time absorbed into the system of secrecy.

DEVELOPMENTAL QUESTIONS AND VARIATIONS

Homosexual identity, then, evolves out of a clustering of self-images which are linked together by the individual's idiosyncratic understanding of what characterized someone as a homosexual. . . . There is no such thing as a single homosexual identity. Rather, its nature may vary from person to person, from situation to situation, and from period to period. (Cass, 1985, p. 105)

The illusion that the homosexualities constitute a simplicity is exposed with the slightest serious examination of the subject area. Even the most commonly named factors in the formation of gender identity—possible prenatal hormonal factors, biological predisposition, intrapsychic dynamics, parental sex assignment, environmental conditioning and imprinting—defy reductionism.

Kinsey et al. (1948) put it this way:

Males do not represent two discrete populations, heterosexual and homosexual. The world is not to be divided into sheep and goats. Not all things are black nor all things white. It is a fundamental of taxonomy that nature rarely deals with discrete categories. Only the human mind invents categories and tries to force facts into separated pigeon-holes. The living world is a continuum in each and every one of its aspects. The sooner we learn this concerning human sexual behavior, the sooner we shall reach a sound understanding of the realities of sex. (p. 639)

In evaluating Richard Ginder's *Sex and Sin in the Catholic Church*, reviewer Fr. John L. Thomas (1975) says:

> Finally [the book] assumes that homosexuality is a condition that pertains to the very essence of the individual and consequently designates a distinctive kind of *being*. But there is no such thing as a homosexual *being*.
>
> What exist are male and female beings who may experience same-sex desires or engage in same-sex activities. But neither desires nor acts constitute *being*. They are dynamic, learnable and unlearnable, mutable in quality and persistence, and always in a state of change and becoming. It is a serious mistake to ignore all the evidence that men and women are amazingly sexually malleable creatures.

The developing body ego is also important in forming sexual identity, which includes a host of sensations, their quality and quantity, and specifically the sensations that come from the genitals. These define the physical and psychic dimensions of the self.

Prenatal and Early Influences

Animal studies have demonstrated that demasculinization of mating behavior is governed by the right hypothalamus. This is accomplished prenatally by using brain implants of steroidal sex hormone (Nordeen & Yahr, 1982). John Money (1984), along with many others, points out the obvious profound implications of this and other prenatal experiments for adult sexual development. "If someone is prenatally programmed so that conformity to either male or female stereotype is difficult, then learning experiences may lead them to develop either a role of trans-sexual gender identity or one of [obligatory] homosexual gender identity" (p. 24).

Bisexuality and the celibate clergy is also a very important area for exploration. I do not have enough data to have any firm impression, yet a career that is dominated exclusively by male power and receives the masculine address "Father," while enjoying the refinement of female nuturance and vestment, makes sense for one who is endowed with both a homosexual and heterosexual psychic disposition. Freud assumed that the human animal is endowed with a bisexual constitution. Although prenatal and biochemical studies are in their infancy, we cannot minimize their import for sexual programming and disposition.

Infantile Sexuality and Identity

Infants experience sexual excitement, boys have erections, and girls lubricate from birth. They discover their own bodies, including their genitals. At about 18 months of age, the toddler usually increases his masturbatory activity. Children commonly experiment in some sort of sexual play with each other and expose themselves. The reactions of parents to all of these activities have lasting effects on the child's body image and sense of self. Excessive parental shame, accompanied by revulsion and rejection, enforces a sense of extreme embarrassment and self-consciousness in the child. A parent's sense of self and each parent's image of his or her partner and of the complementary sex in general are transmitted and cued to the child and incorporated into his or her own sense of self and gender identity—all within the first five years of life. Obviously, gender identity influences sexual object choice later on.

The Negative Oedipal

Freud's oedipal theory is too well known to belabor here. It is generally accepted that the resolution of the early relationships with father and mother has to be accomplished in order to broaden one's social interaction, leave home for school, form a conscience, and generally progress to maturity. For a boy, the impulse to love the mother and reject the father must give way to the need to become like the father and find a love object of his own.

But every child goes through a positive and a negative oedipal. For the boy, the mother becomes the love object, the father the object of fear and rejection. However, the father also alternately becomes the loved one and the mother becomes the feared and rejected one. Both experiences can lead to development or regression.

A Necessary Homosexual Phase of Development

There is another stage of development that is relevant here—the surge of oedipal strivings that recur at the prepubertal stage of development. In fact, at this time occurs an upsurge of all infantile sexuality. In the face of the challenges of approaching adolescence, boys turn to each other and to adult males for masculine reinforcement—often idealized teachers, sports figures, coaches, or ministers. Their fear of women leads them to denigrate anything associated with women or girls as ridiculous or "yucky."

In 1905, Freud recorded this phenomenon in his *Three Essays on Sexuality* (1953a):

> One of the tasks implicit in object-choice is that it should find its way to the opposite sex. This, as we know, is not accomplished without a certain amount of fumbling. Often enough the first impulses after puberty go astray, though without any permanent harm resulting. Dessoir [1894] has justly remarked upon the regularity with which adolescent boys and girls form sentimental friendships with

others of their own sex. No doubt the strongest force working against a permanent inversion of the sexual object is the attraction which the opposing sexual characters exercise upon one another. (p. 229)

Both the negative oedipal and this stage of puberty can broadly be called "homosexual" in that they constitute a turning toward the object of the same sex and away from the complementary sex through devaluation or denigration. It is necessary to pass through these stages on the way to adult heterosexual adjustment. This is why I call it the "necessary homosexual phase of development."

This latter phase is particularly important for understanding celibate practice and development in the Church organization and structure. Much of the homosocial organization of clerical culture is fixed at this stage. It is the culture's natural protection. The power structure of the Roman Catholic hierarchy can be seen psychically only in the context of encapsulating, solidifying, and protecting this stage of development; in this sense, it can rightfully and *only* be called homosexual. If it moves to any other level of psychosexual development, it could not maintain itself in its present structure. These steps of psychosexual development are common to all boys in some variation or other to bring them to adolescence, when psychosexual identity and object choice are usually solidified.

Of the priests in our study, 20 percent expressed concern about their sexual identity or reported homosexual behavior. However, half of that group (eight to 10 percent of the clergy) would tentatively identify themselves as having a homosexual orientation or at least seriously question their orientation or sexual differentiation, basing their judgment on little and oftentime no homosexual experience in their adult life. As a rule, this second group did not act out any sexual behavior with others.

One priest, a psychologist, said that he did not know whether he was homosexual or just underdeveloped. He felt that many of the clergy he dealt with were similarly underdeveloped in their sexual identity. Like many in this category, he tended to be sensitive, productive, and conscientious. Some in this group were highly disciplined and had well developed spiritual lives and consciences. Some of this group supported their celibate resolve and disciplined life-style with psychotherapy. Needless to say, this group with its idealism and sense of sacrifice forms an important core of dedicated religious servants.

Paul Moore Jr. (1976), an Episcopal bishop, can say what many Roman Catholics would be afraid to verbalize, in spite of its applicability to their own clergy: "Historically many of the finest clergy in our church have had this [homosexual] personality structure, but only recently has the social climate made it possible for some to be open about it."

The institutional Church has been instinctively perceptive in soliciting candidates for the celibate priesthood at an early age. Ensuring a better fit into the ecclesiastical organizational and structural reality, it has recruited candidates while they were in their "necessary homosexual phase" of development, when male idealization is high and sexual activity more child-like than adult.

Dozens of examples of informants who reported various sexual behaviors—or only masturbation—could be relegated to this stage of psycho-sexual identity formation. They would not, however, identify themselves as homosexual or have any question about their own identity.

Pseudohomosexuality

An interesting subgroup emerged among the informants. They were marked by the fear that they might be homosexual. They were conscientious and would identify themselves as "gay" if they could only resolve their internal conflict. But they could not. They might have had no adult homosexual experience and were relying on their memories of childhood or adolescent sexual play with friends or family. Some had experimented briefly in adult life with both sexes. They were not caught in preadolescent development. They were more like the college student who fearfully asks, "Am I normal?" They wished to be priests, still held celibacy as an ideal, but wanted to be "like everybody else."

One example is of a 36-year-old priest who was an informant for 11 years of the study demonstrates the point. He joined the seminary at 13 years of age and found the atmosphere supportive and warm, in contrast with his home where his mother had died two years earlier and his father was becoming more and more aggressively and frequently alcoholic. He fit into the seminary program well. The athletic program met his needs and he became first in his year academically. He was sent to Rome for his theological studies, and it was in his first year there that he experienced his first real questioning of celibacy and his vocation. After a brief depressive episode, he regained his enthusiasm for his studies and life.

When he obtained his graduate degree, he was assigned to the Chancery office staff and over the next eight years became increasingly involved in the administrative decisions of the diocese. Then a policy dispute over a financial crisis abruptly ended the personal and political support necessary for him to keep his job. He was suddenly dismissed by the bishop, a man whom he admired and in whom he had found a father figure and, he thought, a genuine friend.

For the first time since he had taken his vow of celibacy 12 years earlier, he began to masturbate. His new assignment in a remote parish afforded him time to "escape"—as he put it—to a large city some distance from his home for several days every few months. It was there that he began to experiment sexually, awkwardly asking bartenders where the "action" was. These adolescent-like ventures brought him both his first heterosexual and his first homosexual contacts (mutual masturbation). His native sensitivity and training combined to make him "Holden Caulfield-like," as he would say of his approach to sexuality. He could not tolerate the pain of his conflicted conscience and curtailed his experimentation after four or five episodes. He did not feel he could leave the priesthood; similarly, he did not feel he could continue to pursue either heterosexual or homosexual liaisons or activity.

After a second parish assignment which brought him professional success, he was reassigned to an administrative position that again recognized and utilized his talents. At 47, he was practicing celibacy, but still feared he was homosexual, although most of his fantasy and ideation was heterosexual.

Some feel we are seeing basic *bisexuality* in this man and in this group. A pertinent observation by Money (1984) is:

> If one travels the manifest path of bisexuality, then, by the age of sexual maturity, one will almost certainly label oneself as homosexual. The explanation of this error is historical. Homosexuality has been considered as a sin on a par with heresy and treason. Sinners are still labeled for their vices and not their virtues. Thus, bisexuals are still singled out, not for their heterosexual but their homosexual actions.

However, I am convinced that Lionel Ovesey (1969) describes more accurately the situation we see frequently among priest celibates:

> The great majority of so-called homosexual anxieties are motivated by strivings for dependency and power. These anxieties ... stem from pseudohomosexual fantasies that are misinterpreted by the patient as being evidences of frank homosexuality. In reality, the sexual component, if present at all, is very much in abeyance. More often it appears to be entirely absent. (p. 31)

The uncertainty of this group persists in the face of little or no sexual experience. Their fear seems to be the salient element. It is difficult to say whether they are truly bisexual and would become oriented to both sexes no matter what the circumstances or environment, or if they are simply a subgroup fostered and held in place by the celibate organization and structure.

Defensive Homosexuality

Many men fear the idea that they may be homosexual. Others are so homophobic that they cannot tolerate the idea of being close to or friendly with a homosexual person. But there are also a few men who can accept more easily the idea of being homosexual than the idea of being heterosexual; they find the latter threatening and fearsome. There are, as Fenichel (1953) pointed out, "reactive forms of homosexuality also, namely, identification with the other sex, for the purpose of denying fear of the other sex" (p. 310).

The first person who helped me understand this entity was referred to my office from the Johns Hopkins sexual clinic in the mid-1960s. I was chosen as his therapist since I was an active priest on the staff of a local psychiatric hospital. This 30-year-old priest was relatively productive in his parish and as a part-time high school teacher. He had had only a few homosexual encounters, with no pattern of sexual activity, and did not feel compelled to act on any of his sexual impulses. He was well regulated in his life-style and talked about his desire to be celibate. He could not see himself being anything but a priest. He was comfortable about identifying himself as a homosexual, in private, but did not openly claim "being gay"—a stance that would have been uncommon and incongruous at that time.

His trouble began when one of the women teachers at the school took a particular liking to him. When she declared her feelings and made a move to hug and kiss him—a response he had no awareness of inviting or provoking—he went into a panic state. He was frightened by the acuteness and vehemence of his physiological responses; they made him think he was going to die. It was a genuine heterosexual panic. His response is hard to explain. But Freud's (1961) observation in 1927 about the threat of castration and various reactions to it is appropriate here:

> Probably no male human being is spared the fright of castration at the sight of a female genital. Why some people become homosexual as a consequence of that impression, while others fend it off by creating a fetish, and the great majority surmount it, we are frankly not able to explain. It is possible that, among all the factors at work, we do not yet know those which are decisive for the rare pathological results. (p. 154)

Over the course of the study I have interviewed a sufficient number of priests with this dynamic to know that it forms one subgroup within the celibate band. This phenomenon does not need sexual activity to keep it in force; it can exist with brief episodic heterosexual experimentation.

In a paradoxical way, defensive homosexuality keeps the priests bound to their vocation and celibacy. They know that sexual activity with another person is a violation of their vow. They cannot rationalize or split sexual behavior from their consciousness; they feel guilt about any sexual activity in which they may become involved. The idea of homosexuality does not interfere with their life choice. As one priest put it, "The Church demands celibacy of homosexuals anyway. If I'm homosexual and I have to be celibate, I might as well be a priest and be useful to the Church." Therefore, to maintain their equilibrium, these men reason that prayer, humility, and reasonable vigilance of their life-style will keep them safe and save their souls. The idea of being heterosexual, with the possibility of a legitimate sexual relationship with an available woman, threatens their equilibrium since it destabilizes their whole life.

Regressive Homosexuality

There are kinds of regressions that serve growth, development, and social stability. Play remains one of these situations throughout life. Men hunt and fish together, have their beer and bowling nights to refresh themselves, and return invigorated to their families and work. This is a homosocial regression generally accepted in society. The men don't do anything overtly homosexual, but their orientation for this brief period is "men only." Only men count, understand each other, and bond together, and they exclude women. Behavior and humor here are very much like the prepubertal boys' clubs.

Freud had a close friend to whom he confided: "The company of the friend, which a special—perhaps feminine—side demands, . . . no one can replace for me. . . ." And "I do not share your contempt for friendship between men, probably because I am to a high degree party to it. In my life, as you well know, woman has never replaced the comrade, the friend." Freud wrote this self-appraisal when his intimacy with Fliess had declined and he could afford to be clear-sighted. In 1910, looking back on the whole fateful attachment, Freud bluntly told several of his closest disciples that his attachment to Fliess had contained a homosexual element. (Gay, 1988, p. 86)

What happens when men live in a homosocial existence? Where do they regress to? After the male bonding and the intense feelings of friendship, they have no wife and family to ease the sexual tension increased by male competition and exchange.

Under tension and pressure, or perhaps under the weight of depressive feelings, some priests regress to a homosexual stage of development—to the prepubertal sexual as well as social exchange. This kind of situation can lead outside the clerical circle into the anonymous and tenuous world of furtive sexual encounters in bars, restrooms, baths, massage parlors, or through hitchhiking. Many priests make a complete psychic split between their sexual behavior and their professional clerical life; this is also true of those who involve themselves in heterosexual behavior. The maturity, judgment, and values lived and expressed in their professional life are entirely abandoned in their "play" world, where they operate almost wholly apart from those values.

A responsible priest of 42 reported that he had periodically over the previous seven years looked for homosexual partners in a series of bars and peep shows, usually after spending time with his good priest friends.

Another priest went twice a month to a hotel for a massage. Although the masseur never touched the priest's genitals, the priest always ejaculated during the massage; it was important to him to have the touch of a male and he therefore avoided the idea of a masseuse.

Although it is most common for the regressive behavior to be split from the clerical life, some priests reported being approached by other priests for sexual contact within the clerical setting—while visiting their parish house, helping with some special function, or on vacation.

Alcohol can be a factor in this regression. Two priest informants took an annual vacation together at a posh beach resort some distance from their homes. Long-time friends, they enjoyed many common interests. At least one night of each vacation, they would drink to the point of drunkenness, come back to their hotel, and masturbate each other—something they did not do at any other time of the year in their association. They never spoke of it with each other. One of the parties in no way considered himself homosexual; the other man felt he had homosexual tendencies, and wanted to be more involved with his friend, but was afraid of being rejected if he broached the subject in any other circumstance.

There can be a compulsive quality to this sexual regression. Men reporting this dimension to their homosexual activity describe the inner force that drives them to seek sexual involvement regardless of (or possibly because of) the danger or possibility of damage. A typical example is the priest who reported returning compulsively to the restroom of a highway interchange, seeking a sexual contact when he knew intellectually that the police were keeping that exact spot under surveillance. Another priest repeatedly picked up sexual partners from among the young men who paraded on the local "meat rack" of his city, in spite of having read in the local newspaper that multiple arrests had been made there for sexual solicitation.

Situational Homosexuality

Doctor Lewis Hill, former medical director of Sheppard and Enoch Pratt Hospital in Towson, Maryland, used to tell his resident psychiatrists, "Man is a loving animal, and he is going to love whatever he is near." The sexual histories of farm boys frequently recorded passing involvements with animals. Sucking calves respond equally to their mother's teat, a finger, or a little boy's penis. This is usually a situational phenomenon dependent on sexual development, social isolation, loneliness, and positive loving feelings for a friend.

What happens to the average man when he is isolated for long periods of time, with restricted affective (social) outlets and limited positive sexual development? One of the early psychological studies NASA commissioned was to project the effect of prolonged periods in space on astronauts. Dependent on one another, one set of factors to be taken into account would be the positive affect that would or could mutually develop when no other loving objects were near. The logical question then became whether homosexual feelings would be aroused eventually after a long time in sexual isolation. Kinsey and colleagues noted the frequency of homosexual contact "among ranchmen, cattlemen, prospectors, lumbermen and farming groups in general" (1948, p. 457). All of these virile and active groups tend to face the perils of nature in a practical way and approach sex the same way.

However, although priests are faced with homosocial isolation for long periods of their life, they are not allowed to accept sex in the same free way some of the above groups might. One would expect and indeed one finds great restraint of sexual activity among clergy as compared to other groups of men. But the homosocial situation does stimulate feelings. Although only 20 percent of clergy report homosexual behavior or identity, 40 percent report having some homosexual ideation at some point during their training or later.

At times the situation rather than the core sexual orientation of the priest dictates his sexual choice. Many reports in this category are similar. A long-time friendship and isolation in a learning or living circumstance lead to a sexual exchange between friends. Subsequent history and development can reveal an essentially heterosexual orientation and choice.

Obligatory Homosexuality

This homosexuality is a state and not necessarily a behavior. It is determined either by genetic endowment or by environmental factors so compelling that the affective orientation toward one's own sex as the primary relational object is irreversible by any known psychological or physical means. In this sense it is determined by nature. More and more biochemical research is examining the influence of hormones on prenatal development (cf. Money, 1984).

In its essence, obligatory homosexuality has nothing to do with behavior or sin. There is nothing immoral about it as a state—a declaration which can, incidentally, be equally valid about heterosexuality. Of course, it is not the norm in any culture, but is a variation of nature and development.

As Nash and Hayes (1965) point out: "Awareness of a homosexual orientation does not imply identity; identity does not imply acceptance; acceptance does not imply commitment" (p. 35). A person who aspires to celibacy will sooner or later have to come to grips with the question of his sexual identity, even in spite of limited or no sexual experience. In fact, sexual activity can be indulged in with less thought than sexual restraint. The latter forces one to rely on inner resources having moorings in one's past and lying deep in one's unconscious, as well as on conscious relatedness to transcendent love objects that can encompass a world.

Since sexual activity of any stripe is forbidden to the celibate, the protected and homosocial environment of the priesthood—where male association dominates, but sexual activity is taboo—can be a haven of peace as well as an arena for productive and loving service. Some who have professed celibacy and practiced it for prolonged periods of time have difficulty identifying themselves as obligatory homosexuals in spite of tremendous inner honesty and self-awareness. Those who do not act out may not be sure of their sexual identity, but use their sexual ambiguity to advantage in the understanding of and ministry to a wide range of persons, both male and female.

There are, of course, those who are aware of their obligatory orientation and have, from time to time, acted on their sexual attractions, either before their pursuit of celibacy or even after taking a vow. Of special concern here is *addictive* sexual behavior. Addiction is troublesome whether the sexual object is male or female, adult or child. In the celibate, oftentimes it violates a trust of office if the priest has gained entrée to and the confidence of another person precisely because he is a priest and presumed celibate (which is often the case in instances of pedophilia). However, even in the cases of anonymous sex, addiction violates self-trust at the deepest level of one's ego. One literally cannot trust oneself.

Sexual addiction among the clergy is described by both the tortured addict and by his victims. The system of secrecy surrounding the sexual behavior only compounds the problem and interferes with breaking the cycle of addiction. The behavior is frequently not dealt with in the confessional. At times, it is part of a cycle of denial; at other times, it is psychically split off from the rest of one's conscious functioning. Even when this behavior is submitted to sacramental confession, it is mostly treated as an "act," separated, or not acknowledged as a pattern of addiction. The "sin" is forgiven, but the state remains.

A priest reported that while he was on temporary assignment at a parish, another priest came to his room, begged to be held, and offered to fellate him. When the first priest declined, the second told him that at times he could not control himself and that he would get into his car and cruise the streets of the city looking for a sexual contact. This behavior had led him to some bizzare and dangerous situations, but he could not stop himself, nor could he predict when the impulse would seize him. This confrontation did eventually lead him to psychiatric treatment and subsequent control of his addiction.

The addictive state is different from compulsive behavior. Addiction can be controlled, but not cured; in the above example, it rested on an obligatory homosexual orientation. A person with an obligatory orientation can go through periods of compulsive behavior which are usually due to stress, depression, or some transient developmental crisis.

A 40-year-old priest who accepted his homosexual orientation and who had had a brief sexual encounter in the army prior to entering the seminary had had no sexual contact with any other person until the death of his mother. He experienced then a resurgence of his sexual drive and sought out sexual contact with a parishioner whom he knew to be actively homosexual. As he described it, there was a real *compulsion* to his behavior. When his mourning for his mother was completed, the compulsion was more easily absorbed and he returned to celibate practice.

The death of a parent, especially a mother, has been reported a number of times as the trigger for either accepting one's obligatory orientation or for acting on the impulses one had either suspected or known.

Committed Homosexuality

There is a group among priests who can be called "committed homosexuals." Their sexual attraction, fantasy, emotional and social preference, and their self-identification or awareness are all congruent. They may or may not practice celibacy, but if they do choose sexual activity, it is invariably homosexual. This can change over time, since all of these factors are interactive and open to development and alteration (cf. Klein, Sepekoff, & Wolf) (1985).

A priest who had contact with our study for 17 years is an example. During part of that time he was assigned to be the superior of the candidates entering his religious community. Situated geographically in an isolated area and separated even from other members of the larger community, he formed strong and affective bonds with his subjects. As the years went on, he developed noticeably feminine characteristics that had not been observed previously, although he was 50 years old.

In his reporting, it became clear that his sexual awareness had been intensified by his isolation and emotional stimulation by successive groups of young men who passed exclusively under his tutelage. He became comfortable with what he termed his "mother" role and demonstrated a tenderness and warmth that had been lacking earlier in his life. This was not unattractive, but it was noticeable to those who had known him in his 30s, when he had given the impression of "macho stoicism." He admitted to one period of sexual crisis that threatened his celibate practice, but was generally observant and developed no pattern of sexual activity with others, although his fantasies were consistently homoerotic.

Among this group are the most observant of religious celibates, self-aware and self-restrained, dedicated to their ideals and selfless in their service to others. They genuinely love humanity and are honest in their internal and external lives. Also represented in this group are part of what Leo Bartemeier called the "silent current within the ministerial mainstream." They are men who have more or less long-term sexual relationships (from three to 20 years) sometimes with other priests, but more commonly with single or married laymen.

The wife of a choir director became concerned when she found out that her husband had had a long-term sexual liaison with their priest. Prior to that point, she had not been aware of her husband's bisexuality or the priest's homosexuality. After her initial shock, she remained tolerant of the friendship and chose not to acknowledge any future sexual activity between the priest and her husband.

Other sexual friendships begin in the seminary and continue through periodic contact over the years. We did not find it common for priests living in the same small groups or parish house to have a close sexual liaison with each other. There may be some, but they were not well represented in our study in the first years. More common is the situation where two men living in a house suspect each other of being an active homosexual, while each knows that he, himself, is. They socialize well and have many friends in common, but they are never sexual with each other and never discuss their activity with the other.

It seems that, most commonly, some distance is necessary for both priests to maintain free of guilt their ministerial work as well as their relationship. In most instances, homosexual activity among these men is ego-syntonic; often they experience no guilt at all. Many never submit their activity to sacramental confession or do so only in the very beginning of their relationship. Their partners tend to be appropriate in terms of age, mutual consent, and circumstance. They do not come to the attention of civil authorities. Because the activity is not disruptive to their work or noticed by the group immediately around them, these men do not command the attention of their superiors.

The sexual activity is completely split off from their lives and religious goals and ideals, or it is rationalized as natural and even necessary for them to carry on their service to the Church. They frame their homosexual activity in much the same mold that they do masturbation—necessary and inconsequential. They do not see it as a threat to their vocations as priests.

One priest in the study did not intend to take the vow of celibacy. He consciously and audibly said "no" when he went through the ceremony preceding his ordination to the subdiaconate. He also wrote clearly in the necessary documents that he did "not" vow celibacy. He has lived a productive ministry over a period of 25 years. As he says, "I wanted to be a priest; I never wanted to marry, but I had no inclination to be celibate either. I decided to live my life as a responsible Christian gentleman. And I have." He has had several sexual friendships over the years, but has never been promiscuous or compulsive in his behavior.

Public exposure is uncommon in this group, but when it happens, it has particular force in disrupting their homosexual pattern or at least their comfort with it. One case in point was Father Charles Coughlin. Dr. Bartemeier was a parishioner of Father Coughlin's in Oak Park, Michigan, from 1928 through the 1940s. Father Coughlin was often a dinner guest in the Bartemeier home, and in the early days, Dr. Bartemeier's wife helped with the household work in the parish house.

One Sunday in 1942, Father Coughlin appeared at the Bartemeier home. He was in a panic state, afraid that his phone and rectory were tapped. He told Dr. Bartemeier that two FBI agents had confronted him after Mass and told him that he would be exposed as a homosexual unless he discontinued his broadcasts and writings against the war. Coughlin's biographer (Marcus, 1973) recounts the incident only as a seizure of documents: "In the late winter of 1942, FBI men, accompanied by moving vans, pulled up to the Shrine of the Little Flower and served the priest with papers authorizing the seizure of the records of all the corporations he had established, along with his personal papers" (p. 208).

It was not the threat of a legal fight that curtailed Coughlin's activity. Ronald Modras (1989) is correct when he elucidates Coughlin's repeated difficulty with religious obedience (p. 222). The threat of sexual exposure, coupled with the timely support of Archbishop Mooney (who disapproved, however, of Coughlin's political activity), gave Father Coughlin the structure but also the pretense of religious obedience to reorder his energies.

Marcus (1973) notes " . . . that questions had arisen about Father Coughlin's sexual morality. It had been rumored that Father Coughlin, as a young priest, was caught in the act of pederasty with another priest, who was defrocked. But the author could locate only an Anti-Defamation League memo entitled *Structure of Charles E. Coughlin's Organization* to attest to this. The memo was neither signed nor dated and is in itself inadequate evidence" (pp. 221–222).

Threat of homosexual exposure and even homosexual entrapment were used by the Nazis to elicit cooperation from some priests in Germany in the 1930s and in Italy during the early 1940s (personal communications).

Questions about the sexuality of New York's Cardinal Spellman have been widely rumored. When I was a student in Rome in 1956, I heard repeated stories about Spellman's days as a student when he systematically courted monsignors who were secretaries to various Vatican officials. It was alleged he would have afternoon tea in their apartments, and would gain entrée into ever more powerful Vatican circles as a result of these trusting friendships. One priest informant gave a firsthand account of his homosexual activity with Spellman, giving credence to the investigative reporting John Cooney (1984) did for his biography of Spellman.

> For years rumors abounded about Cardinal Spellman being a homosexual. As a result, many felt—and continue to feel—that Spellman the public moralist may well have been a contradiction of the man of the flesh. Numerous priests and others interviewed took his homosexuality for granted. Others within the Church and outside have steadfastly dismissed such claims. Finally, to make an absolute statement about Spellman's sexual activities is to invite an irresolvable debate and to deflect attention from his words and deeds. (p. 109)

The therapist who took the aforementioned interviews said he had no doubt that the priest was a reliable informant of his own sexual behavior and had no reason to implicate anyone else falsely, let alone a superior of a Church to which he remained devoted.

The important issue is not any particular churchman's sexual practice, but the fact that sexual activity that is proscribed by Church teaching and disavowed by professors of celibacy can take place at the highest levels of power. There is nothing I could or would say that would detract from all the good Spellman did in his lifetime. There is also nothing I could omit that will alter the truth about sexual practice among celibates, within the hierarchy or not. Cardinal O'Connor, current Archbishop of New York, is quoted in the October 13, 1986, issue of *Time* magazine: "The Holy Father demands that the Truth, whole and unvarnished, be made available to everyone."

The sexual practice of clergy is part of the important teaching truth of the Catholic Church. Example is, as much as or even more than the word, a powerful and effective means of teaching. Celibacy in religious tradition is meant, among other goals, to be a lived example of how to regulate the sexual drive in accord with Christian principles. In the estimation of the general public, celibacy is not merely a legal state of nonmarriage, but a way of life sexually in conformity with Church teaching. It is legitimate to ask not only what is the Church's teaching on sexuality, but how it is lived by Church teachers and leaders.

Especially in the area of the homosexualities, the time has passed when simple denunciation and condemnation can be satisfactory. Labeling homosexuality a "sin" or "essentially disordered" does not aid understanding or responsible sexual practice or abstinence.

In my study, I have made no distinction between priests with or without hierarchical power. But one cannot assume that station and power are keys to sexual orthodoxy in practice or in consistency between word and behavior. In fact, there is ample evidence from a wide range of religious denominations that clergymen can publicly and vehemently denounce sin in others while quietly and repeatedly indulging in it themselves.

Some people assume that *guilt* is an adequate controller or regulator of behavior. It is not. The ego with the sum total of its integrative capacities and object relatedness is the agency that determines behavior (cf. Hartmann, 1958). Too little attention is paid to this reality in the education and formation of men who would be celibate.

There is another subgroup among the committed homosexual population of priests. They are the growing (noticeably, since 1978) and articulate group who are generally allied with gay rights and who talk freely—in surroundings they deem to be nonjudgmental—about their sympathies and even behaviors. They find their support more outside the clergy population than within it. But they also are vocal and often seek out clergy for understanding and support. This group does not split their behavior and their celibate ideal. They frankly disregard celibacy as not possible or desirable for them. The dichotomy in their lives is more between who knows and who does not know their orientation or sexual preference. One wag among this group said that "the unmentionable vice, now mentioned, can't keep its mouth shut."

There are also priests championing the cause of justice for homosexuals who believe in celibacy where appropriate. Father John J. McNeill (1976) has been a pioneer in facing squarely some of the theological questions posed by the reality of the homosexualities and the Church's teaching. Some of this group have declared their own obligatory homosexual orientation, and others are heterosexual or nondisclosed. There is the beginning of a movement via groups of priests in every section of the country who have banded together to support each other in their celibate strivings. Closely guarded as to membership, they operate on many of the same principles as Alcoholics Anonymous.

Latent Homosexuality

A simple definition of latent homosexuality describes it as a true homosexual impulse which can be conscious but is mostly unconscious, and is not overtly acted out. It is beyond the scope or intent of this study to speculate on the number of priests who do not admit a homosexual orientation or who genuinely may not be aware that unresolved homosexual tendencies may indeed motivate their lives and behaviors.

In 1910, Freud made some creative observations about Leonardo da Vinci and his psychic structure, especially the preservation of his relationship with, and fidelity to, his mother (1953a, p. 78). In 1928, he observed of Dostoevsky that "a strong innate bisexual disposition becomes one of the preconditions or reinforcements of neurosis . . . and it shows itself in a viable form (as latent homosexuality) in the important part played by male friendships in his life, in his strangely tender attitude toward rivals in love and in his remarkable understanding of situations which are explicable only by repressed homosexuality. . . ." (1961b, p. 184).

Those observations about Dostoevsky's novels could be applied to the lives of a number of priests, just as Leonardo's homosexual attachment to his mother has echoes in the lives of many priests. In his *Three Essays on Sexuality,* Freud does not equivocate. He says: "The unconscious mental life of all neurotics (without exception) shows inverted impulses, fixation of their libido upon persons of their own sex" (1953a, p. 166). Likewise, in his *General Theory of Neurosis* of 1917 he says:

> I have said that neurotic symptoms are substitutes for sexual satisfaction . . . , and I indicated to you that the confirmation of this assertion by the analysis of symptoms would come up against a number of difficulties. For it can only be justified if under "sexual satisfaction" we include the satisfaction of what are called perverse sexual needs, since an interpretation of symptoms of that kind is forced upon us with surprising frequency. The claim made by homosexuals or inverts to being exceptions collapses at once when we learn that homosexual impulses are invariably discovered in every single neurotic, and that a fair number of symptoms give expression to this latent inversion. Those who call themselves homosexuals are only conscious and manifest inverts, whose number is nothing compared to that of the *latent* homosexuals. (1963, pp. 307–308)

If, according to Freud in 1911, some type of latent homosexuality is generally related to all neurosis, it is the specific and core dynamic conflict of male paranoia: "the wishful phantasy of *loving a man*" (1958, p. 62). I have not observed, nor have I ever heard it said that there is any greater number of paranoids among the celibate clergy than among any other segment of the male population (cf. Meissner, 1978). But anyone who has worked extensively with priests in intensive psychotherapy will resonate with Freud's case history of 1918, *An Infantile Neurosis* (1961a, pp. 7–122). Because the roots of a celibate vocation are of necessity laid down early in life, they will be entangled with early developmental conflicts and relationships. Neurosis is not the inevitable outcome of celibate striving, but there is not one recorded life of a celibate saint that does not include deep self-searching, dark nights of self-awareness, and agonizing struggles for maturity and integrity.

In limiting my observations to the conscious behaviors and orientations of priests, I am not sidestepping the question of latent homosexuality. It is simply unmeasurable. I do think that the spiritual life that many priests pursue faithfully leads them to an intense self-awareness that eventually makes them conscious of their inner psychic dynamic and this in turn gives them the direction and strength to transcend neurosis, whatever its origin, and transform their energies into the loving service of their fellow human beings.

ALCOHOLISM

There was a time when psychological theory branded severe alcoholism as having an underlying latent homosexual personality structure. I don't know of anyone who holds that oversimplification today. Invariably, however, alcohol addiction interferes with sexual function. Many priests report that they come to grips with their sexual behavior and identity once they dealt with their alcohol addiction. Over 50 percent of clergy who are treated for severe alcohol problems have some homosexual concerns. This is an important minority to consider when one approaches the sexual practices of clergy.

In 1966 I decided not to factor alcohol into sexual behavior because it was too potent a variable. At the time, Dr. Robert J. McAllister had completed the first studies on alcoholism in the clergy at the hospital where I was studying (McAllister & VanderVeldt, 1962, 1965, 1986). There is an undetermined number of clergy who have a homosexual problem that is masked by severe alcoholism. I make no estimates from the data I have.

There is an Irish bias that was reported several times: "If Father is an alcoholic, he must be celibate." A drinking problem is seen as a proof of fidelity to the celibate vow and lack of sexual involvement. The studies correlating alcohol use and sexual practice among the clergy are yet to be done. There are a number of treatment facilities for clergy with substance abuse problems which could make a significant contribution to understanding behavior from this vantage.

ACQUIRED IMMUNE DEFICIENCY SYNDROME

By the end of 1985, no priest in the study population had been diagnosed as having AIDS. Two men had test negative for HIV antibodies. Since that time, we have inquired about or contacted several of our informants. Three men have died of AIDS and one has tested positive for HIV antibodies. There is no way for me to engage a great number of the original informants and I can make no estimate of percentages of priests with AIDS. It is obvious, however, that clergy are emerging as a clear subgroup of the homosexual population that has so far contracted AIDS (Leishman, 1987):

> Health officials who deal with sexually transmitted diseases have long been aware of the frequency of homosexuality among Catholic priests. In the words of one such official, "I and most of the public-health directors I've talked to about this subject estimate that in our communities at least a third of Catholic priests under forty-five are homosexuals, and most are sexually active. They almost always engage in anonymous encounters, the highest-risk sex of all, and when they want help they don't come to clinics. I've met with priests in some of the strangest places." (p. 48)

The Task Force on Gay/Lesbian Issues in San Francisco estimates the homosexual population among the Roman Catholic clergy also at 30 percent.

One of the men in the study population who died was actively homosexual. By preference he sought out black sexual partners and contracted syphilis once and anal gonorrhea twice. Although he considered himself homosexual from his early years, he was not active sexually while at the seminary. Two years after his ordination and the subsequent death of his father, he felt himself overwhelmed with loneliness and isolation in his remote rural parish. He planned vacations to large urban areas specifically to experience sex and found himself feeling accepted and safe with black men. His period of promiscuity lasted about three years.

With a reassignment to a more socially stimulating environment, he altered his sexual behavior and found a group of more compatible priests with whom he did not engage in sexual activity, even though he felt they were homosexual. I was unable to be available to this informant when or after he received the diagnosis of his illness. Upon inquiry, I merely received a report that he had died of AIDS.

AIDS is a worldwide problem with medical dimensions like cancer and social dimensions like world hunger. That it is a disease that can be sexually transmitted thrusts it into the moral arena. The danger here is that glib moralizing and homespun theologies—that AIDS is God's curse for sexual sin, for example—or intolerable fears are fostered in the name of religion. Worse still is the real possibility that AIDS will be used as an excuse to hate. Father Joseph Gallagher (1987) has written the most perceptive and balanced Christian response to AIDS to date. The temptation for others to abandon an AIDS patient or for the patient to isolate himself in shame or fear should not be indulged. Likewise, cover-ups in the name of avoiding scandal only increase the problems and encourage irresponsibility rather than accountability.

ESTIMATES OF HOMOSEXUAL BEHAVIORS AMONG CELIBATES

Homosexual Orientation

Homosexual behavior does not coincide exactly with homosexual orientation, as Figure 6.1 illustrates. Approximately half of the priests who would describe themselves as homosexual either practice celibacy or have consolidated or achieved celibacy, and generally have done so in the same proportion as priests who have a heterosexual orientation. The discrepancy between the 10 percent homosexual behavior and the 8 percent orientation is accounted for by the relatively large proportion of situational and transitional behaviors in the unique homosocial atmosphere and monosexual structure of the clerical subculture of men who later accurately identify themselves and function consistently as heterosexual. Also, there is a small percent of men who involve themselves in heterosexual activity who later identify themselves as homosexually oriented.

A percentage of homosexually oriented men do not involve themselves with others, but nonetheless act out sexual fantasy, often via pornography and compulsive masturbation.

Of the 6 percent of priests involved with children or minors, 4 percent have a homosexual orientation (see Chapter 8), but 3 percent are so clearly dominated by their paraphilias that the sexual orientation is secondary. We hold to the estimate that approximately 20 percent of all clergy have some homosexual orientation.

Approximately 10 percent of clergy (10 to 12 percent projected from all sources) involve themselves in homosexual activity.

Four percent of clergy have a stable homosexual orientation and have more or less consistent relationships with little or no guilt attached to their behavior (or at least not sufficient motivation to change it), or sequential relationships that have a stability within the clerical system. Because some of these behaviors involve relationships of genuine friendship and loyalty, without interfering with the practice of their ministry, they are experienced as an aid to the priests' lives and vocations. Some priests

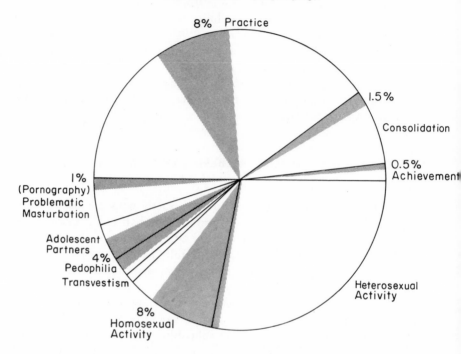

Celibate/Sexual Adjustment
Homosexual Orientation

8% Practice

1.5%

Consolidation

0.5%
Achievement

1%
(Pornography)
Problematic
Masturbation

Adolescent
Partners
4%
Pedophilia
Transvestism

Heterosexual
Activity

8%
Homosexual
Activity

FIGURE 6:1. Celibate/Sexual Adjustment—Homosexual Orientation

in this category do experience guilt about the sexual acts and periodical-lyuse sacramental confession or some means of spiritual direction. However, the pattern and the behaviors remain relatively stable over long periods of time.

Also within this homosexual group are those who are vocal and radically active and feel it is a part of their vocation to be honest about their sexual orientation and that sexual activity is their God-given right. There is a kind of consistency about their internal logic—they refuse to lead a double life. This small but growing faction is truly part of the gay subculture that has been incorporated into clerical life. I did not see evidence of it in any numbers prior to 1978. Some of this group are supported by those who have frankly mental or emotional problems.

Three percent of the clergy act out homosexual behavior as part of a basic mental health problem. Character disorders that involve poor impulse control, excessive narcissism, and depressions are prominent. These disorders are frequently complicated by the use of alcohol. Some of this group come to the attention of Church authorities or the legal system because of their choice of inappropriate partners or circumstances for their sexual activity.

A clear example of a character disorder involving homosexual activity was the priest who maintained an active and prominent life in ecclesiastical circles. When he died suddenly at the age 45 of a heart attack, the priest assigned to put his affairs in order found in the deceased priest's apartment a cache of illegal drugs, including cocaine, a library of pornographic homosexual videotapes, and the names, addresses, and descriptions of the sexual preferences of dozens of young men. In the proceedings following his death, it became obvious that he was as well known in the homosexual bar subculture as he was in Church circles.

A chronically depressed priest, who was conscientious about his clerical duties, periodically sought anonymous and even dangerous sexual contacts. His bouts with sexual acting out coincided with his episodic depressions. The event that brought him to treatment was a frightening encounter in which he submitted for the first time to anal intercourse. On his way back to his place of residence at 2:00 a.m. after a particularly hard period of demanding pastoral work, he entered an all-night pornographic movie house. In the washroom, he propositioned a man; the violence of his own sexual response, including the ripping off of clothing, motivated him to seek psychiatric treatment. In curing his depression, he was also able to choose to modify his sexual behavior. The tragedy is that many of these people do not seek treatment for their depression, but self-medicate with sex.

The narcissistic personality whose relations remain superficial and self-centered can also abuse people sexually. A priest who was a university professor had an inflated view of himself and his importance built on a base of genuine popularity. He repeatedly selected a male student as a companion and cultivated him as a protégé. Once established in the bond, he became envious and demanding, and felt he was entitled to whatever he requested or needed, including homosexual exchanges. These seemingly intimate relationships were interchangeable with anyone who could better fill the priest's needs. The academic process made the temporariness of these relationships seem logical. In truth, the setting was a convenient cover for a superficial and self-serving life-style. The priest was brought to the attention of superiors by a student who had taken the offer of friendship as more permanent and genuine.

As in all segments of society, the borderline personality is finding his way into the ranks of the clergy. Their tendency to overidealize (and/or devalue) can be mistaken for religious enthusiasm. Their basic rage can for a time find worthy objects in the enemies of religion—sin and degradation, abortion, contraception, and even homosexuality. Their tendency to projective identification can be read as good assimilation into the religious mind-set. Even their proficiency at splitting—setting different members of a group against each other—can be rewarded if they succeed in allying themselves with the winning party. It is the poor impulse control and the unhealed scars of separation that lead them to homosexual activity. Their impulsiveness and infantile rage sometimes bring them to the attention of authorities.

Still another 3 percent of the clergy behave homosexually either episodically due to situational stress or as a part of a transitional adjustment reaction. These men have severe or at least moderate guilt feelings in association with their homosexual activities. They really try to control their behavior, mostly because they see it as a contradiction to the ideal they have set for themselves. They are the first to call themselves hypocritical. Men in this group tend to seek spiritual or professional help with what they clearly define as a problem. Some of this group come to the attention of authorities more because of their naivete and ineptness at seeking a sexual outlet, making them easy victims of traps and hustlers that more experienced and cunning people would avoid. This group does not tend to be impulsive, but some can experience periodic transitory compulsions. In a few of this group, there seems to be an unconscious desire to "get caught" or to atone for their "sins" by exposure.

The growth challenge facing this group is apparent if one reflects briefly on the high lifelong ideal that these men have set for themselves; on the young age at which they began their pursuit; and finally on the unique environment that supports them socially and economically while at the same time making them dependent. Sexual maturity is an elusive goal, not necessarily achieved under the most favorable of circumstances. But sexuality is relentless, a natural hankering fueled by a persistent normal curiosity. Although many succeed, sexuality is a difficult drive to fight or to conquer even with highly refined methods of sublimation. This is as true for the man of homosexual orientation as it is for the heterosexually oriented.

Within this group of priests are some who may or may not be obligatory homosexuals. They literally do not have enough sexual experience to resolve for themselves their sexual identity. Their fantasy life is ambiguous, as are their friendships. Their limited sexual play may be heterosexual as well as homosexual. They generally are capable of solid relationships and seek supportive friendships. Their immaturity may lead them to occasional homosexual behavior within the context of these friendships; that behavior in turn is confusing and ego-dystonic as well as spiritually unsettling for them.

Frequently, a sexually more experienced layman or sometimes a fellow priest who is committed to homosexuality picks up the unconscious sexual cues of the person and acts as his teacher or leader. This liaison may exist for a brief time or may be returned to several times over a longer period. This group often seeks assistance to grow through these experiences and will resist establishing a pattern of homosexual behavior.

One middle-aged priest remained persistently immature sexually in spite of heroic efforts to grow. He sought out young men who were hustlers or call boys, using his real name and address. However, he tried seriously to alter this pattern when one of the young men threatened to blackmail him.

Other priests get caught in the trap of making an appointment to "meet" someone they originally encountered in a bar. Later, at the arranged time and place, the priest will find not simply his intended sexual companion, but one or two others who proceed to threaten, assault, or rob him.

Some of these priests get caught in police traps at highway rest stops or other centers of anonymous homosexual exchange. They differ from the other priests who may or may not get caught in that they do not have an established pattern of homosexual behavior or fixed sexual identity, and because the behavior occurs under some transitional stress or growth phase.

Many in this group are pained by their sense of loneliness, and they desire most of all simply "to be held," or to "have someone accept me as I am." They naively look for a relationship among these contacts and some have even recounted a humorous result when they assumed friendship where there had actually been only a "business" deal. One priest's gifts and sentiments sent the hustler into a panic—he thought he was being set up by a government agent.

This group differs from those others who lack a capacity for relationship, or from those so deeply scarred by separation and early deprivation that every relationship futilely seeks the primitive mother.

Some in the group find in a transient homosexual experience the psychic push to complete their adolescent development, thereby resulting in a decent adult heterosexual orientation. They literally complete their adolescent development in their 30s or even early 40s.

The whole range of homosexualities is difficult for both individual clergy and the Church as a whole to deal with. When homosexual orientation and behavior are approached from an exclusively moralistic point of view (good/bad, or thou shalt/thou shalt not), and when the objective reality is ignored (it exists, people *do* behave thus-and-so) in the face of the subjective experience of some of its members and ministers (this is how I feel, think, have lived), the result is that the influence and power the Church has to teach, to heal, and to save persons from unnecessary suffering and injustice are curtailed. In short, to be a moral leader, the Church must deal with the realities of nature (cf. Sipe, 1987, pp. 86ff).

There have always been a substantial number of homosexually oriented men who have given themselves to the service of the Church. There are, of course, some who do not either practice or even care to achieve celibacy. But some find the practice of celibacy possible within the homosocial organization of the Church. Some men achieve celibacy in the monosexual hierarchical structure just as some heterosexually or bisexually oriented men do. A growing number of homosexually oriented and/or sexual active men among the clergy are gaining a voice and visibility—often unwanted—that must be reckoned with.

Chapter 7

THE MASTURBATIONS ___

"Nec tangere nec tangi" ("Neither touch nor be touched")
—Giulio di Medici (1478–1543)

Masturbation is the most common and frequently used sexual behavior of celibates. At times, masturbation is employed with other sexual elements—voyeurism, transvestism, homosexual fantasy, for example—but sometimes it is the celibate's exclusive and relatively infrequent sexual expression.

The first survey of masturbatory activity among celibates that I am aware of was undertaken in the 1950s by a priest from the archdiocese of St. Paul while he was a seminarian.

In 1969, Dr. William Masters told me about a survey of 200 celibates, the results of which revealed that 198 of them reported having masturbated at least once during the previous year. Of the other two, Dr. Masters said, "I don't think they understood the question!"

In the late 1970s, Father Michael Peterson, M.D., a priest of the archdiocese of Washington, D.C., conducted several informal surveys of his own (unpublished work) and spoke of masturbation as an often practiced and usual activity among seminarians and young clergy.

Our study was not a survey, and our findings are more conservative than those described by Dr. Masters. We estimate that 80 percent of clergy masturbate at least occasionally (numbers based on information from clergy sources only).

In the 1980s, many knowledgeable people, including priests, react to these statistics with a "So what?" Unfortunately, the question is not that simple for the serious student of celibacy. Regardless of whether masturbation is frequent or infrequent among celibates, three pressing issues must be faced: first, the assertions that masturbation is essentially pathological; second, the additional assertions that even if it is not pathological—or at least not among the very young—it is an immature activity;

and third, the moral stance that masturbation is sinful because it violates nature and is a selfish activity.

Even those who consider masturbation a basically normal activity, necessary for healthy development, are aware that it can also be a sign of distress or illness. Freud originally considered it "dangerous," and saw it as the cause of neurasthenia—a neurosis marked by anxiety and lassitude.

In clarifying Freud's stance, Fenichel (1954) called masturbation a *normal* symptom, "if it appears at certain intervals and only if sexual acts with objects [persons] are not possible. It is a *pathological* symptom under other circumstances, and has to be understood as a sign that the capacity for satisfaction is disturbed. . . . And really, there is no mental disorder in which the symptom of pathological masturbation does not occur. The psychic value [significance] of pathological masturbation can be manifold" (p. 86). Fenichel's comments are why I refer to the masturbations in the plural—the plural challenges us to distinguish this sexual behavior beyond categories of normal vs. pathological, mature vs. immature, and virtue vs. sin.

NATURE

Masturbation is normal and universal among healthy infants. In fact, it is necessary for development. It would be ridiculous to hold that an infant should discover every other appendage and orifice of his body and selectively neglect his genitals. As early as 1949, Spitz and Wolf wrote about autoerotic activity in one's first year of life. The results of their observations are especially significant since they established the link between good object relationships and the manifestations of spontaneous genital play at that age. They determined that "a certain level of development is a prerequisite for the appearance of genital play" (p. 91), and "the closer the mother-child relation . . . the more infants we find manifesting genital play" (p. 97). By contrast, a parallel link exists between the deprivation of good mothering and the lack of an infant's development. In Spitz and Wolf's words:

> [Autoerotic activities] are absent when object relations are absent; when object relations are so constantly contradictory that object formation is made impossible, rocking results. When object relations change in an intermittent manner fecal play results. When object relations are "normal," genital play results. (p. 119)

Although this infantile autoerotic activity is not masturbation as such, it is both a precursor of and necessary to the establishment of a sense of self. Kleeman (1965) says of self-stimulation in the first year of life, "a slightly different way to conceptualize this is that good maternal-infant relations facilitate the discharge of maturational drive representatives in the form of self-stimulation" (p. 241).

From their observations of infants and children, Margaret Mahler and her colleagues (1975) noted that it is probably of developmental significance that a boy becomes acutely aware of his ability to have erections at the same time that he develops mastery over his own body by walking. A little boy's exploration of his own penis during the first part of his second year seems at first "an experience of unmitigated pleasure. At the beginning of the third year, the masturbation takes on the quality of 'checking their penises for reassurance' " (p. 105).

In normal boys, this self-stimulation leads naturally toward clear masturbatory activity that is appropriate in their third to fifth years. Their self-discovery is progressive and complicated, and is intricately intertwined with their entire developmental process (Kleeman, 1966). It is sufficient for our purpose here to remember that a boy's discovery of his penis has profound implications for the formation of his male identity—i.e., establishment of his core gender identity—and of healthy object relationships throughout his life. It is not a process that ends in infancy. Freud (1953) refers to the "second phase of infantile masturbation" around the fourth year that may continue until suppressed or "without interruption" until puberty (p. 189).

It is generally conceded that adolescence is the ordinary stage of development for the consolidation of one's sexual identity and solidification of career goals. Aristotle believed that adolescent masturbation fostered maturity and manhood (DeMause, 1974, p. 46). It is also common knowledge that masturbation is a well nigh universal activity of normal adolescence. Few authorities in the 1980s would hold otherwise. It is normal at this age, Fenichel (1954) says, because

> [i]t is the best discharge children can have. If tendencies to masturbate do not appear at all, one can be sure that a serious repression has already taken place. And if the educators prohibit masturbation altogether, they push the child into a state of tension, which is difficult to sustain. And more than that: They create in the child's mind the idea that sexual matters are bad and dangerous. They motivate the child to repress his instincts in the future, and in this way cause neuroses and deformations of the child's personality. (p. 85)

PATHOLOGY

As Fenichel has pointed out in the preceding material, masturbation itself is natural; however, it does involve some psychic compromise, and can become pathological. In his words:

But it is true that there are certain other dangers attendant on masturbation—dangers which are mostly less important than the dangers that are caused by prohibition of masturbation—and they become actual only in pathological forms of masturbation.

(1) The tolerance to sustain tensions is diminished if one is accustomed to flee from every tension immediately into masturbation.

(2) If reality is customarily replaced by fantasy, this circumstance causes or increases introversion; that means a general withdrawal from reality. Masturbation may furthermore fixate the disturbance of the subject's relations to his objects, of which it (the masturbation) was a consequence.

(3) If masturbation is performed with a bad conscience and anxiety which prevent its running its natural course, this circumstance has, as I have described, pathological consequences.

But we also said before that a normal person must be able to masturbate if circumstances prevent sexual object relations. . . . (p. 86)

In most priests, masturbation is not a symptom of severe pathology, although clearly some reports can only be understood as involving some degree of it. There are priests for whom masturbation forms the only available means of sexual tension reduction. They only know how to work; play has not been part of their developmental skills, and they are quite restricted in their social interactions.

Another group are those priests who deny themselves nothing in the way of creature comforts and have little capacity to delay gratification in any area of their lives. Sometimes these are men who went through a period of severe self-denial while they were in training and are now compensating themselves for it.

Although a number of priests reported experiencing sexual excitement while they were hearing confessions, few were overwhelmed by the situation. Some reported having a spontaneous emission and one other reported masturbating. In the latter case, the behavior was clearly part of a pathological process.

The stringent religious restrictions on masturbation—because it is deemed "unnatural"—can lead to all sorts of compromises in order to control it. In his account of his own seminary days, Paul Hendrickson (1983) tells of the devout confessor who tried to help his students fight their tendency to masturbate by having them hold a crucifix in one hand while stroking their own genitals with the other—but only to the point of erection. By avoiding ejaculation, the student could evidence his choice between pleasure and his religious goals. The confessor also offered to let the students practice in his presence during confession.

Severe anxiety regarding masturbation can be overwhelming to some priests. They masturbate only under great internal pressure, with no fantasy and with little pleasure. Afterwards they feel compelled to go to confession immediately, sometimes at great disruption to their lives and reality. One priest reported endangering his life by a late night search for another priest to forgive his sin. This kind of tension is pathological. But, as one priest pointed out, he had been taught that a single act of masturbation was sufficient for him to lose his soul and destroy all the good he had ever done. When understood in that context, his anxiety became a logical response to the doctrine he had learned and obsessively obeyed.

The striving to avoid "transgressing nature" leads some priests to elaborate ways of circumventing the law. The rationalization here is that if the priest does not touch his genitals, the masturbation doesn't count; or if he goes only so far in his touching, and then the ejaculation happens "by accident," he is not responsible. Therefore, behaviors such as anal manipulation or scratching, genital pressure on a pillow, encouraging a partial erection, or simply allowing the water pressure of a shower or whirlpool to do the arousing make the experience acceptable. In these instances, the pathology derives not from the masturbation, but from the anxiety that leads to such convoluted reasoning.

In some cases, the anxiety can become so severe that all means of masturbation are impossible for the individual. Such inhibition at the expense of all psychic functioning is neither healthy nor reasonable. One disturbed priest who was hospitalized had been asked prior to his ordination when he confessed masturbating, "When are you going to grow up?" At that moment he vowed never to masturbate again. Over the next 10 years, an increasing amount of his psychic energy was consumed while he kept his vow and in the process lost his effectiveness in every other area of his professional life. During his hospitalization, he had to break his vow to regain his sanity and initiate a satisfying ministry.

Anxiety can cause such a preoccupation with control that extreme means can either be fantasized or actually carried out. Besides fasting, severe asceticism and self-flagellation were a part of some priests' training prior to the mid-1960s. Very few of these priests continue their practices, but some record wishing that they could be castrated to relieve their sexual tension. One celibate did in fact castrate himself, precipitating his admission to a psychiatric hospital.

Although the dynamic is not identical, there is an ancient precedent for castration in the service of celibacy, epitomized by the third century theologian Origen. And of course Abelard (1079–1142) was involuntarily castrated when Héloise's guardian uncle thought Abelard had abandoned her after her secret marriage. The castration was in reprisal for sexually educating the canon's niece, Héloise, and for violating with her the celibacy his position of university professor demanded. The mutilation succeeded in curtailing his sexual activity and ardor, but did little to cool Héloise's devotion for him. She spent the rest of her life in a convent.

Masturbation that usually occurs in conjunction with pathological patterns of sexual behavior is discussed in Chapter 9 on Sexual Compromise. In these instances, the masturbation is secondary to the pathology, and should be distinguished from the behaviors described above.

MATURITY AND IMMATURITY

There are those who say that masturbation is, at best, an immature sexual activity, even if it is not a sign of illness. After talking with hundreds of priests, I have come to the conclusion that sometimes masturbation can be an expression of maturity at any age (and at times may be virtuous).

How does masturbation contribute to maturity? Play and transitional objects hold a very important place in helping a child deal with reality. Fenichel (1954) describes the situation as follows:

> Playing is a very important matter for children. The child learns to master reality by playing. What the child has experienced passively in the past or what he expects to happen in the future—that he plays actively. The tensions which have been set by passive experiences or which will be set by future events, could overwhelm him. But he himself sets this kind of tension in a smaller degree by playing, so that he can learn to master it gradually. Playing is the way to learn to master the world. By playing, a child learns to bear increasing self-imposed tension, becoming thereby slowly able to withstand reality.
>
> But in my opinion it is to a certain degree correct to say that masturbation *is* sexual play. By masturbating the child learns to master sexual tension. One often hears the idea that the masturbating child loses self-control and becomes a victim of his bad instincts. I consider that the opposite is true: if masturbation has no pathological character (as described above) it is a means by which the child learns to control his sexual instincts. (p. 87)

One must be careful to distinguish between masturbation and other forms of play since, as Winnicott (1971) points out, the latter has a quality of sublimation that masturbation lacks (p. 45).

There are priests who can accept that masturbation among infants is an appropriate activity to help the infants traverse the distance between their subjective world and external reality. Without our belaboring psychoanalytic theory, these priests are instinctively aware of psychic equivalents to the beloved mother and her breast. There is, in addition, the need for transitional phenomena to help children cope with reality and the need to endure the pain of giving up things to gain autonomy and build bridges between the subjective and objective so as ultimately to operate as total human beings (Winnicott, 1965, pp. 143–145). They can relate to Fenichel's description of play and mastery.

Likewise, many priests can acknowledge that masturbatory activity in adolescence is age-appropriate behavior. As Winnicott (1965) says, the adolescent "is essentially an isolate. It is from a position of isolation that a beginning is made which may result in relationships between individuals, and eventually in socialization" (p. 81). This isolation colors all the sexual experience of the young adolescent boy who, in his psychic cocoon, does not know what kind of butterfly he will become—homosexual, heterosexual, or frankly narcissistic. Masturbation is part of practicing for an adult sexual life and relationship—future reality tested in fantasy. Or, as Winnicott (1965) points out, "urgent masturbatory activity may be at this stage a repeated getting rid of sex, rather than a form of sex experience" (p. 81). Masturbation can simply reduce sexual tension enough for the adolescent to avoid, at least temporarily, having to make an internal sexual commitment.

Many priests can empathize deeply with this phase of the maturational process and can exist for years in this state of suspended sexuality. Their training period sanctifies their isolation without establishing a truly spiritual relationship or solidifying their sexual identities. Here the adolescent process may be played out, but in super slow motion, one action frame at a time. Other priests delay the whole identity process until after they complete seminary studies, when at some future time the floodwaters of adolescence break through their dam of repression.

A priest had been a successful and affable student during his seminary years, during which time he had not masturbated, and had no memory of *ever* having done so. For the first three years after his ordination, he was relatively happy in his ministry, part of which involved hearing the confessions of adolescents. He became curious about masturbation, as so many of the young people he truly admired confessed to frequent masturbation. The priest began to read books on sex—something he had avoided doing previously. He had, in fact, never allowed himself to think about the whole area of sexuality. At 28 years of age, this man discovered masturbation. Along with it he was inundated by all the thoughts and questions he had been sidestepping. He became profoundly confused, feeling deceived by the teachers and the system he had taken most literally. By confronting his previous denial, avoidance, and overdependence, he began to reevaluate his values in light of his newfound sexuality.

The phenomenon is relatively common whereby repression and denial sustain a man in unchallenged celibacy for long periods of time. It is especially so among some men of superior intellect who do well in their studies and are socially successful within the clerical system, where they are popular with both their peers and superiors. A number of this group of informants registered anger (also adolescent-like) at the system they believed had betrayed them. Having kept all the rules of that system, the men were surprised and felt sabotaged by the force of their internal fire. These were men who thought they had come to terms with their celibacy because of their intellectual success. As one man said, "I have never before had a problem I could not reason my way through." Body, emotion, and sex were foreign territories where all the acquired skills now apparently had no meaning or effectiveness. The coin of the realm had changed.

Some priests react strongly against their own sexual impulses and, at least temporarily, reinforce their resolve by reaction formation. They rebuke with disdain adolescents who confide their masturbations. Harking back to the pathological model, others threaten the penitents with impending insanity if they continue their self-stimulation. Both of these kinds of responses have decreased over the last two decades. Now more priests seem to be in tune with the 1970s cartoon that showed two boys sitting on a curb, their feet planted firmly in the gutter, with one boy saying to the other, "The way I understand it, you go crazy if you don't do it."

The line between pathology and immaturity seems to blur when it comes to masturbation. I remember hearing a retreat master who had long experience both as a hospital chaplain and as a minister to the inner city indigent. He drew a picture of the futility and deprivation of masturbating by telling how these poor souls masturbated even on their death beds while he was administering the last sacraments. The equation in his mind was clear: Masturbation equals deprivation equals death, much in the same way the medical manuals of the 1800s equated all manner of ailment with "the habit," as it was called. Today, what most health care workers who attend the dying know is that masturbation near the time of death is a common phenomenon without moral implication. The process of dying is regressive. Union with the Ultimate Other also entails a trip backward to the womb; thus, the life circle is complete (Schnaper, 1984, p. 282).

Clergy were not alone in relegating masturbation to the category of the pathological and immature. Entrance to the Naval Academy as recently as 1947 was barred to anyone who, on medical examination, was found to masturbate habitually. (How this is discovered on physical examination remains unclear to me.) The Boy Scout Manual dropped its negative reference to masturbation only in 1973.

Quite simply, under ordinary circumstances, masturbation can be a natural, healthy, unselfish act, expected at any stage of life as a part of the process of growth, self-definition and normal sexual function. The basic question really is how well a person relates to reality and to other people.

The place of masturbation in the life of a person vowed to celibacy becomes a serious conundrum. Does it violate celibacy? Two bishops from the same diocese, required to give legal disposition in 1988, were asked that very question. One answered, "Yes," and the other "No." The correct response is probably "Yes *and* no." This issue is addressed in the section below on vice and virtue, and in Chapter 12 on the process of celibacy.

Like the informant described earlier, there are priests who claim to have never masturbated. A small portion of these men are victims of Kallmann's syndrome (see Chapter 10). Others are psychically so defended that they deny or rationalize away their sexual reality; they are not consciously lying. Still others simply *do* lie. Winnicott (1971) warns that anyone who investigates these areas must be prepared for lies. We have records of several priests who indeed had not masturbated either in their adolescence or adult lives. Their profoundly restricted personalities rather than their lack of masturbation led them into a period of severe mental illness. During their treatment, their ability to masturbate was seen as a sign of maturation and growth.

My estimate is that at any one time, 20 percent of priests are involved in masturbatory patterns that are manifestations of sexual immaturity. These patterns may include the pathological elements Fenichel (1954) mentioned: overuse as an exclusive tension-reducing maneuver; isolation and preference of sexual fantasy over sexual reality; and extreme forms of anxiety. This group of 20 percent does not include other forms of sexual behavior that concomitantly involve masturbation.

NOCTURNAL EMISSIONS

In order for the Church's teaching on sex and masturbation to be credible, involuntary or nocturnal emissions would have to provide, in Kinsey's (Kinsey et al., 1948) words, "sufficient release to keep an individual physically and mentally balanced." I have no evidence that this is the case. I hope our study will provide the impetus for further refinement of data from observant celibates to determine the place of nocturnal emissions in the life course of a male. American priests are the logical group to provide this service to science and to clarify a moral position the Church adamantly defends without sufficient cause. Kinsey continues:

It would . . . be of exceeding scientific importance to have histories from a sufficient sample of highly restrained individuals, particularly of those who are celibate. Without such data it is, of course, impossible to depend upon general statements which have been made on this point, especially when they come from persons who are interested in defending moral or social philosophies (Kinsey et al., 1948, p. 528)

As with all sexuality issues, the moral questions surrounding nocturnal emissions are not new. I remember long discussions about them from my own seminary days. A question such as: "If one awakes during the ejaculation and enjoys the experience, does it become mortally sinful?" has a long tradition, at least back to the fourth century. Athanasius treated nocturnal emissions as natural, and did not consider them sinful (Quasten, 1960, p. 328). Timothy of Alexandria, an early writer whose opinions on this matter were confirmed by the Sixth and Seventh Ecumenical Councils, wrote:

> A layman who has suffered a nocturnal emission should not have Communion if this is because he has himself by deliberate choice entertained desire for a woman in his heart. But if the reason is temptation from the demon, then he may have Communion. (Russell, 1981, p. 135)

A third-century cleric, Dionysius of Alexandria, held the same modulated view. Two important elements of moral development were manifest in the controversy: (1) the growing responsibility of the self-awareness that good and evil did not reside outside the self; and (2) the question of what is natural regarding sexual functioning.

Very early in Christian tradition, the celibate ideal was outlined by the Thebaid—monks living in the Egyptian desert. A discourse dating from the fourth century elaborates on the subject, and sets the standard:

1. Take care that no one who has pondered on the image of a woman during the night dare to approach the sacred Mysteries, in case any of you has had a dream while entertaining such an image.
2. For seminal emissions do take place unconsciously without the stimulus of imagined forms, occurring not from deliberate choice but involuntarily. They arise naturally and flow forth from an excess of matter. They are therefore not to be classed as sinful. But imaginings are the result of deliberate choice and are a sign of an evil disposition.
3. Now a monk . . . must even transcend the law of nature and must certainly not fall into the slightest pollution of the flesh. On the contrary, he must mortify the flesh and not allow an excess of seminal fluid to accumulate. We should therefore try to keep the fluid

depleted by the prolongation of fasting. Otherwise, it arouses our sensual appetites.

4. A monk must have nothing whatever to do with the sensual appetites. Otherwise how would he differ from men living in the world? We often see laymen abstaining from pleasures for the sake of their health or for some other rational motive. How much more should the monk take care of the health of his soul and his mind and his spirit. (Russell, 1981, p. xx)

There has been no clear path to the refinement of these issues in moral thought. A ninth-century cleric, John the Faster, still embraced the most severe position by forbidding communion to any man who had experienced a nocturnal emission, regardless of his subjective involvement.

Modern moralists tend to dismiss the controversy as inconsequential and thereby miss a core problem in the theory of sexuality: What is natural? And by missing this question, they avoid the related issue of the place of sexual pleasure in human development.

FASTING

Most ascetic authors draw lines of connection between fasting and controlling the sexual instinct. There is evidence that the link existed early in Christian tradition. It is very probable that some of the early monks were anorectic and experienced the elation and euphoria of negative nitrogen balance, ketosis, or whatever chemical reaction alters mood in severe diet restriction. Recently, Rudolph Bell (1985) explored the effects of anorexia in certain of the female saints.

In talking about his own celibate struggle, Gandhi (1980) said that if a man can control his appetite for food, he can control all of his instincts:

But if it [celibacy] was a matter of ever-increasing joy, let no one believe that it was an easy thing for me. Even when I am past fifty-six years, I realize how hard a thing it is. Every day I realize more and more that it is like walking on the sword's edge, and I see every moment the necessity for eternal vigilance.

Control of the palate is the first essential in the observation of the vow. I found that complete control of the palate made the observance very easy, and so I now pursued my dietetic experiments not merely from the vegetarian's but also from the *brahmachari's* [celibate's] point of view. (p. 30)

Mental attitude as well as dietary restriction is essential to celibate practice. Gandhi (1980) sounds much like the early desert Fathers in his admonitions:

Fasting can help to curb animal passion, only if it is undertaken with a view to self-restraint. Some of my friends have actually found their animal passion and palate stimulated as an after-effect of fasts. That is to say, fasting is futile unless it is accompanied by an incessant longing for self-restraint.

Fasting and similar discipline is, therefore, one of the means to the end of self-restraint, but it is not all, and if physical fasting is not accompanied by mental fasting, it is bound to end in hypocrisy and disaster. (p. 40)

Several of our informant priests who had been P.O.W.'s during the Second World War reported that they experienced either a significant diminution or complete cessation of their sex drive during their capture; their nocturnal emissions also stopped. They associated the change with their severely restricted diet. As one priest said, "During that time, I never once dreamt about sex; I always dreamt about food."

From the 1940s through the 1960s, priests in training were cautioned against the use of certain spices or condiments that might increase their sexual desire or cause nocturnal emissions. There were many jokes and rumors (with some justification in certain places) to the effect that saltpeter was added to the seminarians' food to reduce their sexual response. By and large, fasting was regulated by Church law, during Advent, Lent, and the vigils of certain feasts, for example.

Some religious orders still maintain stricter dietary regimens among their brothers than those followed by other celibates. We have no evidence that the stricter diet causes an appreciable difference in the rate of nocturnal emissions or masturbation in the two groups.

SPONTANEOUS EMISSIONS

There are individuals whose powers of imagination are sufficient to cause an emission. One celibate, 35 years old at the time of his interview with us, could sit in a library, his room, or even Church, and without any physical movement at all could bring on an ejaculation. He struggled greatly with the morality of this ability and worried about his "normality." He would not allow himself to "masturbate" and never consciously used his hand to stimulate himself. He had joined the seminary as a teenager and his first conscious memory of sexual excitement was awakening from a nocturnal emission. Over the years he developed an ingenious compromise by recreating dreams in his imagination. Visual stimulation—especially movies—were invariably sexually arousing to him. He had no other sexual contact or activity.

Another priest frequently experienced an erection while he was saying Mass and, on occasion, had a spontaneous ejaculation at the time of consecration or communion. He was greatly troubled by the experience, since his conscious thoughts were on his prayer and on the ritual he was performing. He was a deeply spiritual man, not neurotic in any observable areas of his functioning. He used confession and incorporated into his spiritual goals occasional masturbation to reduce his excess sexual tension, thereby forestalling the surprise of a spontaneous emission at Mass. At 45 years of age, he felt he knew himself and the rhythm of his life sufficiently to modulate his masturbation in the service of his vocation.

A third priest, in his late 20s, would fall asleep at his desk while preparing a sermon and would awaken at times during an emission. He wondered if he had some unconscious participation in the occurrence and felt he really did not have his sexuality "sorted out yet."

Some extremely conscientious priests who have not allowed themselves to masturbate while awake have reported that they do so "in their sleep." They are half-aware of their involuntary movements on awakening, or they wake up shortly after the experience. All of the men reporting this behavior masturbated prior to their vow of celibacy and have reproduced in sleep the body movements that were part of their previous conscious pattern. The degree of responsibility each feels varies from extreme guilt, as though the act had happened in full consciousness, to guiltlessness— the latter men feeling that the experience is as involuntary as any other nocturnal emission.

There is an ancient story from the Fathers of the desert in which a convert awakens "with his hand full of white fluid." The elder explains to the troubled neophyte that it is merely an unconscious remnant of his former way of life, and does not invalidate his spiritual resolve to follow a life of celibacy. Obviously, there is a continuity in the elements of the struggle to live without directly sought sexual pleasure, just as there is a persistence to the functioning of nature. Culture has only limited influence on the interaction between ideal and nature.

VICE AND VIRTUE

The claim that masturbation can be virtuous may seem revolutionary at first blush, but only the unthoughtful and inexperienced clinician or moralist can hold that it is intrinsically evil and inherently sinful. Sin certainly was the unquestionable epithet attached to "self-abuse," "pollution," or simply "playing with oneself"—mortal sins all. The direst of punishments of Hell would befall one who succumbed to this temptation. A classic pamphlet commonly distributed at the spiritual retreats of teenage boys in the 1950s was entitled *The Greatest Sin.*

One might think that such a title would be reserved for a booklet on genocide, or perhaps rape, or some other injustice against women. Racial injustice or any number of sins against humanity might also come to mind. But no. This was a treatise on masturbation. Generations of young boys became alternately terrified and disappointed that at 13 years of age they had already committed their greatest sin. One can almost admire those brave souls who defied such hyperbole, as well as those who used the book as a how-to manual. A few teenagers had the good sense to recognize the distortion—those who had already developed a firm direction in their sense of self-mastery.

This tradition of crowning masturbation as the king of sins is not recent. It is connected with the attempt to establish power via guilt. In writing about the 14th century, Barbara Tuchman (1978) says of Jean Gerson, the most eminent French theologian of the time:

> He advised confessors to arouse a sense of guilt in children with regard to their sexual habits so that they might recognize the need for penitence. Masturbation, even without ejaculation, was a sin that "takes away a child's virginity even more than if at the same age he had gone with a woman." The absence of a sense of guilt about it in children was a situation that must be changed. They must not hear coarse conversation or be allowed to kiss and fondle each other nor sleep in the same bed with the opposite sex, nor with adults even of the same sex. Gerson had six sisters, all of whom chose to remain unmarried in holy virginity. Some powerful family influence was surely at work here from which this strong personality emerged. (pp. 479–480)

The idea that masturbation is "worse" than fornication is based on the incomplete theology of sexuality that views procreation as the only end of all sexual acts. One can see the lengths to which this lacuna in moral teaching spread in a Vatican document (Rhinelander, 1987) entitled *Instruction on Respect for Human Life in Its Origin and on the Dignity of Procreation: Replies to Certain Questions of the Day.* The collection of sperm through masturbation, even for medically valid reasons, is forbidden. The document states:

> Artifical insemination as a substitute for the conjugal act is prohibited by reason of the voluntarily achieved dissociation of the two meanings of the conjugal act. Masturbation, through which the sperm is normally obtained, is another sign of this dissociation; even

when it is done for the purpose of procreation, the act remains deprived of its unitive meaning: "It lacks the sexual relationship called for by the moral order, namely the relationship which realizes the full sense of mutual self-giving and human procreation in the context of true love."

When translated into practical interaction between two Christian people, those solemn words form a procrustean bed of very undignified make-up indeed. The only Vatican-approved method of collecting sperm for any medical reason is one devised by Dr. Ricardo Asch, as described in the *New York Times* on March 21, 1987:

> The method . . . requires the use of a special condom with a small perforation, which captures some sperm for processing in a laboratory by fertility specialists, while also allowing some of the sperm to escape, a necessary requirement of any treatment program facing the moral judgment of the Church. (Rhinelander, 1987, p. B10)

Anyone who sees this method as more dignified than masturbation as a means of collecting sperm has no realization of what the conjugal act means to most married couples. To have sexual relations in order to pump sperm into a perforated condom for a laboratory sample is both a gross disregard of the woman and an insensitivity to her dignity. She is simply used to obey the letter of a misguided law.

However, seeing masturbation as anything but grave sin poses a major threat to the entire structure of the Church's teaching on sexuality. If all sex outside conjugal intercourse for the purpose of procreation is deemed sinful, a simple, clear-cut, act-oriented morality remains stable and unequivocal. Moral control is secure. Any variation—especially one grounded in male physiology, where ejaculation is physically determinable, if only by nocturnal emission—poses a serious threat to traditional order and control.

Confronting the problem of the masturbations is crucial for the understanding of celibacy. If it is intrinsically evil, as the Church teaches, and yet is so commonly practiced across the broad spectrum of age, celibacy becomes a sham.

GUILT

Priests demonstrate a broad spectrum of guilt reactions to their masturbatory activity—a spectrum that has no demonstrable relationship to the act or its circumstance. One priest may be completely devoid of any guilt feeling after some very pathological masturbatory activity (i.e., in the confessional or in connection with child pornography), while another may have deep pangs of conscience over an isolated incident occurring in complete privacy and in the face of great stress.

For priests, masturbation has always been a subject for jokes among themselves, as well as a fascinating subject of moral exploration, as in "how to deal with it as a confessional matter" when directing others. However, only rarely do priests talk openly in groups about either their own masturbation or any of their other sexual practices. This certainly was true in the 1960s. The climate has changed somewhat over the last two decades. The following is an example from the early 1980s.

About 10 priests were gathered at a parish house for cocktails before dinner. One of the youngest priests announced, "I always like to masturbate when I shower; it makes me feel clean inside and out." The statement caused a conspicuous silence and a series of awkward coughs. For the average priest, masturbation is still a subject that holds guilt and embarrassment, if not confusion and anxiety.

Masturbation can be a concomitant of any of the heterosexual or homosexual orientations or involvements. However, for many priests, it is also their main or possibly *only* sexual activity for extended periods of time.

One group of priests reports no guilt at all about masturbation. These are decent, hardworking men, but would probably not be described as "holy" by anyone. They have very little in the way of a spiritual life, and not a great deal of religious motivation. They are natural men, who can be quite dedicated to the work of the Church, although their strength lies in administration rather than in morality. Masturbation seems to keep them from other forms of sexual involvement, at least for long periods of their lives. Celibacy as a spiritual ideal has little meaning for them and does not become a great obstacle to their daily functioning.

Probably unmatched in any other single group of men is the capability for denial of sexuality found among some priests. As described earlier, on initial inquiry some priests will claim either that they have never masturbated or at least are not doing so currently. Only on subsequent interview will they reveal that there is indeed a history of some form of self-stimulation. Yet these men are not lying. They exhibit a profound denial about their sexual activity because of the anxiety and passivity surrounding it. As they proceed through their interviews and the pattern of their tension and its reduction emerges, they describe behavior that somehow "doesn't count" as masturbation—activity before they go to sleep, when they awaken, while they are bathing or going to the bathroom. The masturbation is subsumed under the other natural function, sometimes not even involving the use of their hands. Since it is not incorporated into their consciousness and usually "just happens" without conscious sexual fantasy, it cannot be incorporated into their spiritual striving. Their resultant guilt feelings are transferred to another activity, i.e., to the way they handle money, or to a general feeling of unworthiness.

Another group of priests, who would be judged as hypocrites if their activity were known, masturbate regularly, using sexual fantasy, while expounding adamantly to others about the sinful nature of both masturbation and other indulged sexual thoughts. Some of these priests quite simply are hypocritical, putting on others a moral burden they themselves refuse to carry. However, the contradiction among other priests is not that easy to categorize. Some have completely split the masturbation off from the rest of their lives, ideals, and values. Although they retain consciousness of both sides of their behavior, there is no link in their awareness between the two. Literally, their own sexual activity is never internally subjected to the critical faculties that are very available for their direction of and preaching to others. Somerset Maugham's preacher in "Rain" is a dramatic portrayal of this dynamic in the extreme. These latter priests' guilt becomes almost overwhelming for them if and when the split is exposed.

Rationalization is another defense some priests use to deal with their own masturbation. They retain a conviction that the activity is sinful and at the same time excuse it as nonsinful. An example is that of one priest who said that if he were able to resist a temptation to masturbate for four days, then there was no sin if he gave in to it after that time. Certainly more humane than other solutions to sexual tensions and somewhat useful in practicing delayed gratification, this reconciliation by merely delaying an act that one teaches to be "intrinsically evil" or "unnatural" is impossible to understand logically.

Some priests do not feel or teach that masturbation is intrinsically evil, nor do they intellectually consider it unnatural. They treat others' concerns about it reasonably and gently. Among this group are those who feel "it is just not a big deal," or that it is "of minor moral consequence." Many priests arrive at this conclusion after years of dealing with the spiritual and moral concerns of lay persons. They are able to treat themselves with the same gentleness and reason they apply to their parishioners.

Other priests use quite a different standard with themselves. They feel tremendously guilty and make every effort to go to confession before they say Mass, or as soon as possible after masturbation. Many times these men have no awareness of sexual fantasy when they masturbate; it is the unconscious sexual fantasy behind their act that causes their feeling of guilt. Therefore, simple reassurance does little to relieve these men of their anxiety, but sometimes spiritual maturity either with or without psychotherapeutic intervention can bring the unconscious fantasy into awareness where it can be subjected to ego integration.

There are those priests who incorporate masturbation into their life of service, who are more or less conscious of their sexual fantasies, and have freely chosen to masturbate as a necessary or good activity in their lives. These men are divided into two distinct subgroups:

The first group is made up of those priests who see masturbation as the lesser of two evils. Although they desire to be celibate, they have found their fantasy life (or in their words, their desires and temptations) too strong, or they have previously wandered into sexual behaviors they found too ego-alien or incompatible with their lives as priests. For them, masturbation has become a substitute for homosexual or heterosexual activity.

Either on their own or sometimes with the understanding guidance of a confessor or psychotherapist, they have learned that masturbation is more ego-syntonic than an involvement with a student, a stranger, or a child would be. By at least isolating their sexual problems in a way that frees some psychic energy, these priests are able to expand the nonconflicted areas of their egos and allow the possibility of more sublimation in their professional lives.

The other subgroup is that of priests who are accepting of both nature and spirit in themselves and in others. They have profound spiritual lives, are conscientious about daily prayer, and submit their every instinct and motivation to introspection and self-analysis. They tend to be mature, solid in self-identity, and with a record of healthy and appropriate relationships with both men and women. They are capable of a high degree of sublimation. Not satisfied with a choice between the lesser of two evils, and with no essential paraphilia or perversion for which to compensate, these men strive for integration in their lives. For them masturbation takes on the quality of virtue. It is consciously willed and directed by love.

One priest reported that his first insight into the real nature of masturbation and its possibility as a virtue, not just the vice he had been taught it was, occurred while he was serving as an Air Force chaplain at a base during the U-2 flights. The temporary duty demanded that the men be separated from their wives—some by half a continent—and have no contact with them or their families by telephone or letter. However, the men were permitted some night or weekend passes to a town near the base. A few of the men confided to the chaplain that they masturbated while thinking of their wives as a protection against the temptation to seek out prostitutes or local girls in the town.

Another priest, in his late 30s, entered treatment for depression. He was creative in his ministry, mature in his interpersonal relationships, and dedicated to his vocation and to his parishioners. A priest friend had recently "burned out," and had had to take a leave of absence from his work. Our priest had many of the same pressures and challenges as his friend, and was afraid he was going to burn out too. However, after a course of brief therapy, his depressed feelings lifted and his enthusiasm and confidence returned.

He thought he was ready to leave treatment, but confided that there was something he "did not want to talk about." Naturally, the therapist encouraged him to pursue that area, and the priest revealed that he masturbated occasionally and was unsure as to what to do about it. This was a most observant, flexible priest, who prayed quite naturally before most of his daily activities—eating, sleeping, studying, and preaching. He had not thought about praying before masturbating. He began to do so at the therapist's suggestion, and once he had incorporated his masturbation into his life goals, he experienced a degree of relief and integration he had never known previously. He said it was only after praying about his masturbation that he really understood the ritual words he uttered daily at the moment of consecration in the Mass, "This is my Body,", It was for him a profound religious experience to identify himself with Christ as a real human being.

Later he reported that his ministry had never before been so energized or meaningful. Subsequently, he shared his insights with some of his priest friends, none of whom had thought of their own masturbating in these terms. They also were encouraged by and grateful for his thoughts.

A like-minded priest who was not in psychotherapy shared the following entry from his journal:

> *I've been thinking a lot about spirit and flesh and the relationship that results. I know that theology splits the two in order to understand them.*
>
> *Now there is the "whole-person." We are spirit-life, or spirit and flesh. What are we going to attach ourselves to? We must be in the flesh but dedicated to the spirit. This has implications for my personal life, Christian living, religious life, and social justice.*
>
> *As for me, I've had to let go of friendships, material things, . . . But the more of those things I let go of, the more I'm left to deal with myself. My supports and crutches are gone, and it's just me and the Lord. . . .*
>
> *Let me share some reflections on celibacy.*
>
> *Masturbation is to celibacy what intercourse is to marriage. Intercourse in marriage celebrates love, forgiveness, dependency, fun, togetherness, unity, and commitment of my body to another. Masturbation in celibacy is not so much a celebration but a reminder of my humanness, dependency on God, humility, loneliness, and commitment of my body to God—it's not as real and concrete as another*

person, but then I believe it can support my growth in dependency on God. It's kind of like saying, "God, it's only me in here, but it's all I have and it's for you and your people."

Intercourse is personal, private, and shared with another person I deeply love and respect. It takes a while for a relationship to move to that point. Masturbation is personal, private, and shared only with myself as a celibate as many things are because that's the life-style. It brings me face to face with myself. Do I still want it? Is it still worth it?

If intercourse in marriage is the ideal sexual response, then masturbation in celibacy is less than ideal—but it is the sexual response celibates are committed to by virtue of their celibate vow. Masturbation as a sexual response may not last all of a celibate's life, just like intercourse may not last all of a married person's life. If celibacy is to have masturbation as a sexual response, then we cannot talk of celibacy by default—there is no such thing.

Letting go is the ideal for the celibate so that the total giving of self to God may be accomplished through my humanity. That God is the desired goal is unquestionable and whatever stands in the way of that can be accepted or seen as understandably necessary for a while but only until I don't need it as a crutch or until I can depend totally on God who gives me life—brings me to life—calls me to life.

I have to live the life of the spirit if I am to understand the struggle of letting go and what it means. . . . I must understand the struggle first and enter into it myself before I can tell people that it's life-giving and good for them. . . .

New life comes when letting go happens. In the end I even pray to let go of masturbation—see it as a necessary part of human growth and development, but not as a desired goal of the celibate life-style— the movement toward.

The majority of American priests in their pastoral practices do not treat masturbation as a gravely serious sin. Although many of them feel guilt about their own masturbation or are confused about it, most priests do masturbate, at least occasionally. This activity can be a symptom of pathology and immaturity, but can also be a sign of maturation and even virtue. It is clear that some priests must masturbate if they are to achieve celibacy. That is a paradox that was most difficult for me to define, but the evidence presented by the lives of many priests makes that conclusion inevitable.

Chapter 8

PRIESTS AND CHILDREN

"He remembered the smell of incense in the churches of his boyhood, the candles and the laciness and the self-esteem, the immense demands made from the altar steps by men who didn't know the meaning of sacrifice."
—Graham Greene,
The Power and the Glory

Priests who have traditionally cared for the education and protection of children can appeal to the example of Christ himself who "took a little child, stood him in their midst, and putting his arms around him, said to them, 'Whoever welcomes a child such as this for my sake welcomes me. And whoever welcomes me welcomes, not me, but him who sent me' " (Mark 9:36–37).

For many priests, work with children and young people is a healthy and productive sublimation of their generative drive. They do perform a parental function and become "father" in the best spiritual sense. St. John Chrysostom (c. 397) exhorted his flock—priests and laity—to tend to the care of children: "The corruption of the world remains unchecked because nobody guards his children, nobody speaks to them of chastity, of despising riches and glory, of the commandments of God" (Quasten, 1960, p. 465).

Monastic and cathedral schools had centuries of experience in teaching young boys prior to the existence of medieval universities. The Jesuits, founded in the 16th century, took upon themselves the mission of educating the masses, not merely the sons of the noblemen and the wealthy. As a result, they had a profound influence on the popular attitudes toward children. "They stressed the notion of childhood innocence, shame, modesty, the need to protect children from adult secrets, and the schooling of children. The Jesuits began to view children with compassion, urged speaking decently to them, ended the practice of children and adults sleeping together and prohibited familiarity between servants and children" (Schetky & Green, 1988, p. 25).

159

This attitude of concern and sexual protection and restraint is generally expected from the clergy. Parents who entrust their children—both boys and girls—to the care of priests as teachers, coaches, club directors, counselors, pastors, or advocates presume that the contact will foster good character and growth in self-confidence, moral values, and spiritual and mental health generally. Those priests who use their positions of trust and the presumption of moral integrity as a cover for their sexual activity with children present a formidable challenge to celibacy.

There is general disdain for those who take sexual advantage of children. Intuitively, the known child molester is treated as immature and inadequate. Matthew's gospel account of Christ's tenderness with children is a unique and prophetic stance in early literature, and adds an admonition against giving scandal to the young: "Anyone who is an obstacle to bring down one of these little ones who have faith in me would be better drowned in the depths of the sea with a great millstone around his neck" (Matt. 18:5–7). There is no equivocation about the inappropriateness of an adult's sexual activity with a child.

WHAT PEDOPHILIA IS AND WHAT IT IS NOT

The *Diagnostic and Statistical Manual of Mental Disorders (Third Edition, Revised)* (American Psychiatric Association, 1987) says of pedophilia that its essential feature is "recurrent, intense, sexual urges and sexually arousing fantasies, of at least six months' duration, involving sexual activity with a prepubescent child. The person has acted on these urges, or is markedly distressed by them. The age of the child is generally 13 or younger. The age of the person is arbitrarily set at age 16 or older and at least 5 years older than the child" (p. 284).

Pedophilia can be either homosexual or heterosexual, but *DSM-III-R* states that "attraction to girls is apparently twice as common as attraction to boys. Many people with pedophilia are sexually aroused by both young boys and girls" (p. 284).

Fred S. Berlin, M.D., (1985) of Johns Hopkins University, claims that pedophilia occurs almost exclusively in men. He also notes that because people do not decide voluntarily what will arouse them sexually, there are great differences among pedophiles as to which partners and behaviors will appeal to them, as well as differences in the intensity of their sexual drive and their ability to resist sexual temptation, or even whether or not they decide the temptation *should* be resisted.

The pedophiliac impulse can either be fixated or regressed (Groth & Burgess, 1979; Groth, 1982). Fixated sexual offenders experience no erotic attraction toward adults and "manifest an arrest in their psychosexual development and maintain a primary psychological and sexual interest in young children who are prepubertal" (Schetky & Green, 1988). They are more likely to victimize boys than girls, and generally first act on their impulses during their adolescence.

Regressed pedophiles are men who find both adults and children erotically appealing, and tend to select female victims. Their tendencies emerge when they are adults and are usually triggered by a stressful sexual situation with an age-peer.

In the United States, the law makes no criminal distinction in its broad category of child molestation between the victim who is an adolescent and the victim who is younger. Pedophilia, on the other hand, is a specific psychiatric term, referring strictly to the sexual abuse of a prepubertal child. Throughout the remainder of this chapter, we will use the term "pedophilia" when referring to young children in order to make that differentiation.

FREQUENCY OF OCCURRENCE

Child abuse is a highly underreported crime. Most victims never reveal what has happened to them. William H. Reid, M.D. (1988) wrote that "careful studies have indicated . . . that child molesters commit an average of 60 offenses for every incident that comes to public attention. These must not be thought of as situational or hidden in some other disorder . . . if they are to be understood completely and treated successfully."

According to Schetkey and Green (1988), "Kinsey *et al.* (1953) . . . found that 24% of a population of 4,441 women had experienced sexual abuse during childhood" (p. 30). Studies of female college students revealed a 19 percent incidence of abuse during childhood and adolescence, and 9 percent among male students.

The percentage of offenders in the general population is unknown and will probably remain so due to the sensitive nature of the problem.

In 1974 the first state laws were passed requiring professionals to report child abuse. This law as well as a nationwide program encouraging children to speak up when they are sexually touched or assaulted have had their results. In 1984, for instance, a member of the United States Senate told the Third National Conference on Sexual Victimization of Children that she herself had been sexually molested when she was five years old.

The laws requiring reporting had a dramatic effect. In 1976 there were 6,000 cases of child abuse confirmed in the United States. In 1985, there were 113,000. Experts in the field estimate that of all the reported cases of child abuse, about 8 percent are false accusations and about 22 percent are unsupported.

Since the early 1980s, the awareness of priests' sexual involvement with children and adolescents has changed dramatically, too. During a 3-year period in the mid-1980s in one psychiatric facility alone, 130 priests were evaluated for sexual concerns and 70 of those were diagnosed as having a problem with pedophilia.

Lawsuits and investigative reporting have highlighted the problem in the American Church. Jason Berry, a Catholic journalist who specializes in Church issues, pursued the case of a priest accused of child abuse in his locality (Berry, 1985, 1987, 1989, in press). Having recorded every case that has come to legal attention, he is probably the single most knowledgeable layman on the current problem of priest pedophilia in the United States. In 1985 he began gathering documentation on dozens of cases and wrote in the *Washington Post* (September 16, 1989) that between 1983 and 1987 200 priests or religious brothers were reported to church authorities, an average of one case per week.

Dr. Leo Bartemeier, who, throughout his entire career, devoted some of his professional energies to the psychiatric treatment of priests, said he thought only 2 percent of Catholic priests could be called pedophiles in the strict sense of the definition. Of this number, three-quarters are homosexual or bisexual, and the remaining quarter heterosexual, in contrast to the general population, where heterosexual abuses outnumber homosexual by two to one. Our study validated those findings.

We also found that, at one time or another, an additional 4 percent of priests are sexually preoccupied with adolescent boys or girls and sometimes approach them. The behavior can be occasional, compulsive, or developmental—the last being those instances where the priest will act out with a child once as part of his (the priest's) developmental experimentation. In this last instance, the behavior is not part of a pattern, but is nevertheless troublesome. Although this group is about evenly divided between heterosexual and homosexual orientations, the homosexual contacts are four times more likely to come to the attention of parents or authorities, especially if the sexual involvement stops short of intercourse in heterosexual cases.

The clergy pedophiliac group probably enters seminary training with a strong sexual attraction toward prepubescent children. This already marked psychosexual deficit is present regardless of what age they are when they enter clerical life. Because their clerical training is generally protective and does not challenge their psychosexual development, many of these men are unaware of the extent of their developmental deficits and sexual tendencies until after ordination. Few of them act out extensively prior to then.

RAMIFICATIONS OF PEDOPHILIA

Pedophilia is an activity that impacts on several diverse yet intertwined social systems. The legal system considers sexual activity with a minor of any age a crime. The religious system views it as irresponsible and sinful. The psychiatric/medical system labels it a perversion or illness. Each system needs to be examined in greater detail for an understanding of pedophilia and therefore of how both it and the consequences of it are to be handled.

Legal

Who is to be held accountable when pedophilia, a crime, is committed by a priest? Robert McMenamin (1985) addressed this question in an article on clergy malpractice.

> There has been an outpouring of claims and lawsuits against Church corporations, Church officials, and the clergy as a result of wrongdoing. One hears the buzz words "clergy malpractice," but the malpractice allegation is but a part of the broader field which includes such items as child abuse, embezzlement, inadequate teaching, paternity, and improper counseling. Normally the clergy have little or no financial resources. Under the well-known "deep pocket" theory, claimants are attempting to assert liability upon the part of Church organizations. . . . For a period of many years, charitable groups and organizations including non-profit groups such as churches were immune from liability. . . . Many claims against churches and church personnel are met with the defense that under the doctrine of separation of church and state, the Church cannot be sued or held liable in a civil court. (p. 3)

On January 1, 1985, the insurance industry adopted an exclusion of coverage for members of the psychiatric and psychological professions for claims arising as the result of sexual contact between the patient and his/her therapist. The exclusion was a reaction to many large payments of such claims by insurance companies in the years immediately preceding the adoption. Six months later an article appearing in the *National Catholic Reporter* stated that "Many dioceses can no longer purchase liability insurance to cover the sexual offenses of clergy, and some sources indiate that molestation lawsuits may cost the Church a billion dollars in the next 10 years—especially if preventative and corrective measures are not taken" (Barry, 1985). Some feel it is quite possible that in the future the insurance industry may extend its sexual exclusion clause to members of the clergy, an action which could threaten the very economic viability of the Church.

Who is liable—an issue apart from who is responsible—when a priest commits a crime? The extent of liability of a bishop or religious superior for a priest who has been incarcerated or suspended, or who is not incarcerated but residing in his jurisdiction for study or work while having been suspended by another has not been defined in the higher courts of the civil law system.

Canon Law has the effect of law over the clergy, but how its relevance will be interpreted *versus* civil law in a specific case will greatly depend on the skills of the participating canon lawyer and the extent of preparation by the civil lawyer. Situations have arisen wherein a district attorney was ready to press criminal charges against the offending priest's superior because he was aware of criminal activity of the priest and failed to report it. At the present time, cases are awaiting settlement in which an attempt was made to sue a bishop, a diocese, diocesan vicars, the metropolitan archdiocese, the pope's representative in the United States, and the pope himself. Thus far, the claims have been covered by various insurance companies without first addressing the issue of the civil jurisdiction in the case. Those days may be coming to a close.

Although sex with any minor is considered illegal, oftentimes there is nothing that the legal system can do to intervene. Girls and boys 15, 16, and 17 years old often have minds of their own about their sexual practices and even adult partners. Also, the question of responsibility or guilt is not always clear.

A 47-year-old priest had a longstanding friendship with a Catholic family who were not his parishioners. He was a warm and physically demonstrative person who was accepted "as one of the family" even on family holidays and vacations. One of the sons, 17 years old, announced that he was going to "live with Father" and did. He was accepted in the parish as "Father's nephew," but he had told his parents that he had been the priest's lover for two years.

The boy insisted that he had had a great deal of sexual experience prior to introducing the priest to sexual activity. The priest insisted that this boy was his first sexual partner. Psychosexually, they were well matched when the boy was 15 to 18 years old. The young man was the one who outgrew the relationship and subsequently developed heterosexual interest in girls his own age. In this instance, it is difficult to say who is the victim. Certainly it is not an attempt to exonerate a 47-year-old priest to say that the teenaged boy was the "older and wiser" person in this relationship. The priest's naivete and his psychosexual arrest were hidden behind the facade of his administrative and pastoral skills and his pleasant personality.

It took a sexually precocious youngster to expose a dimension of the priest's character that was hidden from everyone, including the priest himself. The mother of this boy revealed that she herself was more than casually interested in the priest. Although she had found some of his signs of affection stimulating, she had not talked about them nor offered any sexual response. She held herself responsible for the "sexual" dimension of the relationship she felt. She presumed the invulnerability of the priest's celibate commitment and presumed his sexual innocence until confronted with her son's announcement and confession of his seduction. In fact, if this priest had been more developed psychosexually, he may very well have been able to respond to the mother's unexpressed feelings.

Likewise, there are dozens of examples of teenaged girls who have taken the lead willingly and with a certain amount of pride in a sexual relationship with a priest. The ignorance or neurosis of the priest is no excuse. It is a fact that must be dealt with. Priests should represent the exception proving Kinsey's rule that "older persons are the teachers of younger people in all matters, including the sexual" (Kinsey et al., 1948, p. 167).

Moral

The Catholic Church considers any sex outside marriage to be gravely sinful. Because priests are, by definition anyway, celibate, the Church is reluctant to make official statements about priests' sexual activity. Papal statements on Catholic sexuality are intended to govern the laymen, not the clergy. Thus far, the Church has chosen not to address directly the underlying human sexuality issues of its called servants, and until it does, their moral development will remain undefined and unsupported.

Eugene Kennedy was quoted in a March 20, 1988, article appearing in the *Los Angeles Times*. "[United States bishops] have chosen to take the advice of lawyers on issues that cannot be resolved merely by making the Church legally defensible. It is a very narrow vision of life. Lawyers are not intrinsically interested in morality, but in making their small area no wider than a ledge on which to balance themselves and their clients. Nationally, responsible journalists are beginning to interpret it as a cover-up story, which has a terribly negative potential for the Church. It has failed to examine the conflicts about the human sexuality that throb within it."

Psychological/Pastoral

Dr. Michael Peterson was a priest/psychiatrist who dedicated several years to the treatment of priests with alcohol and sexual problems, especially pedophilia. He said in a report on pedophilia prepared for the American bishops that "we are approximately at the same point in time with pedophilia in the medical/psychiatric world as we were with alcoholism in the late 1950s when the American Medical Association finally agreed that alcoholism was a disease in its own right and not a 'moral weakness' or a 'personality disorder' or 'personality defect'."

In the psychological evaluation and subsequent psychiatric and pastoral care of someone who has sexually abused a child, one needs to keep in mind four questions: 1) Is the behavior homosexual or heterosexual? 2) Is it compulsive? 3) Is it an isolated incident or part of a pattern? 4) Is it fixated or regressed? I will deal with theories as to the causes of pedophilia and with treatment modalities in greater detail in the following sections.

CAUSES

Dr. Berlin has said of pedophilia, "It appears that some men become vulnerable to the development of this type of sexual orientation by virtue of having been sexually active with an adult when they were children, or by virtue of manifesting certain biological abnormalities" (1986).

Dr. Michael Peterson felt more strongly about the latter as a cause: "I would say as a very careful 'thinker' in this area and a person well aware of the scientific research in this area that the etiology of this disorder is most likely biological with a strong contribution of premature, early childhood introductions to sexual behaviors as being the environmental co-etiologic contributor. In simplest terms, it is highly likely that *in utero* a type of programming of the brains of all persons takes place that contributes to the later expression of sexual behaviors in humans. This includes sexual orientation (i.e., heterosexual, homosexual, bisexual), sexual energy level (i.e., libido . . .), and perhaps even erotic age preference (i.e., pedophilia *versus* preference for age-appropriate partners)."

Dr. Berlin has also addressed the biological etiology of sexuality in general, apart from pedophilia:

> Biological factors in animals significantly influence sexually related activities. In some species of birds, normally only males sing, but if a female zebra finch that has been administered estradiol while just an embryo is given androgen hormones as an adult, she will do so also, and will have an increased number of cells in the nucleus robustus archistraitalis and other brain areas (Miller, 1980). She will also display distinctly male courtship behavior. Adult female rats who were exposed to testosterone at a specific time *in utero* will show sexual mounting behavior that normally predominates in male rats. (Money, 1971)

In a pilot study published by the *British Journal of Psychiatry* (Gaffney & Berlin, 1984), the researchers summarized their findings:

The hypothalamic-pituitary-gonadal axis was evaluated in men with pedophilia and non-pedophilia, and in normal male controls, by infusion of 100 mg. of synthetic luteinizing hormone-releasing hormone (LHRH). There were no significant differences among groups in age, height, weight, testosterone, baseline luteinizing hormone (LH) and follicle stimulating hormone (FSH), and FSH response to LHRH. However, there was a significant difference between the pedophilic group and the other two groups in the LH response to LHRH. The pedophiles responded with a marked elevation of LH, when compared with the non-pedophilic paraphiliacs and controls. These data indicate a hypothalamic-pituitary-gonadal dysfunction in pedophiles. (p. 657)

Discussions on the relative importance of heredity and environment in determining behavior are age-old. It is no different in the attempt to assess the etiology of pedophilia.

Kinsey and colleagues (1948) indicated that by the time they are 12 years old, 38 percent of boys have been involved in some form of sexual play, of which 22.7 percent is heterosexual and 29.4 percent homosexual. Obviously, not all of these boys grow up to be pedophiles or adults exhibiting aberrant sexual behavior. A certain amount of childhood experimentation is normal. The tide turns when the experimentation involves an adult. Berlin (1986) said:

There are many additional examples showing that environment and life experiences can play at least some role in the development of gender identity and in the development of sexual orientation and interest. Groth and others have shown that many men who experience pedophilic erotic urges as adults were sexually involved with adults when they were children (Groth & Burgess, 1979). Thus, in treating the pedophile one is in point of fact often treating a former "victim." One is merely treating him later on in his life after the circumstances of his childhood, or the intricacies of his biological constitution, have produced their psychological sequelae. Why sexual involvements with an adult during childhood seem to put some at risk of experiencing pedophilic sexual urges later on in life, but not others, is not known.

In a study on the familial transmission of pedophilia, Gaffney, Lurie and Berlin (1984) found that:

sexual deviancy among the pedophiles' families consisted of pedophilia. In families of nonpedophilic paraphiliacs, sexual deviancy was predominantly a paraphilia not involving children. . . . Pedophilia is found more frequently in families of pedophiles than in families of nonpedophilic paraphiliacs. This indicates specificity in the familial transmission. Thus pedophilia may be independent of the other paraphilias. (p. 546)

Of predisposing factors to pedophilia, *DSM-III-R* (1987) says, "Many people with disorder were themselves victims of sexual abuse in childhood" (p. 285).

Likewise, a large proportion of priests who become either pedophiles or sexually active with adolescents were themselves victims of sexual abuse as children or adolescents—some by priests. It is worth remarking that a number of these men do *not* become abusers, but the fact that many do points to the importance of one's early sexual experience and its relationship to the determination to become celibate.

One celibate who kept his vow with great mental anguish reported that in the course of his psychotherapy he had retrieved the memory of having been sexually abused when he was about five years old by an uncle who lived in his home. The uncle would take him into the bathroom and set the child on his lap, with the boy's bare legs wrapped around the uncle's erect penis; the child would then play with his uncle's genitals. The priest realized how large a part these early experiences and his subsequent reaction formation had played in his decision to become a priest and thereby reject the overwhelming and confusing realities of sex.

Another priest was introduced to sexual play at the age of eight by a cousin who was 16. The younger boy was not only intrigued by the sexual activity, but flattered by his inclusion into a secret world and the special affection of an older boy whom he idolized. The older youth would persuade the younger to help him with his chores and with delivering the newspapers on his route, and would then "reward" him with mutual masturbation. The younger boy curtailed his sexual activity, even masturbation, in midadolescence when he entered the minor seminary. He said it was then that he "vowed" never to do that with another child when he grew up. And he did not. He was, however, bothered for many years of his priesthood by the images of the genitals of adolescent boys, particularly the huge phallus he remembered his cousin possessing. He did not act out his fantasies, but was tormented by his feelings of sexual inadequacy.

A third priest, when he was a 15-year-old seminarian, once experienced anal intercourse with a 25-year-old priest. He, along with other seminarians, were on a summer pilgrimage to a religious shrine. The sleeping arrangements were haphazard and he was assigned to a bed with the older man. Years later he recalled with both excitement and regret his one and only sexual contact with another person. With no other sexual experience with which to compare the contact, it remained a vibrant and troublesome thorn in his flesh. For a brief time in his adult life he became phobic that he would repeat the behavior with some other adolescent.

In speaking about the adolescent sexual experiences of priests, Dr. Leo Bartemeier said that the memory of an intense sexual episode in their lives takes on a particular significance. The deprivation resulting from celibate practice often either enhances the memory or, in some cases, firmly fixates the priest's psychosexual development at a preadolescent or adolescent level.

Although some of these men mature slowly and finally do resolve their identification at more age-appropriate levels, there are others who are impelled to act out with individuals who are essentially on their same level of immaturity and who are directed at least in part by their same sexual orientation. In other words, not all homosexual contact between priests and adolescents involves a man who is of an obligatory homosexual orientation. Nor is all of the behavior compulsive or exclusive. However, it is always problematic—at least for the adolescent who is to some degree the victim of a generational transgression and a violation of trust.

DSM-III-R (1987) underscores Bartemeier's thoughts about the intensity of a sexual experience for a celibate. "Isolated sexual acts with children do not necessarily warrant the diagnosis of pedophilia. Such acts may be precipitated by marital discord, recent loss, or intense loneliness. In such instances, the desire for sex with a child may be understood as a substitute for a preferred but unavailable adult" (p. 285).

Schetky and Green (1988) described the importance of social and physical isolation as a contributing factor to sexual victimization as determined in a study "which indicated that incest and sexual abuse were higher in rural areas. The group of girls who spent their childhood on farms demonstrated the highest rates of victimization. These children were over two-and-one-half times more likely than the rest of the sample to have had an incestuous experience" (p. 34).

Several of these factors come together in the following case example.

A 30-year-old priest completing his doctoral studies was on vacation with his married sister and her family. His two nephews, who were four and six years old, were typically energetic youngsters and were most enthusiastic about the visit of their very important uncle. They demanded his time and attention, which he very willingly accorded them. He genuinely liked them, but became increasingly aware of his own sexual excitement as they hung on him and showered him with their affection. Because he had been so immersed in his doctoral studies and therefore somewhat socially deprived for the preceding three years, he attributed his reaction to his recent sense of isolation. He did not act on his impulse to play with his nephews sexually, but grew more and more concerned when his masturbatory fantasies began to include images of children.

His concern drew him to a psychiatrist, and during his treatment he recalled some repressed memories of having been sexually molested when he was eight years old by a neighborhood boy six years his senior. In therapy he also worked through several other sexual issues. Subsequently, he did not act out any of his fantasies. On follow-up interview 10 years after the disturbing vacation, he was active in his ministry and content with his celibate life, feeling very fortunate to have sought treatment before establishing a pattern of sexual activity. This man's superior intellect and well-disciplined life-style were important supportive factors as he grappled with his sexual identity and conscious attraction for children.

AVENUES OF ACCESS TO VICTIMS

DSM-III-R (1987) says that the pedophile "may limit his activities to his own children, stepchildren, or relatives, or may victimize children outside his family. Some people with the disorder threaten the child to prevent disclosure. Others, particularly those who frequently victimize children, develop complicated techniques for obtaining children, which may include winning the trust of a child's mother, marrying a woman with an attractive child, trading children with others with the disorder, or, in rare instances, bringing foster children from nonindustrialized countries or abducting children from strangers" (p. 284).

Among priests, a setting for child abuse can be the secluded arena of the child's educational facility. Leo Bartemeier himself was witness to both the best and the most troubled of priests' relationships with children and adolescent boys. As a 13-year-old boarding student at a Jesuit high school, he developed a deep admiration for the staff's dedication to the healthy formation of the students. Bartemeier kept lifelong contact with certain of his mentors and felt that he identified closely with the values of these men.

Four years later, however, he experienced the negative side of the coin. While he was a 17-year-old freshman at a Catholic university, he was approached sexually by one of the priest-teachers, whom he rejected as kindly as he could. He said that he began to develop an understanding of the loneliness and dilemma of the celibate as he watched this particular priest's struggles over the years and, with them, the subsequent deterioration of his teaching.

Two avenues of access mentioned in *DSM-III-R* were verified in our study: the family friend and an alliance with a child's mother.

The priest in the preceding section who found himself attracted to his nephews was an unusual man in that he sought treatment before acting out his desires. Like so many uncles and other family friends, the priest relative or priest family friend holds a place of honor and trust with the parents—a position that then becomes both the cover and the occasion for the sexual abuse of their children. One woman in our study reported that as a young teenager she would be sent by her widowed mother to ask their parish priest to come to her mother's bedside. Before accompanying the girl home, the priest would fondle her. When they arrived at her house, the girl would always be given some other errand to run while the priest visited with her mother. Although she was very uncomfortable with the priest's advances, the girl could not easily talk to her mother about them, since she had become aware very soon that her mother's indispositions were a cover for her own sexual liaison with the priest.

Another priest used his prowess in sports to attract young boys to himself. In the process of "horsing around"—usually after a ball game or while skinny-dipping with the boys—the priest would engage in touches that became progressively more sexually explicit. Several times in his career he had misinterpreted the admiration he sensed from children as sexual responsiveness and comfort, when in fact it had been neither. As a result, he had been the subject of a series of complaints that marked his frequent changes of parish assignments.

Altar boys' activities are a common arena for a priest to associate with children. Thousands of Catholic men recall fondly their childish heroism in trekking through the snow or rain to serve at a 6:00 a.m. Mass. They frequently report having experienced a sense of pride and honor at being close to something as sacred as the altar and the consecrated bread and wine. They report a feeling of specialness at having been able to dress up like a priest, hold the golden paten, carry the cross or chalice, and perform services that were off limits even to the holy nuns who taught them in school. Many of their memories are humorous. Some describe trying to please a priest who in retrospect merges with the image of Barry Fitzgerald, while others engaged in a Catholic boy's rite of passage—the boldness of trying out the forbidden altar wine or the unconsecrated communion wafers, or perhaps even sneaking a smoke in the sacristy under the cover of the smell of burning incense.

But for some, the experience of being an altar boy was stripped of its sense of the sacred and deprived of a memory of real fun and community with the other altar boys because these boys were selected by a certain kind of priest for his private sexual service.

Occasionally, the priest does not have to go out looking for his victims. One priest who was not himself sexually attracted to children became aware of the sexual activity of some of his fellow priests when he was sent to a new area to replace a young man of his order. As far as he knew, the move was a routine one. Consequently, he was quite surprised when, within the first few weeks of his new assignment, he was approached on two separate occasions by young boys who made clear their sexual interest in him. When it happened a third time, the priest quizzed one of the young boys as to why they had picked him for their advances. The boy replied that the "other Father gave us five bucks if we'd pull his nail" [fellate him]. When the priest inquired further, he discovered that there had been a succession of priests who had used the local boys in this way. These particular preadolescents were not associated with the Church, but the street tradition in this area was that they could earn money by selling sexual favors and that some priests were especially easy marks.

THE BEHAVIORS

DSM-III-R (1987) notes that

> [P]eople with this disorder who act on their urges with children may limit their activity to undressing the child and looking, exposing themselves, masturbating in the presence of the child, or gentle touching and fondling of the child. Others, however, perform fellatio or cunnilingus on the child or penetrate the child's vagina, mouth, or anus with their fingers, foreign objects, or penis, and use varying degrees of force to achieve these ends. These activities are commonly explained with excuses or rationalizations that they have "educational value" for the child, that the child derives "sexual pleasure" from them, or that the child was "sexually provocative"— themes that are also common in pedophilic pornography. (p. 284)

In our study we found that there also tends to be a strong sexual exhibitionistic component in some of these men; the more immature they are, the stronger that component seems to be. However, we did not find it as an isolated pursuit. *DSM-III-R* categorizes exhibitionism separately, indicating that it is not necessarily a precursor to pedophilia.

Some of our informants rationalized that the sexual activity was educational or helpful to the child. A 60-year-old priest in our study was arrested for child molestation based on incriminating evidence found in his home. There had been no prior complaints lodged against him and his detection had been accidental. The police had been searching for another suspect and were mistakenly given the priest's address by a young boy who was their informant.

The priest had had sexual liaisons with young boys all of the years of his priesthood. Consistently selecting children who were physically or emotionally deprived, he felt that by his friendship and association with them he was offering them genuine love, protection, and guidance along the lines of the Greek ideal, and a chance for a better life adjustment. He did not feel any guilt. Some of the boys would engage in the sexual activity very willingly, sometimes even initiating it. The priest would never hold onto the boys once they reached adolescence, instead encouraging them to participate in school and social activities, and trying to direct them to a level of sexual and emotional maturity that he himself could not attain.

Fred Berlin (1986) echoed the rationalization theme:

> When a person desires sex or falls in love, it is often easy to become convinced that the relationship is good and healthy and not harmful or wrong. Such self-deception may at times be easy for the pedophilic individual in light of the fact that sex with children, though wrong, may not in every instance be damaging (Gilbert, 1976). Some children may enjoy certain aspects of their sexual relationships with an adult, thus facilitating self-deception.

According to *DSM-III-R,* "except in cases in which the disorder is associated with sexual sadism, the person may be generous and very attentive to the child's needs in all respects other than the sexual victimization in order to gain the child's affection, interest, and loyalty and to prevent the child from reporting the sexual activity" (p. 285).

The following case history illustrates this point.

Each year a pastor who was in his 60s selected three eighth-grade girls from his school to help around the parish house, performing such duties as stuffing envelopes, running errands, and doing light cleaning tasks. For these services, the girls would receive tuition reduction and a small salary; it was also well known that there were extra treats to be had, such as candy, ice cream, and occasional trips, all of which made the parish house duty a coveted assignment. From some parents' perspectives, the generous tuition reduction plus the honor of being so closely associated with the pastor made them eager to have their daughters chosen.

When the pastor had begun his tradition, the girls would do their work in groups of two or three, but as time went on, a pattern of singularity developed—one of the girls would emerge each year as the most sensitive (or loving, needy, or vulnerable, as the case might be). She would become Father's special companion and would be able to lie on the couch with him as he took his afternoon nap, exchange kisses and hugs with him, and comfort him with back rubs when his arthritis acted up. The pattern was honed to perfection. Theoretically the association was public, approved by everyone.

Little by little, the genuine affection between the priest and all of the girls was focused on the most suitable candidate, and the subsequent sexual dimension of the relationship receded into a secret area shared only by that girl and the priest. Because the priest did not expose his genitals and did not "deliberately" touch the girl's (although there was playful wrestling during which some contact was made), the victim was left with the conviction that any inappropriate thoughts or feelings were *her* fault, not his. When the priest would ejaculate spontaneously while having the girl's body close to his, he would feign sleep, and if the girl was aware of what had happened, she would believe that "Father hadn't done anything." The priest experienced no guilt about his behavior. He genuinely liked the children, and in his mind, "What happened, happened."

Another important element in this last case example and the one to follow is the depersonalization of the victim and the activity. "What happened, happened" is not a loving exchange between two people who have deliberately selected each other as a sexual partner.

A 40-year-old priest who had a long history of sexual activity with preadolescent and teenaged boys described in detail his method of seduction, and how he had learned it.

As a 12-year-old orphaned boy living with relatives, he was befriended by his local parish priest, who included him in many recreational activities and outings with groups of other youngsters his age. On occasion, the priest would take one or another of the boys to a movie by himself. During the movie, the priest would hold his leg close to the boy's, testing the youngster's comfort with "accidental physical closeness." If the boy responded positively to the gesture, the priest would place his hand on the child's knee, being very careful not to advance too quickly. The process was almost one of conditioning the physical familiarity. If the priest sensed that the boy was comfortable and responsive, on the next outing he might "accidentally" brush his hand against the boy's genitals while passing him a box of popcorn. Through these casual testings of the child's sexual excitement, the priest would know when to proceed to more direct and prolonged sexual fondling. Under the cover of darkness in the theater where no words or looks had to be exchanged, the sex could take place "as if it never happened." It was the pattern used on the priest when he was a child and one that he perpetuated as an adult.

There is some debate as to the frequency of sadism in the pedophilic incident. Berlin said, "Some have argued that pedophilic acts are invariably aggressive (Groth & Burgess, 1979). In the vast majority of cases, this is simply not so. Most pedophiles use no physical force whatsoever. . . . By definition, the issue to be explained in pedophilia is one of sexual and affectional orientation. Pedophilia is not a disturbance of temperament or aggression." *DSM-III-R* states that "sexual sadism may, in rare instances, be associated with pedophilia" (p. 285).

Several informants in our study reported sexual incidents with children and adults incorporating features that could only be labeled accurately as sadistic. Some involved the severe physical punishment of students—usually "paddling"—masking the sexual excitement of the priest. Some of the priests reported masturbating after completing the punishment, while others experienced an ejaculation during it. Some priests would single out a young protégé and under the guise of ascetic or athletic challenge would direct him through a series of intricate maneuvers to train him in discipline and manliness, sometimes appealing to the martyrs as examples. Within the context of these activities, the priests would derive direct or indirect sexual satisfaction. At times, the sexual activity would be part of a final struggle and "initiation," or, as one informant reported, while the protégé endured boot-camp-like paces wearing scarcely more than an athletic supporter, the priest would quietly masturbate.

Reports in the media include examples of priests' sadism toward their victims, one involving a priest who led youth programs and used a paddle, whip, needles, and hot wax to inflict pain on his child victims. One account from the Washington Press described a priest who had been accused of "dressing several young males in the parish in sexually provocative briefs, and engaging in ritualistic sexual fantasies with them that included terrifying imitations of the torture inflicted on Christ and certain other saints."

VICTIMS—THE AFTERMATH

The physical effects on the child victim include the abuses endured in a sexual encounter with an adult, especially penetration in vaginal or anal intercourse, or the pain and scarring from a sadistic episode. Just as serious, however, is the emotional damage the victims suffer. Women who report having been touched, fondled, or otherwise sexually violated by a priest when they were children can recall the overwhelming guilt they experienced about their own sexual feelings. As in an example cited earlier, a young girl will sometimes blame herself for the sexual response of the priest, attributing no desire or intent to him—"What happened, happened."

It is not difficult to empathize with the violated preadolescents struggling with their own sexual development, sitting at Mass on Sunday with the symbol of the community's moral authority before them. Like all other children who at age 11, 12, or 13 are unable to absorb completely their changing body image, their sexual feelings, and their relationships, these girls in addition were deprived of the support, protection, and example of their moral mentors. The adult world that should have fostered their growth instead complicated and impeded it. The priests who abused them not only transgressed the generational barrier and violated a sacred trust, but also trapped the children into incestuous liaisons they may have been trying to avoid—many times unconsciously—at home. The "Father" whom they thought was safe and with whom a spiritual involvement would be a protection from the dangers of family love turned out to be more sexually available than the males at home.

Many nuns who reported early sexual abuse by a priest came from large families and poor circumstances. In their eyes, the Church had great stature and power. Early involvement with parochial school activity and Church work with the parish priests were seen by them as ways out of poverty and a legitimate distancing from their chaotic home environments.

Typical of this history is that of a woman who was one of 12 children in her family. From her early years until puberty she slept in one bed with four of her siblings—both boys and girls, since her parents made no effort to segregate the sexes. She became increasingly uncomfortable not only with this situation, but also with the drunkenness and harshness of her father. At 10 years of age, she gained a measure of distance from the rest of her family by declaring that she was going to join the convent. Thereafter, she was allowed to spend time working in the Church sacristy instead of doing chores at home. Later on, she was permitted to sleep alone on a couch on the porch; the explanation that it was part of her ascetic preparation for life in the convent became an acceptable rationalization for all parties. Her brothers, who had been sexually assertive with her and her sisters, now left her alone. Apparently the threat of violating someone intended for the Church was stronger than any incest taboo. A future nun in the family became an honor for all of them.

The girl was a sweet child, and quickly endeared herself to the Church staff. She was conscientious in her sacristy work and partook in daily Mass and communion. The parish priest often spent time talking with her after she had completed her tasks, presented her with gifts of a rosary and a daily missal, and sent fruit and candy home with her for her whole family. So when the priest first hugged her, she accepted it as a gesture of his genuine and appropriate affection. She did not associate it with the drunken gropings of her father or the adolescent intensity of her brothers, which had frightened her and which she had rejected. The contrast between the poverty of affection in her turbulent home and the warm, peaceful glow of the Church made the gentle advances of the priest seem not wrong to her.

Her contact with the priest eventually became sexual and continued regularly until she left home for a convent boarding school at age 14. Despite this, her affection for the Church, her vocation, and the priest remained intertwined until she became an adult nun. Only with great pain was she eventually able to separate her sense of violation from the elements of support the priest had extended to her.

Many women report grade-school experiences of having been touched or kissed by a priest. The sexual element that becomes so apparent to them from their adult perspectives had not been evident to them as children. Under the guise of playfulness and obscured by the children's expectation of the priest's nonsexuality, he could, as one woman put it, "cop a feel that I would have slapped a boy's face for."

Younger children are more trusting, less suspicious, and less sexually experienced than their adolescent brothers and sisters, all of which makes them more vulnerable to a priest's sexual play.

Ferenczi, a colleague and friend of Freud, described the effects of sexual abuse on the psyche of the child-victim.

> The overwhelming power and authority of the adults render them silent: often they are deprived of their senses. Yet that very fear, when it reaches its zenith, forces them automatically to surrender to the will of the aggressor, to anticipate each of his wishes and to submit to them, forgetting themselves entirely to identify totally with the aggressor. (Schetky & Green, 1988, p. 28)

Sometimes the results of the abuse are irrevocably tragic. The June 7, 1988, issue of the *National Catholic Reporter* included a story about a $10.5 million suit before the New York Supreme Court's appellate division brought by the parents of a 12-year-old boy who had hanged himself after having been molested by a religious brother at a Boy Scout camp.

Some victims of child abuse are taught by the experience to depersonalize sex. In the earlier example of the priest who abused young boys in the movie theater, the victim never had the chance to face his abuser or talk to him while it was happening. After the movie, life went on as though the incident had never happened. The young girl involved with the priest who feigned sleep after his spontaneous ejaculation was also unable to talk to her abuser.

Some victims escape into the world of celibacy to avoid dealing with sexual episodes in the future. Many victims become abusers themselves; and sometimes the two responses overlap.

When priests are the abusers, "the effects" according to Michael Peterson (personal communication), "are long lasting and go well into adulthood.

This is well documented though it may well be difficult to predict the extent of the effects in particular cases. We are speaking not only of psychological effects but also the spiritual effects since the perpetrators of the abuse are priests or clerics. This will no doubt have a profound effect on the faith life of the victims, their families and others in the community."

A recent article in the *Seattle Times* (May 24, 1988) quoted a woman who said that it was very confusing trying to explain to her children why one priest, who said Mass at the altar, wasn't allowed to talk to them.

Other questions arise when the abuser is a priest. How will the child be able to perceive the Church and clergy in the future as unselfish, loving representatives of the Gospel and Body of Christ? What happens to the child's perception of the sacraments as administered by the clergy? As an adult, will the victim come to view the hierarchy of the Church as hypocritical and weak for not having prevented the abuse or putting a stop to it once it was discovered? Depending on how widely the situation is known among the child's family and acquaintances, how many other ancillary victims will there be for each abused child?

TREATMENT

The most important issue in considering the treatment of pedophilia, especially among the clergy, is how the pedophiliac treats himself—how he handles his sexual desires and whether or not he recognizes them as inappropriate.

Many priests do give in to their urges, rationalizing the behavior as educational for their victims, as discussed previously.

Others will recognize their urge as inappropriate, become fearful of the behavior it demands, and avoid compromising situations for years. The child who had been abused by his uncle became a priest, hoping that the vow of celibacy would keep him from repeating the behavior. The priest who had engaged in mutual masturbation as a child with his adolescent cousin was tormented throughout his ministry by images of the genitals of adolescent males, though he did not act out his desires. The priest who, as a teenager, had been subjected to anal intercourse by an older priest on a church outing always remembered the incident with excitement and fear. Without other sexual experiences to reduce the impact of it, he found it intensified as the years went on.

Another priest used reaction formation to combat his pedophilic urges. He was in his mid-30s when he was assigned to be chaplain of an orphanage. This position was usually reserved for a priest close to retirement age, but was given to him because he had been in delicate health. The nuns who staffed the institution were enthusiastic about this younger man who would be saying their Mass, hearing confessions, and generally enlivening the atmosphere. They willingly supplied him with every comfort they could afford to insure "Father's health."

As the priest regained his physical strength, he grew increasingly nervous, complaining to his superiors that he was bothered by all the "female attention," and that he missed the "man's world" he had known in the seminary and in his prior assignments. However, to his closest priest friend he confided that he found himself sexually excited by the children who were always eager to hold his hand, sit on his lap, or hug him whenever he had any association with them. Eventually his anxiety escalated to such a degree that he had to be reassigned. Subsequently, he cultivated the reputation of not liking children, a reputation reinforced by his avoidance of any contact or activity with them or with young people.

At times these men become greatly troubled by their sexual activity and concerned over their own loss of self-control as well as the damage they have inflicted on the children involved. Therefore, some of their activity comes to the attention of other priests through the confessional, or of psychiatrists through psychotherapy. Occasionally, a priest will seek help prior to acting out his desires, like the priest who found himself attracted to his young nephews on a vacation with his sister and her family. More often, however, the fits of pedophiliac guilt are all too fleeting, and the pedophile who so desperately wants a relationship cannot sustain the adult demands of either a psychotherapeutically or spiritually directed attachment which might offer him a modicum of insight or help in working through his problem.

Most active pedophiles do not "turn themselves in" to therapy or confession. Many do not share their concern with anyone else, and seek anonymity by limiting their partners to persons who have no connection with their work or ministry. Others avoid confiding their behavior because they simply do not experience any guilt in connection with it.

For those who do seek help, Berlin said (1986) "Treatment, therefore, may have to involve helping a person stop rationalizing, as well as helping him to try to develop strategies for more successfully resisting sexual and affectional temptation." He discussed four major treatment modalities (1985):

Psychotherapy
According to Berlin (1985):

Therapy utilizes the process of introspection to try to figure out what went wrong, with the expectation that newly acquired insights will help to overcome the problem.... [However], it is doubtful that persons can come to fully understand the basis of their own sexual interests through the process of introspection alone. . . . There is little convincing evidence to show that the traditional psychotherapies alone are an invariably effective means for treating pedophilia. (p. 85)

We have found in our study that even in the best of circumstances, therapeutic or spiritual attachments by themselves are inadequate in dealing with the confirmed pedophile whose compulsion requires a multifaceted mode of intervention to control it. The transient incident of an adult-child sexual contact can be dealt with in spiritual direction or psychotherapy if it is genuinely an incident only, and not part of a pedophiliac process.

Behavior Therapy

According to Berlin (1985),

This approach is less concerned with the historical antecedents of pedophilia than with the question of what can be done about it. Common to most behavioral approaches is the attempt to extinguish erotic feelings associated with children, while simultaneously teaching the individual to become sexually aroused by formerly nonarousing age-appropriate partners. . . . There is insufficient evidence that such changes invariably carry over into the nonlaboratory situation. (p. 85)

Surgery

This can be either neurosurgery, or removal of the testes to reduce the offender's testosterone level, and thereby his sexual libido. Although extreme, studies have shown that either procedure works.

Medication

Substituting drugs for castration as a means of lowering the pedophile's testosterone level has been successful in controlling the behavior. Most pedophiles are also encouraged to attend group counseling sessions as well (similar to Alcoholics Anonymous) "in which the men are expected to acknowledge their temptation to engage in inappropriate sexual behavior" (Berlin, 1985, p. 85).

DSM-III-R is not encouraging about the course of pedophilia:

[It] is usually chronic, especially in those attracted to boys. The frequency of pedophilic behavior often fluctuates with psychosocial stress. The recidivism rate for people with pedophilia involving a preference for the same sex is roughly twice that of those who prefer the opposite sex. (p. 285)

Basic to all treatment modalities for pedophilia is that the pedophile must acknowledge his problem and seek help. The trouble with most of the sexual activity of celibates is that it is seen by both the perpetrator and the Church authorities as an "act" (or sin) that can be resolved by confession and a firm purpose of amendment. A much more finely tuned assessment of the priest's total developmental history and his personality structure is needed to intervene effectively and help him come to grips with his sexual behavior.

CHANGES IN THE CHURCH'S AWARENESS OF THE PROBLEM

There are basically two reasons for the Church not having assumed a more active role in dealing with its clergy who abuse children. First, Church authorities have not been aware of the magnitude of the problem until the last decade or so. Part of this lack of awareness is due to ignorance on the part of the medical/psychological community and the population as a whole, and part is due to the Church's tendency to stick its head in the sand on matters sexual.

Second, a system of secrecy runs throughout the Catholic Church when it is faced with the choices of either recognizing and confronting the sexuality of clergy or ignoring it and hoping it will go away. Again, there are several reasons for the existence of the secret system.

1. The Church, like everyone else, was not well informed on pedophilic behaviors and inclinations, and did not realize the compulsive implications of the disorder. Only recent laws requiring the reporting of child abuse have brought the frequency of those incidents to the attention of legal authorities, forcing the Church to take a hard look at these occurrences within her own ranks. The tendency of Church authorities not to get involved in the sexual behaviors of priests is now a crime if the behavior involves a child.
2. Scandal from clergy is anathema to the Church, which needs to be respected and wants to remain so in the community as an example of moral leadership.
3. Concerns for the dwindling supply of clerics have placed the Church in a position of ignoring the rights of priests' sexual victims, whether they are adults or children.

Let us now look in greater detail at each of the two reasons for the Church's lack of involvement in the treatment of pedophile priests.

Lack of Information about Pedophilia

In a recent mandatory meeting of priests called for by their bishops (and the nation's bishops) to discuss the issue of pedophilia, one elderly priest was puzzled over the concern and commotion surrounding the subject. He said he thought a pedophile was a kind of machine.

Coined in 1912 by Krafft-Ebing (p. 555), the term "pedophilia" is relatively new in spite of the fact that it represents an age-old practice. Kinsey and colleagues in their landmark study on the sexuality of the human male (1948) did not have much to say about pedophilia.

> Older persons are the teachers of younger people in all matters, including the sexual. The record [of 2749 cases of preadolescent sex play] includes some cases of preadolescent boys involved in sexual contacts with adult females, and still more cases of preadolescent boys involved with adult males. Data on this point were not systematically gathered from all histories, and consequently the frequency of contacts with adults cannot be calculated with precision. (p. 167)

Dr. Benjamin Karpman's book *The Sexual Offender and His Offenses: Etiology, Pathology, Psychodynamics and Treatment* (1954) contained the following warning: "The sale of this volume is restricted to the medical and legal professions; to ministers and educators; and to adult students of the psychological, biological and sociological sciences."

Mohr, Torner and Jerry (1964) said of pedophilia, "There is doubtless no subject on which we can obtain more definite opinions and less definite knowledge" (p. 3).

The definitive *Comprehensive Textbook of Psychiatry—Second Edition* (Freedman, Kaplan, & Sadock, 1975) which was in press in 1974, the year in which the first law was passed requiring incidents of child abuse to be reported, contained only a few paragraphs on pedophilia, including the following.

> The pedophile is usually visualized as the "monster on the corner" who is ready to pick up innocent children. Thus, schools and parents warn children never to take rides with strangers. There are a number of individuals who are pedophilic in their orientation and who do commit predatory acts and go after young children. However, by far the greatest amount of pedophilic behavior is in families or among friends and neighbors. Often it is a one-time activity in which a male who has been denied or deprived of adult female sexual gratification becomes intoxicated and turns to the children. . . . Often, his pedophilic behavior will be expressed after a fight with his wife or a put-down by a friend or neighbor. The wife not only

denies her husband sexually but also may berate him and make him feel less than a man. . . . Cases of pedophilia typically involve alcohol and a berating wife. The pedophile needs to leave home to find companionship and sexual satisfaction. He chooses an immature sexual object because of his fear of the castrating, aggressive, mother-wife adult female. (p. 1542)

The *Synopsis* of the *Comprehensive Textbook,* published a year later, still did not indicate that pedophilia was a crime, saying only that it was a practice "in which a child is used for sexual purposes" (p. 1320). The 1978 *Harvard Guide to Modern Psychiatry* (1978) does not even mention pedophilia.

The subject of adult sexual contact with children or minors is more emotionally loaded than any other area of sexual behavior and, as Mohr et al. (1964) said, less researched. Since 1974, the legal system has been forced to contend with the problem and it is usually the justice system that brings it to public attention. Those eventually convicted of child abuse by the legal system are usually spurned and denigrated by other convicted criminals. There have been attempts to decriminalize and popularize sexual activity between adults and children, but they have been largely ineffectual in moving the general conscience to look kindly on this behavior.

Catholic parents in the 1980s are more alert to the possibility of sexual abuse by a priest, an unthinkable or at least unmentionable notion in the 1960s. In 1985, one informant in our study related the experience of grade school children lined up in Church to receive the sacrament of reconciliation (confession). The line was long on one side and very short on the other. When the nun encouraged some of the children to shift to the line in front of the other priest's confessional, they were reluctant to do so. Finally one of the boys spoke up loudly, "My mom told me not to go to him. He's a wimp." That kind of awareness and response would not have happened 20 years earlier.

The System of Secrecy

The lack of information about pedophilia is intertwined with the Church's system of secrecy. As Michael Peterson (personal communication) said:

"Pedophilia" and related deviant disorders is an area which has been closeted in Western Civilization for centuries. Most individuals and organizations, including the Church and bishops, who were ever confronted with the issue of illicit sexual relationships between adults and children responded in a manner they thought to be responsible in an effort to protect the injured child and aid the offending priest. It is now known, because of strides in the clinical field, that perhaps those actions insofar as they aided, comforted or enabled the sex offender to continue his secret life were irresponsible and injurious to the sex offender. Though psychological study is still in its infancy in some respects, much more is known about the long and short term traumatic injury inflicted on the victim.

Prior to 1983, in the United States the Catholic Church authorities handled problems of child abuse that came to their attention in much the same ways families did—in secrecy and by denial and rationalization. Consider a family example:

During a large family gathering, a male family member playfully but passionately embraced and attempted to French kiss his grand niece who was 13 years old. The girl objected, but no one in the group intervened, in spite of the fact that several family members present had been approached sexually by the same relative when they were children. It was an open family secret that no one wanted to deal with. They kept on talking and laughing, responding to the playfulness rather than to the obvious sexual dimension of the approach or to the distress of the youngster.

Another example: A married man was reported to the police for touching the genitals of a nine-year-old playmate of his son. It was only then that more than 20 relatives confided to each other that they had been sexually approached by him—some as long as 15 years prior to the reported incident—or at least knew of his sexual activity. But again, no one had said anything.

During the time course of our study, there were several ways the Church family handled pedophilia when it came to the attention of bishops or religious superiors. The offending priest was remonstrated, sometimes given time to make a retreat (repent), and usually transferred to a different parish or parochial assignment. Or else, there were a few psychiatric institutes run by religious to which a priest might be sent.

In 1983 the picture changed with the beginning of lawsuits against the Church when a priest was known to have abused a child or minor.

In 1985, there were 30 cases of priests involving at least 100 children before the courts, which would have required $400,000,000.00 from the Church if all the cases had been upheld.

In the May 30, 1986, issue of the *National Catholic Reporter* the following appeared:

> One year after the story of a pedophile priest in Lafayette, Louisiana, first came public [the case of Gilbert Gauthe, a priest who confessed to raping and sodomizing at least three children], the Church here—ravaged by scandal, multimillion-dollar lawsuits,

charges of cover-ups and incompetence, and anguish on every side—
will never be the same.... Few of those involved deny that the
wider trauma may well have been avoided if the diocese had acted
more quickly and more openly when the tragedy first began to
build. [The pastor] of the diocese's largest parish ... , reportedly
wielding considerable influence, explained that when the problem
arose, the Church reacted in a traditional ecclesial fashion, closed
itself off in a clubby circle and attempted to deal with the matter
internally, with no due process for anyone. Only this time, it did not
work. This time, by all accounts, the modern world reached into the
Church through the processes of civil and criminal litigation and
held it accountable....

Lafayette Bishop Gerald Frey said a series of seminars on child
abuse was held for all the clergy in the diocese last August. [He said]
"One of the problems is that the people who have *this* problem are
extremely clever at covering their tracks.... You have to be more
constantly alert and aware of the possibility of this and to act immediately when there is even a suspicion of it." That is a lesson Frey
learned at great cost. He first heard of Gauthe's problem in 1974.
The priest—now serving 20 years at hard labor in a Louisiana
prison, without benefit of parole—went on to molest at least three
dozen children (some say the actual figure is closer to 100) before
Frey relieved him of his ministry in 1983. Frey lays much of the
blame to his own ignorance. "Even the professionals—psychologists,
psychiatrists, lawyers—are telling me that they're learning a lot
about pedophilia that was not known some years back." (p. 6)

The *Baltimore Sun* on February 10, 1988 said, "The Roman Catholic
Church, faced with increasing reports of child molestation cases involving
priests, said yesterday that dioceses are taking measures to crack down on
offenders.... In December the San Jose [California] *Mercury-News* published a series of articles that said while national awareness of child abuse
is increasing, the Catholic Church 'continues to ignore and cover up cases
of priests who sexually molest children.'"

On April 4, 1988, the *National Law Journal* reported, "Attorney Jef-
frey R. Anderson said 'the priest is put in a position of power and authority. If he's a pedophile, he will abuse compulsively until, ultimately, that
abuse is discovered because his victims are many in number.' Mr. Anderson says the Church's 'institutional' response has been to appease families,
keep it from the police, and transfer the priest to another parish where the
abuse begins again."

On June 7, 1985, the *National Catholic Reporter* published the names
of priests then involved in lawsuits involving pedophilia. Included in the

list was a San Diego monsignor accused of molesting an altar boy. The Church paid the boy's family $75,000 to preclude court costs. The monsignor was transferred but not removed from his diocesan status.

The New York Times (June 12, 1988) ran a story referring to a case in Seattle of a parish priest who had a 20-year history of allegations of pedophilia and had been in treatment for 10 years. In Seattle, "some parents here say the Church has been more concerned with protecting [the priest] than helping the victims. 'This priest has a 20-year history of sexual contact with children, and they still returned him to a parish full of young kids,' said a member of that parish. 'The Church says they were protecting his confidentiality. I say it was old-boy secrecy.' "

On October 27, 1988, the *Baltimore Sun* published these two stories: "The Archdiocese of Washington [D.C.] has made a secret six-figure settlement with a 20-year-old man who accused the Church of negligence after he was molested by a Roman Catholic priest several years ago, the *Washington Post* reported yesterday." And, "the Roman Catholic Archdiocese of Baltimore was sued by parents charging their son was sexually molested by a priest whose deviant behavior was 'actively covered up and concealed by Church officials.' It was the second suit involving this priest."

Although in 1985 several national publications had investigative reporters trying to tie isolated regional stories on priest molesters into an exposé, most backed off from the task by 1989. Jason Berry is the one investigative reporter following the story to its conclusion. All three major television networks and CNN have given the subject of child molestation by priests a great deal of attention, as evidenced by the coverage on shows such as 20/20, Donahue, Geraldo, Larry King, and Oprah.

THE FUTURE

As mentioned earlier, the first step in treating a priest pedophile is that he must admit needing help. As Berlin (1986) said:

Although it is not the pedophile's fault that he has the sexual orientation that he has, it is his responsibility to deal with his sexuality in a manner that does not put innocent children at risk. However, in order for him to be able to do this and to be held accountable by society, adequate treatment facilities must be made available, facilities where a person can seek out help without fear of stigmatization, ridicule, retaliation, or unwarranted distain. Only under such circumstances can one expect an individual to talk candidly about the innermost aspects of his own sexuality.

Treatment must be immediate. If the priest himself tries to suspend his sexual habit, his superiors would be well advised to set aside any misplaced feelings of guilt of their own and urge him to seek professional treatment. It is beyond the ability of most clerical authorities to probe into the roots of this problem and to solve it by nonpsychiatric means.

As recommendations for the future, Robert McMenamin (1985) wrote:

> It appears that an open disclosure and discussion of problems is preferable to secrecy. It also appears that immediate help should be offered to any damaged individual. Preventive measures such as careful selection and continuing education of church personnel is indicated by the extraordinary number of tort wrongs committed by church personnel. (p. 6)

According to Canon 1342 of Church law, a priest against whom criminal allegations have been made and supported, or even suspected of being supported, can be suspended from his duties without a trial and by means of an extrajudicial decree. Such a suspension would be a protection for potential victims as well as for the Church.

Unfortunately, four factors compound or foster the problem of pedophilia and the Roman Catholic clergy:

1. The lack of basic education about sex and celibacy creates a situation where adolescence is protected or postponed, or where the celibate priesthood becomes a hiding place for unresolved sexual conflicts.
2. The atmosphere and structure of the Church and its priest-education system tolerate and in some cases encourage sexual regression and fixation.
3. Preference for secrecy obviates accountability on the part of the priest and his superiors.
4. The lack of credibility in the Church's teaching on sex fosters primitive mental defenses such as denial, rationalization, and splitting.

The Church of the future is going to have to examine carefully its current positions in moral theology and reassess its basic statements, many of which have been codified and accepted without question for years—or perhaps centuries. To survive, it must engage in such a reassessment.

Chapter 9

SEXUAL COMPROMISES ___

"I am not at all optimistic that celibacy is in fact being observed."
—*Franjo Cardinal Seper*
Archbishop of Zagreb
Rome, 1971

Priests are part of that segment of the male population who "cannot marry." The Church presumes that this is a self-limitation because of a call to give up all to follow Christ. That *all* includes an overdependence on material things (religious poverty in some form); sexual sin and even marriage relationships, as well as any directly sought sexual pleasure (chastity); and a *weltanschauung* that presumes that the will of God is the supreme law and that it is sometimes expressed through legitimate authority (obedience).

For some priests these ideals are formalized in vows. However, with or without the vows, the histories of all clerics—saints and sinners alike—are ultimately measured against these gospel ideals. It can be most accurately stated that the approach to the ideals is a history of the compromises made in reaching them. Success is proven only by acknowledging honest failures.

It is sublimation of the sexual instinct that makes celibacy possible, yet over the period of our study I observed several areas of failure in accomplishing that sublimation. These areas are essentially victimless or at least there is no direct victim. The most common modes of sexual expression involve pornography and transvestism, with fewer occurrences of exhibitionism and bestiality. Before proceeding to these individual issues, a few words are necessary about the unique sexual role of the priest and his relationship with women.

WHAT IS NORMAL?

Celibacy, because it depends on a "grace," is a supernatural vocation. Certainly it is not *natural* for the average man to remain celibate. Celibacy is not the norm for society; in that sense it is not normal. Even if not in disaccord with his vow, is it normal for the celibate priest to view pornography? The *Report of the Commission on Obscenity and Pornography* (1970) stated:

> Approximately 85% of adult men and 70% of women in the U.S. have been exposed at some time during their lives to depictions of explicit sexual material in either visual or textual form. Most of this exposure has apparently been voluntary, and pictorial and textual depictions are seen about equally often. Recent experience with erotic materials is not as extensive as total experience, *e.g.* only about 40% of adult males and 26% of adult females report having seen pictorial depictions of sexual intercourse during the past two years. (p. 19)

According to these figures, regardless of the *morality* of viewing pornography, in itself it cannot be called *unnormal* adult behavior. The priest who is determined to eschew marriage or sexual contact with another person may find himself in the position of what Dr. Benjamin Karpman (1954) called "the normal pervert," an appellation that will not be welcomed by clergy or psychiatrists, but which is instructive for one who is trying to understand the sexual behaviors of men vowed to celibacy. Karpman pointed out that behaviors that are essentially pathological in their extreme form, are acceptable "in milder forms and degrees, especially if they are indulged in as a subsidiary part of normal relations; as a sort of preliminary, they should be regarded as falling within the framework of the normal" (p. 416).

He also pointed out that "children indulge in all sorts of sexual experimentations which include perversion" (p. 416). As I have said earlier, one of the problems of celibate education is a propensity or proclivity to leave childhood sexual orientation unexamined. Those who are inclined to write off celibacy itself as a form of pathology will not be interested in fighting through to an understanding of the dilemmas, behaviors, and vagaries of one who is striving for maturity, even sexual, without the benefit of the mating and marital experiences. The observer will need tolerance and empathy with the educational and growth struggles of a minority whose "handicap" is a supremely high spiritual ideal. A priest attempting celibacy does not necessarily develop psychosexually in the same way or at least at the same rate as the average man. I will say more about these matters in Chapter 12 on the process of celibacy. At this point it is useful to consider Karpman's (1954) position as it applies to priests. He defined the normal pervert as

... one who, despite the handicap imposed by an unorthodox and socially unacceptable sexual orientation, does manage to live an otherwise normal life according to general standards of ordinary behavior. He is really no different from the individual who suffers from a physical handicap and who nevertheless contrives to make for himself a way of life that is generally useful and attended with more than an ordinary amount of satisfaction. But while the victim of a physical handicap is praised for his efforts, the victim of a psychosexual handicap is condemned. The principal reason is because the victim of a physical handicap is regarded as having suffered a misfortune, while the victim of a psychosexual handicap is labeled a pervert as though his psychosexual handicap were a matter of voluntary choice and deliberate selection. . . . (p. 417)

THE PLACE OF WOMEN

A question related to celibate compromises is that of the place of women in the life of a priest who does not want to be sexually or affectively involved. The place of the priest's mother is often enhanced by devotion to the "Blessed Virgin Mother Mary." This spiritual emulation tends to fixate the priest in the role of a son who is affiliated with a male-centered "idolatry." Monica Furlong (1987) contended that this structure of the Church justifies men's right to dominate all women. The male child for whom mother is the center of his affective universe becomes very special in the real or imagined reciprocity of his mother's love. Furlong put it this way:

> The Christian feminist contention is that the Churches are hung up on a sort of male-centered idolatry which in turn justifies a belief that men are superior with the right to dominate women (there are other tragic assumptions around all this—the right to dominate nature, for one). Yet no true mutuality is possible within a framework of domination and subordination, attractive as it is to those who find intimacy difficult. (p. 1084)

By revising their view of Christian womanhood, women are challenging the traditional structure of power that has become inextricably interwoven with celibacy. A celibacy that is dependent on immature sexual identity will be threatening to women and, equally as important, will be frightened of them (*cf*. Karl Stern, *The Flight from Women*, 1986). Women's experience of the Church and their articulation of it are helping the priest experience his own gender conflicts and have them exposed in bold relief. Questions of sexual identity can be manifest in behaviors involving pornography, transvestism, and exhibitionism, among other things.

Gender identity—the sense that one is male or female—is laid down very early in life. Sexual identity—the sense of *how* masculine or feminine one is—also begins in the first year of life but becomes increasingly focused from the third year of life through adolescence, building on gender identity. The place of the mother and her expressions play major roles in forming these identities. The mother's response to her baby and her facial cues of approval or displeasure are crucial to identity formation. Again, Furlong (1986) made a powerful analogy of women's experience of the Church as it impinges on a woman's identity:

> To gaze upon the face of the Church our Mother (psychoanalysts nowadays often describe the face of the mother as being like a mirror in which the child learns its identity) has been for many Christian women of this generation an extraordinarily painful and life-changing experience, one that it was at first enormously tempting to deny, as some women still do deny it. (p. 1083)

From the clerical point of view, what this attitude amounts to is really rejection. Furlong (1986) confirmed that it is not "the rejection of our ideal and idealized selves of course—for Christianity had always been strong on those—but the rejection of the living, breathing, subjective people that we are" (p. 1083).

If sexual development does not mature, not only is sexual identity stifled or delayed, but untimely "childhood" behavior becomes overly attractive, often in an attempt to solve the immaturity. In outlining the development of childhood sexuality, Sterba (1968) underscored the prominence of vision as a source of excitation. He said:

> Looking at the naked body, particularly at the genitals or buttocks of others, produces, from a very early age, intense pleasure satisfaction. Even with adults, the sight of the loved object is frequently the first source of excitation. In the case of perversion, the erotogenic pleasure in looking leads to scoptophilia. Being looked at when naked also often excites intense, even ecstatic pleasure of an undoubtedly sensual nature in children. (p. 55)

The knowledge that seeing erotic material can be sexually stimulating was recognized in ancient ascetic tradition, which counseled "custody of the eyes" as a protection against sensual temptations. Today it is accepted that both the desire to see pornography (voyeurism, certainly) and the desire to be seen (exhibitionism) have their roots deep in infancy.

FEAR OF WOMEN

If the use of pornography is coupled with the fear of women as it was frequently demonstrated to be by those who reported to us, the probability of fixation at immature levels of psychosexual development becomes more likely. Devotion to the idealized Blessed Virgin only serves to enhance early concepts of other women as dangerous and, therefore, desirably inaccessible. Freud, Abraham, and other students of psychosexual development have pointed out the importance of fear in inhibiting development.

> The fear of women in all pregenital cultures is the denied fear of the maternal object, who by her oral seduction becomes the castrating mother. Freud's . . . concept of the universality of the "repudiation of femininity" was based upon castration anxiety and penis envy, characteristic only of the phallic phase. It may be, perhaps, more accurately interpreted as the repudiation of the pregenital mother, "the most dangerous enemy." (Sarlin, 1975, p. 367)

In some priests, the sexual flame of curiosity is actually fanned by their fear, their attempt to overcome it, and by their sexual inexperience. The Report of the Commission on Obscenity and Pornography (1970) applied to the priests in our study as well as to the general population when it stated:

> Most patrons of adult bookstores and movie houses appear to have had less sexually related experiences in adolescence than the average male, but to be more sexually oriented as an adult. This high degree of sexual orientation in adulthood encompasses, in addition to pictorial and textual erotica, a variety of partners and a variety of activities within a consensual framework. Activities most frowned upon by our society, such as sadomasochism, pedophilia, bestiality, and nonconsensual sex, are also outside the scope of their interests. (p. 134)

Many people would question the value of pornography as an educational element in any man's life, let alone that of a dedicated celibate. Pornography is a fact, an ancient fact and in some cultures an art form, but not in Christian tradition. "An erotic art, Foucault said [in *The History of Sexuality*], is the usual way for a civilization to make sense of its knowledge about sex. He pointed to the existence of such artistic expression in Etruscan, Roman, Arabic, Persian, Indian, Chinese, Japanese, and many other civilization but not, alas, in the Christian" (Sipe, 1987, p. 89).

The feminists make a point about the exploitation of women in pornography. As Alan Soble (1986) said:

> The feminist critique of pornography can be summarized in four theses. First, some of the *content* of pornography is sexist. It depicts the abuse of women, and often, even when the sexual acts are not cruel, it is degrading. Second, pornography supports sexism and has

other objectionable *effects.* Pornography perpetuates sexual stereotypes, undermines the quality of sexual relationships, and . . . pro-
motes a social climate in which assault is tolerated. Third, the
production of pornography involves the exploitation of women.
Fourth, the *consumption* of pornography is propelled by exploitation; the producer of pornography takes advantage of manipulated
men. (p. 150)

In *Presentations of Gender* (1985), Robert J. Stoller discussed some of
the manifestations of gender disorders and their impact on women:

> When we look closely at the behavior that makes up a man's perver-
> sion—when we get an in-depth subjective description of the erotic
> behavior—we find, regardless of the overt form of the behavior, that
> he is under pressure from envy and anger toward women. . . . The
> evidence is found in the fantasies these men have that they are de-
> grading women. Examples are rape, coprolalia (dirty language as an
> erotic stimulant), voyeurism, fetishism, exhibitionism, pedophilia,
> necrophilia. In all these you will find evidence of uncertain manli-
> ness. And so, though there may be no desire to put on clothes of the
> opposite sex or otherwise to behave (or fantasize behaving) as a
> member of the opposite sex, in the perversions is nonetheless buried
> unsureness of gender identity. (Classical psychoanalysis discusses
> these issues in terms of "castration anxiety," a concept I find too
> anatomic, too stripped of identity connotations.) (p. 18)

The feminist arguments hold some special significance for the priest
whose sexual experience and education are limited, and who is, therefore,
unduly influenced by what he does see and hear. A priest's unresolved
fear of women often manifests itself in a harsh and denigrating attitude
toward them that has multiple pastoral and even theological ramifications. Excerpts from Pope John Paul II's apostolic letter, "On the Dignity
of Women," published in the September 30, 1988, *New York Times,* ex-
emplify the Church's increasingly positive *teachings* on the nature and
roles of women. Yet it will not be until the opinions of women are heard
and heeded by the Church that it will develop a healthier mode of educating and evaluating its priests.

WHAT IS PORNOGRAPHY?

Speak no evil, do no evil, but see what you can.

In his book, *Sexual Excitement,* Stoller (1979) defined pornography
rather objectively:

By pornography I mean material made available (openly or secretively) for those who derive sexual stimulation from representations of sexual objects and erotic situations rather than from the objects and situations themselves. These materials may consist of writings, drawings, paintings, sculpture, ceramics; private performances, recorded or spoken; performances for an audience, such as recitations, plays, dance, religious rites, performances in which one is a participant. (p. 27)

In *The Joy of Sex: A Gourmet Guide to Love Making,* Dr. Alex Comfort (1972) discussed the substitution aspects of pornography and defined it as:

[the] name given to any sexual literature somebody is trying to suppress. Most normal people enjoy looking at sex books and reading sex fantasies, which is why abnormal people have to spend so much time and money suppressing them. The only drawback of the commercial stuff is that because it is based on fantasy, and often inexperienced fantasy at that, it's not much help with sex practice. Depiction of any of the range of sex behaviors we've described helps people to visualize them; porno stories tend to be dull, repetitive, and a strain on credulity; frankly antisocial fantasies about torture and so on worry legislators and others for fear they might induce idiots to imitate them—it's equally possible that by enabling not very bright people to fantasize their unacceptable needs vividly they help to keep them from acting them out, but there is no good evidence one way or another. (p. 208)

John Money's (1986) *Lovemaps* defined pornography more subjectively:

The best empirical definition of pornography is that it is explicitly depicted erotic and sexual material that generates in a viewer, reader, or listener who has access to it, a sense of being sneaky, surreptitious, and illicit, provided access to the same material by the same person at a younger age would have been prohibited, prevented, and punished. (p. 167)

Money (1986) also quotes Supreme Court Justice Potter Stewart's "famous dictum on defining hard-core pornography: '. . . perhaps I could never succeed in intelligibly [defining it]. But I know it when I see it. . . .' " (p. 166).

Martha Freud, Sigmund's wife, "thought her husband's psychoanalytic ideas 'a form of pornography' " (Gay, 1988, p. 61). Others may see the psychiatrist as a kind of voyeur. Indeed, probably all the helping professions, including medicine and ministry, demand a quality of character that can tolerate an intimate view of other persons' sexual problems and lives. At times, there may be a very fine line dividing pastoral concern from prurient interest. It is simply an occupational hazard that each professional must deal with responsibly.

In this chapter, I am treating pornography and voyeurism not in their respective psychiatric diagnostic categories, but instead I am addressing the behaviors they generate. Thus, I will group the two.

According to Tollison and Adams (1979), although the data on voyeurism are scarce, several facts are known: (1) The behavior is limited to males; (2) the voyeur usually displays deficits in heterosocial skills; and (3) masturbation plays a critical role in development and maintenance of the behavior (p. 228).

Priests deprived of a sexual outlet can turn to pornography and in that sense exhibit the behaviors of voyeurism. In our study, an increasing number of priests between the late 1960s and the 1980s reported exploring both visual and literary pornography. For most of these priests, the incidents were part of their attempt to supplement faulty sex education or were merely forays into their sexual immaturity.

Over the past 20 years, pornography has become more available to everyone, including priests. Adult bookshops with their bright signs have proliferated across the United States landscape with a familiarity similar to the markings of the interstate road system.

Legal, familiar, and accessible hard-core pornography has become almost stylish. Johnny Carson can joke and speak openly about viewing *Deep Throat* and *Behind the Green Door* before millions of television viewers. The growth of the VCR industry in the 80s has made these and thousands of other films dealing explicitly with every form and manner of sexual activity available to interested persons in the comfort and privacy of their homes. A number of priests have responded just like the public in general with curiosity and experimentation. Some reported that by "seeing" some sexual activity they were, for the first time, confronted with their own sexual interest and orientation.

For example, a 32-year-old priest who had entered the seminary in his teens and whose sexual experience was limited to occasional masturbation, observed one night from his rectory window a teenaged couple "making out" in a car parked close by. There was a dance in the parish hall and this couple had sneaked past the chaperons to their rendezvous. The angle of view and the lighting favored the priest's observation and he stood in the dark of his room transfixed by the thrashings and obvious passion of the young couple. He found himself more sexually stimulated than he had ever been in his life and he masturbated. After this experience, he went through a phase of visiting pornographic bookshops and, later, peep shows. He was fascinated with the female body and became aware of how much he wanted to make love with a woman. Although this period lasted several years and was distressing and confusing to the priest, it finally was incorporated into his sexual maturation.

The use of pornography is often accompanied or followed by masturbation. Sometimes it is a prelude to or reinforcement of other sexual activities, including homosexuality and pedophilia.

In *The Psychoanalytic Theory of Neurosis,* Otto Fenichel (1945) said the following:

> In lovers of pornography one frequently meets two contradictory, reassuring attitudes: (1) The fact that sexual details are described in print proves the objective existence of sexuality; by the mechanism of "sharing guilt" it relieves guilt feelings by making sexual fantasies more "objective." (2) Nevertheless the feared sexuality is not quite real; it is enjoyed in empathy by reading about it in a book, not by experiencing it actually, and thus it is less dangerous.
>
> Masturbation with the help of pornographic literature is nearer, in one respect, to normal sexuality than is masturbation without it, the book being a medium between sexual fantasy and sexual reality. In adolescents or persons with perverse inclinations who are ashamed of admitting their wishes, the book or picture may simply represent a substitute for a sexual partner. (p. 351)

One of the finest first-person descriptions of the use of pornography and its process in a priest's life could have been written by any one of a dozen priests in our study, but it was not. It was published anonymously under the pen name "Father Augustine" in *America* magazine (October 1, 1988):

> I first began to "act out" sexually about 20 years ago. That was in the late 1960s when the so-called sexual revolution was just getting under way and when pornography became widely and easily available. It was with pornography that my addiction first manifested itself, and my addiction has continued to center on it, although it has developed other manifestations.
>
> I had been ordained about 10 years, felt happy in my vocation as a priest and a member of a religious order and had received my first permanent assignment. I went about that assignment in a large Midwestern city with all the zeal I could muster "for the kingdom of God." I now understand that my zeal contained within it the core of what I consider my primary addiction: workaholism.

I soon began to subordinate in practice (though not in theory, of course) all my time and energies to achievement in my ministry. Just why I *had* to achieve, I now see, goes back to my childhood and adolescence, but at the time, I was not even aware that it was a problem. I, in fact, thought of it as a virtue.

I shaved time off my prayer and fitted God into my schedule in the few moments I could spare. Friends and recreation suffered in the same way. I, in effect, was shutting down on the affective, humane side of my vocation. The fact that I was attaining immense success in my ministry only fed the ills concealed in my zeal. I had time for everybody and everything except myself.

My prurient interest in pornographic magazines and movies grew accordingly, and I found myself with some frequency in the bookstores and cinemas that fed it. Even at this early stage of addiction, my denial had sufficiently developed to allow me to walk out of these situations with a relatively clean conscience. What devastated me in those early years, however, was that two or three times a year I would go on a binge—spending hours in the cinemas, buying the literature, bringing it home where I consumed it and masturbated over it.

This led on the "mornings after" to thoughts of suicide and to anguished visits to confessionals where I prayed I would find a priest who would not recognize me. Every confession brought the firmest resolutions that I would never, never do it again. But within a few months the pattern repeated itself, resulting in the same self-hate and the same firm but utterly ineffective resolutions. By this time I had, for obvious reasons, given up the practice of a "regular confessor."

One year during a retreat I became painfully aware of the pattern and of the fact that my resolutions were getting me nowhere. I needed help, and God gave me the strength to talk to another priest about what was going on in my life. The priest could not have been more surprised, for my life gave absolutely no evidence on the outside that anything was wrong. I was, in fact, admired by him and by many others as a colleague who "had it all together."

I have to admit that as I told my story I surprised myself. The person I described did not seem to be *me*. Although like most human beings I had struggles with my sexuality while I was growing up and even during my years in the seminary, neither I nor others saw any cause for particular alarm. I believed all along—and continue to believe—that I had a genuine call from God to serve in the priesthood and religious life. But things were happening in my life to make it seem to be the worst of hypocrisy. The image of Dr. Jekyll and Mr. Hyde often flashed through my mind.

The priest was kind and compassionate. He suggested a number of standard spiritual remedies, and especially insisted that I be open with him about everything that was going on. I count that interview as the beginning of my recovery, for I had become an expert at keeping secret even from myself the deep and dark forces that were at work in me. Nonetheless, my acting out did not cease. In fact, its frequency and intensity increased, especially after I was transferred to another large city where I once again could not bring myself to talk about my problem to those who might help me. The shame was overpowering.

I began to have some physical contact with others who sought the same sexual thrills as I did, but the real center of my disease continued to situate itself in various forms of pornography and masturbation. I occasionally had several weeks during which I felt I had everything under control, but as time went on my binges became more frequent, more prolonged, more devastating, more reckless. Alcohol became one of my preferred "props" to help me get the sexual highs that were gradually becoming more elusive.

By this time I had mastered the art of hiding my secret activities, but I could at least vaguely see what others could not. My life was careening out of control. I began to miss work and to feel obsessed for days on end. I could not, however, stop doing what I so much hated. Given the places that I frequented unremittingly, it is a miracle that I was not mugged, knifed or arrested.

After a particularly frightening experience one night when I thought I was recognized by someone at a pornographic movie, I told one of my superiors about it—and about everything else. As the months passed I continued to try to keep in touch with him, wrenching though these interviews were. I remember weeping bitterly in his presence on several occasions; but despite the compassion and good advice I received, I still could not stop. (pp. 190–191)

This priest demonstrated the pattern and progress of growing absorption with pornography. First he confided the incident, as sin, to his confessor. Quicky he moved to the second phase where he sought out an anonymous confessor to whom he told isolated transgressions of his conscience. Third, he indulged his interest and avoided telling any priest about his activities. At this point, the problem had moved deeper and deeper into the system of secrecy, more and more isolated from the priest's religious ideals or perhaps completely split off from them. The visual stimulation led not only to masturbation but also to sexual contact with other men or with women.

Frequently there are men or boys around adult bookshops and peep shows who are willing or eager to exchange sexual activity. If the store is in an area of bars, prostitutes are often also available. It does not take long for even the shy inexperienced clergyman who is seeking pornography to find that it is usually surrounded by people who are ready to enact what the books describe and the movies depict.

One 55-year-old priest in our study came to our attention not in his lifetime, but because of his death by a heart attack in a pornographic movie theater. His church superiors were anxious to keep the site of his death out of the newspapers, which they were able to do. The facts of his sexual pattern were revealed in the aftermath. He had kept a complete record of all the foreign ships that docked at a seaport near his home. Certain foreign seamen frequented the pornographic movie theater that he had become accustomed to visiting once a month, the visit always coinciding with the shore leave of a foreign ship. All of his sexual activity had involved pornographic films in conjunction with homosexual contact with sailors in the theater. It can be assumed that this had been the sole sexual activity of this methodical priest, who had kept such a meticulous accounting of his adventures. The rest of his life had been equally well regulated and documentable.

Although pornography can lead a priest to sexual contact with others, it may also follow or substitute for that contact. A priest who had had a prolonged sexual affair with a woman when he was in his 30s renewed his vow of celibacy when she died and did subsequently refrain from sexual activity. His collection of pornographic literature and pictures, which he began after her death, may be viewed as the exception—a sublimation and, although untraditional, his way of seeking celibacy. Since he was a teacher and scholar, he incorporated his hobby into his other interests in an intellectual way—he became an authority on Henry Miller.

There are a number of priests who practice celibacy and even eventually achieve the state who use modern cinema and literature very well. Literally, they learn from it in a mature way. They are rarely interested in the pornographic because of its lack of person and event. In pornography, the only object is a penis or a vagina; the only event is the orgasm. Persons of spiritual and intellectual depth and maturity are fascinated by life and are usually bored quickly by pornography.

For some priests, pornography is an occasional or passing interest as a victimless outlet for their sexual tension. A few become addicted. There are a few who relish their role as censors and crusaders against pornography. A layman reported his aversion to the enthusiastic cleric who was trying to elicit his help on a church committee to stamp out pornography for the protection of the youths of the area. With a wild gleam in his eye, the priest had said to the layman, "You should *see* what they *show!*" The layman noted also that many of the committee members spent a disproportionate amount of time reviewing and riling against the material to be stamped out.

The following editorial appeared in the October 6, 1984, *Baltimore Sun* regarding the Reverend Jerry Falwell:

> From his mass-mail factory in Lynchburg, Virginia, he has just sent to the faithful a most unusual solicitation containing an envelope with a warning to prepare for a "shock." The shock turns out to be two photographs—one of the transvestite Sister Boom-Boom and the other of two men kissing with "tongues entwined, openly in public," to use Mr. Falwell's own description.
>
> Prudently, the minister urges the photos be destroyed at once, lest they fall under the gaze of children. But it turns out that the two photographs are only teasers for even more "unbelievable" pictures. "For $25 or more," Mr. Falwell wrote, "I will send you a Photo Journal of my San Francisco experience, featuring pages of pictures taken by my 17-year-old son Jonathan, who went incognito into the streets."
>
> From this astonishing sales offer, as well as from his TV sermons, it is reasonable to wonder if Mr. Falwell has developed something close to an unhealthy obsession with an activity that to the average American is rather remote.
>
> Mr. Falwell's ploy recalls a high-ranking judge I once knew who would startle lawyers who came to his chambers by thrusting upon them a large collection of pornographic magazines—ostensibly to show just how bad things had gotten since Earl Warren became chief justice.

For the average priest or the average religious layperson, pornography is not the object of prolonged or undue interest. The most apt similarity to the interested priest is the adolescent—curious and afraid of sex, relatively inexperienced, yet eager to learn about it and not quite certain of an avenue that is both safe and acceptable to his conscience.

Because so many priests during the late 1960s and beyond have been exposed to some pornography and yet it so rarely persists in isolation without masturbation, and even with homosexual or pedophilic activity, we make no estimate of pornography as a sexual outlet. Suffice it to say that many have been exposed, but only a few are addicted. From our observations, we have to agree with the *Report of the Commission on*

Obscenity and Pornography (1970) that "Research to date thus provides no substantial basis for the belief that erotic materials constitute a primary or significant cause of the development of character deficits or that they operate as a significant determinative factor in causing crime and delinquency" (p. 243).

The Attorney General's conclusion as reported in the May 14, 1986, *Baltimore Sun* that "substantial exposure to materials of this type bears some causal relationship to the level of sexual violence, sexual coercion, or unwanted sexual aggression in the population so exposed" does not hold true for our informants, despite the fact that it caused many a great deal of distress and soul-searching. However, although it does not lead to violent behavior in priests, pornography does little to soften their view of women or to tame the violence toward them that some may feel. "Wrestling with the devils" of their own unconscious brought some scars along with knowledge and in certain cases was a step toward their maturation.

EXHIBITIONISTIC BEHAVIOR

In contrast to voyeurism, where sexual pleasure is achieved by seeing, exhibitionism is a mode of deriving sexual pleasure from *being* seen. More specifically, it is defined "as the exposure of the sexual organs to the opposite sex in situations in which exposure is socially defined as inappropriate, and is carried out, at least in part, for the purpose of sexual arousal and gratification. . . ." This definition rules out instances in which the exposure is seen as appropriate (Tollison & Adams, 1979, p. 237).

Alex Comfort (1972), that champion of casual sexual attitudes, said "the self-adhesive label gets stuck on people who for a variety of reasons can get their sex in no other way, and show their genitalia to strangers. This would be a harmless but unrewarding activity (these timid characters are by definition not rapists) if people weren't shocked or frightened by it, though it's a disability to the fellow who can't get further than that" (p. 232).

In our study group, not one case of exhibitionism as defined by Tollison and Adams appeared. Dr. Bartemeier had consulted with two cases prior to 1960 and some clinicians who reviewed our conclusions said that they had known of some as well, but it is safe to say that as an unvarnished disorder it is rare among priests vowed to celibacy. Other researchers have pointed out that in the population generally "the peak of exhibitionism is in the 20s, and it decreases rapidly in the 30s; over the age of 40 the symptom occurs only in rare instances. Although the peak of the exhibitionist's behavior is around age 25, the onset of symptoms has two major periods, one in midpuberty, and the other in the early 20s. Exhibitionists as a group are young; offenses occurring at an older age frequently indicate other factors, such as alcoholism, organic deterioration, or another sexual deviation, especially pedophilia" (Mohr et al., 1964, p. 127).

There was one priest who took great delight in walking nude from the bathroom to the bedroom in his parish house when he felt the housekeeper, whom he disliked, had invaded his upstairs domain. Although it was mean-spirited, the housekeeper was intrigued as well as frightened, but it lacked real sexual excitement on his part. He had other problems.

Several reports of incidents where priests who were drunk exposed themselves inappropriately were reported, but none proved to be a pattern, and control of the alcoholism seemed to eliminate even these incidents. Exhibitionism that is a factor in pedophilia is correctly dealt with under that disorder, one that proves more troublesome both to the offender and his treatment as well as to the victim.

Since celibacy is dependent on the more or less successful sublimation of the sexual instinct, one has to be aware of the partial and derivative ways in which a person seeks to be celibate. We learn from the spectrum and not merely from the extremes of success and failure.

I have to take careful note of exhibitionistic behavior, not because the ranks of the clergy are filled with "flashers", but because of the psychic dimension of this element of sexual development manifested in many clerical histories, although this use of the term "exhibitionistic" has to be distinguished from the strict clinical diagnostic category. As Tollison and Adams (1979) said, clinical exhibitionism "also differs somewhat from the more general usage of the word . . . [which denotes] anyone who enjoys showing off his or her body and being admired and desired for his physical attractiveness" (p. 237). The clerical office puts men on exhibit; they become public figures and command the attention of throngs of sometimes adulatory people. Some men exploit this aspect of their vocation. Other men who were exquisitely aware of the inner workings of their hearts and minds (by way of long-term daily meditation) humbly acknowledged the part played in their ministry by their love of attention.

The traditional way of understanding exhibitionistic behavior was to see it as a result of unresolved "castration anxiety."

> In exhibitionism a denial of castration is attempted by a simple overcathexis of a partial instinct. Exhibitionism in children certainly has the character of a partial instinct; any child derives pleasure from the display of his genitals and, in pregenital times, of the other erogenous zones and their functions. . . . Perverts regress to this infantile aim because the stressing of this aim can be used for denial of a danger that is believed to be connected with normal sexuality. (Fenichel, 1945, p. 345)

Fenichel then pointed out three ways in which this underdeveloped sexual (and personality) expression serves a man.

1. It calls upon the reactions of others to reassure one in the face of his own inner doubts about his masculinity.

2. Inspiring fear in the other, one does not have to be afraid of himself ("identification with the aggressor"). One priest who had exhibitionistic fantasies when he masturbated was a remarkably dramatic preacher and had been a popular retreat master at one time in his career. In his parish he carefully arranged the lighting to focus only on a large crucifix and himself in the pulpit. In one of his favorite presentations, he would prostrate himself before the crucifix, "casting himself at the feet of Christ." The whole of his drama would reach a crescendo when he would speak about sin and God's response. "He will hate you! He will hate you! He will hate you!" he would shout at the top of his voice, pounding the pulpit with his closed fist (a surprisingly clear masturbatory gesture) before a rapt and terrified audience. This particular presentation would always give him a great sense of relief and reassurance.

3. An imagined element of magic exists in which the distinction between male and female disappears. "In this sense the exhibitionist acts like the transvestite; he 'acts' the girl who shows her penis. . . . In reassuring the individual against castration the partial instinct of exhibitionism may engage all of the sexual energy, thus facilitating the repression of the other parts of infantile sexuality, especially of the Oedipus complex" (Fenichel, 1945, p. 346).

The elements of unconsolidated and ill-resolved gender and sexual identities are eminently important to the understanding of some aspects of celibacy. We have only glimpses of the fantasy lives of priests, but from the information gathered in our study, I feel it is safe to say that there are some who, like the men Stoller (1985) observed in his work, are "under pressure from envy and anger toward women. The evidence is found in the fantasies these men have that they are degrading women" (p. 18). In the case of priests committed to celibacy in whom direct sexual behavior may be minimal, it is in fantasy that their relative levels of sexual anxiety are revealed to them. The new diagnostic category takes this into account when it includes as exhibitionism not only the man who acts on his urges, but also the man who is "markedly distressed by them" or who masturbates while "fantasizing exposing himself" (*DSM-III-R*, 1987, p. 282). A great deal of work needs to be done to clarify satisfactorily this area as it applies to celibates.

TRANSVESTISM

Dr. Bartemeier and I had long discussions about the meaning of transvestism for the Catholic priest. He felt that only those could be considered to have a problem with cross-dressing who became sexually excited when "arousal and facilitation or attainment of orgasm are responsive to, and dependent upon wearing clothing, especially underwear, of the other sex" (Money, 1986, p. 272). Indeed, we had a sufficient number of informants report behavior strictly defined as transvestism to conclude that 1 percent of Catholic clergy make this sexual compromise. Bartemeier felt that it was of no consequence that the ministry occasionally demands that one wear skirts or flowing robes, which, from a secular point of view, could be feminine. The silks, satins, brocades, laces, and ermines required in some ceremonies are no more than a uniform to the vast majority of clergy.

A deeper understanding of the clerical transvestite, as in the understanding of the other manifestations of sexual compromise, requires an examination of transvestism in its strictest clinical sense as well as a look at the psychosexual developmental dynamics underlying it.

Of the definitions of transvestism I have encountered, Stoller (1985), in his *Presentations of Gender*, most closely encompasses all of the elements found in our reports.

> The term *transvestism* has been used for any cross-dressing. (In fact, such a vague clinical concept can seem precise only if one transforms it with the scientific-sounding Latin.) I restrict it, however, to those, again biologically normal, who put on clothes of the opposite sex because the clothes are sexually exciting to them. Though this fetishism can occur in childhood, usually it is first manifested at puberty or later in adolescence. It is almost always found in men who are overtly heterosexual, of masculine demeanor, in occupations dominated by males; and it occurs only intermittently, most of the subject's life being spent in unremarkably masculine behavior and appearance. (p. 21)

A priest in midlife had collected a series of costumes throughout his career. Sometimes he used them in his teaching and sometimes in his role as a host for both private and parish-related parties. The clothes were not exclusively feminine, but often were ambiguous, including King Solomon-like flowing robes or the garb and earring of a pirate, or occasionally the dress of some Shakespearean character. However, he never exhibited his most exotic outfits in public, reserving them instead for himself while relaxing in the privacy of his room. He enjoyed wearing very tight corset-like garments, especially those that held his genitals firmly, under every costume.

Nothing is known about the early development of his behavior. His parents had died when he was a child, and he had spent some time in an orphanage prior to his placement with an older couple whom he described as attentive and loving. He was conscientious about his work in every regard; he entertained many and offended no one. His insecurity about his own masculinity and his attitudes toward women were his private crosses.

Another priest of similar age was the product of an unhappy home. He spoke of his father as harsh but ineffective and his mother as overprotective and frowning. He entered the seminary in high school in part as a way out of his family's conflicts. He was an excellent athlete with an unquestionably masculine face and form, so much so that it was nearly impossible to conjure the mental image of him dressed in any of what he described as a "closetful" of women's clothing. No one had ever seen him dressed up. His living arrangement allowed him complete privacy. He would return to his home at night, put on feminine finery, have his meal, and relax before the television or with a book.

Although he had no desire to change his behavior, two fears had brought him to psychiatric care. The first was that he might be involved in an accident and someone would discover his secret wardrobe; the second was his growing urge to steal women's lingerie. He had been able to assemble his other clothes on buying trips out of town, but even there he could not bring himself to purchase undergarments, the very items he found most sexually exciting. They held a more direct fetishistic quality for him and therefore conflicted the most with his vow of celibacy.

A third example is that of a hardworking priest who was concerned about his masturbation. He was very troubled and felt tremendous guilt; no confessor had been able to console him, even those who told him that masturbation was "natural" or that he had too delicate a conscience. Because the priest's episodes were relatively infrequent, it was difficult for a confessor to fathom the depth of the anxiety and remorse each incident caused this tortured man.

However, what this priest failed to confide was the mode of his sexual activity. He would sustain long periods of sexual abstinence and then would be overcome by an urge to put on women's clothing, especially pantyhose, a corset, or any other tight-fitting undergarment, being careful not to touch his penis with his hand. When he was younger he had thought such touching was the essence of the sin of masturbation, and thought if he could avoid touching himself he would not be guilty. Nevertheless, in struggling against the binding undergarment, he would have an erection and ejaculate. He had been the product of a broken home and had always felt that his mother would have been happier if he had been a girl, a thought he found abhorrent. He reasoned that as a priest he could at least take care of her.

Another priest, who had a flair for the dramatic in his own personality as well as in his activities coaching the drama students, sustained a long-term involvement with amateur theater productions and told us of his early awareness of his desire to dress in women's clothes. His mother was a seamstress and would get him to play the dressmaker's dummy when she was exercising her craft. At first he had not wanted to work with her, but recounted that eventually he experienced a closeness, warmth, and sense of fun with her that he had never had before. His sexual fantasies always revolved around those moments, and his behavior was an attempt to relive them. I believe Stoller (1985) was correct when he said "if a man is a transvestite—a fetishistic cross-dresser—his childhood can be expected to differ from the constellation described for very feminine boys" (p. 137). This was true of the informants in our study.

St. Jerome, who died in 420, was one of the most colorful Fathers of the Church. He was a staunch and implacable proponent of clerical celibacy. His stature is established as a scholar who spent a half-century translating the Scriptures. His sexual life found no autobiographical witness like his contemporary, St. Augustine, but there are provocative intimations that are worthy of a psychohistory. A thousand years after his death, part of Jerome's life was immortalized in the incomparably beautiful illustrations in The Belles Heures of Jean, Duke of Berry. Jerome was a learned man versed in the pagan philosophies. The story goes that he had a dream in which he promised to give up his secular studies. In that dream he was scourged by two whip-wielding angels in the sight of God on His throne. The manuscript reads:

> Then the Judge ordered a severe beating. Jerome cried out: Lord have mercy on me, if I read these [profane] books again I shall have denied Thee. Then, dismissed, he suddenly regained consciousness in streams of tears and found terrible scars on his shoulders. (Meiss & Beatson, 1974, Fol. 183v)

The commentators remarked that:

> Jerome made public his resolution taken in a dream, and many years later it was used against him by Rufinus, who ridiculed him for his classical quotations. The saint was not, however, seriously troubled; his attitude to dreams had changed. "Can dreams," he asks, "be used in evidence? . . . How often have I dreamed that I was dead and in the grave . . . How often have I flown over mountains and crossed the seas! Does that mean that I am dead or that wings grow from my sides?" (Meiss & Beatson, Fol. 183v)

In the same source is recorded and depicted the famous incident where Jerome appeared in the monks' choir wearing a woman's dress. Biographers have called the occurrence a mistake on Jerome's part, saying that he fell into a trap set by monks who were jealous of his popularity with rich Roman women—friendships that were the subject of much gossip. According to biographers, an evil monk substituted a woman's dress for Jerome's habit, and in the dark Jerome put it on, not realizing what it was. Whatever the motives or facts of the incident, it propelled Jerome to leave Rome, never to return. He subsequently spent four years in the desert and was known to wear a hair shirt rather than soft garments. Under a miniature of Jerome in the desert reads an inscription taken from one of his letters to his student, Eustochium:

How often as I dwelt in that waste, in that vast solitude burnt away by the heat of the sun, which provides a terrible abode for monks, I imagined myself among the delights of Rome. My twisted limbs shuddered in a garment of sackcloth. (Fol. 185v)

In another of Jerome's letters, he described being tempted by dancing girls:

Daily I wept, daily I groaned, and when overcome by sleep I resisted, my bones, scarcely holding together, were bruised by the ground. Although my only companions were scorpions I often imagined I was surrounded by dancing girls, who kindled the fires of lust. (Fol. 186)

The miniature showing Jerome translating the Bible indicates accurately that his life's work did not really begin until he had extricated from himself some thorn of the flesh. Metaphorically, he removed a thorn from the paw of a lion, who subsequently became his docile companion. The text under this miniature reads:

Having, therefore, done penance in the wilderness for four years, Jerome went to dwell like a domestic animal at the manger of the Lord in Bethlehem where, remaining chaste, he labored for fifty-five years and six months at the translation of the Bible and the Holy Scriptures. (Fol. 187v)

Jerome's life makes sense if we understand his episode of cross-dressing not simply as a trick of wicked monks, but as a manifestation of his sexual development that must be reconciled with his brilliance and later sanctity. His asceticism and hair shirt, although not entirely uncommon practices at that time in Christianity, can be seen as a reaction to having been caught in behavior that was little understood in religious form at that time.

It is not idle speculation to search the lives and writings of saintly celibates to reconstruct their psychosexual development. I believe that sound scholarship can verify from Jerome's own writings a far clearer picture of his sexuality and celibacy than has been painted thus far.

I also believe that the disagreement Dr. Bartemeier and I had over the importance of the transvestite element in the priesthood was grounded in our differing perceptions of the formation of gender and sexual identities. Bartemeier would agree without reserve with Fenichel (1945) who said,

> The homosexual man replaces his love for his mother by an identification with her; the fetishist refuses to acknowledge that a woman has no penis. The male transvestite assumes both attitudes simultaneously. . . . He fantasies that the woman possesses a penis, and thus overcomes his castration anxiety, and identifies himself with this phallic woman. Hence the fundamental trend of transvestism is the same as that found in homosexuality and fetishism: the refutation of the idea that there is a danger of castration. However, the identification with the mother is established not by imitating her object choice but rather her "being a woman." (p. 344)

The essence of transvestism, Fenichel reiterated, is "identification with the woman, as a substitute for, or side by side with, love for her" (1953, p. 169).

The challenge to establish one's masculinity and the struggle then to remain celibate are not simple matters. Freud believed in the inherent bisexuality of humans, but he did not espouse gender equality. He, with all thinkers of his time, thought of the male gender as the superior biological and psychological sex. The persistence of this stance is important, if not indispensable, for understanding the current celibate structure. However, a more fully reasoned sense of the development of masculinity actually explains more accurately how celibacy operates and the problems it faces.

The idea of male superiority is necessary to keep the male matrix unassailed, to preserve the male exclusivity of the hierarchical structure of the Church, and to validate the homosocial organization of the clergy.

Stoller articulated the shift in thinking about the development of masculinity. We will deal with this in greater depth in Chapter 12 on the process of celibacy. However, I want to note this important shift here, where it bears on behavior which, although a sexual compromise, is neither heterosexual maturity nor homosexuality. In Stoller's (1985) words:

> Freud said that masculinity was the natural, original mode of gender identity in both sexes. He believed that it resulted especially from the boy's heterosexual, and the girl's homosexual, first object

relationship with mother—together with the inherent superiority of having a penis. The new theory, however, says that the first form of gender identity (preceding object relationship) is one of being merged with—of not distinguishing one's anatomic and psychic boundaries from—mother. This preverbal "identification" can comfortably augment the creation of femininity in a girl, but in a boy it becomes an obstacle to be surmounted if he is to grow into a separate, masculine person. These processes favoring femininity place the boy's, not the girl's, core gender identity at risk. (p. 181)

This process of differentiation begins in the first year of life. We will see presently how celibacy grapples with the demands of consolidating masculinity while foregoing sexual activity. The history of celibacy also shows some failure in achieving gender and sexual identities. Transvestism is a significant compromise that can help us understand some priests' dilemmas and their unconscious attempts to be men but not too sexual. Again, it is Stoller (1979) who explained this dynamic in his analysis of sexual excitement, describing the male struggle to be both separate and yet related to women.

> Then, for instance, he can put on her clothes (transvestism), feel that he is inside her skin, and at the same time—especially because of the sharp, precise delineating power of an erection—still be a separate creature while inside her skin. . . . The garment that excites the transvestite is thus a microdot: (1) phallic women exist: the transvestite, with his penis under the woman's clothes, is living proof; (2) the garment stands for a whole woman—mother—one can be close to, a cure for separation anxiety; (3) inside the garment, the fetishist is a woman, (4) but one with a penis, (5) and therefore still also a male, (6) free to pick up his masculinity again when he chooses, (7) safe from women's threats to harm his maleness and masculinity or to abandon him; (8) he can then, in the same instance, be both (imagine himself to be) separate from and at one with mother, (9) and so be superior to anyone who is only a female or only a male; (10) with all these mental acrobatics, he runs no real risks, (11) and yet ends up with a storm of pleasures that are engrossing, dependable, repeatable, (12) for a fetish, unlike humans, is totally cooperative, nonjudgmental, uncomplaining, and, when cast off, does not retaliate. All that, I suggest, can be crammed into one erection. (pp. 172–173)

For some priests, celibacy holds them safely in a stage of development where it is not necessary for them to define their sexuality. They can be close to a woman (inside her skin) without running the risks of rejection; they can maintain a sense of masculinity without indulging in the external aggression needed for sexual activity with another. For these men, external, inanimately mediated reassurance gives them gratification while preserving a certain equilibrium. Their sense that at least they are not involved sexually with anyone else saves their appearance of celibacy or maintains abstinence for relatively long periods of time, even if this security comes from the "cloth."

Here again, the value of our exploration is not in its conclusions but in its questions: How is transvestism related to celibacy and how do celibates consolidate their sense of masculinity? What meanings do the robes of office play? Is there an element in clerical reality that gives credence to the cliché "Clothes make the man"?

PRIESTS AND ANIMALS

Among our informants were three cases of patterned sexual behavior with animals that can only be classified as paraphilia because each priest demonstrated persistent and exclusive sexual urgings and activity with animals. These examples came to light only because each of the priests was concerned and troubled enough about his behavior to seek help. One history was traced to early experiences on a farm. No projection of estimates of this kind of sexual activity is attempted from the information here, but the question of bestiality among celibates should remain open.

SUFFERING AND SEXUAL VIOLENCE

Anyone not acquainted with Catholic tradition may not appreciate the close link between sex/celibacy and suffering/martyrdom instilled in average Catholics and taken most seriously by some boys aspiring to the priesthood. One priest told of being encouraged to take scalding baths to temper his passions. He was to endure water as hot as he could possibly stand and was not to tell anyone of his ascetic practice lest it lose its value. David Plante (1986) opened the Preface to his novel, *The Catholic,* with this image:

> A young nun told us one morning during catechism class how missionaries from France had been captured and tortured by the Indians in America. The Indians stripped the missionaries naked, tied them to stakes, then pressed red hot tomahawks to their flesh. This was done to them because they were Catholic and loved God. The nun's face, in her fluted wimple, was flushed. My knees were shaking.

Plante concluded the Preface with the confrontation of his childhood sexual identity on the eve of his first communion.

> My brother and I concentrated, with bright halos of attention, on one another's prepubescent members, and I said, suddenly, "Ainque les Peaux Rouges ont cela" ("Only Red Skins have this"). My brother didn't deny it. We were different from anyone else.

Celibacy is an ascetic practice of the first order, and its relationship to love and suffering needs to be explored. Perhaps nowhere is the interplay between the beauty of the ascetic ideal and the gruesomeness of the fleshly reality more graphically portrayed than in the artistic renditions of *The Belles Heures* (Meiss & Beatson, 1974): St. Bartholomew was skinned alive (Fol. 161); St. Stephen was stoned (Fol. 162); St. Sebastian was transfixed with arrows (Fol. 165v); St. Francis was marked with the bloody wounds of Christ (Fol. 171); St. John (Fol. 212 and 212v), St. Paul (Fol. 215v), and St. Denis (Fol. 166v) were all gloriously and adeptly beheaded; St. Lawrence was grilled like a piece of meat (Fol. 162v). Women were depicted in even more grisly detail as they defended their virginity: St. Agnes was led to a brothel (Fol. 175); St. Ursula and her companions were slaughtered (Fol. 178); St. Lucy (Fol. 179v) and St. Catherine (Fol. 19v) were beheaded; St. Cecilia was beheaded after being boiled in oil (Fol. 180); and St. Agatha had her breasts cut off with large pincers (Fol. 179).

The psychological implications of these examples are clear. Celibacy in the service of the love of God is worth any suffering.

One of the most pregnant statements of Robert Stoller's (1979) study of sexual excitement follows.

> Sadomasochism is, I think, a central feature of most sexual excitement. My hunch is that the desire to hurt others in retaliation for having been hurt is essential for most people's sexual excitement all the time but not for all people's excitement all the time. (p. 113)

The potential ramifications of Stoller's hunch are tremendous. It causes one to pause at St. Augustine's insistence that no sexual excitement could be wholly separated from all trace of sin. Suffice it to say here that there is some connection between violence and sex, as well as some sense of "doing violence" to oneself in the service of celibacy. Both are mysteries yet to be explored.

In 1985 priests were no more nor less victims of violence than the general population. They have been robbed, murdered, and their cars vandalized while they were minding their own business. The atmosphere in which the priest exists has changed drastically from the 1960s to the present. In 1960, few rectories had bars on their windows; most churches could remain open and unguarded from the first Mass in the morning until they were locked at 6:00 or even 9:00 p.m. by the custodian or the parish priest. Even an inner city priest had few qualms about making a sick call late at night. I remember answering a hospital call after midnight in 1965, walking unafraid the six dark city blocks between the church and the hospital. By 1985 the priest needed the protection of his car (or a policeman) and often would defer the call until morning, if possible. The Roman collar worn by Spencer Tracy and Pat O'Brien as sufficient protection against the guns of thugs (cf. Keyser & Keyser, 1984) was not an effective shield in 1985. Today, priests are as fair game as anyone else for violence in our society.

Murder

What is of most concern is the avoidable violence to priests. Several priests, in recounting their histories to us, remarked, "I'm lucky I didn't get myself killed" (see also the chapter on the homosexualities). Two priests did not live to be able to say that. Both murders were reported to the press simply as random robberies; both victims, however, were well known to informants—one had been a psychiatrist and the other a parish pastor.

The first victim was a priest in his mid-30s who, for a period of 5 years, periodically sought out casual sex, usually in public restrooms. He would suffer a paroxysm of severe guilt after each encounter and would vow never to seek another. His resolve would last for several weeks or months, until, as he described to a friend, he would feel a building tension and a growing preoccupation with the meeting place, the image of white tiled walls and floor, the memory of the mixed smells of disinfectant and human bodies, and the thrill of the danger. In retrospect, he could see that the desire was several days in the building, but the final thrust to action almost always took him by surprise. He would "find" himself in the area rather than "plan" to be there. His heart would pound; he would salivate; the place itself took on a significance. There was something akin to Hemingway's Nick Adams in his search for clean, well-lighted places, which, ironically, led to his senseless murder.

In all other regards, this man's life as a priest was unremarkable. He was responsible enough and sociable enough, and in no obvious way could his proclivity be detected in his work. He was generally perceived as the kind and conscientious priest that he was.

The other priest who was murdered was noticeably successful in his ministry, if judged by the prestige and regard he enjoyed. He had entered therapy a few months prior to his death, consumed with a feeling of loneliness that no association or friendship within his priesthood could assuage. In fact, the more success he achieved and the more generally popular he became among his peers, the more his feelings of loneliness and desperation grew. At times in the depths of his despair he would cruise the streets for a companion, and would occasionally invite a stranger into his living quarters. These exploits were sexually motivated. When he was found murdered in his office, the crime was attributed to robbery, as the priest was fully clothed and some cash was missing. However, the priest's pattern had been known by his psychiatrist and suspected by a few of his priest friends.

Suicide

Generally, the idea of suicide is not associated with priests and I have no data on how their rate of suicide compares with that of dentists and psychiatrists, for example, who have the highest recorded rates among professionals. In the 1950s I learned from Dr. Francis Braceland, an eminent Catholic psychiatrist, that earlier in his life he had mistakenly believed that nuns and priests were almost immune from the act of self-destruction. He said that a bitter experience had taught him otherwise.

The refinement of understanding between religion and psychiatry over the past decades has made representatives of both professions more realistic about the mental health of religious people (McAllister, 1986). Depression, for instance, knows no religious boundaries. In fact, there seems to be a strong depressive component to the psyches of seriously religious people. Certainly, a depressive-like encounter is necessary to the pursuit of celibacy, as I will show in Chapter 12 on the process of celibacy. Four of the five reports of suicide we reviewed were intrinsically bound up with the sexual conflicts in pursuing the celibate ideal. Suicide is always a tragedy, and no less so among the clergy; however, among them it probably also has some special symbolic power, contradicting the message of hope inherently implied by ministry.

A priest in his mid-30s sought the help of a Catholic psychiatrist specifically because of his doubts about celibacy. He was successful in his priesthood and was considered an "exciting intellectual" by those who knew him. He had entered the seminary in college after some brief periods of dating. He was genuinely popular wherever he studied or served. After a decade in the priesthood, he still found himself questioning his sexual identity and had a tremendous desire to experience dating again.

His choice of a psychiatrist was truly unfortunate, because this psychiatrist was not only unaware of the depth and complexity of the priest's celibate struggle, but also had the monumentally poor judgment to encourage the priest simply to date and aided him in meeting women who would supposedly help the priest sort things out. Occasionally the psychiatrist and his wife would even accompany the priest on his outings. Rather than helping, the escapades only led to a deeper feeling of desperation and confusion on the priest's part.

When the priest consulted a second psychiatrist, he was even more convinced that there was no way out of his dilemma and was terrified that he was "going crazy." The second psychiatrist was able to see beyond the smiling and even jaunty manner in which the priest presented himself to the tortured soul within. However, the priest's manner did fool most of his friends and some other professionals into thinking that his confusion was temporary, superficial, or merely intellectual. Most missed the agony, which, in this case, certainly did not look like ordinary depression. One priest friend who talked with him the week before he died reported that he had been greeted by the laughing remark, "You're only welcome today if you have brought a gun."

The day before the priest died, another priest friend encouraged him to "forget the guilt and just get involved with a woman; that's what I do." He could not have known that it was exactly the wrong kind of support for his friend, who by this time had become so entangled in his despair that he feared the prospect of hospitalization. Terrified of the possibility of ending up as a chronic mental patient, he killed himself. One who knew this man's struggle intimately found him a heroic religious figure, "who struggled manfully and fought the good fight. He served and saved many others, but could not save himself."

Another priest was hospitalized for severe depression, torn between his love affair with a young woman and his very religious family who were counting on his continuing priesthood. During his hospitalization, the woman sent him passionate letters declaring her love for him and encouraging him to leave the ministry, a move he knew he could not make. His best priest friend advised him to incorporate the relationship into his priest life, as he himself was doing with another woman. After his release from the hospital, the priest tried to do just that, struggling with the relationship while hopelessly trying to maintain celibacy. When he began to experience another severe depressive episode, he swallowed an overdose of medication and died.

A priest in his early 40s became increasingly distressed by his sexual fantasies, and suspected for the first time in his life that he might be homosexual—a prospect so abominable to him that he began having panic attacks which crippled his work and life. He had always been a sensitive man, described as "high strung" by those who knew him well. He was also a very active, prolific worker. He never gave anyone a chance to know the dynamic behind his fear, but he apparently killed himself because of it. No one could find any evidence that he had ever acted out sexually.

On the other hand, a priest who was involved in sexual liaisons that were about to become public and cause a considerable scandal in his area drove his car into an abutment, killing himself. He had left a note to a priest friend telling him exactly what he intended to do. In contrast to the first two priests described above who could not reconcile their celibate vows with what they saw as the hypocrisy of their sexual activity, this priest very comfortably incorporated it into his ministry over a long period of time. It was finally the threat of discovery that destroyed his ability to deny and to split his sexual functioning off from the rest of his life.

The fifth incident of a priest's suicide presented itself more vaguely as a vocational problem. The priest could neither leave the priesthood nor dedicate himself to it. His family and friends experienced him as nervous but not self-destructive. He appeared to be a spiritual man and a loner who took no one into his confidence.

I said earlier in this chapter that celibacy has martyrdom as its historical antecedent. The ideal that one should be willing to sacrifice everything—life itself—in the service of one's fellow humans is in the imitation of Christ. It is difficult to see this ideal at work where suffering is glorified for its own sake or where self-abnegation leads not to service and love but to waste and death by one's own hand.

Alcoholism is another manifestation of waste and self-destruction. Its relationship, if any, to the priesthood and celibacy is yet to be determined, but it must be looked at in the broad context of sadomasochism as well as in the narrow focus of slow suicide.

The mystery of the priesthood is not merely the history of individuals, but a reality that transcends persons and times. To what extent individuals may be sacrificed or may sacrifice themselves for the preservation of discipline or structure is not clear in individual circumstances, even if an ascetic or theological ideal were clear. An ideal may be measured by those who fail to achieve it, but the idea that suffering in and of itself is good or salvific is a misrepresentation of the life of Christ as well as of those who blazed the trail for a celibate life-style.

Chapter 10

THE SEX DRIVE _____

"Some celibate priests don't find women all that attractive sexually.
They can do without them rather easily."
—Fr. Andrew Greeley, 1983b

Do men who seek celibacy differ in the degree or strength of their sexual drive from those who seek marriage?

This simple question is very complex and difficult to pursue, much less answer, for several reasons. First, subjectively, the internal sense or urgency for sexual gratification is an unreliable indicator, if only because one who is dedicated to total abstinence will receive *any* sexual urge differently from one who has available to him sanctioned sexual outlets. Second, no objective studies—on testosterone levels in the general male population, for instance—are available for comparison with the celibate population. Finally, cultural influences also affect how one expresses his sexual drive.

Furthermore, these three factors—subjective, psychological, feelings; biological and biochemical endowment; and behavioral, environmental forces—not only vary in different men, but vary within the same man at different times and in different situations. These factors, as well as the spiritual, influence the sexual drive and can seriously complicate a priest's celibate life.

It is with the second of these factors—biological and biochemical endowment—that I would like to deal in this section.

KALLMANN'S SYNDROME

Kallmann's syndrome is hypogonadism—small genitalia (penis and testicles)—associated with anosmia, a congenital lack of a sense of smell.

F. J. Kallmann and colleagues (1944) first described the familial occurrence of the two symptoms, and related the hypogonadism to a specific gonadotropin deficiency due to a deficit in the hypothalamus. The syndrome was named for him. Patients with Kallmann's may also have a eunuchoid body type and lack secondary sexual characteristics—their voices can fail to deepen, their beard growth may be scanty, and the normal male hair distribution may be sparse. Color blindness may be present as well, and sometimes enlargement of the breasts (gynecomastia).

Other researchers expanded on Kallmann's work and found other clinical abnormalities that may or may not be present in all cases. However, common to all persons with Kallmann's syndrome are infertility and erotic apathy extending to all forms of sexual behavior, including masturbation. These patients typically have never had the experience of "falling in love," with all the attendant emotion and physical passion that are normally invested in the loved one. They speak of both as an outsider would (Males, Townsend, & Schneider, 1973).

According to studies done at Johns Hopkins Hospital, the intelligence level of Kallmann's syndrome patients is normal and may even tend toward a higher than normal I.Q., with a superiority in the verbal areas. However, Hopkins researchers acknowledge that both trends need verification on a sample larger than their 13 patients (Bobrow, Money, & Lewis, 1971).

In conducting our research of priests and listening to their stories, I became aware of a small group of 15 men with an unusually low or absent sexual drive and suspected that they may have had Kallmann's syndrome. Because of lack of detail, 10 of them must remain only tentatively categorized, but five certainly can be classed as having the syndrome, including one who was clinically diagnosed at Hopkins.

Our five men with Kallmann's consisted of four ordained priests and one man who was not ordained. One thing that makes Kallmann's interesting to the student of celibacy is that it raises the question of strength of sexual drive in its most extreme form. We have no data to prove that men who represent the lower end of the spectrum of sexual drive are more inclined to seek the celibate life than others, but this possibility does arise. Unfortunately, at the present time, we do not have the objective tools to measure sexual drive, and are dependent on subjective reporting.

One might think that the complete lack of sexual drive represented by Kallmann's would free the priest from all sexual concern. This is not borne out by our observations, as demonstrated by the case histories of the five Kallmann's patients in our group.

Case 1

This priest had been ordained less than two years when he sought consultation. His concern was the size of his genitals. Although he was a large man with a typically pyknic body type, his penis measured less than 5 centimeters long. His anosmia made him indiscriminate in his diet and he tended to be overweight. He had been in the seminary from the age of 13, and because he was the student rather than the athlete, he was not exposed to the open shower situation of a typical high school or college. It was only after his ordination to the priesthood and subsequent parish assignment that he began to feel he was "somehow different" from other men. He was generally happy in his work, had no sexual desires or contact with anyone, and after brief psychotherapy seemed satisfied with himself and able to develop the preaching and administrative duties at which he excelled.

Case 2

This priest was in his mid-30s and was noted at the university where he taught for the brilliance of his lectures as well as for the embarrassingly crude sexual jokes he told at often inappropriate times. Although not an athlete, he was conscious of his weight and ran and exercised to keep himself in shape. He got into trouble with the school administration when he was observed having male graduate students sleep with him on occasion. When interviewed, he stated that he had no [sexual] feeling, only a "sense of warmth and closeness" to the students, and could see nothing wrong with his actions. He did wonder, however, about his bed partners who became sexually excited and he was curious about their ejaculations.

He was not interested in psychotherapy, but did find a priest confessor who was understanding of his limitations and able to help him regulate his uneasiness with sexual matters. By the time of his follow-up interview, his behavior had been modified, but his verbal displays had diminished only slightly. It seemed that his jokes were his way of trying to master an unknown and puzzling territory—much the way of prepubescent boys.

Case 3

This priest was in his 50s and was the rector of a major seminary when he came to our attention. An exemplary and dedicated scholar and administrator, he was noted for his unsurpassed lectures on celibacy and the priestly life. By all accounts, he articulated the ideals masterfully. A mild heart attack caused him to pay some additional attention to his physical health. He had a typical pyknic body build and tended to be overweight. On subsequent physical examination, his hypogonadism was noted.

Prior to this time, he had no awareness that his genitalia were different from those of other men. Almost all of his life he could relate to a "sense of being special," which he associated with his vocation to the priesthood. His anosmia and color blindness were minor deficiencies that he became aware of as a young student. He had long since adjusted to them and considered them less incapacitating and even minimal in comparison with his left-handedness.

His health crisis coincided with a movement called "the third way" among young priests and seminarians in the late 1960s and 70s. The movement involved their development of close friendships and dating-like behaviors with women. As a supreme idealist in matters of celibacy, this priest could see nothing wrong with this behavior. In fact, he briefly became an exponent of it, at least in theory. He could not understand that there was any particular danger as long as one kept one's ideals. On the other hand, as rector, he was extremely hard on anyone who transgressed the ideal and actually became sexually involved with women. He literally could not understand how anyone could be sexual "after he had made up his mind" to be celibate. As a result, some of the faculty became critical of his lack of patience and understanding with some of the students' struggles with sexuality. Subsequently he retired from his administrative post and returned to his scholarship and teaching.

Case 4

This 40-year-old priest was a popular professor in his community university. He was the head of his department and had the services of a full-time secretary. Because he was thoughtful and kind, he quite naturally paid attention to the concerns and persons of his secretaries. He was puzzled, then, when a succession of them grew emotionally involved with him and misinterpreted his gestures of friendship as having an intimate and even sexual meaning, to which he was oblivious.

He had been an excellent student from the minor seminary through graduate school and was happy in his vocation. He was comfortable with women and enjoyed their friendship, companionship, and sharing. He could see no conflict with having women come to his room and even giving him a massage late at night.

Confronted by his superior, who could not understand such naivete in one of his brightest community members, the priest agreed to an evaluation. His lack of any history of sexual feelings, his congenital anosmia, and his body type established the diagnosis of Kallmann's. Since this man was productive and satisfied in his vocation, endocrine studies were not recommended. He profited from psychotherapy and developed sufficient insight to guard himself from being misunderstood by his women friends.

Case 5

Although we have avoided including nonordained students in our study, one exception seems useful here. A 19-year-old undergraduate was being treated for Kallmann's with hormone therapy at a university medical center because he had felt humiliated by his lack of secondary sexual characteristics. With hormone therapy, his beard developed and his voice deepened sufficiently to make him fit in with his classmates; there was even some penis growth that reinforced his self-confidence. However, he was facing the reality of his sexual deficit and during one psychotherapy session, said, in tears, "I don't know what the guys mean when they talk about being horny." One can see how a celibate culture might offer a viable albeit painful alternative.

With so few examples of Kallmann's in our study, we can make no estimate of the percentage of clergy who may have it. Our experience and that of others suggest that Kallmann's syndrome is not rare and in all likelihood goes undiagnosed in many individuals. And the seminary system that accepted students as freshmen in high school could have provided a haven for these men as well as a challenging environment for their intellectual abilities.

SUBCLINICAL HYPOTHYROIDISM

Although hundreds of patients in the United States each year are treated for low sexual desire, I have never known of a celibate priest to seek such treatment. I have, however, interviewed celibates who have been treated for chronic, subclinical hypothyroidism—a condition involving general apathy and a tendency for the patient to gain weight. In the mildest form of the condition, these symptoms may be the only ones experienced, or the patient may remain completely asymptomatic. Diagnostically, the condition is confirmed by laboratory studies (T.S.H.); it does not appear on the ordinary thyroid tests (T3 and T4). It does affect the sexual drive.

I believe this is a commonly undiagnosed condition among celibates. Those who have been treated noted a marked increase in their sexual desire. (Parenthetically, at the other extreme, we have seen priests whose *hyper*thyroidism was a significant factor in the operation of their sexual-celibate lives. Mania and depression can both have a significant impact on the sexual drive.)

Recent research has examined the relationship between beta-endorphin levels and lack of sexual desire. Endorphins are found mainly in the pituitary gland, act primarily as hormones, and are associated with alterations in autonomic reactions. At higher levels, they seem to be able to "rob the entire psychological response of its intensity and pleasure, and secondarily account for a lack of desire. . . . Ejaculation can occur without feeling. . . . the common denominator psychological feature [is] found to be a feeling of satiation and indifference to a fundamental biological imperative, sexual desire" (Chapman, 1984).

Naturally, a low sexual desire can make sexual abstinence easier, but by no means does it assure the achievement of celibacy. We have interviewed a number of priests whose sexual desire is limited—and by average standards severely so—who nevertheless do involve themselves in sexual activity even if it is on a very restricted and occasional basis. If, for instance, a priest experiences sexual excitement twice each year and each time seeks a sexual outlet, he is 100 percent sexually active. That contrasts sharply with the celibate who may also seek a sexual outlet twice a year, but who experiences sexual excitement on a weekly or daily basis.

Characterological factors, ego strengths, relationship patterns, and patterns of defense are all operative in the maintenance of celibacy. And although biochemical deficiency may make sexual abstinence easier in some cases, it contributes nothing to the virtue of chastity or to sexual maturity.

Chapter 11

WHEN PRIESTS BECOME FATHERS _____

> "My hope is that when He comes again, He will still be human enough
> to shed a clown's gentle tears over the broken toys—that once were
> women and children."
>
> —Morris L. West
> The Clowns of God

BIRTHS

In some cases, sexual intercourse leads to conception and birth, in spite of caution, contraception, and the conscious intent *not* to have a baby. Nine unplanned or unexpected pregnancies that produced live births by women involved with priests were reported between 1960 and 1980. Marriage between the priest and the child's mother did not occur in any of the nine incidents.

Also significant is a report in 1966 by a staff member of a large archdiocesan foundling home that six of the residents at one time were nuns, all waiting to deliver. The father in each case was a priest. I hold the report entirely reliable, but I was unable to interview any of the principals at the time. I make no estimates of percentages from these cases.

One priest, at age 32, was the epitome of naivete in matters sexual. He reported that at the time of his ordination at age 26, he believed that every act of intercourse created a pregnancy. He comforted himself that since he would not have wanted more that five or six children if he had married, celibacy would not be such a great sacrifice for him anyway. He experienced seminary life positively, threw himself into his parish assignment with enthusiasm, and was well received, especially by the young people in his parish community. A 17-year-old girl in one of his high school release-time classes developed a strong attraction for him. He reacted in a fashion more befitting an adolescent than a man in his 30s. Since he was active and observant in all areas of his clerical life, the

222

"crush" seemed to other observers to have been absorbed, when in fact it flourished as a growing relationship for a year.

During its second year, the relationship gained the attention of some parishioners and other priests in the parish house. The couple was seen walking together hand-in-hand, sitting very close at the local community softball games, and being overattentive to each other at parish functions. By the time the priest was formally called on the carpet for his demeanor, he had learned that not every act of intercourse ends in pregnancy; soon after, however, the girl did become pregnant. The small Catholic community responded with both shock and understanding. The priest was reassigned to a parish some distance away. The girl, now 19, went to a large city to a home for unwed mothers. She remained in that city and later married someone she met at her work there.

The naivete of this man was dramatic, but only in degree. Report after report of priests' sexual involvements with women are marked with a quality of remarkable ingenuousness, in part due to the priests' great denial of sexual feelings. This quality becomes a two-edged sword: the childlike innocence of the young priest's sexual inexperience is perceived correctly, making him both attractive and vulnerable. Again, the unpredictable onset of the priest's delayed adolescent development makes his psychosexual maturing difficult—or at the very least complicated—for himself and for others.

Another informant was the mother of a priest. One day a woman appeared at her door carrying a baby. "I would like you to meet your grandson," she said. Having only one son—a priest—the mother was flabbergasted and unbelieving. When she confronted her son, he finally admitted his ongoing relationship with this woman, who in fact was married. An interesting facet of this case history was that this child was only one of three born to the woman and priest. The woman's husband was tolerant of her relationship with the priest. He was willing to bring up the children and act as if convinced they were indeed his own. The priest and the wife were open and clear about their relationship to the priest's mother, who eventually accepted both the relationship and her grandchildren. The priest's career was not interrupted by his sexual friendship or the pregnancies, nor was his companion's marriage appreciably affected.

Another case involved a young seminarian who, at 18 years, sought the identity of his biological parents. He knew he had spent the first three years of his life in an orphanage before living with his adoptive family. His adoptive parents were supportive, but his efforts encountered one resistance after another from the Catholic Charities' officials through whom he had been placed for adoption. He pursued their clue that his father was dead and found that the man had been a priest. Finally, he was able to locate his biological mother—still living, but very protective of the fact that she had conceived a child out of wedlock. She was not willing to include his existence in her current life, but was helpful to him in confirming the identity of his father and supplying some personal history that made the seminarian quite proud of him and his clerical accomplishments.

Another case also came to light in the context of a family mystery. The son of a divorced couple was sent to live with his grandparents in a large city. The household also included an unmarried aunt and her son. The newcomer to the household began to suspect that his cousin's father was the parish priest. The grandparents, knowing the truth, were eager to keep the secret and had participated in the cover story that their daughter had been secretly married to a soldier who left her pregnant and then died. When it was clear that the young grandson saw through the ruse and observed the ongoing relationship with the priest, he became a threat to the stability of the family. The grandparents panicked and made him promise to perpetuate the cover story.

The most common pattern reported is that the pregnancy destroys the relationship, each party usually going his or her own way. The child is most commonly given up for adoption. I have seen that the experience for certain priests can be incorporated into renewed dedication to celibacy in the tradition of St. Augustine. It can, however, also serve as no more than a rite of passage that produces a more cautious and sexually aware man.

ABORTION

Official Vatican teaching on abortion is clear and unequivocal. Abortion is forbidden. The only exception is when the life of the mother is clearly endangered. Luker (1984) records:

> The earliest American Catholic stand on abortion was that of Francis P. Kenrick, the Bishop of Philadelphia, who, in 1841 declared that there were no "therapeutic" indications for abortion. Two deaths, in his view, were better than one murder. (pp. 58–59)

Most bishops today would not hold to that rigorous a standard. An early testimony to the Church's position is from Athenagoras of Athens (Quasten, 1950):

> "When we say that those women who use drugs to bring on abortion commit murder and will have to give an account to God for the abortion, on what principle should we commit murder? For it does not belong to the same person to regard the very fetus in the womb as a created being, and therefore an object of God's care, and when

it has passed into life, to kill it; and not expose an infant because those who expose them are chargeable with child-murder, and on the other hand, when it has been reared, to destroy it. But we are in all things always alike and the same, submitting ourselves to reason and not ruling over it. . . ."

[Quasten says] It is very important that Athenagoras refers here to the fetus as a created being. According to Roman law of that time it was not considered a being at all, and had no right to existence. (pp. 234–235)

This was in A.D. 177. But the circumstances were not simply one of doctrinal exposition. The Christian minority was under severe persecutory attack and one of the arguments against them was that they were baby killers. (In later centuries, this same accusation would be used by the Christian majority to assail the Jewish minority.)

In an attempt to justify his community, Hippolytus of Rome (active from A.D. 215 to 235) attacks Pope Callistus for his laxity not only in ordaining priests who had been married two and three times, but in looking with mercy on sinful bishops as well as pardoning adultery and fornication after penance. But he vents his real wrath on women who call themselves Catholic after an abortion:

"He [Pope Callistus] permitted females, if they were unwedded and burned with passion at an age at all events unbecoming, or if they were not disposed to overturn their own dignity through a legal marriage, that they might have whomsoever they would choose as a bedfellow, whether slave or free, and that a woman, though not legally married, might consider such a companion as a husband. Whence women, reputed believers, began to resort to drugs for producing sterility, and to gird themselves round, so as to expel what was being conceived on account of their not wishing to have a child either by a slave or by a paltry fellow, for the sake of their family and excessive wealth. Behold, into how great impiety that lawless one has proceeded, by inculcating adultery and murder at the same time! And withal, after such audacious acts, they, lost to all shame, attempt to call themselves a Catholic Church." (Quasten, 1953, p. 206)

Abortions were not unknown even in the Middle Ages, when Christianity held its greatest social and political sway. *Artes muliebres* (women's arts) were the closely guarded secrets passed on from woman to woman and included mixtures that allowed women to remain barren (Duby, 1983, p. 268).

Throughout this report, I have aimed to have priests speak for themselves about their own celibate/sexual practice. I have taken equal care to allow women to speak for themselves, both theoretically and by practical exposition, especially in regard to abortion and childbirth.

Although there is a significant, substantial, and vocal group that supports the Vatican view on abortion, the majority of Catholics do not without reservation endorse it. Dr. Ralph Lane analyzed survey data gathered between 1972 and 1982 by the then Chicago-based National Opinion Research Center. About 90 percent of Catholics approve of legal abortion, at least under certain circumstances. Chittister and Marty (1983), found in their local but landmark study of Christian belief as applied to practice that

> . . . almost three-quarters (70%) of the population accept abortion, only 15% believe that it should be entirely a matter of personal choice. Almost half (45%) would permit abortion only in extreme cases. Whatever their definitions of "extreme," this 45% does not look upon abortion casually. Nor is it a matter of clear consensus even among the majority who accept abortion as sometimes moral. But it is, at least in Minnesota, admissible in the church community, even to more than one-third (35%) of the Roman Catholic population, to more than three-fourths of the Lutherans (77%), Baptists (78%), and Covenant Church members (78%).

A closely reasoned position articulated by Dr. Elizabeth R. Hatcher, (1983, 1989) a Catholic woman staff physician from the Menninger Foundation, represents a view not uncommon among lay Catholics:

> Most moralists would agree that the subjective morality of abortion is affected by a host of variables: the degree to which the woman understands what she is doing, the medical problems involved, the motive, the stage of pregnancy, the question of whether the woman consented freely to the intercourse that produced the pregnancy, whether she tried to use a responsible form of contraception, what socioeconomic pressures she may be under, etc. Given a real case and asked to decide the degree of evildoing (if any) with respect to this abortion, we would have to assess all those circumstances.
>
> Attackers of legal abortion would simplify this issue by reducing it to the proposition that human life with all the rights of an adult begins at conception. But this proposition cannot be proven. Moreover, for Catholics it "is not, strictly speaking, a matter of dogma," as moral theologian Bernard Haring concedes, however reluctantly. Learned geneticists have supported this proposition in testimony before Senate committees—and equally learned scientists have disagreed. The proposition cannot be proven because the evidence is ambiguous. The morality of abortion is almost inescapably a subjective issue.

I do not perceive the issue in terms of "pro" or "anti," of "life" or "not life," or "abortion on demand" or "no abortion." I think in terms of a continuum of life from viral to bacterial to vegetative to animal to human, and a continuum of human life from one generation to the next. Since our brain functions make possible most processes of organ and system physiology (except heartbeat) and constitute everything that is "human" about us (our consciousness of pain, our emotions, our thinking, our self-reflection), I think it is safe to define human life as beginning with the start of brain function (EEG waves) near the start of the second trimester. "Almost 90% of abortions in the United States are performed during the first trimester"—before the start of fetal brain function (Katchadourian & Lunde, 1980).

But I do not accept abortion on demand for first-trimester pregnancies; nor do I reject abortion after the first trimester. Pregnancy is a complex interdependence of the already-established adult life of the woman (and the lives of her family and her community) with the developing life of the fetus. The real needs of both the woman and the fetus must be regarded. In the unfortunate case where needs conflict, a judgment call must be made.

Some examples. An irresponsibly pregnant unwed teenage girl might worsen her problems by an irresponsible abortion six weeks into her pregnancy. Her sexual activity may be a symptom of an emotional problem. Counseling may show her that carrying her child to term would be a fulfilling, responsible act. But in this early phase of pregnancy the final choice, made after reasonable deliberation, should be the woman's.

A different case. A responsibly pregnant married woman with children may suffer *hyperemesis gravidarum,* morning sickness so severe that she must be hospitalized (one case in 200 pregnancies). This condition can become so acute that she will die without an abortion (Katchadourian & Lunde). In this case, an abortion seems morally necessary. Since morning sickness occurs mainly in the first six to eight weeks of pregnancy, such an abortion is probably not taking a human life.

After the first trimester, the reasons for abortion must be grave, since now the needs of the developing *human* life are outweighed by the needs of already-established human lives. A threat to the physical survival of the mother seems a justifiable reason for late abortion. The ethical principle that the end does not justify the means has been used against such abortions. This principle is indefensible here, since we are forced to choose between the lesser of evils, and to do nothing is as much a human act as to intervene. Moreover, the indifference to the meaning and value of the mother's life in these circumstances reflects church sexism.

Catastrophic fetal disease also seems a justifiable motive for late abortion. "About 5 percent of all infants born live will have some sort of serious birth defect or will develop mental retardation" (Katchadourian & Lunde, 1980). It is fortunate that chronic villus biopsy, which permits diagnosis of many fetal diseases early in pregnancy, is now quite safe and accurate.

I define catastrophic fetal disease as a permanent condition that will take the child's life before adulthood or destroy its capacity for self-care. An example is Tay-Sachs disease, a degenerative disease of the nervous system. "By about eight months [after birth], symptoms of severe listlessness set in. Blindness usually occurs within the first year. Afflicted children rarely survive past their fifth year" (Curtis, 1979). No one, the child least of all, is served by such a birth. The emotional and financial cost to the family is staggering.

Many unjustifiable abortions doubtless take place. We need good demographic research on this issue. My hunch is that good education not just about sex, but about sexuality, is associated with a lower abortion rate. I wonder whether it can be shown that abortion causes emotional scars or suicidal tendencies in women, or whether both the abortion and the emotion problems (if they exist) are results of some deeper, underlying cause. I want women, especially those having more than one medically unnecessary abortion, to be impartially counseled when contemplating abortion.

A practical reason for a permissive abortion law is that, legal or not, women will have abortions. Before the 1973 Supreme Court decision, "Kinsey found that about 23 percent of the white women he sampled had an illegal abortion by the time they finished their reproductive years" (Katchadourian & Lunde, 1980). Illegal abortions endanger the lives of women while profiting organized crime.

The issue is not whether to allow abortions. They will take place whatever the law. The issue is how to manage a situation that can be either a serious medical dilemma or a symptom of important sociopsychological problems—or both. And in the last analysis, the issue is decided in the consciences of individuals. (Private communication)

Abortion as a doctrinal issue has not received open debate even in Catholic academic circles, where there is clearly a variance of opinion and reasoning. The celibate clergyman is poised between a clear doctrinal and disciplinary stand on the part of Church authority and, on the part of his Church members, either defiant or reverent disagreement and deliberate, thoughtless, or reluctant behavior. Many priests do not think much about abortion. Some are leaders of movements to champion and amplify the Church's current stance; and a few are persistent in seeking to clarify the issues both doctrinally and pastorally. Some priests involved in pregnancies choose abortion; their reasoning may be more akin to Hatcher's than the Vatican's, or it may be thoughtless panic.

Five cases of priests involved in the choice for abortion of the fetus they fathered were reported, all between 1980 and 1985. Although I make no estimate of percentage of behavior from this sample, I have consulted with four psychiatrists from widely dispersed geographic areas, who are well acquainted with clergy life; all had themselves known of similar instances.

One priest who had an ongoing and stable sexual relationship with his housekeeper, impregnated her twice and each time they decided to abort the fetus. Neither was willing or able at the time to alter their living circumstances to make the care and raising of a child possible. Although both had their regrets, they felt family obligations, the priestly vocation, and avoidance of scandal outweighed other moral considerations.

Another priest had a two-year love relationship that grew out of a work assignment. The woman was an active member of a Protestant parish. When she became accidentally pregnant, she was eager to marry and raise their child. When the priest refused, the woman agreed with some reluctance to terminate the pregnancy rather than lose the relationship entirely.

A young woman in graduate school became sexually involved with a visiting professor—a priest. She became pregnant just as she was about to complete her studies and he was to return to his tenured position at his university. They both agonized extensively over the decision, but in the end chose abortion. She was not eager to cut short her career at that particular point in her life, while he was very conscious of the negative effects a pregnancy and his departure from the priesthood would have on his ailing mother, who was financially and emotionally dependent on him. These rationalizations did not relieve any of the genuine pain of their decision, nor account for the unconscious striving of both of them to be free to marry.

The fourth instance was reported by a woman who was irate and regretful after the abortion she chose. She was involved in a long-term sexual relationship with a priest who was being promoted consistently up the ecclesiastical ladder. She was both secure and proud of his professional accomplishments and supported his work with sacrifice and enthusiasm. She was shocked and disappointed when she found out she was pregnant. He was furious. She quickly sought an abortion out of fear, rather than thinking through clearly or talking over with him her decision. Her anger later was at his failure to support her when she needed it most, as well as at all the unresolved unconscious factors surrounding the relationship and pregnancy in the first place. She continued the relationship with the priest, feeling that the abortion was her punishment for it.

The fifth instance is recorded for our study by the woman involved and speaks for itself:

> *I met Father Mark about two years after my divorce from my husband, Jim, who had been a Protestant pastor. I had always been drawn to the Catholic Church, even when I was a child—which is another whole story—but when I was dating my husband, he told me I'd have to stay Protestant if I wanted to marry him. Protestant pastors couldn't have Catholic wives. So after my divorce there weren't any obstacles any more to my taking instructions in Catholicism and I signed up.*
>
> *I made my decision to join the Church too late to be part of the already-in-progress instruction class, and I had a real crazy travel schedule with my job, so I was relegated to once-a-week-whenever-I-was-in-town sessions with Father Mark, who was the assistant pastor.*
>
> *My initial reaction was disappointment because I always pictured myself sitting at the feet of a patriarch type and here I was with a man who was just my age—35 at the time. I'm mentioning this so you'll understand that I didn't choose to take instructions from Father Mark because I was interested in him—that really hadn't entered the picture at all.*
>
> *My instructions went pretty quickly. Because of the 11 years I had spent married to Jim, I already had a good grasp of the sacraments, and both Mark and I relaxed pretty quickly into talking about how the particulars of the Church were applied to reality in the world. We found that we saw life the same way, and even knew a lot of the same people—he had traveled in some of the same circles either a year ahead of or a year behind Jim and me, and it surprised both of us that we had never bumped into each other before. We began to laugh a lot—thought the same people were terrific and the same people were idiots—he was so different from my husband, from whom I had obviously grown distant enough to divorce.*
>
> *I couldn't tell you exactly when I realized that I was in love with Mark or he with me. Jim and I had known quite a few priests during our marriage, and I guess I had demythologized them unlike people who grow up in the Catholic Church. Mark also told me how much he valued our time together, since I was "different"—a real person to him, probably also because of my own clergy background.*

Right after I was brought into the Church on Easter, Mark asked if I would go to a ball game with him. I said I didn't realize priests could date. He said he had never had a date in his life, but couldn't see any reason for us not to do things together—we had become friends after all. I was delighted that our relationship was going to continue.

I know now that we were both kidding ourselves. After two years on the singles scene, I had grown to hate all the bullshit out there, and saw Mark as such a refreshing change—I really thought I could compartmentalize our friendship and treat him like I treated my girl-friends. God only knows what lies he was telling himself.

He seemed to be everything that Jim was not—or rather every-thing that I had thought Jim was and then found out he wasn't. I was probably trying to replace Jim, who had been such a dismal failure as a husband, and whose existence reminded me of my dis-mal failure as a wife. Mark I guess was going to be the new Jim— my second chance—my opportunity to "get it right" this time. Mark was kind and honest and warm and funny and nurturing—all the things I thought Jim was when I first knew him.

After a few months Mark and I became lovers. Mark had never been to bed with anyone before, and always cried and said it could never happen again after we made love. We tried all kinds of schemes and bargains to keep him celibate—we'd spend more time outside my apartment, or not have drinks, or only "go so far," like a couple of teenagers. Except that the more sexual we became, the guiltier he got, and then he became so paranoid about being seen with me and having people suspect the truth about us, that if we wanted to see each other at all, it had to be in my apartment. And then we'd both pretend to be surprised when we'd end up in bed. I remember dumb things like during one of our periods of being ab-stinent, Mark suggested that we go stretch out on my bed, because it would be more comfortable up there, or that we take a shower to-gether because it was a sticky night. Some celibacy! And then the old guilt trip and script would kick in, and he'd blame me for going along with him—like I was supposed to stop him when I loved him and wanted to sleep with him.

The longer I stayed with Mark, the more I doubted my own sex-uality and sexual reality testing. Here I was—having been married all those years, and having had a normal heterosexual adolescence, being made to feel guilty by someone who had the emotional and sexual mindset of a 14-year old. Mark was like the worst of all my teenage years—a kid inside a man's body. And yet I loved him—I guess I couldn't accept that he had about 20 years of catching up to do. He was so wise in so many other areas—and I refused to accept that he was really two people—(1) the priest with all the priestly qualities I had grown to admire; and (2) an adolescent who was cheating on his girlfriend—or in this case, his wife, the Church.

The real killer, however, was in the third year of our relationship when I became pregnant—a diaphragm failure. It took Mark a while to accept that I really was pregnant—he kept hoping all the tests were wrong. I told him we had four choices (1) I could have the baby and raise it with my other two children; (2) I could have the baby and give it up for adoption; (3) We could marry and raise the child together; (4) I could have an abortion. Without batting an eye, he told me to have the abortion. He couldn't marry me, couldn't help raise the baby, couldn't face what people would think of him if they knew.

I was so sad and mixed up, I did have the abortion. Mark wouldn't come with me to the hospital. One of my girlfriends did. That night he came by my apartment—he wanted ME to comfort HIM. I couldn't believe it. He dissolved into a pool of tears about how could this have happened to HIM when he had tried to be so good his whole damn life. I remember that I needed some milk for the kids—they stayed with their dad for a few days during all this— and I asked Mark to drive me to the nearby market to get some. I wasn't supposed to drive for a few days. Do you know he refused? He was afraid of what people would think if they saw me in his car! Here I had just aborted his baby about 12 hours before that and he's worried about my face in his car window.

As a footnote, I should mention that Jim knew about the abortion and was a lot more understanding and probing about it than Mark. Jim has never thrown it in my face, never told the kids; he talked to me for hours about whether or not I really wanted to go through with it. And I had divorced him. Still a good decision, but he was there for me in this instance when his replacement was acting like a bowl of mush. Old mush.

I don't think I'll ever get over having chosen to destroy that baby. I read about how other women have this experience too—this regret and guilt. I look at my existing children, and wonder how this one would have turned out. I hope I don't spend eternity in Hell because I killed somebody. I worry about that a lot. I've talked to my priest who is now a bishop, and he's said there are no sins that are unforgivable. He even told me to stay away from Mass for a couple of weeks because right after my abortion the Church was having its big *"right to life" campaign and he thought that would be pretty tough for me to take.*

There's another punch line to all of this. I stayed with Mark another year after the abortion—don't ask me why—I guess I felt he owed me something. Then out of the clear blue sky one day he told me he was never coming back—he had gotten a big promotion and had to give me up to get it. And he left. He's been gone now for four years, and I keep seeing in our local Catholic newspaper that he's on this committee and that committee, having received this award and that award—a real star.

They bought him. I think he's just like one of these sleazy characters in an Andrew Greeley novel—a better priest for having known a woman. Greeley has yet to address what happens to the women after the priest has cast them off and learned from them.

I wonder if Mark ever thinks about me or the baby. Or if I have been replaced by someone else. Or if he worries about going to Hell. He always used to say he felt like such a hypocrite when he slept with me and then celebrated Mass the next day.

I think he's a bigger hypocrite now.

After several years, I interviewed this woman again. She says that she deeply regrets the abortion and that, if she had to do it over, she would choose to raise the child herself.

Dedicated religious women are increasingly vocal about the right and need to be heard—certainly when issues touch them directly and essentially. There is a theme of disregard of women—from gentle neglect to flagrant abuse—that runs through many accounts of the practice of priestly celibacy-sexuality. The words of Sister Margaret Ellen Traxler (1979) have to taken seriously:

Men of the Church have yet to understand a basic principle, namely, that they have no right to tell women what to do with their bodies. That principle is already understood in the new and growing women's consciousness, and men of the Vatican will have to understand and respect it.

Part III
THE PROCESS AND THE ATTAINMENT _____

Chapter 12

LIVING WITH CELIBACY __

"The celibate has only one true friend—Jesus Christ"
—Fr. Thomas Verner Moore, M.D.
1877–1969

If one dismisses celibacy as unnatural or abnormal, one is restricted to categories of mystery or pathology to explain its structure and process. To be sure, the goal of celibacy is not usual, but that in itself does not render it ipso facto pathological. To clothe celibacy in the garments of its religious idealism, as is most customary in the literature, or conversely to rip its religious vesture and expose its naked historical imperfections does little to reveal its essential dynamic. Regardless of one's limited comprehension or understanding of an ideal, there is an instinctive admiration for another's undivided dedication to it. Profound sacrifice in the pursuit of altruism is heroic and admirable even if not imitable.

Those who confuse celibacy with simple sexual abstinence will fail to realize that celibacy involves a complex process of development. Even if one cannot define it or trace it accurately, the serious student of celibacy soon becomes aware that there must be an inner dynamic to the practice of this discipline and the pursuit of this ideal.

WHAT IS THE PROCESS OF CELIBACY?

Two subquestions are related to this primary one: (1) How does one achieve sexual identity *without* sexual experience? (2) How does one integrate celibate practice *after* sexual experience?

In other words, how does one come to the solid awareness, conviction, and reality that "I am a celibate person"? Clearly, celibacy as I have defined it in Chapter 4 is a process that involves the whole person because it involves essential elements of identity.

Since celibacy is the redirection of sexual energy from its original goal of direct discharge to both delayed and derivative gratification, it cannot be attained by a simple act of the will. The achievement of celibacy involves a series of developmental tasks that are ongoing, overlapping, and interactive. Also, since priestly celibacy is a lifelong process, it involves stages of refinement toward completion and integration.

After analyzing the celibate search from hundreds of priests' stories, I have come to formulate the process in a tripartite interactive model (Figure 12:1).

1. It involves developmental relationships and patterns, many of which precede any celibate intention but vitally influence the sexual/celibate pattern.
2. There is a process of internalization of the celibate ideal from intention to achievement.
3. There is a sequential process that involves the refinement of the forces from awareness to integration.

In presenting these dynamics—one centrifugal, one centripetal, and one linear—I warn the reader to avoid thinking of this unfolding process as a neatly segmented reality which the schematic presentations might imply. The illustrations represent a perspective on sexual reality from a celibate vantage in the tradition of William James's view of the phenomenal world as "one big buzzing blooming confusion" (Pruyser, 1984, p. 106).

DEVELOPMENTAL RELATIONSHIPS

At the core of the celibate search and process is the achievement of a relationship rather than the absence of one. The operative dynamic is centrifugal (Figure 12.1). The true celibate is able to forge a real and durable relationship with the transcendent. Having done so, he will develop the capacity to realize expanding potential, which, when the relationship is of sufficient satisfaction and meaning, will produce a firmness of identity in the face of the deprivation of direct sexual satisfaction.

Naturally, this developed capacity for a relationship of such depth and magnitude is preceded and conditioned by the parent-child and especially the mother-child bond. No voice has been stronger or clearer in the past quarter-century in delineating the steps of ego development than that of Margaret Mahler (1979). Her work forms a paradigm for psychological insight into the process of spiritual development.

Just as psychological development does not occur simultaneously with physical birth, spiritual birth is not concomitant with either physical or psychological birth. Spiritual "rebirth" is a traditional biblical concept: "Unless a man be born again he cannot enter the kingdom" (John 3:3). This transformation to a new phase of awareness or existence is mediated by a transcendent power—nonphysical and all-encompassing. Spiritual re-

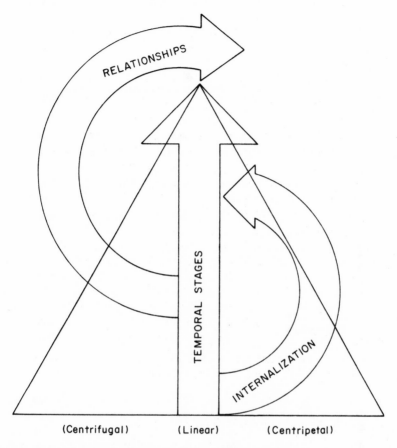

RELATIONSHIPS

TEMPORAL STAGES

INTERNALIZATION

(Centrifugal)   (Linear)   (Centripetal)

FIGURE 12:1. Interactive Dynamic of the Celibate Process

birth puts the believer in an essential and personal relationship of enduring meaning and significance through which he reacts with all other beings in his path.

Celibacy is possible only to the degree that this relationship becomes
effective. One life story after another in our case histories of men searching for celibacy verified this core reality: the process and possibility of
celibacy are essentially entwined with the capacity for a refined relationship with the unseen of ample force and measure to organize one's existence and energies. As one priest wrote, "Only those who see the invisible
can do the impossible." It is the connection with the Ultimate Other that
undergirds, infuses, and crowns the celibate quest. In the tradition of Erik
Erikson, this conceptualization sees the life cycle as a journey from the
Primary Other through and with Significant Others to the Ultimate
Other (see Figure 12:2.).

1. The Primary Relationship

One can hardly overemphasize the importance of the first three years of life for the development of personality and character in later life. The roots of self-image are firmly established in the first two years when the awareness of identity "is maintained by comparison and contrast" and when the predictability of the rhythm of gratification/frustration associated with the loved and loving mother lays the foundations for object constancy and therefore meaningful and satisfying relatedness (Mahler, 1979, pp. 5–6). "The wordless appeal" of the toddler to the mother for love, praise, the expressions of longing, the search for meaning in the newly discovered and expanding world, the wish for sharing and expansion (all Mahler's words, p. 11) and how the mother responds to these early needs will forever mark the person who seeks and must find all of these same elements in spiritual and celibate relationships.

An ongoing loving and supportive bond with an adequate mother, living or dead, seems to be a factor in many celibates' lives. It is not, however, invariable or essential. Some celibates report exactly the opposite: an inadequate or rejecting mother. Whereas for the former, the positive experience is enhanced, continued, generalized, and reproduced in the context of the church and the world, for the latter, deprivation is compensated for, and equilibrium and constancy are found in Mother Church. The institution of the church provides the possibility of compensation, restoration, and regeneration.

One priest who practiced celibacy for years traced the roots of his continuing struggle to an inadequate early relationship with his mother:

> As far back as I can remember, I've never gotten a word of encouragement from her. If I displeased her in any way, she would accuse me of *deliberately* harassing her. She was constantly disappointed in me—except my priesthood. I think she found her own self-image and worth as the mother-of-the-priest. She would not understand if I were anything else. If I were to leave the priesthood, she would have a serious depression. I see her rarely but call her every couple of weeks or so. But I'm loaded with resentment toward her—confused feelings like I let her down, like she let me down; why the hell didn't she see that I needed love and why do I feel this way about a poor old lady?

This man goes on to report how his priesthood (his "crusade") and sense of well-being and righteousness, which comes with serving a cause, have sustained him. He is, as he says, "relaxed and happy" in his ministry. Community and Mother Church have been nourishing and supportive. The frustrations of celibacy were partially compensated for by these re-

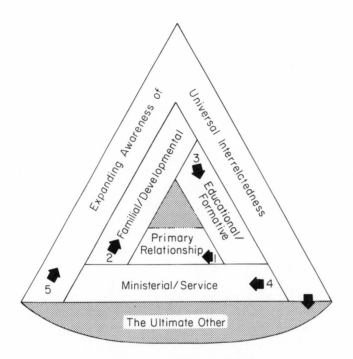

Process of Celibacy – Developmental Relationship

FIGURE 12:2. Developmental Relationships in the Process of Celibacy

warding relationships that he could not hope for or duplicate in any other forum.

Not all early deficits can be rehabilitated by celibate alliance, but I have been amazed by the mystery of celibate healing which many priests reported. I have been, however, equally moved by the tragic, torturous, and futile efforts some priests had to make in attempting to compensate for early developmental deficiencies. The limits of nature were stretched beyond endurance in their celibate search. Grace had too little to build on.

Object constancy is most significant for later spiritual growth, especially for establishing what traditionally is called the "presence of God." The awareness of this presence is both necessary and fundamental for celibate development. It is obvious how directly this presence parallels a child's need to retain the mental image of his primary relationships and to be able to recall them for equilibrium as he ventures out into the world.

One thing is absolutely predictable: The quality of all subsequent bonds will be marked by the core primary relationships of the would-be celibate. Those who select candidates for ministry and who train men for celibate dedication are well advised to help them appreciate fully the importance of this endowment for their future growth and interactions.

2. Familial/Developmental

The family can provide the lifelong model for warm, close sharing and for emotionally satisfying relationships that do not involve sexual exchange. It is not accidental that "brother," "sister," as well as "father" are appellations and paradigms of celibate functioning.

During preadolescence, home and family form the base of a boy's "intellectual and affective life. . . . He uses his friends and companions in the secret pursuit of knowledge about the body and its sexual functions, as partners in sexual games, and in the enactment of sexual fantasies" (Harley, 1975). The histories of many celibates confirm how very significant this early period is in the formation of their sexuality and impulse toward celibacy. Sexual arousal is indiscriminate, and infantile sexuality is a kind of defense against genitality and growing up sexually. The preadolescent boy can have greater fear of the mother than of the father. He can therefore more easily turn away from girls (his mother) and turn toward his father (or other idealized men like priests) for reinforcement of his budding masculinity. Many priests trace their impulse to study for the priesthood from this time in grade school. For this reason a great deal of effort was expended during the 1940s through the 60s to encourage priestly vocations from this age group.

Many celibates find themselves years later trying to bridge the gap between the prepubertal sexual experience and growth and their adult intellectual and spiritual values. For some men, adolescent asceticism sealed their sexual development at this stage. This explains—but only in part—the relatively higher rate of sexually nondifferentiated, bisexually, and homosexually oriented men among the clergy. Some years after the completion of their studies, the thread of development reemerges to be woven into the fabric of the celibate garment. Celibate identity that is grounded in an avoidance or delay of adolescent sexual conflict will invariably be ambiguous.

Greenacre and others have written about the "prepuberty trauma" that is utilized to explain a boy's inability to enter into heterosexual activities in adolescence. Harley (1975) writes, "this prepuberty trauma of the boy consists of an unconscious provocation of an overt homosexual experience with an older boy or man. When he reaches adolescence, the boy then uses the fact that he had been 'homosexually assaulted' as the rationalization for his homosexual proclivities and concomitant heterosexual difficulties."

Several priest informants who served on seminary faculties in widely separated geographical areas reported the frequency of this phenomenon among their students. The exact nature of the sexual experience is not as significant as the familial context in which it occurred and the degree to which it is psychically available to the adult for incorporation into his value system and his celibate life-style and discipline. For some few celibates, early sexual play is the fountainhead of their process of sexual differentiation and identity.

One priest who later became an American citizen entered training for the priesthood in his home country at five years of age—a custom with centuries-old tradition and very common in his homeland. It is clear from his account that both maternal and paternal roles were fulfilled by the priests and brothers who performed all of the educational, health care, and homemaking services for their charges. Even from this skewed and unusual environment, firm sexual identity and heterosexual orientation are clearly possible.

3. Educational/Formative

Prior to 1975, many priests began their studies for the priesthood during their high school years; others began seminary training in college; and fewer still started after graduating from a nonseminary college or even after a period of time in the working world or after training in another profession. The shift toward later rather than earlier entry into seminary training is clearly progressive from 1960 to 1985. Earlier entry into studies took advantage of the natural idealism of adolescence about which Anna Freud (1944) and others have spoken (Blos, 1962; Freud, 1966). The reasons for the semiseclusion and protective schedules behind the seminary walls were the solidification of the clerical identity and the "preservation of chastity."

We found no celibate—except a few suspected of having Kallmann's syndrome—who denied ever having any sexual experience, even if it was relegated to this period of his life. In fact, for some men this activity formed the prototype of their understanding of others and remained for them a valuable set of calipers with which to measure their own subsequent feelings and reactions. When I observed this, I was reminded of wise mystics who can find the meaning of the universe in a blade of grass—a rare but beautiful thing to encounter.

The formation of bonds of security and emotional and economic sustenance also provided the basis of a brotherhood of lasting shared values and ideals. After more than 50 years of celibate living, one priest said, "I cannot imagine another profession that could supply such love and support."

Priests commonly report, however, that the specific challenges to their sexual identities were not confronted in their education and formation. Sex was not dealt with as a lived reality and it surfaced later in the priests' 20s and early 30s. Instead, both denial and rationalization were fostered in the process of seminary training.

There is no question that sexual activity during seminary years is far more restricted than among men of equal age and education elsewhere. It is not unusual for men to abstain from all sexual activity, including masturbation, during their seminary training; however, there is no overwhelming correlation between sexual abstinence during training and later celibate achievement.

The purpose of the satisfying support in a system of both discipline and fraternal relationships is designed to foster an internalization of those two entities. Both are necessary to sustain celibate practice.

4. Ministerial/Service

If celibacy is to thrive, it must be able to withstand the rigorous demands of unrequited loving service. Great satisfaction as well as monumental frustration can accrue to the unselfish attention to the community. The ability to foster and maintain essentially ministerial and service relationships that have enduring and comprehensive meaning for the celibate test his view of Man and God to ultimate depths. What eyes of faith it takes to see Christ in each human and to depend on the transcendent for one's vision and comfort in the face of daily challenge! All ecclesial literature abounds with encouragement and warning for the celibate who has progressed to this level of development in his quest.

It is during this long period that the celibate heroes are made and the sexual compromises that threaten integrity are tested. Great humanitarian and institutional deeds can be provided by those whose ministerial relationships are not totally infused by celibate sublimation. Just as other important bonds are formed and tested (with mother, family, or friends), so too the ministerial/service relationships and patterns are programmed, furthered, and refined by daily demands and interactions.

Some pastoral situations provide a missionary-like setting wherein the demands of service are extremely clear-cut and the sources of gratification global (i.e., progress of the community group) rather than individual. Such situations were reported more often as sustaining as well as exacting.

The degree to which these ministerial relationships flourish is related to the quality and mastery of earlier stages of relational achievement. The isolate and the person of rigid ego adaptation—even if they have attained a record and degree of sexual control and abstinence—are not well defended against the pressures and demands of service. For them, a period of sexual experimentation tends to be destructive of general relatedness since it cannot be incorporated into their celibate identity. Instead, it is inclined to abort the celibate quest altogether or, more commonly, leaves their ministerial rigidity intact and establishes a split-off sexual life. Inflexibility is not a good support for celibate exercise.

Celibacy and the achievement of celibate relationships require a personality of fluid ego adaptation. The awareness of the transcendent and the creativity required to live one's life and serve in accordance with that awareness demand a man of unusual inner resourcefulness. He must also possess a strong capacity for the memory of relatedness as well as for the projection of as yet unrealized relatedness, i.e., hope. This flexibility, demonstrated by many active celibates, revealed an independence of spirit and will which was not overly contingent upon institutional props.

A great deal of work must be done to understand the link between institutional alignment and celibate bonds. At best, dedication to the "community" of the church is a correlative of good celibate adjustment. At worst, it is an immature reliance on a power structure and a failure of differentiation which makes every relationship hollow. Indeed, hollow relationships do not reinforce celibacy but rather lead to sexual activity that is either problematic or unhealthy, or both. With the accumulation of priests' stories, at times I was forced to ask myself the question: "Does one have to be a little bit anticlerical to be a good celibate?"

One thing is certain: The man of creative adaptability can more easily incorporate noncelibate experience without rationalization or splitting. Some priests felt that a period of noncelibacy, honestly dealt with, had enhanced their eventual celibate practice and enriched their subsequent ministerial/service relationships.

5. Expanding Awareness of Universal Interrelatedness

In our estimation, lived celibacy leads to greater similarity than dissimilarity between celibates and noncelibates in this one regard: Many men described the experience of a greater inner interrelatedness with all human beings as their celibate identities solidified. Several times this phenomenon took on the quality of a "religious experience." I first became aware of this interrelatedness around a cluster of men who described near-death experiences (Sipe, 1974) and how these had affected them. The keys to such an experience are its subsequent impact on one's life and its sustaining quality.

One man described a month-long "high" during which he had an acute awareness of both the presence of God and his own oneness with others. The time was vivid to his recall even after several years had passed. His subsequent productivity and accomplishment were visible, public, and remarkable.

Usually such an episode follows a period of turmoil or felt disintegration. It comes suddenly, unexpectedly, and in such diverse places as a busy street, at home in the middle of the night, on a beach, or in an airplane. In an instant, the one having the experience can see things in a unity that he had not previously known. Whether coupled with an incident or not, many celibates reported a sense of cognizance that could be labeled "universal interrelatedness." They were clearly able to transcend emotionally their institutional and cultural barriers. The experience did not seem to be parochial or provincial and had a quality of transinstitutionalism in spite of a firm sense of clerical identity.

This feeling of relatedness appears to be the natural outcome of the process of celibacy and the refinement of one's relationships. It is the culmination of a progression whereby sincere, devoted, and highly motivated men seek the highest spiritual ideal of love and service to humankind. They arrive at this point only by coming to terms with the sexual dimensions of their lives rather than by avoiding them. These men are self-aware and can recount subtle shades of sexual feelings which were generated in their ministries—the kind of Socratic love and parental responses which were roused in certain interactions. The richness of their inner lives and motivations gave an analytic clarity and integration to all of their relationships.

INTERNALIZATION

As priests describe their experience of celibacy/sexuality, one is challenged to comprehend the second dynamic of the process: a centripetal movement from *intention* or attraction to *goal* and integration (Figure 12.3). What motivates a man to sacrifice his sexuality? Naturally, one may say, "the love of God"; but if this is the only reason one can give in recounting the development of his celibacy, he ironically is very suspect both in his self-critical capacity as well as in his honesty. The determination to be celibate is usually adjunctive to and derivative of some perceived good or advantage. It is mediated by a person or the image of a persona whom one wants to be like. The advantages of education, prestige, or opportunity, if not power, are commonly mentioned as early motivating factors as well. The first step toward the internalization of celibate identity is very significant since it prefigures all the stages to follow.

1. Celibate Image and Intention

This first step involves the formation of an image and the awareness of an intention. It announces the direction of the process toward achievement and includes the separate but interrelated tasks of comprehension, conversion, self-control, and commitment.

The image of the celibate is usually formed through the family, church, or school where the celibate model was extolled or revered. (Conversely, it may have been the negative image that was sought out in opposition to the perceived wealth, prestige, or power of one's own family's values.) In any case, one comprehends the image in personal terms.

Comprehension is the cognizance of a meaning of life and of one's existence that is "one's own." That cognizance may or may not be validated by a wide segment of social groups. It might be called the sense of vocation: One finds a place for oneself in the scheme of things. At first, it may just be a vague awareness that one "should be" a celibate. The awareness is a cornerstone because over the subsequent decades of the man's life, it will support the expanding edifice that is his place of service.

I have never ceased to be amazed at the young age at which many celibates record their first such awareness of their vocation. Many have memories dating from their fifth year of life. There are a number of celibates who know that the priesthood was a resolution of their oedipal strivings. Several celibates recounted a consciousness that each could be a "father" of commanding authority—one to whom their own fathers could give obeisance. At the same time, they could identify with the loved mother and preserve a special relationship with her.

Several celibates came to a knowledge of their life goal after serving in the armed forces during World War II or the Korean conflict. Either in the discord about them or in their own hearts, they witnessed deprivation or degradation that they could no longer tolerate. Some men sensed a futility in the direction of their lives and felt they could "do better." Invariably, the example of some person whose life they viewed as meaningful was the impetus for their "seeing the way." The example of a celibate was a universal element in nearly every history of a man who chose that route for himself.

Some priests spoke of the Depression of the 1930s and the economic hardships and insecurities suffered by their families as a counterpoint to the stability and advantage they perceived among their parish clergy. "Celibacy," one priest good-naturedly said, "seemed like a fair exchange at the time."

Death in a family can be a powerful force in the rearrangement of values and in the interpretation of meaning. The death of a parent, especially prior to one's adolescence, was a factor in the lives of a number of our informants who had practiced celibacy for many years or who had at last achieved it. It almost seemed that the death of the loved one reinforced the reality of the transcendent persona who loved them and was part of the unseen reality.

Even the threat of the death of a parent or loved one can be the precipitator of a comprehension of reality which invites a celibate response. One priest who had practiced celibacy for 16 years told of his initial awareness of his vocation. He was in the fifth grade of a Catholic school; his mother was hospitalized at the time. While praying for her recovery, he felt that

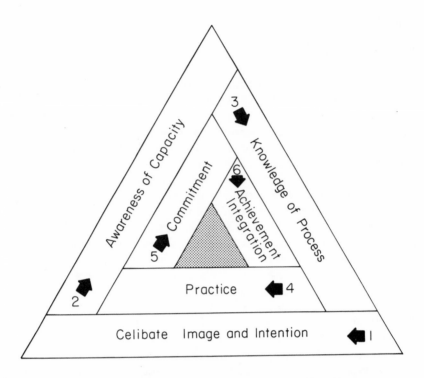

The Process of Celibacy - Internalization

FIGURE 12:3. Internalization in the Process of Celibacy

he should be a priest, but he was also acutely aware that part of him was equally resistant to the idea.

The perception of the conflict seems to be an important factor in the validity of the resolution. Many celibates relate the agony of the initial formation of their celibate intent.

2. Awareness of the Capacity to be Celibate

How does a man know if he has a capacity for celibacy and not merely an admiration for a personally unattainable ideal? First, he must know himself and his ability to enter into and sustain relationships. Second, he must have some knowledge of the process that supports that ability.

Since the Council of Trent, the seminary training period has been meant to inculcate into the young aspirant a pattern of life which will develop the necessary internal discipline to sustain celibate practice. Three other factors support motivation toward the priesthood: (1) economic dependency; (2) the position of specialness in a social setting; and (3) a measure of power. In some way these factors do achieve a certain realization, at least temporarily. Many men report that regardless of subsequent sexual activity, the period of their seminary training was relatively free of it.

In the assessment of their vocation, most men experienced it primarily as a call to the priesthood and only secondarily to celibacy. That meant that a sense of inner change or the need for it was already present in their initial awareness of the vocation. However, invariably it involved—though perhaps vaguely—the need to be sexually restrained. With many, their capacity for celibacy was first confronted by an experience of conversion.

Conversion or *metanoia* is an ancient concept that involves not merely a comprehension or cognizance of life's meaning but also a change in heart or behavior that reflects that new awareness. It is, therefore, a test of capacity. In the same way, the cognizance of a transcendent reality and a "presence" that one can count on leads to the next step—the translating of that reality into behavior that reflects the relatedness. The reevaluation of one's past life produces a sense of one's imperfections or a consciousness of one's sinfulness and unworthiness; yet it also yields a gratitude for being part of such a relationship. "Accepted," "validated," "loved," and "chosen" are the feelings, frequently expressed, that lead to the conversion or the sense that one's life has not been good enough.

Frequently, sexual feelings or alliances are reevaluated then. The younger one was when this part of the process was experienced, usually the more vague is the sexual context of the conversion. However, it is inevitably present, no matter how ill-defined. Some priests relate many years later how their childhood sexual play was the chief element in their self-evaluation and conversion. Those who were older at the time of their conversion or who had had more sexual experience than others up until that point felt more guilt, specifically for their sexual activity. At this stage, these variables all play a part in the test of one's ability for sexual control and sublimation.

A priest who had practiced celibacy for nearly 20 years explained that although he felt he had a capacity for celibate dedication, he felt he needed a strict and structured atmosphere for his life since he had lived a sexually active and free existence prior to his conversion. There are others who, although they have had very little sexual experience prior to their conversion, are acutely aware of their sexual desires and their potential capacity for acting on them.

3. Knowledge of the Process (How to be Celibate)

Control, or the ability to influence one's existence and environment, is part of the task of and reward for the celibate quest. The image of the athlete in training is borrowed from the Bible and St. Paul and has inspired many celibates. There is a justifiable pride in accomplishing a difficult feat—one that takes discipline, practice, sacrifice, and a willingness to engage a powerful, unrelenting opposing force. Regulating one's sexual instinct surely involves all of the above.

The question is *how*? Traditionally, the *system* has been depended upon to instill the necessary self-control and skills to achieve celibacy. A seminary was a finely tuned program based on monastic tradition which did indeed foster a sense of self-denial, order, community, and shared values. Ironically, the system has not proved to be particularly successful in inculcating lifelong celibacy. Sixty-eight percent of men religious respondents to Greeley's (1972) study of priests agreed with the following statement: "The traditional way of presenting the vow of chastity in religious formation has often allowed for the development of impersonalization and false spirituality." Supposedly 80 percent of the same group felt they were well aware of the "implications" of their vow of chastity (p. 364).

According to the informants I interviewed, training programs and the ecclesial system failed them in their knowledge of how to be celibate in three ways: (1) the avoidance of sexuality; (2) dependence on a system of secrecy; and (3) a lack of personal witness. Celibacy cannot be practiced without confronting one's own sexuality as well as the whole subject in a realistic way. The sociologist Father John L. Thomas told me, "A celibate should know everything there is to know about sexuality. short of experience." I know from years of teaching in Catholic seminaries how difficult it is to teach human sexual development to candidates for the priesthood. Is Fr. Thomas's ideal attainable?

In the seminary, when sexual tensions, temptations, or personal questions arise, they are handled by secrecy—in the confessional or counseling office. If sexual behavior or acting out comes to the attention of authorities, invariably it is dealt with in the most clandestine manner possible to avoid scandal. Many an idealistic, serious, well-intentioned seminarian, as well as many a naive one, actually goes through his training feeling that there is a sex-free zone enjoyed by all his comrades and teachers, disturbed only by his own thoughts or temptations (and, perhaps, one exceptional story or incident that he knows of). This was very much the characterization of seminary experiences recounted prior to the mid-1970s.

The presumption that the seminary faculty is celibate is perpetuated without the necessity of personal witness. The faculty enjoys the same system of avoidance and secrecy that their students have. One priest who had a position of some authority said that he indeed had presumed the celibate practice of his seminary faculty while he was a student. Subsequently, he learned unequivocally that nine of his instructors had had sexually active lives while performing their official tasks well or admirably. Within the seminary, there is no tradition of personal witness: "This is what celibacy means to me. This is how *I* practice it and have achieved it." St. Augustine's penetrating *Confessions* has served generations of priests as a convenient hiding place as well as a source of inspiration.

4. Practice

The sustained intention to be celibate—even with a capacity for sublimation and control and backed up by a solid knowledge of sexuality and how it impinges on one's being and behavior—needs practice to achieve reality. If virtue were merely not perpetrating vice, prisons would be bastions of holiness. If celibacy were merely the absence of sexual activity, some of the ranks of the married would have to be reclassified as celibate. The path from intention to integration is not traversed without risk. As I illustrated in Part II of this volume, entitled "The Practice versus the Profession," not all those who profess celibacy officially practice it. The question here is what is an abandonment of the celibate goal and what is part of the necessary learning process and the refinement of one's ideals.

Many priest informants who spoke forthrightly about their sexual/celibate development recounted what they considered to be their failures or transgressions. Many of their stories revealed heroic struggles and tender and humane reminiscences with loving gratitude for relationships or incidents that temporarily broke their vow but led them back to the pursuit of celibacy—chastened but wiser. As far as I can tell, it is impossible to codify this paradox of spirit and struggle wherein "sin" may indeed serve the ends of growth, maturity, and, finally, virtue.

Many psychiatrists who have treated priests speak of the challenging experiences they witness in a priest's sexual involvement—healthy by standards of human sexual development yet a violation of the man's conscience and explicit church norms. Conscientious confessors witness the same struggle. The important thing for the person wishing to practice and achieve celibacy is that the struggle remain an honest part of the celibate search—not hidden in denial, justified self-servingly by rationalization, or split from one's ministerial life. All of these maneuvers tend to derail the process of celibacy, at times irrevocably. It is one thing to ally oneself with David justifying his hypocrisy to Nathan, and quite another to sing the *Miserere* with him.

It takes delicate and unflinching self-assessment to distinguish between a *felix culpa*—which leads to greater spiritual awareness and dedication—and a pattern of compromise and self-indulgence. The literature on celibacy is almost exclusively inspirational and idealistic. Yet real-life witness and history neither destroy the ideal nor lessen the inspiration. The lack of this real dimension in the literature and teaching of celibacy becomes glaring as one tries to explore the practice and process of celibacy. The Thomas Merton archives in time may have more to contribute toward filling this gap (see Mott, 1984, pp. 435–454).

There are stories of incredible sexual misuse of others in the pursuit of the practice of celibacy. Some priests are quite open in admitting their former "ignorance," "arrogance," "folly," and "naiveté." A few priests clearly were victimized by a cunning and experienced person who deliberately set out to become sexually intimate with a priest. Some people with quite complex motivations assigned themselves the task of sexually educating the blatantly uninitiated. I interviewed several women who felt almost a sense of obligation to teach a priest about sex; one took great pride in the number and hierarchic rankings of priests for whom she had provided the first heterosexual encounter. Another woman, eager to bring priests "out of the closet," was active in setting up inexperienced priests with laymen who were comfortable in their own homosexual life-styles.

Whether a period of sexual involvement is merely a passage (i.e., an incident to be understood as part of the paradoxical and difficult pursuit of an ideal), whether it is an abandonment more or less temporary of the celibate search, or whether it is the initiation of a sexual pattern wherein celibacy has little or no real meaning, can be determined only on a person-by-person basis. There are priests who also report a very rigid and obsessive-like period in which their self-absorption with the avoidance of sex was so energy consuming that they lost all freedom and fire for their life of service. Priests also speak of times when it was easier to practice celibacy than to face the risks of confronting their own sexual identities and of times when it was more difficult and stressful to do so.

5. Commitment

The initial stage of the celibate process is the determination that the relationship—or the vocation—is worth the sacrifice. Like the call of the burning bush to Moses (Exodus 3) or the words of Jesus, "Come follow me and I will make you fishers of men" (Matt. 4:19), this is the thrilling alignment of one's energies in the service of the cause and in unison with one who commands the attention and energies of one's existence. At base, it is the willingness to serve which validates the commitment. Those who are primarily or largely self-serving will be betrayed in the end by their sexual instincts. An excessive desire for acclaim will leave celibate striving undefended in the face of inevitable confrontation.

In his autobiography, Gandhi (1957) notes the relationship between the practice and commitment phase of celibacy:

As I look back upon the twenty years of the vow, I am filled with pleasure and wonderment. The more or less successful practice of self-control had been going on since 1901. But the freedom and joy that came to me after taking the vow had never been experienced before 1906. Before the vow I had been open to being overcome by temptation at any moment. Now the vow was a sure shield against temptation. The great potentiality of *brahmacharya* daily became more and more patent to me. (p. 209)

Commitment to a cause that is essentially of another demands a level of integrity and self-honesty of unusual magnitude. The temptation to compromise is ubiquitous, as is the tendency to rigidity—both of which ill prepare one to meet the demands of growth in service. Once a colleague at the Menninger Foundation commented on the healthy adaptation of a celibate of singular note as a man "possessing the quality of tempered steel—strong and flexible."

It is also this commitment that serves as the example to the community of believers. The single-minded devotion to the cause and the undivided attention to the service of religious conviction are needed and admired in the human community. It "enriches a nation," as Gandhi pointed out.

A certain level of commitment is involved even in the first stage—intention—and is refined and tested through the successive stages. However, real commitment cannot be accomplished without sexual/celibate knowledge and the risk/practice of celibate service *in vivo*—in real life, interacting with real people. Growing commitment inspires a stability and predictability of response and behavior based on a fine-tuned and more or less accurate self-perception. It is apparent how interdependent this phase is on a model of relationships. The commitment is not to some abstract ideal but to a person. This, of course, demands that one's own personhood be clear, including one's sexuality.

6. Achievement and Integration

The achievement of celibacy is not the accidental passage of sexual feelings into the oblivion of physical senescence. One cannot be celibate by accident. One has to achieve it, since celibacy involves the integration of one's identity without the ongoing support and benefit of a sexual friendship. The person who has achieved celibacy can be said to be an integrated human being with knowledge of both self and reality. The use of his energies in the service of life is consistent, transparent, and tested by life. Many priests are reluctant to claim the "achievement" of celibacy. They are always waiting for the next temptation or period of stress that might reactivate their imagination.

However, sexual abstinence can also tend to reinforce itself. I do not know if this is in part a physiological phenomenon or if the success of sublimation becomes so effective in some people that the sexual drive is truly disenfranchised. A number of older priest informants reported contradictory experience of prolonged sexual abstinence—one group stating that temptation to sexual activity and sexual interest itself diminished with prolonged periods of abstinence, the other group maintaining that sexual interest and enticement remained high although their discipline and commitment became easier to maintain despite increased periodic internal pressure.

Internalized celibacy is not directly apparent; its accomplishment is integrated into the man's life goals and meanings. The lifelong or prolonged discipline is not external, as is the flagellate's. The focus is not the subjection of the senses but rather the life system and productivity that reinforce the celibacy. There is no question that each man in our study had a system of discipline, parts of which were probably more apparent to the inquirer than to the celibate since for the celibate the system seemed to be such a natural part of his life. Prominent in the system was a routine of prayer. I was struck by the amount of time devoted each day to prayer and how it was placed to meet individual needs and schedules. One man made a "holy hour" each noon, during which time he could defend himself from professional demands since it was his lunch hour. He said people could better understand his being unavailable to take calls because of lunch than because he was "just praying."

Other men reserved the early hours of the day for the bulk of their prayer. Most often, however, the system of prayer was also woven throughout the day in short periods—times during which the men would pray the rosary or spend some moments in recollection and self-examination. Not a man among them was afraid to be alone; even the most sociable in temperament commented on their ability to be at peace by themselves.

Celibate integration was also marked by vital intellectual interests, sometimes in areas quite esoteric for men of the cloth, such as mechanics, astronomy, or another avocation at least symbolically appropriate—sheep husbandry. Golf was mentioned as a common interest among priests, as it is among other professional men in the United States. However, it does not seem to correlate with the achievement of celibacy in any particular fashion the way some other activities do.

When asked what factors fostered his successful celibate dedication, one elderly priest responded tersely, "fishing." He said he trusted priests who fished; in fact, fishing and gardening were mentioned prominently by priests who considered themselves successful celibates.

Sex does not disappear entirely from consciousness even after years of celibate dedication. One 78-year-old man said that he did not watch certain things on television, citing the June Taylor dancers as an example, because he found them "unnecessarily stimulating." However, another priest of similar age and equal discipline and devotion relished an occasional visit to Radio City Music Hall with its Rockettes, not finding them sexually tantalizing. He did say, though, that he avoided certain literary productions that he thought might "distract" him.

Those priests who reported having had a good deal of sexual activity prior to their vow of celibacy or early in the process of their celibate search could admit to the availability of their memories. Nevertheless, only a few had to manufacture extraordinary or heroic means such as fasts or physical deprivation to "preserve" their achievement. As one priest said, "Life has a way of keeping me humble."

TEMPORAL STAGES

Although celibacy can become an integrated reality after a period of time, there seems to be a series of stages through which the seeker must pass. From the men we interviewed, we got a firm impression that the stages cluster around certain time periods. Therefore, this model is a linear one (see Figure 12:4).

1. Initial Awareness/Depression: Gain/Loss

Every man who wanted to be celibate described an initial awareness, however vague, of a sense of loss. One mature priest who had traversed most of the stages of celibacy said that there were moments at each stage when he had experienced what he called "an instant stab of genital grief." I was tempted to characterize each stage as a kind of depression, but in the end I decided that the term carried too much of a one-dimensional mental health quality to it. However, the first inner determination to be celibate always has this depressive quality to it, no matter how positively the allied goods of the priesthood and study are perceived. Interestingly, this experience does not always precede one's determination to be a priest or even coincide with it. We interviewed some priests who had not experienced even this first stage—but then they were not practicing celibacy either.

Not all men conceptualized the downside of this stage as having to do with sex, but I am convinced that this sense of loss has much to do with the men's blurry anticipation of the future lack of a sexual outlet and the oblation of a sexual relationship. In men of unusual intuition, the perception seemed accurate regarding the direct sexual component of this stage, i.e., they were aware at the time of foregoing a future sexual relationship, and their memory of this stage was quite clear.

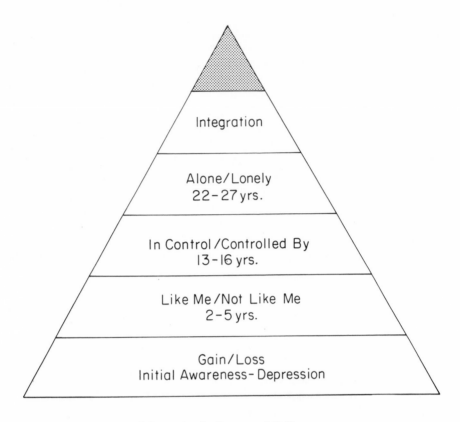

FIGURE 12:4. Temporal Stages in the Process of Celibacy

In others, there appeared to be a good deal of secondary revision, i.e., in light of subsequent experience and reflection, they realized that the sacrifice of intimate sexual relationships was required. This later realization only confirms the essential sexual component of the original experience. One priest said, "I realized that I would have to live my life like a man who was deprived of an arm or leg. I would do the best I could, but nothing would give me the use of a limb I didn't have." He and others expressed experienced knowledge of the gospel meaning of being a "eunuch for Christ." With men like this, the choice was conscious, not merely denial, filled with a keen awareness of what it was they were giving up.

The core depression is an inner battle, a sense that one *must* follow a certain path that is abhorrent or at least disagreeable. The *must* is not of the compulsive kind—as if one cannot help oneself or is moved by external forces. Nor is it of the nature of the loss of liberty, for the choice can be accompanied by a tremendous sense of inner freedom and determination, which, unfortunately, in itself will not alleviate the depression. Any celibate, when pressed, will be able to recall this depressive stage that may last from a week to several months—rarely as long as a year. It is usually followed by a feeling of quiet peace that can be quite memorable. "Joy," "peace," and "security," are words often used to describe the resolution of this initial sadness.

People of deep religious temperament often have an underlying personality component that can be called mildly depressive. The Greeks used the term "melancholic" to identify one of the four basic personality types. This kind of person, sensitive to the inner life and given to intellectual rumination, is well represented among devout men and women.

2. Like Me/Not Like Me

Priests report a post-training phenomenon that commonly occurs sometime between the second and fifth years after ordination (i.e., post-vow). For the priest, it constitutes an awareness of the degree and the manner in which people outside the clerical environment are "like me" or "not like me." Some of these clergy were relatively isolated from the secular world from perhaps three to 13 years prior to their ordination. Often, the ordination itself marks a dramatic shift in surroundings from the sequestered religious system to an open, semireligious, or even frankly secular environment. The young man who was encapsulated and protected to some degree by a group of men who shared his beliefs, education, and ideals and who behaviorally marched more or less to the same officially regulated cadence now finds himself among people often of widely varying education and religious practice, even if of his same faith traditions. His chosen drum beat is only one rhythm vying for orchestration. He must now simultaneously fit in and hold his own. Reflecting on this period of his life, one priest said, "I trained with the angels and then had to fight on the devil's own turf."

Especially since 1960, there has been a conscious effort in the church to bridge the gap between theoretical training and practical application. An interesting paradox comes to mind: Is it that the young priests are not prepared for the work, or is it that, closed to the mystery of celibacy, the world is not prepared for the young priests? My years of observation have convinced me that the apparent deficit in the transition from education to active service is not one of pastoral technique but one of sexual and celibate identity in light of the pastoral demands.

The period after ordination is not necessarily a conscious jolt. It all seems so natural; it is the achievement of a training goal. At least initially, most of the men feel personally well prepared. Even in circumstances where priests continue to live in a rather restricted environment, there is greater freedom and responsibility after ordination. People—even fellow priests or religious—put a new kind of demand on the celibate: he is expected to sustain a sort of intimate sharing and a response to inner needs which only comes with the expectation, "You will help."

The intimate sharing with parishioners, the self-revelations that people make to their priest, and the discovery of what people are really like all confront the young celibate with an awareness of how much he has changed or not changed since he began his training. Many priests ordained prior to 1970 tell of the hours they spent in the confessional, particularly prior to Christmas and Easter. They relate how their traditional views of sexuality and the sinfulness of certain sexual behaviors were challenged by the existence of good people whom they had come to know and respect whose sexual lives they were now privy to or could surmise.

"Everyone has a sex life except me," said a young celibate in this stage of his search. "I'm not sure I want to spend my whole life sleeping alone," said another man who had vowed celibacy three years earlier. Both statements reflect the necessary confrontation of the celibate with the reality that most people are not like him and that his own self-definition is not in opposition to others even though it is distinct.

The most successful negotiation of this stage of celibate internalization involves a solidification of one's celibate self by role definition and by identification with the community of celibates.

It is not infrequent that a certain amount of sexual experimentation is indulged in at this stage. Some men will use the experimentation as a period of testing their sexual identity. This activity may involve a few incidents or it may be a brief abandonment of celibate practice in some of the ways I have discussed in this book, only to return to a celibate search with renewed determination. Other men at this time assume a stance of functional adherence to their ministerial life but embark on a pattern of sexual activity which obviates any real celibacy. Still others will give up the priesthood to return to secular life and sexual practice.

3. In Control/Controlled By

Clerical celibacy exists in a framework of authority; the power structure in turn supports a man living within it. Sooner or later the ties with authority must be clarified, absorbed, internalized, and in one sense desexualized. (Some people may argue with that term; I will leave it to others to analyze more thoroughly this aspect of celibacy.) If we take only one facet of the authority structure—the *filial*, where the Church and her superiors assume the parental roles of protector, nurturer, and role model—we can see that sooner or later one must leave to become his own man. By so doing, his conviction, values, goals, and behaviors fall under his own control and there will be progressively less dependence on and devotion to externals. This movement is an internal one beyond authority; it is necessary for mature celibate practice.

Celibates most commonly report this stage clustering in the 13th to 16th years post-vow, although we have examples of it much earlier and much later. There is always an adolescent-like quality to this phase of celibate resolve. One realizes, as does an adolescent, that he cannot hope for all that he had expected from his "parents"; with this dissolution of the mental construct of external control, the celibate is threatened with a new freedom. The extremes of response are to reject internalization and become a toady—a stance that does little to enhance celibacy and at times becomes a cover for a sexual relationship or even deviant behavior—or to rebel mindlessly, rejecting all authority and sexual restraint at the same time.

Especially for men who have been truly celibate into their 30s, this is a period of real trial. They have genuinely cast their lot with the celibate fraternity, sharing interests, fate, economy, spirituality, and often esthetics—just like a family. Now they find themselves on their own in an emotional way they have never experienced before, with a disillusionment of major proportions.

A number of our informants reported their first conscious discovery of masturbation at this stage of their development. One priest had had an unusually successful course of studies and work into his 30s. His personality, intelligence, humor, and ability to translate policy into human terms had made him a favorite of teachers, students, and church authorities. He was the perfect organization man. The death of a powerful man in the church whom he had loved like a father and his subsequent replacement by a person who resented our informant's prestige and popularity precipitated in him a crisis leading him to experience a period of sexual confusion like none he had sustained previously.

Although some stories are of deep personal affiliation and then disenchantment with a particular authority figure, many are not dependent on one person or circumstance. Rather they are the progressive awareness of where the supports for celibacy must ultimately rest—in the self. *Humanae Vitae*, a 1968 encyclical condemning artificial birth control, provided a crisis impetus for many priests. It was the most commonly mentioned catalyst in many of the men in our study who were at this stage of celibate refinement. Questioning the credibility of the church's teaching on this facet of sexuality precipitated a revolution of celibacy also—not in every instance to the detriment of celibacy. One 40-year-old priest who was jarred by a teaching to which he in good conscience could not subscribe reevaluated and rededicated himself to celibacy at that same time, stating, "That church [meaning those who teach that all means of birth control are sinful] is not the church to which I belong."

Movement beyond external authority to greater internalization is the salient factor at this stage of celibate development. To navigate it well, one must reach a new level of relationship with the transcendent and in one's self-identity. One man reported that it was at this stage of his life that he really learned courage. As he said, "You can't count on anyone else if you are looking for a triumph over a biological imperative!"

The intensification of reliance on one's spiritual life increases rather than decreases as time passes. The relationship with the celibate fraternity deepens but is less dependent if this stage is mastered. Productivity increases as the celibate retrenches. Literary accounts of priests' lives by sensitive authors like J. F. Powers, Graham Greene, and Georges Bernanos reveal the process of the struggle. There is a novel by Edwin O'Connor entitled *The Edge of Sadness* (1961) that describes beautifully the mood of this period.

St. Ignatius Loyola (1491–1556), the founder of the Society of Jesus, the largest order of religious priests, was a master of celibate psychology. He required that after 12 or 13 years in training his followers spend a year in reflection and rededication. His intuitive awareness that there was something significant in this point in time and experience for the celibate which needed to be addressed is borne out by the witness of numerous priests who had no contact with his ideas.

4. Alone/Lonely

"Lonely" is one of the most frequent replies when one asks a celibate how he feels. Loneliness is a lifelong struggle for anyone who is serious about maintaining a deep relationship. It makes one aware of the untraversed and untraversable chasm that separates even people who love one another.

Loneliness is a deeply personal privation that takes on different colorings at different times in life. Its roots are in the first relationship with mother, who ideally was neither too close nor too far from the child. A mother who could accept a child as a partner in fulfilling his own needs and who was centered in herself but present to the baby is an appropriate model of the human-transcendent interaction. A priest who has enjoyed a training and ministerial career that involved similar support from the church and her authorities will be well prepared for this stage of the celibate process.

To some degree, each of the previous stages dealt with loneliness. Each stage involved a separation. Each contained a risk because it demanded a shift in the way the celibate related to himself, to other people, and to the primary object of his affection—the transcendent.

There inevitably comes a time in the celibate's search when he has to rise above loneliness to a stage of aloneness. It is the final step in resolving the illusion that primal merging is possible.

More must be said about the distinction between "lonely" and "alone." To be alone in the way that I intend means that one is able to accept the reality of one's self and destiny, which requires a sense of the reality of the transcendent and one's dependence on and relationship with that reality. It is not only a stance beyond community and beyond authority, it goes beyond productivity. It is at this stage that the single-mindedness required "on account of the kingdom" is tested to its limit.

This stage is best defined by celibates who have been ordained for more than two decades (22 to 27 years) when they are confronted with the question, "Is it worth it?" Doubt that the sacrifices made and the work done have been of real value to anyone is probably the core of the crisis, coupled with the awareness that to enter more deeply into celibacy obviates any possibility of a meaningful companionable relationship in old age. Men in the throes of this crisis report discouragement at seeing wizened old men grow cranky or dependent on alcohol as a way of combatting their bitter loneliness.

By this stage, most priests have developed healthy celibate friendships and have been observant of their celibate discipline. Whereas passion needed temperance at earlier stages of development, at this stage it is the lack of sexual companionship rather than sexual discharge that threatens the celibate commitment. "The pearl of great price" and the heart's being where one's treasure is are analogical attempts to describe the unswerving dedication to the service of others which is required to negotiate this stage of celibate growth.

The person who cannot tolerate true aloneness cannot move beyond this level of celibacy and therefore remains vulnerable to sexual compromises even after years of discipline. Here celibate resolve requires a level of sexual identity and dedication to purpose which remains constant in the absence of external support. At this stage, many priests cannot make this final step or are faced with the choices they made at earlier stages when they fought passion and loneliness. The unfortunate term "celibate marriage" reflects the option some priests take when faced with the spectre of an aloneness they cannot fathom.

The aloneness embraced by those who are able to do so is neither antisocial nor schizoid. It is rather based on sexual resolution, a deep relationship with the transcendent, and an ability to see the transcendent in other people. When I asked one man how he had grown through this stage, he smiled and quoted Gandhi: "If you can't find Christ in the person next to you, you can't find him anywhere."

5. Integration

There is something mystic about men who have integrated celibacy firmly and unequivocally into their being and behavior. The awareness of the transcendent in themselves and others, past and future, comes together in them and in their work. At times, they do record moments that might be called ecstatic or classed as spiritual peak experiences, but the real test of their resolve is in their daily lives. They have a spiritual transparency— they indeed are what they seem to be. They are not without the faults or idiosyncrasies developed in pursuing a rarefied form of existence and service. But they also typify what is written about in the literature as a true eschatological witness. These men point to life beyond and to values not yet achieved. They have triumphed as much as humans can over the biological imperative. They exercise a freedom of service to their fellow humans unbound by any institutional restraints. They are what they set out to be: men of God.

It is easier to find men who will relate their celibate/sexual struggles than it is to find men who can talk in the first person about their achievements and integration. This in part is because integration is accompanied by a deep sense of humility and in part is because these men are a minority. The tendency to deal with celibacy only in idealistic and legalistic terms rather than in terms of process and personal history militates against a realistic literature that genuinely supports celibacy. These men both validate the process and approach the ideal.

We need more direct witness from these men. For me to become more biographical at this point would expose the best examples to recognition against their wishes. It is my hope that this formulation of a model of celibacy will encourage more celibates to expose the process of their own search. What I do know from the few men in the study who can unquestionably be categorized as having integrated celibacy beyond all of its stages is that they have transcended the self to a level beyond sexuality, when "male and female, and also Jew and Greek" no longer have meaning.

Chapter 13

THE ACHIEVEMENT OF CELIBACY _____

What would happen if men remained loyal to the
ideals of their youth?
                              —*Ignazio Silone*, Bread and Wine

If you had cut Andrew Pengilly to the core, you
would have found him white clear through. He was a
type of clergyman favored in pious fiction, yet he actually did exist.
                              —*Sinclair Lewis*, Elmer Gantry

Classical literature about celibacy is fraught with presuppositions about the achievement of the ideal. The assumption that the ideal-achieved is the ordinary state is the starting point of most presentations. The reality of this assumption is not so easily taken for granted by the serious practitioner of celibacy. "How is it possible?" was a question posed by many students in their last years of training for the priesthood. The majority of our informants are witness to a stretch for the ideal rather than a firm grasp on it.

This report has tried to avoid assumptions in favor of an accurate portrayal of the state of celibacy as it exists. We remain convinced that such a representation is more supportive of those who strive for the fulfillment of the ideal than are depictions that avoid the real difficulty in its attainment or that offer simple ascetic schemes for success.

At any one time, 2 percent of vowed celibate clergy can be said to have achieved celibacy—that is, they have successfully negotiated each step of celibate development at the more or less appropriate stage and are characterologically so firmly established that their state is, for all intents and purposes, irreversible. These truly are the eunuchs of whom Christ spoke in the New Testament (Matt. 19:12). Even more, they are from among that group who have made the decision for celibacy, as Balducelli (1975) describes it, from the beginning, surmounting the crisis of intimacy in favor of celibacy; the crisis of responsibility resolved by community; and the crisis of integrity resolved by permanent commitment (pp. 219–242).

263

There is also a group of men, 6 to 8 percent, who, although their course of celibate practice has not been without its missteps and fumblings and, for some, serious reversals in the past, enjoys a present condition so refined and in which the practice of celibacy is so firmly established that the group can be said to have consolidated the practice of celibacy to such a degree that it approaches the ideal.

This group represents those who clearly have the charism of celibacy. It also includes brave, courageous, and devoted men who say that, although they feel they lacked the charism, they have embraced—even if at times unenthusiastically—the discipline required by a church they love because of a work they truly feel is their own.

Even the reader who is accustomed to think only in terms of the ideal may be open to considering the realism of these figures if he or she recalls that these groups are added to the 40 percent estimated to be practicing celibacy (Figure 13:1).

The average person is not scandalized by the portrayal of clerics by Chaucer (1934 ed.) in *The Canterbury Tales*. The Monk has an aversion to the quiet and seclusion of his monastery, and he is consumed with his interest in material things, good food, and worldly pleasures. Chaucer's Friar is frankly evil and cunning—using the confessions he hears as a ruse for financial profit. Another implication is clear—he is sexually familiar with another man's wife. The Pardoner, that special envoy of Roman power, is drawn as an unattractive homosexual. The nun's priest betrays his vanity and vacuousness in his story of the cock and the fox. The canon's alchemy and duplicity are exposed by his yeoman.

None of these characters is unbelievable and each has his parallel in modern-day ministry. However, just as true to life is the Oxford cleric—the serious student who aspires to the ministry and church office—and the Parson—the poor and devoted parish priest, of whom Chaucer says:

This fine example to his flock he gave,
That first he wrought and afterwards he taught;
Out of the gospel then that text he caught,
And this figure he added thereunto—
That, if gold rust, what shall poor iron do?
For it the priest be foul, in whom we trust,
What wonder if a layman yield to lust?
And shame it is, if priest take thought for keep,
A shitty shepherd, shepherding clean sheep.
Well ought a priest example good to give,
By his own cleanness, how his flock should live. . . .

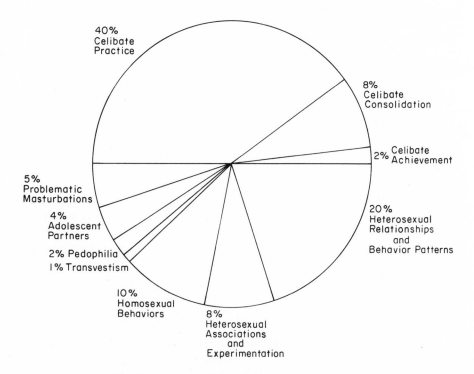

40%
Celibate
Practice

8%
Celibate
Consolidation

2% Celibate
Achievement

5%
Problematic
Masturbations

4%
Adolescent
Partners

2% Pedophilia

1% Transvestism

20%
Heterosexual
Relationships
and
Behavior Patterns

10%
Homosexual
Behaviors

8%
Heterosexual
Associations
and
Experimentation

FIGURE 13:1. Celibate/Sexual Adjustment: Estimates of Behavior

There is nowhere a better priest, I trowe.
He had no thirst for pomp or reverence,
Nor made himself a special, spiced conscience,
But Christ's own love, and His apostles' twelve,
He taught, but first he followed it himself. (pp. 16–17)

The questions remain: Who are the men who succeed in celibacy? How do they approach the ideal of celibacy? What is involved in their success?

Over the years, I have found them to be almost universally humble and very reticent about claiming "success" for themselves. Contrary to what might be expected, I found in them that a sense of humanness and flexibility of character were far more common than rigidity. Also remarkable was their general sense of good humor rather than the wizened anger and resentment some might expect among sexually deprived persons.

A discipline and purposefulness were evident in their lives in place of the harsh practices one imagines as ascetic. Judging from the men with whom I have spoken, I have come to agree with the Franciscan theologian,

Fr. Martin Pable (1975), who recast celibate asceticism into a positive statement about life that refuses to be encapsulated by popular presuppositions. Humanness unbounded by sexuality, love beyond loneliness, sexual identity grounded in real generativity, and transcendent awareness and activity are all open to the celibate and are the reward of his discipline (pp. 266–276).

Often, the men who are the best examples of celibate achievement have the hardest time describing "how" they do it. They may mention some practice of prayer, or even a hobby or interest that has sustained them, or the example of others, but somehow celibacy becomes for them a natural consequence of who they are, what they love, and what they are devoted to.

Interviewing these men led me to look for the supports they established internally and used externally that fostered their development and made celibacy possible for them. What distinguished their lives from those of priests who did not practice or achieve celibacy? Was it merely a difference in character, opportunity, or motivation? Certainly, each of these factors does play a part.

ESSENTIAL ELEMENTS OF CELIBATE ACHIEVEMENT

Originally, I identified four elements that were universally present in all the celibate achievers I had interviewed up to that point—the early 1970s: prayer, work, community, and service. Men of diverse circumstances, from librarian to missionary, scholar to urban activist, all demonstrated a well-defined system of prayer that was an integral part of their day and existence. Each man was productive and, even if pressured by particular situations, was happily working. Each had a clear idea of whom he considered to be his community and family; the Church as such did not always rate as paramount, but every man looked to a group of specific people to whom he felt devoted. Finally, each man's life was one of meaningful service. Presuming generally good mental health and physical aptitude, I believe that it is within these four areas that the keys to understanding the successes and failures of celibate adjustment are to be found.

In order to expand my understanding of the system of celibacy within the Catholic priesthood, I began to examine early spiritual writers who mediated a celibate life-style for others. Surprisingly, little explicit reference to celibacy exists in the rules formulated by these writers. At first I was discouraged by the omission, only to realize later that the absence itself supported my own observations rather than dismissed them. I quite naturally turned first to the Rule of St. Benedict (1980 ed.), because it was the most familiar to me and because historically it occupied the premier place in propagating the celibate way of life within the monasteries and among the secular clergy as well. It did so especially through Popes Gregory I (540–604) and Gregory VII (1020–1085).

The Benedictine, Gregory I, called the Great, enforced celibacy for all the clergy without exception and even deposed offending prelates. His *Liber Regulae Pastoralis* (*Pastoral Care*) written in 591 (1950 ed.) proposed the norms of pastoral care to be provided by the secular clergy. For a thousand years, this book was traditionally handed to each bishop upon his consecration. The norms presumed a celibate ministry.

Gregory VII, who was also trained under the Rule of Benedict, as part of the Cluniac reforms reestablished celibacy as a requirement for all clergy in the Western Church:

> With the object of rooting out moral abuses in the Church and freeing it from lay control, he first reinforced, at his Lenten synods of 1074 and 1075, his predecessors' decrees against clerical marriage and simony. This provoked great resistance, especially in France and Germany, but special legates armed with overriding powers were able to overcome most of it. (Kelly, 1986, p. 155)

After studying this rule, I identified 10 instead of four essential interrelated elements that support celibacy as a way of life (Sipe, 1983). Later, I could identify them as addressing three main areas of human need: the spiritual, the psychological, and the physical (Sipe, 1990). I hold that these elements are present in the lives and the codification of the experience of every celibate rule maker.

The most significant religious codifier in the past 500 years has been Ignatius of Loyola (1491–1556). His profound spiritual experience is transmitted in his *Spiritual Exercises* (1978 ed.), which do not necessarily demand a celibate response but rather form a solid base for the transforming religious experience or orientation indispensable to celibacy. Further, it is from this base that he founded his Society, the Jesuits—a way of life that contains all the essential elements mentioned above.

To put the matter in a contemporary framework: These religious traditions endure and continue to draw men and become for some of them a structure within which they can successfully sublimate their sexual drives. This is because the structure demonstrates how one can supply sufficient biopsychosocial reinforcement to make human development possible and religious aims realistically attainable (see Figure 13:2). The ten elements that support celibate achievement are: work, prayer, community, service, attention to physical needs, balance, security, order, learning, and beauty.

1. Work

"What are you going to do when you grow up?" "What are you going to be?" are the kinds of questions that plague and inspire the young. Everyone has to do something; everyone has to be something. Everyone has to work. A man's celibacy is inextricably bound up with work, with the fact of work as mastery—the productive use of one's energies and time—rather than with a particular task.

The variety of work that can absorb the vitality of a celibate is amazing. Many celibates, however, are not satisfied with the priestly functions of sacramental minister, teacher, or plant administrator; their individual interests can range from the theoretical and ecclesiastical areas of their primary training to photography, fly-tying for fishing, or gardening. I include under this rubric of work some activities that others might number as hobbies because I have found that celibates seem to know the value of time and productivity and find these activities related to their work/mastery energies.

2. Prayer or Interiority

I have never interviewed a man who has attained celibacy without finding in him a rich and active prayer life. This is so intimately bound up with celibate practice and achievement that Dr. Bartemeier taught me always to inquire first about the prayer life of a priest when making a clinical assessment. A celibate's prayer life will reveal the capacity, quality, and nature of his relationships not just with transcendent reality but also with other significant human beings and his self-concept as well.

There will be complaints about the next observation I am about to make, but state it I must because I have found it to be consistent: I have not come across one man who has achieved celibacy who has not devoted at least one and a half to two hours daily to prayer. The danger in this comment is that it will be perceived in a mechanistic way or as some kind of litmus test of celibate practice; there are those who spend considerable time in prayer and yet are not celibate. There can also be periods of scanted prayer even in the observant; nevertheless, a regular and meaningful prayer life was invariably a component mentioned by those who had achieved celibacy.

There does not seem to be any shortcut or substitute for time devoted to interiority during which one is in touch with a reality beyond self. Many of these men described how the time spent in prayer became a priority for them, increasingly so as they confronted challenges to their lives and ministries.

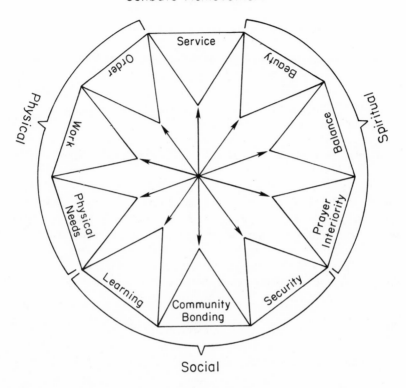

Model Structure for
Celibate Achievement

FIGURE 13:2. Model Structure for Celibate Achievement

3. Community

The importance of interiority leads quite naturally to the third element found among men who have achieved celibacy: a sense of themselves as part of a community. They seemed to know the answer to the Gospel question: "Who is my mother and brothers and sisters?" In some with a very highly developed religious personality, we found an awareness of the family of humanity, and in others an awareness of oneness of self with all creation.

This consciousness in this group was not theoretical or ephemeral. The men had a deep sense of persons: people to whom they were committed and people on whom they could rely. One man, despite being incapacitated by physical injury and disgruntled and gruff with those around him, clearly manifested the depth of his allegiances. In short, strong object relationships with a wide variety of persons seem to support celibate achievement.

4. Service

All of these three elements—work, prayer, and community—are united in the awareness of service as a meaningful existence. In other words, all is "on account of the kingdom." Whatever the work, the prayer form, or the community for the particular celibate, the effort is beyond the self.

Some mentioned that it was not always easy to be conscious of this reality. They pointed out that at times it was tempting to be the "served" and special one, receiving or directing the service of others. They were also aware that such a shift—so acceptable culturally—was a danger to maintaining that which was essential to their rightful calling.

5. Physical Needs

Many adults think of sexual gratification as a primary physical need along with those of home, food, and clothing. They accordingly spend a good deal of their time and effort on taking care of these necessities. Many celibates are forced to spend more time than they would like on taking care of their physical needs even though they admit that they are generally well cared for. Some priests felt their living standard was reasonably commensurate with (or better than) that of the people they served.

We found a wide variety of adjustments in this area, not so much in the essentials as in the details left to taste and quality. Some priests savored exquisite food, whereas others seemed quite indifferent to its quality. Some also enjoyed an alcoholic drink, whereas others were abstinent. A few said they had had a problem with alcohol in the past, but no addictive alcoholic was represented in the group of celibate achievers. (I believe that active alcoholism is incompatible with the achievement of celibacy.)

Not all of the achievers were lean; several portly gentlemen confessed that they had struggled with a weight problem all of their adult lives. There were some who said that food and drink remained the areas of their greatest and most persistent combat. I was left with the impression that this was a group of men who knew themselves, knew their limits and needs, and fulfilled them appropriately and with gentleness. One man stated it clearly, "If I don't assure myself enough legitimate pleasure, I'm liable to seek the illegitimate."

Indeed, there were some men for whom the word "ascetic" seemed the first obvious description, but they lacked the force of reaction formation that one often sees in the fanatic or youthful enthusiast. There was a quiet discipline about their lives and I observed consistently an accompanying tolerance of others and their needs, along with an understanding of their different ways of meeting them.

I believe that for these priests the process of learning to assess their own limitations and needs and of finding appropriate ways to overcome and meet them not only bestowed self-satisfaction but also contributed to their appreciation of the human condition of the people they loved and served. Several times I had the pleasure of observing the openness and uncritical acceptance these celibates demonstrated for the behaviors of deprived persons and underprivileged parishioners. The priests seemed to understand poverty as a condition rather than focusing on acts of thievery, for example. They had empathy for the cold, unloving, and harsh environment that demoralizes people whom others labeled as immoral, irresponsible, or perverted.

Several times I recalled Victor Hugo's bishop and his silver candlesticks in *Les Misérables*. I felt that a number of the men I interviewed really did look at the world's unfortunates with the attitude "There but for the grace of God go I."

6. Balance

Another element I identified not only in the codes of the spiritual writers but also in the lives of the celibate achievers was balance. It is the psychological and spiritual quality that probably ensures the flexibility necessary to juggle the inner and outer daily and seasonal demands. Not only does balance moderate the physical instincts and their legitimate satisfaction, it also assures sufficient prayer and quiet to restore the consciousness of one's goals and values, and limits the tendency to overwork.

I met a few of these men fortuitously as they were struggling with a considerable amount of inner anguish. In some instances, a man needed a neutral and supportive arena in which to sort out his inner confusion. In every instance, I could describe the experience they were undergoing as "a dark night of the soul." The process outlined by St. John of the Cross is an apt comparison.

From these men, I learned to ask informants about their specific periods of special stress. All had undergone the periods I have described in the preceding chapter. Sometimes combined with one of those temporal stages of celibate development and sometimes independent of them, the periods were characterized as deep internal struggles, filled with confusion and disorganization.

Several of my psychiatric colleagues could understand these periods only in traditional psychiatric terms. However, several other colleagues, who had wide experience with religious, knew what I was talking about when I said that there was a "different" quality to the struggles of these men. I found Kazimierz Dabrowski's (1964) concept of positive disintegration helpful in defining these periods. He outlined the process as follows.

The developmental instinct, therefore, by destroying the existing structure of personality, allows the possibility of reconstruction at a higher level.

In this procedure we find three phenomena which are to some extent compulsory:

1. The endeavor to break off the existing, more or less uniform structure which the individual sees as tiring, stereotyped, and repetitious, and which he begins to feel is restricting the possibility of his full growth and development.
2. The disruption of the existing structure of personality, a disintegration of the previous internal unity. This is a preparatory period for a new, perhaps as yet fairly strange and poorly grounded value.
3. Clear grounding of the new value, with an appropriate change in the structure of personality and a recovery of lost unity—that is, the unification of the personality on a new and different level than the previously held one (pp. 2–3).

This is not far removed from some of the thinking of St. Augustine and other spiritual writers. I have found that many celibates must expand the bounds of traditional thinking in order to integrate their celibate practice with the reality of their lives. Meister Eckhart (1981 ed.) is a spiritual writer whose work helped me comprehend the progress toward inner balance that informants described. An abstract thinker, Eckhart was interested in the sources of universal being and connection and in the relationship of an individual being in God and God in being. A celibate's sense of detachment and his understanding of sin as part of life and spiritual process are areas in which understanding aids the struggle to balance celibate values.

One informant related that his practice of celibacy was incomplete, split off, and uncommitted until he was 40 years old. At that time, he was hospitalized and nearly died. In his recuperative period, he experienced a self-evaluation the core of which was one whole night that he spent in his sickbed meditating on the Lord's Prayer. Not conscious of the passage of time that night, he has since maintained a sense of the meaning of every word and phrase in the prayer and he credits to that experience his enduring celibate practice and the balance he has kept in his life. He had not read the writings of St. Teresa of Avila prior to his illness; when he finally did study them, he was astonished that her description of the prayer of quiet echoed so accurately his own decisive spiritual encounter.

7. Security

Security is a universal human requisite for growth and for the development of adequate coping mechanisms. As I have said elsewhere, "the sense of stability, enduring circumstances, rootedness in interpersonal relationships, with bonds to time, place, and practical realities, are fundamental to personal growth and development" (Sipe, 1983, p. 434).

In part, this is integral to the vow of celibacy. I have already quoted Gandhi's experience of celibacy before and after he took his vow. The prayer, work, community alliance, and service so essential to celibate practice are sealed by the internal commitment expressed in a vow. The commitment establishes the inner security and allegiance that manifest themselves especially in relatedness.

This element is closely allied with the community mentioned earlier, but it is also an expansion of it. The core community, like the nuclear family, is the base from which one reaches out and to which one can retreat. One's identity is confirmed by the essential relationships, but security in that identity allows one to expand.

The base for security is laid down in early childhood in attachment and separation—especially to and from the mother. The resolution of the process is strong object constancy and the solidification of identity and relationships. This resolution then forms a model for problem-solving and coping skills in the face of evolving challenges to one's security in new contexts.

There will be an ebb and flow of problems and confrontations in any life cycle, and the celibate is not immune from them. His commitment should provide him an overarching relatedness that sustains him through reversal and crisis. Many celibates have testified to this reality in their experience. Some felt that at some point they had been betrayed by those they believed they had had a right to count on, only to find a deeper sense of self in recovering from the betrayal.

Somewhere in the struggle, the celibate must discover a mutuality of durability, one that can span his life cycle. Although mediated by others, its core is internal, secure in the commitment to the transcendent. Many men spoke of their test of "faith." When analyzed, it was not a test in the traditional sense of doubt about the existence of a God, but rather in the value and meaning of the relationship upon which they had built.

Security is both the father and the child of intimacy. As the product of intimacy, security is based on the interaction of trust, self-disclosure, and shared pleasure. In speaking with priests, I am frequently struck by their references to loneliness. In many histories of those who have failed in the celibate practice are accounts of backfired attempts at legitimate intimacy. Overeager, misplaced trust and indiscriminate self-disclosure led to frustration or sexual acting out. Sometimes these attempts were followed by rejection within the celibate circle.

All celibate achievers had someone to whom they felt they had confided the essence of themselves, and most had been the recipients of such disclosure. Above all, they all maintained self-respect and the respect of others, the great reinforcements to security. Security seemed also to allow tolerance of differences and the expansion of one's circle of trusted friends, both clerical and lay.

Security also means the discovery of places to be oneself within the circle of relationships involving mutual interdependence. This is perhaps one of the most difficult tasks for a celibate: how to be celibate when recreating and when not involved with official duties; how to be a celibate on an equal plane with those who are not.

Many informants recounted how associations that began with the promise of mutual respect for the other's commitment ended with sexual compromise. Nonetheless, many of the achieved celibates had forged alliances and friendships that did fulfill the promises.

Fr. Noel Mailloux, O.P., said to me that failure to find the right work assignment was most disruptive with respect to establishing adult, secure, human relationships for the celibate. As an example, Mailloux described the situation in which a young celibate is assigned to a parish or to pastoral work into which he enthusiastically throws all his energies. Often this assignment is abruptly terminated, and the young priest is transferred. In this new situation, the young man invests less of his energies into relationships, anticipating a second additional set of painful separations.

The danger is that with each new parish, the priest becomes increasingly isolated in his official persona and consequently is progressively more vulnerable to a sexual liaison. Celibate achievers, however, seemed to know what others did not: how to achieve relationships of broad mutual satisfaction and respect that enhanced their celibate identity without imposing on it clerical trappings.

I have emphasized this element of security because it seemed to be the confirmation of the integrity of these priests' celibate identities. These men functioned as celibates and felt they were consistently "themselves," regardless of circumstances or surroundings. They did not change into a different kind of private persona distinct from their public image and they did not split off their personal life from their stated values.

8. Order

I never met a celibate achiever who lacked a sense of order in his daily and seasonal life. I encountered a few whose system of order was so idiosyncratic that at first it appeared to be disorganization—or, in one case, chaos—but on further examination I discovered that this was not the case.

While balance means a spiritual quality regulating the inner competing needs, order responds to the regulation of time and energy, whether in prayer, work, study, hobbies, or recreation. If one cannot organize his time and energy, one is deprived of the satisfaction of mastery and achievement—those very elements of productivity which make the sacrifice of sexual gratification possible.

Perhaps it is not surprising that celibates who have legislated for others arrange the days and the seasons of a celibate's life by way of systematizing an order of prayer. In houses of training, to some extent, and in some established religious communities, the official regimen of prayer sets aside specific times of day around which all other aspects of daily life, work, recreation, and meals fit.

The important lesson to be learned from this ordering is that the daily, seasonal, and annual cycles of prayer recitations measure out human life into manageable segments and make synchrony with vital rhythms possible. Celibacy that is insistently assailed by recurring human desire and buffeted by a hostile culture can only maintain itself a moment or a day or a season at a time. Order not only fosters productivity, but is a conscious regulation of one's time and energies, which obviates unnecessary challenges to their values and intentions.

Ordering of work, hobbies, interests, associations, and friendships, as well as of prayer, are all part of the challenge for the celibate. Here, again, rigidity is less successful than is flexibility. One who can reorganize his life to meet changing demands is better equipped to maintain internal order than one who is wedded to an established routine that must be abandoned entirely in the face of new circumstances.

Several informants told us that they learned their lesson on how to organize their lives only after the failure of a system on which they had previously relied too heavily, in most cases an external ordering. Some of these men reminded me of the accounts of successful prisoners of war—men who, in solitary confinement, learned to segment and regulate their days, devising ways, even under severe deprivation, of finding meaning and endurance by providing a makeshift structure to their lives.

9. Learning

Not all men who achieved celibacy were scholars, but the learned were overrepresented in this group. I can say that, by and large, this was a group of men who were interesting because they themselves were interested in many things and many people. A certain level of intellectual achievement was traditionally required for ministerial studies. Certainly, intelligence and successful celibate attainment are not correlative, but the love for learning and intellectual curiosity probably are. It is difficult to be a good celibate without continued learning. Many priests have told me that it is impossible. They rest their case on the need for both intelligent ministry and intellectual and spiritual growth—practical as well as theoretical.

One priest repeated the advice he had heard from a celibate whom he admired: "The only two things a priest needs are the Bible and the *New York Times*," the timeless and the timely, intelligently mediated for the people one loves and serves.

The denial of sexual pleasure by itself does not lead to intellectual achievement, but the dedication of one's life to the service of others, even to the extent of sexual self-denial, does.

10. Beauty

There is a need for legitimate pleasure that takes the form of beauty in many celibates' lives. This is absolutely clear when celibates band together in stable communities. Even those confounded by the practice of celibacy can admire its artistic productions. What I said about monastic history applies in some degree to all celibates:

> A love for beauty seems to flow naturally from the conditions provided by monastic living. The order and balance in day-to-day living, reverence for learning, and attention to simple human needs, form a psychological synergism easily demonstrable in monastic history. They give rise to a number of expressions. For example, liturgical prayer led to its natural enhancement through psalmody and gesture. The practical necessity of providing permanent, stable housing allowed for architectural achievements. The task of copying manuscripts led to the art of embellishment and illumination. In short, it seems that the monastic spirit cannot be indulged without a natural sublimation into beautiful as well as practical forms. (Sipe, 1983, p. 343)

This is, of course, a derivative quality. However, learning and beauty are cultural achievements that inspire people to think about the transcendent and about values that are of immeasurable worth. Celibate achievers did tend to be rather more culturally literate than not. Some had a deep love for music, others for art or drama. Some could translate these appreciations into their ministries; others could only use them directly for their own sustenance.

When I shared this observation with the eminent theologian Godfrey Diekmann, he pointed out to me that the first visual portrayal of Christ was in the form of Apollo, the god of beauty.

This then is the celibate structure that is manifest in the lives of celibate achievers. They created it and, in turn, they are created by it. The structure, rather than producing one kind of person, yields a wide variety of individuals. The refined aesthetes of profound gentleness as well as the rough-and-ready action-oriented are both represented. The quiet, unobtrusive and unassuming man as well as the much noticed leader has likewise achieved celibacy. Some of these men said that they have always felt that they had a same-sex orientation, although they lacked experience. Others spoke at length about their periods of sexual stress and temptations toward women during the course of their celibate striving.

I have encouraged several informants to write autobiographies of their sexual/celibate achievement. Some just laughed in response, but none has accepted the challenge. The refusals are a loss to those who would like to understand and support the celibate ideal. They are also a great deficit in the propagation of the ideal and the education of those who are inspired to follow the celibate path. Having such limited written witness to what lived celibacy is like and how it is achieved by ordinary men makes it not only unattractive but also unbelievable.

WHO WILL FOLLOW?

The recurring question is: Who will follow the celibate path that is inextricably bound with religious life and, at least currently, with the Roman Catholic priesthood? Vocations to the priesthood have declined in recent decades; many reports have said that celibacy is a major stumbling block. I personally believe that the crisis is far deeper than that. At core, it is a spiritual dilemma of which sexuality and celibacy are important elements. Also at the vortex of the crisis are justice and the credibility of authority.

There have been official attempts to understand and renew the lagging spirit of the religious and priests in the United States. Pope John Paul II wrote to all of the U.S. bishops on April 3, 1983, setting up a commission to study religious in this country. On February 22, 1989, he wrote to all of them again, this time with a report of the commission's findings. The report was assembled after much listening to and dialoguing with men and women religious. It indicated that there is serious concern about the life of celibates, but great fear in addressing directly the questions that count. Pious generalities are reiterated without any original and careful analysis of the core conflicts presented. Authority and official teachings become the saving plank offered to a drowning person.

The National Conference of Catholic Bishops produced a wise document, *The Program of Priestly Formation* (1982). The document deals with the foundation of the priest's college studies and with the major seminary years—the last four years of training prior to ordination or, more specifically, the professional part of training.

The document is sage and thoughtful in its treatment of celibacy. Unfortunately, its suggestions have not been successfully implemented in any training center, as far as I know. There is, for example, no seminary in the United States, training priests, which has so much as a one-semester course on celibacy or on the necessary correlative material of human sexual development.

One problem with training young men for celibacy and to be moral leaders in the area of human sexuality is the enduring controversy between Augustinian thinking—which implies that all sexual pleasure is at least tinged with evil—and the view of sexuality as a part of good nature. Cassian, writing from 420–426, was a celibate who preserved the wisdom of the early celibates of the desert and concluded from them that sexuality was woven into the fibers of our beings:

> When a thing exists in all persons without exception . . . we can only think that it must belong to the very substance of human nature, since the fall, as it were, "natural" to man . . . when a thing is found to be congenital . . . how can we fail to believe that it was implanted by the will of the Lord, not to injure us, but to help us. (Brown, 1988, p. 420)

"How do *you* do it?" is a fair question from any seminarian to his celibate professors or his bishop. It is an extremely difficult question to field, but unless more men who support celibacy as an important spiritual practice put their explicit example on the line, the practice will wither. St. Augustine's *Confessions*, the first example of a real autobiography in Western literature, gave weight to his judgments about all sexuality precisely because of his personal and unstinting honesty.

Men will follow Christ if they can find persons who have already done so with honesty and joy. Nothing is more powerful than example. Nothing exerts more authority than simple truth lived.

The problem of the selection of priests is not new. St. Paul lays it out well:

> A bishop must be irreproachable, married only once, of even temper, self-controlled, modest, and hospitable. He should be a good teacher. He must not be addicted to drink. He ought not to be contentious but, rather, gentle, a man of peace. Nor can he be someone who loves money. He must be a good manager of his own household, keeping his children under control without sacrificing his dignity; for if a man does not know how to manage his own house, how can he take care of the church of God? (I Tim. 3:2–5)

He wrote similarly on another occasion:

> As I instructed you, a presbyter must be irreproachable, married only once, the father of children who are believers and are known

not to be wild and insubordinate. The bishop as God's steward must be blameless. He may not be self-willed or arrogant, a drunkard, a violent or greedy man. He should, on the contrary, be hospitable and a lover of goodness; steady, just, holy, and self-controlled. In his teaching he must hold fast to the authentic message, so that he will be able both to encourage men to follow sound doctrine and to refute those who contradict it. (Titus 1:5–9)

Some advocates of a married clergy will quickly point out Paul's presumption of such. This is beside the point here—namely, the high moral standards required of any clergy. There is no lack of statement of ideals. There is, however, reticence to put oneself on the line, so to speak, in ways that people can hear and to which they can relate.

The crucial problem is that the Church exacts high standards in theory without actually having enough effective means of supporting those who would subscribe to them. This is most certainly true of celibacy.

A study completed in the 1970s of the characteristics that people value most in their clergy revealed nine elements, listed here in the order of descending importance:

1. The willingness to serve without looking for acclaim.
2. Personal integrity.
3. Personal, lived religion; he should set a good example.
4. Competence and a sense of responsibility.
5. Community leadership.
6. Be an empathetic counselor.
7. Be a thinker (student).
8. Able to perform under pressure.
9. Acceptance of ongoing need for personal growth.

These are criteria that should be taken seriously by both celibate and married clergy. There is no proof that celibates can fulfill these requirements better than the married clergy, but it is also not clear that a married clergy has an advantage in doing so.

In 1982, a group in Nebraska under the leadership of Dr. Donald Clifton, an educational psychologist, developed a test instrument for future clergy, the Priest Perceiver Interview. Selection Research Incorporated, of which Clifton is the founder, has pledged itself, in the account of Sr. Jo Ann Miller, who was instrumental in developing the test for prospective priests, to "study intensely for 50 years the thought patterns of people who make a significant difference in the lives of other people" (Miller et al., 1984, p. 105).

The creators of the testing process defined and selected "successful" priests, interviewed them, and analyzed the thought content from the recorded interviews. Their interview structure merits credibility and correlates well with the popular perception of people who know the test candidates well. Nowhere, as far as I can tell, is there any direct assessment of sexual/celibate adjustment. This does not invalidate the test, but it is, of course, an important omission since many of the priests we interviewed would merit unflinching endorsement as successful priests and yet have maintained a full sexual life on the side.

The Priest Perceiver Interview lists 14 themes that are divided into three foci. The first focus involves the question "*Can* this person be a priest?" In order to qualify, the following five criteria must be met, according to Miller (1984, pp. 105–107):

1. Consciousness of the presence of God.
2. Positive human relationships.
3. Capacity to enable others' growth.
4. Empathy for the feelings of others.
5. Courage to face resistance.

The second focus has to do with motivation and addresses the question "*Will* he do it?" The five themes listed here are:

6. Mission or sense of purpose.
7. Hope and optimism for the future.
8. Loyalty to tradition.
9. Community builder.
10. Ego awareness or a solid sense of self.

The third focus is based on the assumption that the style of ministry will be dependent on personality type and poses the question "*How* will he do it?"

11. A candidate may exhibit a style that emphasizes focus-setting priorities, goals, and persisting to completion.
12. Another candidate is called the arranger, good at facilitation and management.
13. The "Omni" is the intellectual adventurer.
14. The candidate who is endowed with superior verbal ability is called the Conceptual.

The questions remain: How do these spiritual leaders, whether celibate or married, integrate their sexuality with their ministries? What is the sexual/celibate capacity of a candidate? I hope that this work will aid those who are ferreting out the future leaders and educating them to deal directly, honestly, and intelligently with the areas of their prospects' sexuality and celibacy.

Chapter 14

THE FUTURE OF CELIBACY: RITUAL AND REALITY _____

"I am a man" answered Father Brown gravely; "and therefore have all devils in my heart. Listen to me. . . . "
—G. K. Chesterton
The Hammer of God

"Toute est grâce."
—Georges Bernanos
The Diary of a Country Priest

At this point, I trust that it is clear to the reader that my search for the meaning and prevalence of celibacy has conferred on me a sense of realism about human nature and its struggles and yet has enhanced my sense of admiration for the spiritual power and service manifest by those who undertake the process of celibacy and follow through to its full integration. I recall telling my analyst how impressed I was with the depth of self-awareness I observed in some of the men who had achieved celibacy. At the time, I credited them with a kind of "self-analysis," an achievement she viewed skeptically, with the comment, "Freud's achievement was unique!" But I persist in my conviction that celibacy practiced and achieved still has a great deal to contribute to the understanding of the human condition and the advancement of humankind.

For those who feel that the deficits and failures of celibate practice invalidate it entirely, I say with Freud, "No one like me who presumes to wrestle with the dark forces within can hope to come through the struggle unscathed" (Freud, 1905/1953a). In spite of its history of faults and betrayals, celibacy's achievements on behalf of the human race are substantial, and I predict they will continue. Certainly, what we witness in celibacy achieved is a sublimation at work in which the sexual drive re-

281

tains great intensity and force though not directed to its original aim. Instead it is at the service and disposal of culture. The historian Peter Gay (1986) is accurate when he says,

> Freud was the first to naturalize sublimation, that indispensable piece of psychological work, in the mental sciences. But he did not sort out all its intricacies, did not even fathom them. Sublimation is desexualization, the withdrawal of erotic energies for other purposes, their employment in other forms. But it is often accompanied by projection, the unconscious act of endowing external objects—a work of art, nature, anything—with sexual qualities they do not really possess. (p. 256)

Even Freud, like Homer, "nods." The challenge to celibates is to *sort out* and define more elegantly the nature and potential of sublimation. (cf. Hartmann, 1964, pp. 215–240)

My research has generated some light on the questions of clerical celibacy. It has also brought me face to face with some related questions about religion and human sexuality. Most of the questions have been aired previously, but I think they merit refocusing in light of the sexual/celibate practice of those who lead. These unsolved questions related to five areas: the equality of the sexes; the Gospel norm; married priesthood; the credibility of the Church's sexual teaching; and, most fundamentally, the question of Christian anthropology i.e., the sexual nature of human beings.

CELIBACY AND THE EQUALITY OF THE SEXES

What is so easily missed about celibacy is its natural tendency toward equality, as I pointed out in Chapter 12. The preservation of the male matrix and the monosexual structure of power is not essential to celibate practice and achievement. However traditional, this matrix and structure may not even be necessary for the power structure of a church hierarchy.

Clerical celibacy historically has often attempted to maintain itself at the expense of women and women's rights. It is clear to me from the men I interviewed that the majority of those who have achieved celibacy or who enjoy the charism are not threatened by women or women's rights. Those who are more insecure in this discipline tend to have greater problems with both. In fact, the whole thrust of celibacy, if followed to integration, transcends traditional categories of masculine and feminine, of ruler and ruled, of friend and alien. It is directed to oneness.

I agree with Riane Eisler (1987) when she says, "Human evolution is now at the crossroads. Stripped to its essentials, the central human task is how to organize society to promote the survival of our species and the development of our unique potentials" (p. 186). I also believe that authentic male celibate striving is essentially supportive of the organized future she envisions precisely because celibacy is nurturant, life-sustaining, and enhancing (symbolized by Eisler's "chalice") rather than destructive or controlling (Eisler's "lethal blade") (pp. 185–203).

I hold to this hope in spite of the challenges to celibacy vested in the male matrix and in the monosexual structure of the hierarchy, which do not foster sexual maturity or responsibility. Celibacy by its nature, as I have tried to demonstrate in analyzing its process, leads the subject to partnership with all human beings. In the transcendent, male and female are not distinct.

In defining the Church as the *People of God,* the Roman Catholic Church during the Second Vatican Council (1962–1965) struck the death knell to inequality between celibate and married, male and female. This definition of Church opens the way for the evolutionary forces moving toward the fulfillment of the Kingdom where "There is no longer male or female, Jew or Greek, slave or free"—where all are one (Gal. 3:28).

WHAT IS THE GOSPEL IDEAL FOR SEX AND CELIBACY?

There is no question that the ideal of celibacy has been pursued in Western culture by some men and women since the time of Christ (Gryson, 1970). The history of Western civilization, peopled with intellectual giants and bold liberators, thoughtful curators, and institutions of beauty and value, is partially dependent on and indebted to celibate practice and organization. For all its shortcomings, the history of celibacy belies Freud's judgment on the subject. As Peter Gay (1986) points out:

> Freud was intent on showing in the very paper in which he developed his idea of sublimation, [that] excessive self-restraint only produces neurotic suffering. Total celibacy, he said, usually makes "well-mannered weaklings," not "energetic thinkers, bold emancipators or reformers." (p. 257)

Mother Teresa of Calcutta is a woman admired by a secular public for her bold, innovative, and untiring moral leadership. She clearly links her energetic achievements with her celibacy. Gandhi made the same connection between his practice of celibacy and his service to his country. Incidentally, I think that Erik Erikson's (1969) evaluation of Gandhi's celibacy is inaccurate because of his lack of understanding of the process of celibacy (pp. 122–123).

There is no question that celibate striving has been distorted and misused in the course of time. I have tried to indicate as fairly as I could some of those permutations. Some early Christian communities made Christian life synonymous with celibacy (Voobus, 1951). But this thrust toward celibacy was not limited to early Christianity or to Roman Catholic tradition. American Protestant groups like the Shakers made celibacy and conversion to the Christian ideal one and the same (Foster, 1981). The French Protestant community of Taizé is a contemporary example of the celibate tradition.

The Episcopal Church has, more than other mainline Protestant traditions, wrestled with the place and value of celibacy from the time of the Reformation (Coffin, 1977) through the beginning of the century (Hawks, 1935). John Henry Cardinal Newman (1801–1890), who was part of the Oxford Movement that in its early days espoused celibacy, found his way into Roman Catholicism. Charles Kingsley, the Episcopal theologian, contemporary of Newman and fellow member of the Oxford Movement, struggled in his early life with "that terrible question of 'Celibacy versus Marriage' " (Gay, 1986, p. 302) before he championed marriage and sexual love as a dimension of God's love.

In some ways, the controversy over the value of celibacy seems to have settled little over the centuries. Conflict about the Gospel ideal persists (Foresi, 1969; Hebert, 1971) and will persist not only in Roman Catholicism but for any serious student of Christianity precisely because celibacy challenges assumptions about sexuality in the same way that shadows challenge light. If there were no shadows, the nature and the glory of light itself would be diminished.

In our society, there is no realistic framework offered by a teaching that labels as "sin" any sexual activity outside marriage for the developing or even mature single person. In a sense, those leaders who teach this are really legislating a kind of celibacy prior to marriage for all believers. I have found during the study that many priests are naturally empathetic with the young unmarrieds. They instinctively relate to the ambiguity of their struggle. It is because of this dilemma that many young people reject all religion. This is the only area of human behavior that the Church treats with this level of rigidity and "irreformability."

Informed experience (validated by pastoral practice) shows that there can be sexual acts free of sin within marriage—acts not open to the transmission of life—or even outside the marital state. The most difficult area of celibacy to reconcile theoretically has been the practice of the masturbations among priests. In 1983, I was sharing my findings with a young historian from Cambridge University. He listened attentively and said, "Oh! My! What you are really asking is, 'Does the Pope masturbate?' " It was not my question, but the force of it struck me deeply. The questions about sexual activity outside marriage have not been adequately faced by most teachers and leaders.

Scripture scholarship has neglected the exploration and implications of the sexuality of Christ (McBrien, 1980, pp. 532–538) and the apostles

(Sipe, 1973). Jesus Christ, celibate or not, could not have developed to maturity without erections and ejaculations, and there is no reason to think that these natural functions would have been devoid of sexual pleasure for him.

Of course, it is absolutely necessary to explore as thoroughly as possible the sexual/celibate adjustment of St. Paul, precisely because his explicit New Testament witness to celibacy is the only one we have. Scripture scholarship and the psychological sciences have advanced to the point where a responsible psychosexual history of Paul may soon be feasible. Briefly, one comment will indicate the challenge inherent in understanding Paul's sexuality. His reference to a "thorn in the flesh" (2 Cor. 12:7) brings scriptural commentaries to take great pains to deny any sexual component. All commentators say that the nature of the affliction is "unknown" and then go on to speculate about "epilepsy, malaria, stammering, and blindness. . . . Jung suggested that the blindness was psychogenic" (Black & Rowley, 1975, p. 968). Father Fitzmyer (Brown et al., 1968), an eminent scholar, writes:

> This affliction was relatively permanent, as the present subjunctive of the verbs suggests. It is possible, however, that when Paul wrote 2 Cor., the affliction was no longer with him. Three general interpretations of the nature of this affliction have been given: persecution, disease, and concupiscence. . . . The last of these seems necessarily excluded, for concupiscence is something that afflicts everyone to some degree. Moreover, it is difficult to conceive that Paul had not earlier been bothered by such inclinations more or less habitually. As for the general nature of this affliction, modern exegetical opinion generally opts for some physical malady. It is called an "angel of Satan. . . ." (p. 289)

Given the experience of our study, I would not so quickly or definitively rule out sexual concern. Recurrent fantasies of past pleasure with masturbation would certainly be considered an "angel of Satan" to the dedicated celibate who wished all Christians to be like himself—unencumbered by marriage and sexual attachments. Getty (1982) writes:

> The function of this affliction is clearly to humble Paul. It serves as a weapon of Paul's perennial enemy, Satan, and reminds Paul that he is vulnerable. Paul's temptation is to not accept this, and he persistently asks that it be removed. (p. 117)

This is exactly the function that masturbation has served for a myriad of priests who have reflected on their own sexual/celibate development. I will leave it to others to argue the case.

THE QUESTION OF A MARRIED PRIESTHOOD

Marriage of the clergy is in itself no solution to the problems inherent in either celibacy or ministry. The primary reason is that there is no credible theology of sex extant in Christian tradition (Sipe, 1987). It simply has not yet been developed and a married clergy (and laity) are as hampered by this deficit as are celibates.

The Protestant Reformation, which generally enhanced theological and scriptural authenticity and genuinely challenged religious theory and practice, left to its married ministry in contemporary America no more convincing legacy of thought about Christian sexual practice than exists among Roman Catholic priests. The Episcopal Church conducted a study of its clergy in the 1960s. The Methodist and Presbyterian Churches have also paid careful attention to the pressures and problems of their clergy during the time I continued my study of celibacy. There is, I venture, no knowledgeable authority in any of these confessions who would hold that marriage eliminates the sexual problems of ministers (cf. Fortune, 1989).

Protestant and Catholic ministers could contribute to the understanding of problems inherent in Christianity, ministry, and sexuality if they could share honestly their experience of life and ministry.

The question of married priests is not a new one. The debate raged in the Middle Ages and there were informed theologians on both sides (Barstow, 1982). As I said earlier (Chapter 3), in the aftermath of the Reformation, which raised the question of a married clergy to a test of faith, canonical legislation in Catholicism won out over reason because the arguments could not be more subtly nuanced than pro or con, heretic or orthodox. Barbaro (1969) records the legislation that solidified celibacy as a requirement for the priesthood. The reconstitution of celibate practice for Catholic priests was indebted more to the Jesuits than to any other single agency. Their efforts were paralleled by the development of a married clergy—pastors and theologians—in the Protestant tradition.

The Second Vatican Council raised expectations that a married priesthood could and would coexist as equal alongside celibate ministers within the official embrace of Mother Church. The Synod of Bishops held in Rome in 1971 dashed all hope that such a situation would be quickly realized (cf. Schillebeeckx, 1988, pp. 211–236). In fact, Mother Church, or at least the Vatican acting in her stead, closed an embrace around celibates that squeezed many out of the active ministry.

The years between 1962 and 1971 produced serious voices echoing the medieval debates—"Pourquoi le célibat du prêtre?" (Lavallée, 1964). Many openly advocated a married priesthood or at least questioned the necessity of celibacy as a discipline for all clergy (Hermand, 1965). These sentiments reiterated some of the concerns of the Catholic bishops from around the world that indeed the discipline was not always being observed and that the charism of celibacy was not universally manifest in ministry (Blenkinsopp, 1968). Very quickly, the ranks grew of priests and nuns who left their ministries in order to marry, and they gave voice to their experience and convictions (Colaianni, 1968).

Two realities of marriage and celibacy challenge people concerned about religion: (1) the Gospel tradition, and (2) moral leadership and credibility in matters of human sexuality. The Gospel tradition—Christ himself and some of his followers—espoused celibacy; some of the followers were married. This was true both of ministers and of the faithful at large. The benefits of celibacy to the Christian message have been largely lost in Protestantism, just as the value of a married clergy has been resisted in Roman Catholicism. Both traditions suffer from this incompleteness in defiance of the clear example of the early Christian communities. This condition will probably be remedied automatically if the second issue—that of moral leadership and credibility—is addressed.

HOW CREDIBLE IS THE CHURCH'S SEXUAL TEACHING?

Religious leaders claim a right to voice moral standards. They are not God or incarnate sons of God and their judgment should not be divinized. But they stake their claim on their role as servants among the People of God—the community. Religious leadership should, of course, validate its words by its example, but even if that is lacking, its teaching must be straight and credible. Theologian William M. Shea (1986) outlines the "tangle of issues" that Roman Catholic leadership has failed to deal with credibly. They all have to do with sexuality.

> They are: family life, divorce and remarriage, premarital and extramarital sex, birth control, abortion, homosexuality, masturbation, the role of women in ministry, their ordination to the priesthood, the celibacy of the clergy, and the male monopoly of leadership. Some have suggested that sex is, at bottom, the issue that clogs up our Catholic calendar. Fear of women, and perhaps hatred of them, may well be just what we have to work out of the Catholic system. (p. 589)

The strands of the customary church rationale about such matters form a seamless cloth—remove one and the whole fabric is weakened. This is why the questions about celibacy—really understanding its practice and process—are so threatening, as is any debate on contraception or abortion, or the masturbations, or the place of women. Religious leaders, when threatened with unsettling questions, are tempted to respond with pronouncements.

In spite of these official pronouncements, however, the questions of the Church's teaching on human sexuality are far from resolved. In fact, we are merely at the embryonic stage of a comprehension of Christian sexuality and a viable theology of sex. Quite simply, the Roman Catholic Church's official teaching on human sexuality in its present state is not credible— that is, the teaching cannot be validated by an act of faith, by human experience, or by the sincere informed conscience of believing Christians.

There are responsible theological voices seeking to harmonize controversies between bishops and theologians regarding the ordinary magisterium—that is, who has the authority to modify noninfallible teaching (Curran, 1986; Granfield, 1987). But in fact, ordinary believers have a voice and a part in articulating truth.

As theologian Fr. Patrick Granfield (1987) paraphrases official Church teaching, "The Christian faithful have the right and 'even at times a duty' to make known their opinions to bishops and to other Christian faithful on matters which pertain to the good of the Church" (p. 160). The magisterium, or teaching authority of the Church, belongs to the pope and his bishops by reason of their office *and* to theologians by reason of their scholarly competence. But there is also a validating function of the Christian community and that is the *sensus fidelium*—the actual belief of Christians throughout the centuries. This sense of the faithful is *also* one of the norms of theological truth (McBrien, 1980, pp. 68–72).

There is no area of faith and morals where the faithful have a greater right to be heard than in the area of sex and marriage. A life involving sexual activity is the faithful's normal state for salvation, just as non-marriage and celibacy have been the established norm for the pope and bishops. Most Christians are called to live their lives in a sexual context. Thus, teachings about sexuality vitally concern them in a very practical way because, as Granfield (1987) reminds us: "Christian truth is not an abstraction, but exists only in the living faith of the people" (p. 148); or as Fr. Virgil Michel, the Benedictine liturgist and theologian, used to say: "Any theology that is not a lived theology is no theology at all." Pronouncements that ignore theological scholarship and the *sensus fidelium* have little hope of enduring moral force or effective intellectual (or faith) assent (cf. Chittister and Marty, 1983). "The level of the efficacy of a Church doctrine is linked to the level of its reception," states Granfield (1987, p. 149).

All the confusion surrounding human sexuality cannot be clarified by acts of faith in the official papal pronouncements. Believing the earth is the center of the universe will never make it so, at least astronomically.

The history of thought has demonstrated how new thinking—the shift in a paradigm or model, as Kuhn demonstrates in his landmark *Structure of Scientific Revolutions* (1962)—is often resisted by authority. It literally shakes things up. Pietro Redondi (1987) has shown that opposition to Galileo was based not so much on scientific grounds as on theological insecurity and political controversies. In short, authority can be threatened by changes in thinking and new paradigms that it perceives as possibly engendering loss of control.

An excellent, if painful, example of this phenonemon is the question of birth control. Pope Paul VI set up an advisory group to report on the problems surrounding it. The majority report delivered to him in 1966 favored the acceptance of contraception as a legitimate form of birth control and made no moral distinction between chemical and mechanical means. A majority of theologians on the commission, as well as other experts in medicine, economics, and sociology, supported the arguments for a change in Church teaching.

The minority report that was accepted and acted upon in the form of an encyclical two years later reinforced the concept of the Church's "irreformable" teaching. Fear of a loss of confidence in its moral leadership and doubts about its ability to control other sexual abuses motivated this decision. The current pope, John Paul II, has gone the limit in defending what a majority of the Catholic faithful reject when he stated that sexual intercourse even within marriage is not only incomplete but even "ceases to be an act of love" if contraception is used (NC News Service, Aug. 22, 1984).

The credibility of the Church's teaching is a vital concern to celibate popes and bishops, as well as to theologians. The noncelibate faithful, for whom sex and marriage are part and parcel of their vocation, are not merely interested bystanders and silent recipients of papal pronouncements on sex. Their experience and knowledge are essential to any deeper, more complete understanding of human nature.

This community of believers forms the *sensus fidelium* mentioned earlier. Their active part in the reception, formation, and validation of Church doctrine is not reducible to morality or faith by vote, but it is essential. Even Joseph Cardinal Ratzinger, a preeminent Vatican spokesman, concedes that assent by a significant group of committed Christians is necessary for the authenticity of doctrine. "Where there is neither consensus on the part of the universal Church nor clear testimony in the sources, no binding decision is possible. If such a decision were formally made, it would lack the necessary conditions and the question of the decision's legitimacy would have to be examined" (Granfield, 1987, p. 150). Most of the Church's teachings about sexuality are in this category.

Some may say that an act of faith should be enough to reconcile official teaching and personal conscience. An act of faith can certainly be reasonable, but as theologian Fr. Karl Rahner (1975) points out, "The act of faith is not unreasonable, because it presupposes the signs of credibility and their rational comprehension" (p. 512).

The trouble with attempting an act of faith regarding the present teaching of the Church on sex is that the signs of credibility are violated. Pronouncements do not conform to the sexual nature of man for several reasons. (1) The teaching is based on an archaic anthropology. (2) There is no realistic moral framework in which the developing and even mature single person can work out his or her sexual potential. (3) Informed experience (validated by pastoral practice) shows that there can be sexual acts that are free of sin even outside the marital state. (4) Scripture scholarship has neglected the exploration of the sexuality of Christ and the apostles. (5) The Church has chosen to speak essentially in the prophetic voice (thou shalt/shalt not) in isolation from the objective voice and the lyrical voice.

When Churches and moral leaders choose to speak about sexual matters essentially in the prophetic voice (thou shalt/shalt not) in isolation from the objective and lyrical experience, people do not listen. The commands lose a sense of reality and meaning. I will not repeat here the arguments I put forward elsewhere for the necessary development of a unified language to deal with human sexuality (Sipe, 1987). Suffice it to say that the moral credibility of religious leadership, whether celibate or married, is hampered by the lack of an accurate language that takes into account also the biological, psychological, and social realities of sexuality.

WHAT IS THE SEXUAL NATURE OF THE HUMAN BEING?

John Cardinal O'Connor, current archbishop of New York, unwittingly named the core of the problem of sexuality, celibacy, as well as of marriage, when he said, "In moral and spiritual matters I didn't create the truth. It is inherent in the *nature* of things." It is the question of sexual nature that has not yet been fully addressed.

Father Philip Keane (1975), author and moral theologian, when writing about celibacy, said,

> What this issue really comes down to is a question of anthropology, a question of how tightly together the human person's body and soul should be linked from an anthropological viewpoint. In former times many types of Christian anthropology made too great a separation of body and soul in the human person with the result that sexuality was seen primarily as a bodily function having little or nothing to do with human personality. Such a position was obviously inadequate and today most Christian philosophers would hold to fairly tight linkage of body and soul in the human person. (p. 289)

Although Charles Kingsley decided against celibacy and felt that men were "unsexed" by its practice even in the service of religion, he did categorize the problem correctly, saying that the whole question was an anthropological one. He saw the "two great views of man ... (1) a spirit embodied in flesh and blood, with certain relations, namely, those of father, child, husband, wife, brother, as necessary properties of his existence ... (2) spirit accidentally connected with, and burdened by an animal" (Gay, 1986, pp. 301–302).

The moral and spiritual truth of which Cardinal O'Connor speaks is not separate from biological, psychological, and social truth. None of these, as each impinges on the sexual, can be easily or apodictically defined. This does not mean that truth is relative; but the human brain, through which truth is apprehended, is not entirely developed yet, as Ludwig Von Bertalanffy (1971) stated:

> [There is] the general human predicament. It is the dualism of man in a natural and a symbolic (or cultural) world. As I once expressed it, man's forebrain has developed splendidly, and this made possible the evolution from stone axes to atom bombs, from fetishism to physics. The brainstem of man, however, seat of emotions, instincts, animal drives, did not evolve but remained pretty much the same since the dawn of man and his ape-like ancestors. . . . Here is the reason that we have an almost superhuman intellect which created atomic physics and bombs, combined with the subhuman instincts of a savage or angry ape. (p. 118)

Although Edward O. Wilson's (1978) theories of sociobiology are controversial when applied to human nature, the questions he raises are important for celibate and sexual adjustment: just how genetically determined *is* a human being, not only in sexual but even in social behavior?

Theologians will probably applaud Wilson's assertion that some sort of religious instinct is inborn (p. 175)—a view not far from some of St. Augustine's conclusions. They will also agree that love and sex in humans are biologically linked, as are certain temperamental differences between men and women (pp. 128–135).

Agreeing or not, moral and spiritual leaders, celibate or no, need to contend with the evidence that reproduction is not the primary purpose of sex among human beings. Love, fostered and supported by sexual consolation, serves to bond parents long enough to raise children.

> [Natural laws] are biological, were written by natural selection, require little if any enforcement by religious or secular authorities, and have been erroneously interpreted by theologians writing in ig-

norance of biology. All we can surmise of humankind's genetic history argues for a more liberal sexual morality, in which sexual
practices are to be regarded first as bonding devices and only second
as means for procreation. (Wilson, 1978, p. 142.)

Wilson links the growing evidence that homosexuality is biologically
predetermined, or at least influenced, with the impulse toward altruism.
Societies need individuals free of family obligation for special service to
the community (p. 143).

At any rate, there is evidence that altruism among animals is genetically
controlled. It serves the chances of survival of the group. There is great
significance for the understanding of the nature of celibacy in determining
how "natural"—genetically determined—is the capacity to make sacrifices, even to give one's life, for the good of others.

Regardless of the unanswered questions about the biological and social
nature of sexual/celibate adjustment, it is clear that the current Catholic
teaching is based on an archaic anthropology.

An Archaic Anthropological Model

What view of human nature is consistent with the Church's teaching on
sexuality? A basic violation of credibility exists at the core of the Church's
pronouncements on sexuality. Dependence on an archaic anthropology
calls into question the concept of human nature underlying all of the
Church's teaching on sexuality.

Schematically put, the Church's official teaching on sex is that all directly sought or welcomed sexual pleasure (thought, word, desire, or action) outside marriage is gravely sinful and that every act of sexual
intercourse within marriage must remain open to the transmission of life.

How can this teaching be supported by the "nature" of sexual beings as
known and experienced by thoughtful Christians? It imposes a system
that makes grave sin inevitable and even necessary.

There is only one way to demand intellectual assent, to justify such assertions, and to make the teaching coherent and internally logical: appeal
to an outmoded anthropological model. I am indebted to Margaret Mead
for the seed of this idea. In a private conversation in 1966 about psychoanalysis and anthropology, she said that Freud's oedipal theory makes
sense only if we postulate a prehistory anthropology that assumes a life
cycle of 12 to 16 years. Otherwise the oedipal threat has no reality base
but is rather merely a psychic figment. Although I was involved in a study
of celibacy and the Church's sexual practice at the time, it took me nearly
a decade to realize the importance of this observation for Catholic theology and sexual theory.

Even if I were to question Mead's theory that prehistory human beings were limited by a life span of 12 to 16 years, there is no reason to think that the steps of early sexual development recognized today were not present in our forebears.

Sexual activity and interest begin at birth in some form or other. An infant discovers his or her genitals the same way he/she discovers other interesting appendages and cavities such as the nose, toes, fingers, mouth, ears, nostrils, and anus. There are special reactions in the genitals, also from birth (erection/lubrication), which enhance and command the attention of the infant and his/her peers and elders.

Socialization within the family matrix (clan) demands some channeling and restricting of behavior and instinct. The child must redirect its infantile sexual striving from its original object (mother, father) to one acceptable to the clan. At the point when childhood sexual activity (premoral) is submitted to understanding (the age or reason) and community responsibility (the formation of conscience), the person is ready for mature sexual involvement. In primitive humans, these activities coincided with physical sexual maturity and the capacity to propagate the species at approximately 5 to 7 years of age, thereby allowing enough time for the nurturance of children before menopause and senescence, which occurred from age 9 to 12. A long life of 16 to 18 years was the reward of the very hardy and lucky (see Figure 14.1).

All of the Church's teachings are consistent with this (*and only this*) understanding of human nature. Such a scheme leaves no room or need for sexual development outside marriage. Sexual practice and readiness are all accomplished in prerational and therefore premoral circumstances prior to the formation of conscience. (Choice of family size is not an option, but also not a question.) The scheme also requires that the marital state immediately follow the resolution of infantile psychosexual development (which at one time was probably the state of human affairs). Therefore, at the point when one is ready to "leave father and mother" (the resolution of the oedipal), one is ready to "cling to a wife."

The Church's teaching on human sexuality, in spite of its internal logic, is not credible because it is consistent only with this archaic anthropology. It has echoes of inherent truth, but its view of *human nature* is not validated as experienced and lived by reasonable and informed Christians today. The Church's view of human sexual nature is quite literally underdeveloped. It is understandable that the official Church would cling to an incomplete and outmoded sexual teaching at a time when there was no coherent and comprehensive cognizance to substitute. However, in spite of current confusion and legitimate controversies in sexual studies and theology, the time has passed when clearly inadequate models can

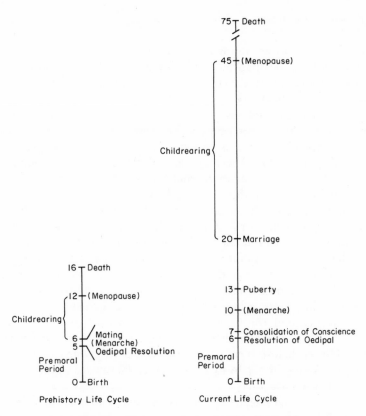

FIGURE 14:1. Sexual Development: An Anthropological Model

support official pronouncements. We can tolerate indecision while the Church develops a theology of sex. But who can give credence to pronouncements that are clearly incredible?

CONCLUSION

Celibacy has been a factor in the spiritual development of Western culture. Likewise, it is part of the spiritual ecology of America, whether or not it is widely appreciated or acknowledged. This report has been addressed to the general public in the hope of furthering a deeper understanding of and sensitivity for the struggles, the strengths, the passions, and the possibilities of this ancient practice.

Celibacy's vitality and life-giving potential are dependent not on its ritual but on its reality. Any reform or revitalization of a part of the ecosystem is dependent on the mobilization of other related parts of the system in the service of establishing balance. Celibates alone cannot reform or revitalize the practice of celibacy. There is a mutual interdependence between the married and the celibate Christian. They are each enhanced by the achievement of the other as they seek to penetrate and master the common reality that generated and nurtures both—human sexuality.

REFERENCES _____

Alexander, Franz G., & Selesnick, Sheldon T. *The History of Psychiatry: Psychiatric Thought and Practice from Prehistoric Times to the Present.* New York: Harper & Row, 1966.

American Psychiatric Association. *Diagnostic and Statistical Manual of Mental Disorders, 3rd ed., revised.* Washington, DC: American Psychiatric Association, 1987.

Aries, Philippe, & Béjin, André. *Western Sexuality: Practice and Precept in Past and Present Times.* New York: Basil Blackwell, 1985.

Augustine, Father. Help and hope for the sex addict. *America,* 1 October, 1988.

Balducelli, Roger. The decision for celibacy. *Theological Studies,* 36: 219–242, 1975.

Barbaro, Ermolao. *De Coelibatu, De Officio Legati.* Firenze: L. S. Olschki, 1969.

Barstow, Anne Llewellyn. *Married Priests and the Reformed Papacy: The Eleventh-century Debates.* New York: E. Mellen Press, 1982.

Bartemeier, Leo H. In Paul E. Johnson (Ed.), *Healer of the Mind: A Psychiatrist's Search for Faith.* Nashville, TN: Abingdon Press, 1972, pp. 59–77.

Baum, Gregory. Catholic homosexuals. *Commonweal,* 99: 479–482, 1974.

Bell, Alan P., Weinberg, Martin S., & Hammersmith, Sue Kiefer. *Sexual Preference: Its Development in Men and Women.* Bloomington, IN: Indiana University Press, 1981.

Bell, Rudolph M. *Holy Anorexia.* Chicago: University of Chicago Press, 1985.

Benedict, St. *The Rule of St. Benedict,* Timothy Fry (Ed.). Collegeville, MN: The Liturgical Press, 1980.

Berlin, Fred S. Pedophilia. *Medical Aspects of Human Sexuality,* 19: 79–88, 1985.

Berlin, Fred S. Pedophilia: Diagnostic concepts, treatment, and ethical considerations. *American Journal of Forensic Psychiatry,* 7(1):13–30, 1986.

Berlin, Fred S., & Coyle, Genevieve S. Sexual deviation syndromes. *The Johns Hopkins Medical Journal,* 149: 119–125, 1981.

Bernanos, Georges. *Diary of a Country Priest.* New York: Macmillan, 1962.

Berry, Jason. Pedophilia. *National Catholic Reporter,* 7 June 1985.

Berry, Jason. Homosexuality. *National Catholic Reporter,* 27 February 1987; 7 March 1987.

Berry, Jason. *Washington Post,* 16 and 17 September 1989.

Berry, Jason. *And Lead Us Not into Temptation: The Scandal of Pedophilia,* in press.

Bieber, Irving, et al. *Homosexuality: A Psychoanalytic Study.* New York: Basic Books, 1962.

Bishops Committee on Priestly Formation. *The Program of Priestly Formation.* Washington, DC: National Conference of Catholic Bishops, 1981.

Bishops' Committee on Priestly Life and Ministry, National Conference of Catholic Bishops. *The Health of American Catholic Priests: A Report and a Study.* Washington, DC: United States Catholic Conference, 1985.

Black, Matthew, & Rowley, H. (Eds.). *Peake's Commentary on the Bible.* London: Thomas Nelson and Sons, 1975.

Blenkinsopp, Joseph. *Celibacy, Ministry, Church: An Enquiry into the Possibility of Reform in the Present Self-understanding of the Roman Catholic Church and Its Practice of Ministry.* New York: Herder and Herder, 1968.

Blos, Peter. *On Adolescence.* Glencoe, IL: Free Press, 1962.

Bobrow, Nanci A., Money, John, & Lewis, Viola G. Delayed puberty, eroticism, and sense of smell: A psychological study of hypogonadotropism, osmatic and anosmatic (Kallmann's syndrome). *Archives of Sexual Behavior,* 1: 329–344, 1971.

Boswell, John. *Christianity, Social Tolerance, and Homosexuality: Gay People in Western Europe from the Beginning of the Christian Era to the Fourteenth Century.* Chicago: University of Chicago Press, 1980.

Brown, Gabrielle. *The New Celibacy.* New York: Ballantine, 1981.

Brown, Peter. *The Body and Society: Men, Women and Sexual Renunciation in Early Christianity.* New York: Columbia University Press, 1988.

Brown, Raymond F., Fitzmyer, Joseph A., & Murphy, Roland E. *The Jerome Biblical Commentary, Vol. II: The New Testament and Topical Articles.* Englewood Cliffs, NJ: Prentice Hall, 1968.

Bynum, Caroline Walker. *Jesus as Mother: Studies in the Spirituality of the High Middle Ages.* Berkeley, CA: University of California Press, 1982.

Carnes, Patrick. *Out of the Shadows: Understanding Sexual Addiction.* Minneapolis, MN: CompCare Publications, 1983.

Cass, V. C. Homosexual identity: A concept in need of definition. In J. P. DeCecco & M. G. Shively (Eds.), *Origins of Sexuality and Homosexuality.* New York: Harrington Park Press, 1985.

Chapman, J. D. Neuroendocrinologic developments in sexuality: Beta-endorphins in sexual phase disorders. *J. A. D. A.,* 84: 368–371, 1984.

Chaucer, Geoffrey. *Canterbury Tales.* (Tr. J. U. Nicolson). Garden City, NY: Doubleday, 1934.

Cherfas, Jeremy, & Gribbin, John. *The Redundant Male: Is Sex Irrelevant in the Modern World?* London: The Bodley Head, 1984.

Chesterton, G. K. *The Penguin Complete Father Brown.* New York: Penguin Books, 1981.

Chittister, Joan D., & Marty, Martin E. *Faith and Ferment.* Minneapolis: Augsburg, 1983, p. 30.

Clark, Keith. *An Experience of Celibacy: Creative Reflection on Intimacy, Loneliness, Sexuality and Commitment.* Notre Dame, IN: Ave Maria Press, 1982.

Code of Canon Law. Washington, DC: Canon Law Society of America, 1984.

Coffin, Edward. *A Refutation of M. Joseph Hall.* Ilkley, England: Scolar Press, 1977.

Colaianni, James F. (Ed.). *Married Priests and Married Nuns.* New York: McGraw-Hill, 1968.

Coleman, Eli. Assessment of sexual orientation. *Journal of Homosexuality,* 14: 9–24, 1987.

Comfort, Alex. *The Joy of Sex: A Gourmet Guide to Love Making.* New York: Simon and Schuster, 1972.

Cooney, John. *The American Pope: The Life and Times of Francis Cardinal Spellman.* New York: Times Books, 1984.

CORPUS. First National Conference on a Married Priesthood. Washington, DC: American University, 1988.

Cozby, Paul C. Self-disclosure: A literature review. *Psychological Bulletin,* 79: 73–91, 1973.

Cullmann, Oscar. *Peter: Disciple, Apostle, Martyr: A Historical and Theological Study,* 2nd ed. Philadelphia: Westminster Press, 1962.

Curran, Charles E. *Faithful Dissent.* Kansas City, MO: Sheed and Ward, 1986.

Curtis, Helene. *Biology,* 3rd. ed. New York: Worth, 1979.

Dabrowksi, Kazimierz. *Positive Disintegration.* Boston: Little, Brown, 1964.

Davis, Henry Joseph. *Moral and Pastoral Theology, Vol. 4.* New York: Sheed and Ward, 1938.

DeMause, L. *The History of Childhood.* New York: Psychotherapy Press, 1974.

Duby, Georges. *The Knight, the Lady, and the Priest: The Making of Modern Marriage in Medieval France.* New York: Random House, 1983.

Easwaran, Eknath. *Gandhi, the Man.* Berkeley, CA: Blue Mountain Center of Meditation, 1972.

Eckhart, Meister. *Meister Eckhart: The Essential Sermons, Treatises, and Defence.* (Tr. Edmund Colledge & Bernard McGinn) New York: Paulist Press, 1981.

Editorial. Homosexual love. *Commonweal,* 110: 484–485, 1983.

Eisler, Riane. *The Chalice and the Blade: Our History, Our Future.* San Francisco: Harper and Row, 1987.

Erikson, Erik. *Gandhi's Truth.* New York: W. W. Norton, 1969.

Fenichel, Otto. *Psychoanalytic Theory of Neurosis.* New York: W. W. Norton, 1945.

Fenichel, Otto. *Collected Papers, First Series.* New York: W. W. Norton, 1953.

Fenichel, Otto. *Collected Papers, Second Series.* New York: W. W. Norton, 1954.

Foresi, Pasquale M. *Celibacy Put to the Gospel Test.* New York: New City Press, 1969.

Foriliti, John. *Early Adolescents and Their Parents: Growing Together.* Washington, DC: National Catholic Education Conference, 1984.

Fortune, Marie M. *Is Nothing Sacred? When Sex Invades the Pastoral Relationship.* San Francisco: Harper and Row, 1989.

Foster, Lawrence. *Religion and Sexuality: Three American Communal Experiments of the Nineteenth Century.* New York: Oxford University Press, 1981.

Foucault, Michel. *The Archaeology of Knowledge and the Discourse on Language.* New York: Harper and Row, 1972.

Foucault, Michel. *The History of Sexuality.* New York: Pantheon Books, 1978, 1:57.

Fox, Robin Lane. *Pagans and Christians.* New York: Alfred A. Knopf, 1987.

Franklin, Robert. Accolades and ironies. Minneapolis *Star Tribune,* 18 September 1988.

Freedman, Alfred M., Kaplan, Harold I., & Sadock, Benjamin J. *Comprehensive Textbook of Psychiatry,* 2nd ed. Baltimore: Williams & Wilkins, 1975.

Freud, Anna. *The Ego and the Mechanisms of Defense, rev. ed.* New York: Grune and Stratton, 1944.

Freud, Sigmund. *Complete Psychological Works, Vol. 7 (1901–1905).* London: Hogarth Press, 1953a.

Freud, Sigmund. *Complete Psychological Works, Vol. 13 (1913–1914).* London: Hogarth Press, 1953b.

Freud, Sigmund. *Complete Psychological Works, Vol. II (1910).* London: Hogarth Press, 1957.

Freud, Sigmund. *Complete Psychological Works, Vol. 12 (1911–1913).* London: Hogarth Press, 1958.

Freud, Sigmund. *Complete Psychological Works, Vol. 17 (1917–1919).* London: Hogarth Press, 1961a.

Freud, Sigmund. *Complete Psychological Works, Vol. 21 (1927–1931).* London: Hogarth Press, 1961b.

Freud, Sigmund. *Complete Psychological Works, Vol. 16 (1916–1917).* London: Hogarth Press, 1963.

Freud, Sigmund. (1909). Family romances. *Standard Edition, Vol 9.* London: Hogarth Press, pp. 235–241; 1966.

Friedan, Betty. *The Feminine Mystique.* New York: Dell, 1967.

Furlong, Monica. A sense of rejection. *The Tablet,* 10 October 1987.

Gaffney, Gary R., & Berlin, Fred S. Is there hypothalamic-pituitary-gonadal dysfunction in paedophilia? A pilot study. *British Journal of Psychiatry,* 145: 657–660, 1984.

Gaffney, Gary R., Lurie, Shelly F., & Berlin, Fred S. Is there a familial transmission of pedophilia? *Journal of Nervous and Mental Disease,* 172: 546–548, 1984.

Galdston, Iago (Ed.). *The Interface between Psychiatry and Anthropology.* New York: Brunner/Mazel, 1971.

Gallagher, Joseph. *Voices of Strength and Hope for a Friend with AIDS.* Kansas City, MO: Sheed & Ward, 1987.

Gallagher, Joseph. The sadness of being gay. In *The Business of Circumference.* Westminster, MD: Christian Classics, 1988, p. 248.

Gandhi, Mohandas K. *An Autobiography: The Story of My Experiments with Truth.* (Tr. Mahadev Desai). Boston: Beacon Press, 1957.

Gandhi, Mohandas K. *All Men Are Brothers.* Krishna Kripalani (Ed.). Ahmedabad: Navajivan Publishing House, 1960.

Gay, Peter. *The Bourgeois Experience: Victoria to Freud. Vol. II: The Tender Passion.* New York: Oxford University Press, 1986.

Gay, Peter. *Freud: A Life for Our Time.* New York: W. W. Norton, 1988.

Getty, Mary Ann. *Collegeville Bible Commentary: First Corinthians; Second Corinthians.* Collegeville, MN: Liturgical Press, 1982.

Gilbert, A. N. Buggery and the British Royal Navy 1700–1761. *Journal of Social History,* 10: 72–76, 1976.

Goergen, Donald. *The Sexual Celibate.* New York: Seabury Press, 1974.

Goodich, Michael. *The Unmentionable Vice: Homosexuality in the Later Medieval Period.* Santa Barbara, CA: Ross-Erikson, Publishers, 1979.

Gould, Stephen Jay. *The Flamingo's Smile: Reflections in Natural History.* New York: W. W. Norton & Company, 1985.

Granfield, Patrick. *The Limits of the Papacy.* New York: Crossroad Publishing Co., 1987.

Greeley, Andrew M. *The Catholic Priest in the United States: Sociological Investigations.* Washington, DC: United States Catholic Conference, 1972.

Greeley, Andrew M. *Cardinal Sins.* New York: Warner Books, 1981.

Greeley, Andrew M. *Thy Brother's Wife.* New York: Warner Books, 1982.

Greeley, Andrew M. *Ascent into Hell.* New York: Warner Books, 1983a.

Greeley, Andrew M. Priests, celibacy and *The Thorn Birds. TV Guide,* 31: 4–6, March 26, 1983b.

Greene, Graham. *The Power and the Glory.* New York: Viking Press, 1946.

Gregory, Pope. *Pastoral Care.* (Tr. Henry Davis). Westminster, MD: Newman Press, 1950.

Groeschel. Benedict J. *The Courage to Be Chaste.* New York: Paulist Press, 1985.

Groth, N. A. The incest offender. In S. Sgroi (Ed.), *Handbook of Clinical Intervention in Child Sexual Abuse.* Lexington, MA: Lexington Books, 1982.

Groth, N. A., & Burgess, A. Sexual trauma in the life histories of rapists and child molesters. *Victimology: An International Journal,* 4: 10–16, 1979.

Gryson, Roger. *Les Origines du Célibat Ecclésiastique du Premier au Septième Siècle.* Gembloux: J. Duculot, 1970.

Haering, Bernard. *Shalom: Peace: The Sacrament of Reconciliation,* rev. ed. New York: Image, 1969.

Haering, Bernard. The Curran case. *Cross Currents,* Fall: 332–342, 1986.

Harkx, Peter. *The Fathers on Celibacy.* De Pere, WI: St. Norbert Abbey Press, 1968.

Harley, Marjorie. Some reflections on identity problems in prepuberty. In J. E. McDevitt & C. F. Settlage (Eds.), *Separation-Individuation: Essays in Honor of Margaret S. Mahler.* New York: International Universities Press, 11, pp. 385–403, 1971.

Harley, Marjorie. Psychoanalysis of the Prepubertal Child. Unpublished paper, 1975.

Hartmann, Heinz. *Ego Psychology and the Problem of Adaptation.* New York: International Universities Press, 1958.

Hartmann, Heinz. *Essays on Ego Psychology.* New York: International Universities Press, 1964.

Hatcher, Elizabeth R. The Menninger Foundation. Private communication to the author, based on a Letter to the Editor, *Community Times.* Reisterstown, MD, 10 February 1983. (Revised for inclusion, 1989.)

Hatterer, Lawrence J. *Changing Homosexuality in the Male: Treatment for Men Troubled by Homosexuality.* New York: McGraw-Hill, 1970.

Hawks, Edward. *William McGarvey and the Open Pulpit: An Intimate History of a Celibate Movement in the Episcopal Church and of Its Collapse, 1870–1908.* Philadelphia: Dolphin Press, 1935.

Hebert, Albert J. *Priestly Celibacy: Recurrent Battle and Lasting Values.* Houston, TX: Lumen Christi Press, 1971.

Hendrickson, Paul. *Seminary: A Search.* New York: Summit Books. 1983.

Hermand, Pierre. *The Priest: Celibate or Married.* Baltimore: Helicon, 1965.

Hoffman, Richard J. Vices, gods, and virtues: Cosmology as a mediating factor in attitudes toward male homosexuality. In J. P. DeCecco & M. G. Shively (Eds.), *Origins of Sexuality and Homosexuality.* New York: Harrington Park Press, 1985.

Hoge, Dean R. *The Future of Catholic Leadership: Responses to the Priest Shortage.* Kansas City, MO: Sheed & Ward, 1987.

Hoge, Dean R., Potvin, Raymond H., & Ferry, Kathleen M. *Research on Men's Vocations to the Priesthood and the Religious Life.* Washington, DC: United States Catholic Conference, 1984.

Hollender, Marc H. The 51st landmark article. *Journal of the American Medical Association,* 250: 228–229, 1983.

Howe, Irving. Introduction to *Bread and Wine* by Ignazio Silone. New York: Signet, 1986.

Hudson, Walter W., & Ricketts, Wendell A. A strategy for the measurement of homophobia. *Journal of Homosexuality,* 5: 357–372, 1980.

Ignatius, St. *The Spiritual Exercises* (Tr. David Fleming). St. Louis, MO: The Institute of Jesuit Sources, 1978.

Illich, Ivan. *Gender.* New York: Pantheon Books, 1982.

Instruction on respect for human life in its origin and on the dignity of procreation: Replies to Certain Questions of the Day. Vatican Paper, 10 March 1987.

Jenkins, Ray. Jerry Falwell's feelthy pictures. *Baltimore Sun* Editorial, 6 October 1984.

John Paul II, Pope. Reporting on the Commission's Study of United States Seminaries, 3 April, 1983.

John Paul II, Pope. Letter to the bishops in the United States on religious orders. *Origins,* 13 (7 July 1983).

John Paul II, Pope. *The Baltimore Sun,* 28 January 1984.

John Paul II, Pope. Letter to the bishops of the United States of America, 22 February 1989.

John, St., of the Cross. *The Collected Works of St. John of the Cross* (Tr. Kieran Kavanaugh and Otilio Rodriguez). Washington, DC: Institute of Carmelite Studies, 1973.

Jurgens, W. A. *The Priesthood: A Translation of the Peri Hierosynes of St. John Chrysostom.* New York: Macmillan, 1955.

Kallmann, F. J., Schoenfeld, W. A., & Barrera, S. E. The genetic aspects of primary eunuchoidism. *American Journal of Mental Deficiency,* 48: 203–236, 1944.

Karpman, Benjamin. *The Sexual Offender and His Offenses: Etiology, Pathology, Psychodynamics and Treatment.* New York: The Julian Press, Inc., 1954.

Katchadourian, Herant, M.D., & Lunde, Donald T., M.D. *Fundamentals of Human Sexuality, 3rd. ed.* New York: Holt, Rinehart, 1980.

Keane, Philip. Sexuality in the lives of celibates and virgins. *Review for Religious,* 34:2, 1975.

Keller, Evelyn Fox. *Reflections on Gender and Science.* New Haven, CT: Yale University Press, 1985.

Kelly, J. N. D. *The Oxford Dictionary of Popes.* New York: Oxford University Press, 1986.

Kelly, Timothy. *An Indian Journal (Visit to the Dalai Lama 1986).* The Scriptorium, Vol. 26. Collegeville, MN: St. John's Abbey, 1988.

Kennedy, Eugene C., & Heckler, Victor J. *The Catholic Priest in the United States: Psychological Investigations.* Washington, DC: United States Catholic Conference, 1972.

Kennedy, Eugene C. *Father's Day.* Garden City, NY: Doubleday, 1981.

Kennedy, Eugene C. Asexuality. *National Catholic Reporter,* 14 November 1986.

Kennedy, Eugene C. The problem with no name. *America,* 158: (23 April), 423–425, 1988.

Keyser, Les, & Keyser, Barbara. *Hollywood and the Catholic Church: The Image of Roman Catholicism in American Movies.* Chicago: Loyola University Press, 1984.

Kinsey, Alfred C., Pomeroy, Wardell B., & Martin, Clyde E. *Sexual Behavior in the Human Male.* Philadelphia: W. B. Saunders, 1948.

Kinsey, Alfred C., Pomeroy, Wardell B., Martin, Clyde E., & Gebhard, Paul H. *Sexual Behavior in the Human Female.* Philadelphia: W. B. Saunders, 1953.

Kleeman, James A. A boy discovers his penis. *The Psychoanalytic Study of the Child,* 20: 239–266, 1965.

Kleeman, James A. Genital discovery during a boy's second year: A follow-up. *The Psychoanalytic Study of the Child,* 21: 358–392, 1966.

Klein, Fritz, Sepekoff, Barry, & Wolf, Timothy J. Sexual orientation: A multi-variable dynamic process. *Journal of Homosexuality,* 11: 35–49, 1985.

Knowles, David. Canterbury Cathedral Chronicle, 65: July, 1970.

Krafft-Ebing, R.v. *Psychopathia Sexualis.* Brooklyn, NY: Physicians and Surgeons Book Company, 1934.

Kraft, William F. *Sexual Dimensions of the Celibate Life*. Kansas City, KS: Andrews and McMeel, 1979.

Kramer, Heinrich, & Sprenger, James. *Malleus Maleficarum*. New York: Dover Publications, 1971.

Kuhn, T. S. *The Structure of Scientific Revolutions*. Chicago: University of Chicago Press, 1962.

Landis, J. Experiences of 500 children with adult sexual deviants. *Psychiatric Quarterly Supplement*, 30: 91–109.

Langsley, Donald G. Community psychiatry. In Harold I. Kaplan, Alfred H. Freedman, & Benjamin J. Sadock (Eds.), *Comprehensive Textbook of Psychiatry, 3rd ed., vol. 3*. Baltimore: Williams and Wilkins, 1980, p. 2860.

Lavallée, Fleury. *Pourquoi le Célibat du Prêtre?* Lyon: Chronique Sociale de France, 1964.

Lea, Henry C. *An Historical Sketch of Sacerdotal Celibacy, 2nd ed.* Boston: Houghton Mifflin, 1884.

Leishman, Katie. Heterosexuals and AIDS. *The Atlantic Monthly*, 259: 39–48, February 1987.

Lerner, Harriett Goldhor. *The Dance of Anger*. New York: Harper and Row, 1986.

Lewes, Kenneth. *The Psychoanalytic Theory of Male Homosexuality*. New York: Simon and Schuster, 1988.

Lewis, Sinclair. *Elmer Gantry*. New York: Harcourt, Brace & Co., 1927.

Luker, Kristin. *Abortion and the Politics of Motherhood*. Berkeley, CA: University of California Press, 1984.

Mahler, Margaret S. Separation-individuation. In *Selected Papers*. New York: Jason Aronson, 1979.

Mahler, Margaret S., Pine, Fred, & Bergman, Anni. *The Psychological Birth of the Human Infant: Symbiosis and Individuation*. New York: Basic Books, 1975.

Males, James L., Townsend, John L., & Schneider, Robert A. Hypogonadotropic hypogonadism with anosmia—Kallmann's syndrome: A disorder of olfactory and hypothalamic function. *Archives of Internal Medicine*, 131: 501–507, 1973.

Marcus, Irwin M., & Francis, John J. *Masturbation from Infancy to Senescence*. New York: International Universities Press, 1975.

Marcus, Sheldon. *Father Coughlin: The Tumultuous Life of the Priest of the Little Flower*. Boston: Little, Brown, 1973.

Marmor, Judd (Ed.). *Sexual Inversion: The Multiple Roots of Homosexuality*. New York: Basic Books, 1965.

Marshall, Donald S., & Suggs, Robert C. (Eds.). *Human Sexual Behavior: Variations in the Ethnographic Spectrum*. New York: Basic Books, 1971.

Masters, William H., & Johnson, Virginia E. *Human Sexual Response*. Boston: Little, Brown and Company, 1966.

Masters, William H., & Johnson, Virginia E. *Human Sexual Inadequacy*. Boston: Little, Brown and Company, 1970.

Masters, William H., & Johnson, Virginia E. *Homosexuality in Perspective*. Boston: Little, Brown, 1979.

Masters, William H., Johnson, Virginia E., & Kolodny, Robert C. *Masters and Johnson on Sex and Human Loving*. Boston: Little, Brown and Company, 1982.

Maugham, W. Somerset. *"Rain" and Other Short Stories*. London: Readers Library, 1933.

McAllister, Robert J. *Living the Vows: The Emotional Conflicts of Celibate Religious*. San Francisco: Harper & Row, 1986.

McAllister, R., & VanderVeldt, A. Psychiatric illness in hospitalized clergy: Alcoholism. *Quarterly Journal for the Study of Alcoholism*, 1962.

McAllister, R., & VanderVeldt, A. Factors in mental illness among hospitalized clergy. *Journal of Nervous and Mental Disease*, 1961.

McAllister, R., & VanderVeldt, A. Psychiatric illness in hospitalized Catholic religious. *American Journal of Psychiatry*, 1965.

McBrien, Richard P. *Catholicism, Vol. I*. Minneapolis: Winston Press, 1980.

McBrien, Richard P. Homosexuality & the priesthood: Questions we can't keep in the closet. *Commonweal*, June: 380–383, 1987.

McLaughlin, Loretta. *The Pill, John Rock, and the Church: The Biography of a Revolution*. Boston: Little, Brown and Company, 1982.

McMenamin, Robert W. Clergy malpractice. *Case and Comment*, 90: 3–6, 1985.

McNeill, John J. *The Church and the Homosexual*. Kansas City, MO: Sheed, Andrews and McMeel, 1976.

McNeill, John J. Homosexuality: Challenging the church to grow. *The Christian Century*, March: 242–246, 1987.

Meiss, Millard, & Beatson, Elizabeth H. *The Belles Heures of Jean, Duke of Berry*. New York: George Braniller, 1974.

Meissner, W. W. *The Paranoid Process*. New York: Jason Aronson, 1978, pp. 653–654.

Miller, J. A. A song for the female finch. *Science News*, 117: 58–59, 1980.

Miller, Jo Ann, et al. How to identify a future priest. *America* (18 February 1984).

Miller, Jean Baker. Women and power. In *Work in Progress*, Wellesley, MA: Stone Center for Developmental Services and Study, Wellesley College, 1982.

Modras, Ronald. Father Coughlin and the Jews: A broadcast remembered. *America*, 160(9):21;9–222, 1989.

Mohr, J. W., Turner, R. E., & Jerry, M. B. *Pedophilia and Exhibitionism*. Toronto: The University of Toronto Press, 1964.

Money, John. Clinical aspects of prenatal steroidal action on sexually dimorphic behavior. In C. H. Sawyer & R. A. Gorski (Eds.), *Steroid Hormones and Brain Function*. Berkeley, CA: University of California Press, 1971, pp. 325–338.

Money, John. Bisexuality and homosexuality. *Sexual Medicine Today*, 24 February 1984.

Money, John. *Lovemaps: Clinical Concepts of Sexual/Erotic Health and Pathology, Paraphilia, and Gender Transposition in Childhood, Adolescence, and Maturity*. New York: Irvington Publishers, 1986.

Money, John. *Gay, Straight, and In-Between: The Sexology of Erotic Orientation*. New York: Oxford University Press, 1988.

Money, John, & Ehrhardt, Anke A. *Man and Woman, Boy and Girl: The Differentiation and Dimorphism of Gender Identity from Conception to Maturity*. Baltimore: Johns Hopkins University Press, 1972.

Moore, Paul J. *Time*, 7 June 1976.

Moore, Thomas Vernor. *Dynamic Psychology: An Introduction to Modern Psychological Theory and Practice, 2nd ed.* Philadelphia: J. B. Lippincott, 1924.

Moore, Thomas Verner. *Consciousness and the Nervous System*. Baltimore: Williams & Wilkins, 1938.

Moore, Thomas Verner. *Cognitive Psychology*. Philadelphia: J. B. Lippincott, 1939.

Moore, Thomas Verner. *Prayer*. Westminster, MD: Newman Press, 1943.

Moore, Thomas Verner. *The Nature and Treatment of Mental Disorders*. New York: Grune and Stratton, 1943a.

Moore, Thomas Verner. *Personal Mental Hygiene.* New York: Grune and Stratton, 1944.

Moore, Thomas Verner. *The Driving Forces of Human Nature and Their Adjustment: An Introduction to the Psychology and Psychopathology of Emotional Behavior and Volitional Control.* New York: Grune and Stratton, 1948.

Moore, Thomas Verner. *The Life of Man with God.* New York: Harcourt Brace, 1956.

Mott, Michael. *The Seven Mountains of Thomas Merton.* Boston: Houghton Mifflin, 1984.

Murphy, Paul I., & Arlington, R. Rene. *La Popessa.* New York: Warner Books, 1985.

Myrick, Fred. Attitudinal differences between heterosexually and homosexually oriented males and between covert and overt male homosexuals. *Journal of Abnormal Psychology,* 83: 81–86, 1974.

Nash, J., & Hayes, F. The parental relationships of male homosexuals: Some theoretical issues and a pilot study. *Australian Journal of Psychology,* 17: 35–43, 1965.

National Catholic Reporter, April 1976.

National Center for Health Statistics. *Health, United States,* Washington, DC: U.S. Government Printing Office, 1983.

National Conference of Catholic Bishops. *The Program of Priestly Formation, 3rd ed.* Washington, DC: United States Catholic Conference, 1982.

National Conference of Catholic Bishops. *A Reflection Guide on Human Sexuality and the Ordained Priesthood.* Washington, DC: United States Catholic Conference, 1983.

National Conference of Catholic Bishops. Partners in the mystery of redemption: A pastoral response to women's concerns for church and society, 12 April 1988, Washington, DC. *Origins,* 17(45):757–88.

Nickalls, John L. (Ed.). *The Journal of George Fox, rev. ed.* Philadelphia: Religious Society of Friends, 1985.

Nicoli, Armand, Jr. *The Harvard Guide to Psychiatry.* Cambridge, MA: Harvard University Press, 1978, 1988.

Niebuhr, Gustav. Broken vows: When priests take lovers. *The Atlanta Journal,* 15 April 1989.

Nordeen, E. J., & Yahr, P. Hemispheric asymmetries in the behavioral and hormonal effects of sexually differentiating mammalian brain. *Science,* 218: 391, 1982.

Nugent, Robert. *A Challenge to Love: Gay and Lesbian Catholics in the Church.* New York: Crossroad, 1983.

O'Connor, Edwin. *The Edge of Sadness.* Boston: Little, Brown, 1961.

Ostow, Mortimer. (Ed.). *Sexual Deviation: Psychoanalytic Insights.* New York: Quadrangle/ New York Times Book Co., 1974.

Otene, Matungulu. Celibacy in Africa. *Review for Religious,* 41(1): 14–21, 1982.

Ovesey, Lionel. *Homosexuality and Pseudohomosexuality.* New York: Science House, 1969.

Pable, Martin W. Psychology and asceticism of celibacy. *Review for Religion,* 34:266–276, 1975.

Pagels, Elaine. *Adam, Eve, and the Serpent.* New York: Random House, 1988.

Peake's Commentary on the Bible. Black, Matthew, & Rowley, H. H. (Eds.). London: Thomas Nelson and Sons, 1962.

Peele, Stanton, & Brodsky, Archie. *Love and Addiction.* New York: Signet, 1975.

Pfliegler, Michael. *Celibacy.* London: Sheed and Ward, 1967.

Plante, David. *The Catholic.* New York: Atheneum, 1986.

Priests who date: The third way. *Newsweek,* December 3, 1973.

Pruyser, Paul W. The diagnostic process in pastoral care. In A. W. Richard Sipe & Clarence J. Rowe (Eds.), *Ministry and Pastoral Counseling, 2nd ed.* Collegeville, MN: Liturgical Press, 1984, pp. 103–116.

Quasten, Johannes. *Patrology, Vol. I: The Beginnings of Patristic Literature.* Westminster, MD: The Newman Press, 1950, pp. 234–235.

Quasten, Johannes. *Patrology, Vol. II: The Ante-Nicene Literature after Irenaeus.* Westminster, MD: The Newman Press, 1953, p. 205.

Quasten, Johannes. *Patrology, Vol. III: The Golden Age of Greek Patristic Literature from the Council of Nicaea to the Council of Chalcedon.* Westminster, MD: Newman Press, 1960.

Raguin, Yves. *Celibacy for Our Times* (Tr. M. H. Kennedy). St. Meinrad, IN: Abbey Press, 1974.

Rahner, Karl (Ed.). *The Encyclopedia of Theology.* New York: Seabury Press, 1975.

Redondi, Pietro. *Galileo Heretic.* Princeton, NJ: Princeton University Press, 1987.

Reid, William H. *The Psychiatric Times,* April, 1988.

Reiss, Ira. *Journey into Sexuality: An Exploratory Voyage.* New York: Prentice-Hall, 1986.

Report of the Commission on Obscenity and Pornography. Washington, DC, U.S. Government Printing Office, 1970.

Reuben, David. *Everything You Wanted to Know about Sex but Were Afraid to Ask.* New York: D. McKay, 1969.

Rhinelander, David. Vatican ban sidesteps one procedure. *The New York Times,* 21 March 1987.

Ricoeur, Paul. Wonder, eroticism, and enigma. *Cross Currents,* 14(2):133–66, 1964.

Rock, John. *The Time Has Come.* New York: Alfred A. Knopf, 1963.

Russell, Norman. *The Lives of the Desert Fathers.* Kalamazoo, MI: Cistercian Publications, 1981.

Russell, D. Incidence and prevalence of intrafamilial and extrafamilial sexual abuse of female children. *Child Abuse and Neglect,* 7: 133–146, 1983.

Sacred Congregation for the Doctrine of the Faith (S.C.D.F.). *Declaration on Certain Questions Concerning Sexual Ethics.* Washington DC: US Catholic Conference, 1976.

Sacred Congregation for the Doctrine of the Faith (S.C.D.F.). *Letter to the Bishops of the Catholic Church on the Pastoral Care of Homosexual Persons.* Washington DC: US Catholic Conference, 1986.

Sanderson, Margaret H. B. *Cardinal of Scotland: David Beaton c. 1494–1546.* Edinburgh: John Donald Publishers, 1986.

Sarlin, C. N. Cultural and psychosexual development. In Irwin M. Marcus & John J. Francis (Eds.), *Masturbation from Infancy to Senescence.* New York: International Universities Press, Inc., 1975.

Schetky, Diane H., & Green, Arthur H. *Child Sexual Abuse: A Handbook for Health Care and Legal Professionals.* New York: Brunner/Mazel, 1988.

Schillebeeckx, Edward. *Celibacy.* New York: Sheed and Ward, 1968.

Schillebeeckx, Edward. *The Church with a Human Face.* New York: Crossroad, 1988.

Schnaper, Nathan. The Talmud: Psychiatric relevancies in Hebrew tradition. In A. W. Richard Sipe *Hope: Psychiatry's Commitment.* New York: Brunner/Mazel, 1970.

Schnaper, Nathan. Care of the critically ill and the dying. In A. W. Richard Sipe & Clarence J. Rowe (Eds.), *Psychiatry, Ministry and Pastoral Counseling, 2nd ed.* Collegeville, MN: Liturgical Press, 1984.

Seltzer, Benjamin, & Frazier, Shervert H. Organic mental disorders. In Armand M. Nicholi, Jr. (Ed.), *The Harvard Guide to Modern Psychiatry.* Cambridge, MA: Harvard University Press, 1978, p. 308.

Shea, William M. The Pope our brother. *Commonweal,* 7 November: 586–590, 1986.

Silone, Ignazio. *Bread and Wine.* New York: Signet, 1986.

Singer, Irving. *The Nature of Love. 1. Plato to Luther,* 2nd ed. Chicago: University of Chicago Press, 1984.

Sipe, A. W. Richard. The Sexuality of the Apostles: An Eisegetical Exploration. Baltimore: Loyola College Lecture Series, 1973.

Sipe, A. W. Richard. Memento Mori: Memento Vivere in the Rule of St. Benedict. *The American Benedictive Review,* XXV(1), 96–107, 1974.

Sipe, A. W. Richard. The psychological dimensions of the Rule of St. Benedict. *American Benedictine Review,* 34:4, 1983.

Sipe, A. W. Richard. Sexual aspects of the human condition. In Paul W. Pruyser (Ed.), *Changing Views of the Human Condition.* Macon, GA: Mercer University Press, 1987.

Sipe, A. W. Richard. Outpatient response to sexual problems of Catholic religious. *Bulletin of the National Guild of Catholic Psychiatrists,* 32:42–57, 1988.

Sipe, A. W. Richard. Pastoral care of religious. *Dictionary of Pastoral Care and Counseling.* Nashville, TN: Abingdon Press, 1990.

Smillie, Wilson G., & Kilbourne, Edwin D. *Preventive Medicine and Public Health,* 3rd ed. New York: Macmillan, 1962, p. 205.

Soble, Alan. *Pornography: Marxism, Feminism, and the Future of Sexuality.* New Haven, CT: Yale University Press, 1986.

Socarides, Charles W. *The Overt Homosexual.* New York: Grune & Stratton, 1968.

Spitz, Rene A., & Wolf, Katherine M. Autoerotism: Some empirical findings and hypotheses on three of its manifestations in the first year of life. *The Psychoanalytic Study of the Child,* 3/4: 85–120, 1949.

Steinmann, Anne, & Fox, David J. *The Male Dilemma: How to Survive the Sexual Revolution.* New York: Jason Aronson, 1974.

Sterba, Richard. *Introduction to the Psychoanalytic Theory of the Libido,* 3rd ed. New York: Robert Brunner, 1968.

Stern, Karl. *The Flight from Woman.* New York: Farrar, Straus and Giroux, 1965.

Stoller, Robert J. *Perversion: The Erotic Form of Hatred.* Washington DC: American Psychiatric Press, 1975.

Stoller, Robert J. *Sexual Excitement: Dynamics of Erotic Life.* New York: Simon and Schuster, 1979.

Stoller, Robert J. *Presentations of Gender.* New Haven, CT: Yale University Press, 1985.

Task Force on Gay/Lesbian Issues, San Francisco. *Homosexuality and Social Justice, Reissued Report.* San Francisco: Consultation on Homosexuality, Social Justice, and Roman Catholic Theology, 1986.

Teresa of Avila. *The Way of Perfection* (Tr. E. Allison Peers). New York: Image Books, 1964.

Tetlow, Joseph A. *Studies in the Spirituality of Jesuits: A Dialogue on the Sexual Maturing of Celibates.* St. Louis, MO: American Assistancy Seminary on Jesuit Spirituality, 1985.

Thomas, John L. Book review of Ginder, Richard: *Sex and Sin in the Catholic Church.* Englewood Cliffs, NJ: Prentice-Hall, 1975. In *National Catholic Reporter,* 12:11.

Thompson, Larry. A new study of gay males supports the Kinsey report. *Washington Post,* January 24, 1989.

Tollison, C. David, & Adams, Henry E. *Sexual Disorders: Treatment, Theory, and Research*. New York: Gardner Press, 1979.

Traxler, Margaret Ellen. *New Directions for Women*. Englewood, NJ: New Directions for Women, October, 1979.

Tripp, C. A. *The Homosexual Matrix*. New York: Signet, 1975.

Tuchman, Barbara. *A Distant Mirror*. New York, Alfred A. Knopf, 1978.

Veyne, Paul. *A History of Private Life, Vol I: From Pagan Rome to Byzantium*. Cambridge, MA: Belknap Press, 1987.

Visser, Fr. Jan. *London Clergy Review*, May, 1976.

Von Bertalanffy, Ludwig. System, symbol and the image of man. In Iago Gladston (Ed.), *The Interface between Psychiatry and Anthropology*. New York: Brunner/Mazel, 1971.

Voobus, Arthur. *Celibacy: A Requirement for Admission to Baptism in the Early Syrian Church*. Stockholm: Estonian Theological Society in Exile, 1951.

West, Morris. *Devil's Advocate*. London: Heinemann, 1959.

West, Morris. *The Clowns of God*. New York: Bantam Books, 1981.

Williams, Walter L. *The Spirit and the Flesh: Sexual Diversity in American Indian Culture*. Boston: Beacon Press, 1986.

Wilson, Edward O. *On Human Nature*. Cambridge, MA: Harvard University Press, 1978.

Winnicott, D. W. *Family and Individual Development*. London: Tavistock Publications, 1965.

Winnicott, D. W. *Playing and Reality*. New York: Penguin Books, 1971.

Wittkower, E. D., & Dubreuil, Guy. Reflections on the interface between psychiatry and anthropology. In Iago Galdston (Ed.), *The Interface between Psychiatry and Anthropology*. New York: Brunner/Mazel, 1971.

World of the Desert Fathers: Stories and Sayings from the Anonymous Series of the Apophthegmata Patrum. Oxford: SLG Press, 1986.

Young-Bruehl, Elisabeth. *Anna Freud: A Biography*. New York: Summit Books, 1988.

Zilbergeld, Bernie, & Ullman, John. *Male Sexuality: A Guide to Sexual Fulfillment*. New York: Bantam Books, 1978.

ADDITIONAL READINGS ⎯⎯⎯⎯

Auget, Jean Paul. *Structures of Christian Priesthood: A Study of Home, Marriage, and Celibacy in the Pastoral Service of the Church.* New York: Macmillan, 1968.

Bassett, William, & Huizing, Peter (Eds.). *Celibacy in the Church.* New York: Herder and Herder, 1972.

Bertrams, Wilhelm. *The Celibacy of the Priest: Meaning and Basis.* Westminster, MD: Newman Press, 1963.

Bishops Committee on Priestly Life and Ministry. *A Reflection Guide on Human Sexuality and the Ordained Priesthood.* Washington, DC: National Conference of Catholic Bishops, 1982.

Bishops, United States. *Statement on Celibacy.* Washington, DC: National Conference of Catholic Bishops, 1969.

Congregatio pro Institutione Catholica. *A Guide to Formation in Priestly Celibacy.* Washington, DC: United States Catholic Conference, 1974.

Conner, Paul M. Celibate love. *Huntington Sunday Visitor,* 1979.

Coppens, Joseph. *Sacerdoce et Célibat: Études Historiques et Théologiques.* Louvain: Peeters, 1971.

Dubay, Thomas. *And You Are Christ's: The Charism of Virginity and the Celibate Life.* San Francisco: Ignatius Press, 1987.

Ford, Josephine Massingberd. *A Trilogy on Wisdom and Celibacy.* Notre Dame: University of Notre Dame Press, 1967.

Frein, George H. (Ed.). *Celibacy: The Necessary Option.* Symposium on Clerical Celibacy, University of Notre Dame. New York: Herder and Herder, 1968.

Gallagher, Chuck, & Vandenberg, Thomas L. *The Celibacy Myth: Loving for Life.* New York: Crossroad, 1987.

Gay, Peter. *The Bourgeois Experience: Victoria to Freud, Vol. I: Education of the Senses.* New York: Oxford University Press, 1984.

Gentili, Egido. *L'Amour dans le Célibat.* Paris: Lethielleux, 1970.

Grevy-Pons, Nicole. *Célibat et Nature, Une Controverse Médiévale: A Propos d'un Traité du Début du XVe Siècle.* Paris: Centre National de la Recherche Scientifique, 1975.

Gustafson, Janie. *Celibate Passion.* San Francisco: Harper and Row, 1978.

Hemrick, E. F., & Hoge, D. R. *Seminarians in Theology: A National Profile.* Washington, DC: United States Catholic Conference, 1985.

Huddleston, Mary Anne (Ed.). *Celibate Loving: Encounter in Three Dimensions.* New York: Paulist Press, 1984.

Hughes, Royce. *The Jesus Man.* Rome: M. Spada, 1977.

Kiesling, Christopher. *Celibacy, Prayer, and Friendship: A Making-Sense-Out-of-Life.* New York: Alba House, 1978.

Kraft, William F. *Sexual Dimensions of the Celibate Life.* Kansas City, KS: Andrews and McMeel, 1979.

Küng, Hans. *Life in the Spirit.* New York: Sheed and Ward, 1968.

Lienhart, Archille. *Célibate et Sacerdoce.* Paris: Les Éditions du Cerf, 1961.

McGoldrick, Desmond F. *Living the Celibate Life: An Essay in the Higher Psychology of Faith.* New York: Vantage Press, 1969.

McNamara, Jo Ann. *A New Song: Celibate Women in the First Three Christian Centuries.* New York: Institute for Research in History: Haworth Press, 1983.

O'Neill, David P. *Priestly Celibacy and Maturity.* New York: Sheed and Ward, 1965.

Oraison, Marc. *The Celibate Condition and Sex.* New York: Sheed and Ward, 1967.

Paul VI, Pope. Encyclical Letter on Priestly Celibacy: Sacerdotalis Caelibatus. Washington, DC: United States Catholic Conference, 1967.

Raguin, Yves. S. J. *Celibacy for Our Times.* St. Meinrad, IN: Abbey Press, 1974.

Thomas, Gordon. *Desire and Denial: Celibacy and the Church.* Boston: Little, Brown, 1986.

Thurian, Max. *Marriage and Celibacy.* London: SCM Press, 1959.

Trautman, Donald W. *The Eunuch Logion of Matthew 19:12.* Rome: Catholic Book Agency, 1966.

Vatican Congregation for Religious and Secular Insititutes. Essential element in church teaching on religious life. *Origins:* 13:133–142, 1983.

Von Hildebrand, Dietrich. *Celibacy and the Crisis of Faith.* Chicago: Franciscan Herald Press, 1971.

Wade, Joseph D. *Chastity, Sexuality, and Personal Hangups: A Guide to Celibacy for Religious and Laity.* Staten Island, NY: Alba House, 1971.

Zissis, Theodoros N. *The Fathers' Arguments on Celibacy and Their Sources.* Thessaloniki: Patriarchal Institute for Patristic Studies, 1973.

INDEX

311